**The Estate
of Social Knowledge**

**The Johns Hopkins Symposia
in Comparative History**

The Johns Hopkins Symposia in Comparative History
are occasional volumes sponsored by the Department
of History at the Johns Hopkins University and the
Johns Hopkins University Press comprising original
essays by leading scholars in the United States and
other countries. Each volume considers, from a
comparative perspective, an important topic of current
historical interest. The present volume is the
nineteenth. Its preparation has been assisted by the
James S. Schouler Lecture Fund.

THE
ESTATE
OF
SOCIAL
KNOWLEDGE

Edited by

JoAnne Brown and

David K. van Keuren

The Johns Hopkins University Press
Baltimore and London

The Johns Hopkins University Press
701 West 40th Street, Baltimore, Maryland 21211
The Johns Hopkins Press Ltd., London

The paper used in this book meets the minimum requirements
of American National Standard for Information Sciences—
Permanence of Paper for Printed Library Materials,
ANSI Z39.48-1984.

Library of Congress Cataloging-in-Publication Data

The estate of social knowledge / edited by JoAnne Brown and
David K. van Keuren.
        p.   cm.—(The Johns Hopkins symposia in comparative
history) Includes bibliographical references and index.
    ISBN 0-8018-4060-0 (alk. paper)
    1. Social sciences—United States—History—19th century.
2. Social sciences—United States—History—20th century.
3. Social sciences—Great Britain—History—19th century.
4. Social sciences—Great Britain—History—20th century. I.
Brown, JoAnne, 1954-11. van Keuren, David Keith.   III. Series.
H53.U5E85   1991
300'.9—dc20   90-39696 CIP

■ Contents

FOREWORD   *George W. Stocking, Jr., and David E. Leary*   vii

INTRODUCTION   *David K. van Keuren and JoAnne Brown*   xi

1. The Estate of Political Knowledge: Political Science and the State
   James Farr   1

2. The Great Desert of the American Mind: Concepts of Space and
   Time and Their Historiographic Implications
   Andrew Kirby   22

3. From Natural History to Social Science: Disciplinary Development
   and Redefinition in British Anthropology, 1860–1910
   David K. van Keuren   45

4. Mathematics and the Economics Profession in Late Victorian England
   Margaret Schabas   67

5. The Ideas of the Past as Tools for the Present: The Instrumental
   Presentism of John R. Commons
   Jeff E. Biddle   84

6. Quandary of the Quacks: The Struggle for Expert Knowledge in
   American Psychology, 1890–1940
   Jill G. Morawski and Gail A. Hornstein   106

7. Mental Measurements and the Rhetorical Force of Numbers
   JoAnne Brown   134

8. The Domestication of "Culture" in Interwar America, 1919–1941
   John S. Gilkeson, Jr.   153

9. Eugenics among the Social Sciences: Hereditarian Thought in
   Germany and the United States
   Robert N. Proctor   175

10. The "American Creed" from a Swedish Perspective: The Wartime
    Context of Gunnar Myrdal's *An American Dilemma*
    Walter A. Jackson   209

11. The Politics of Ethnicity in Social Science
    Rubén Martinez   228

CONTRIBUTORS   253

INDEX   257

▪ Foreword

The last several decades have witnessed a remarkable development of the historiography of the various disciplines that, in different historical and ideological contexts, have been variously called "moral," "social," "behavioral," and "human" sciences. The present volume is an outgrowth of a summer institute held in 1986 at Stanford, California, under the co-sponsorship of the Center for Advanced Study in the Behavioral Sciences and the Social Science Research Council, with funds provided by the Andrew W. Mellon Foundation. The institute was planned and organized by George W. Stocking, Jr., of the University of Chicago and David E. Leary, then of the University of New Hampshire. Entitled "The History of Social Scientific Inquiry: Disciplinary and Interdisciplinary Perspectives," it was envisioned in part as a kind of stocktaking, analogous in a general way to the 1957 conference on "Critical Issues in the History of Science," which, a generation ago, marked a new phase in that related field of study.

In the decades since 1957, the history of social scientific inquiry has developed with a double impulse, to a great extent along specifically disciplinary lines. On the one hand, the reaction against positivistic models dominant in the 1950s and 1960s stimulated a critical historical in-

For a more detailed discussion of the institute's organization and syllabus, see George W. Stocking, Jr., and David E. Leary, "Summer Institute on the History of Social Scientific Inquiry," *ISIS* 78, 291 (1987): 76–79; "The History of Social Scientific Inquiry: A Report on an Interdisciplinary Summer Institute," Social Science Research Council, *Items* 40, 3/4 (1986): 53–57; "Summer Institute on the History of Social Scientific Inquiry Held at Behavioral Science Center in Stanford, California," *Journal of the History of the Behavioral Sciences* 21 (January 1987): 94–96.

In addition to the contributors to the present volume, the participants in the institute included Kevin Breault, Antoine Joseph, Robert Richards, Raymond Seidelman, Alan Sica, Leigh Star, Shirley Washington, and Michael Woodard.

terest among practitioners of particular social science disciplines; on the other, professional historians moved beyond traditional intellectual history and history of science into areas already marked by disciplinary boundaries. The 1986 institute itself reflected this disciplinary focus, inasmuch as its organizers were, respectively, historians of anthropology and of psychology. However, it was envisioned as a first attempt to treat in a relatively systematic fashion the variety of substantive, conceptual, and methodological issues cutting across work in individual disciplines and to consider the possibilities of a more general interdisciplinary history of social scientific inquiry.

The twenty younger scholars chosen for the institute represented a cross section of the social scientific disciplines and the various impulses to their history. Their prior participation in the historical movement out of which the institute grew varied considerably. At one extreme, there were intellectual and cultural historians with no advanced training in the social sciences; at the other, there were practicing social scientists interested in placing recent developments in their disciplines in a broader historical context but with no prior experience in the history of the social sciences. In between were a group of social scientists with serious interests in the history of their disciplines and a group of professional historians of particular social science disciplines.

The success of the institute stemmed largely from the fact that its members were an extremely capable and talented group who brought with them a wide range of relevant competencies and a considerable body of their own prior research. The members quickly developed a high degree of social solidarity and collective intellectual commitment, and their varying historiographical, theoretical, and critical orientations produced unusually lively discussions. There were sharply stated differences on many issues (the utility of the concept of "methodological values," the usefulness of quantification and the legitimacy of "scientizing" approaches, the heuristic value of a distinction between internal and external factors, etc.), and there was a tendency sometimes for these to coalesce into a division between ardent critics and not-so-ardent defenders of positivistic social science. However, the lineup on most issues varied, and even the most strongly held positions were sharpened, modified, and enriched in response to the continuously reelaborated presentation of opposing views.

Aside from taking stock, the institute was envisioned also as a means of identifying a group of younger scholars who might play an important role in the future historiography of social scientific inquiry. Developments since then have highlighted this aspect of the institute's agenda. In the final days of the institute, there were several discussions about the possibility of creating a volume of essays by the members. The editors of the present volume were successful in gaining the support of the Johns Hopkins University Press and Department of History in sponsoring a symposium of the potential contributors in May 1988, at which preliminary drafts of the papers were presented and discussed. Although neither of the two institute organizers participated in the symposium or in the planning of the present volume, we are both very pleased to be able to reclaim a small place in its realization.

In the short period since 1986, the historiography of social scientific inquiry has developed in significant ways. There has been a broadening of impulse—reflected, for instance, in the Group for Research in the Institutionalization and Professionalization of Literary Studies (GRIP), in a heightened activity of research and publication outside the United States, and in the founding of a journal entitled *The History of the Human Sciences*. But the problems of disciplinarity and interdisciplinarity that motivated the 1986 institute have by no means lost their salience. The present attempt to reconsider the various boundaries of the estate of social knowledge will surely be an important contribution to the development of an integrated historiography in the decade to come.

GEORGE W. STOCKING, JR.
Professor of Anthropology
Director, Fishbein Center for the
History of Science and Medicine
University of Chicago

DAVID E. LEARY
Professor of Psychology
Dean of the Faculty of Arts
and Sciences
University of Richmond

■ Introduction

DAVID K. VAN KEUREN and JOANNE BROWN

The identification of the social sciences as a distinctive component of learning dates back at least to the French Enlightenment. The marquis de Condorcet, author of the *Esquisse d'un tableau historique des progrès de l'esprit humain,* used the occasion of his inaugural address to the Académie Française in 1782 to herald the birth of a new moral science based on the precepts of *les sciences physiques.*[1] The union of sciences and letters, established on the application of a common methodology, was, Condorcet declaimed, a crowning achievement of the age. One consequence of the resulting revivification of learning was the genesis of a *science morale* directed to the study of human society. It was to be based on the same careful observation of facts, use of exact language, and achievement of analytical certitude that characterized studies within the physical realm. Scientific method, Condorcet averred, had restored unity within the sphere of learning. Its application to the analysis of human affairs, moreover, had generated an entirely new branch of knowledge.

Condorcet later joined those who united at the close of the decade to form the Society of 1789. Their goal was to apply the principles of the moral sciences to the task of creating a new constitution for France.[2] Thus, at the same time that the Estates General were being called into session by Louis XVI, leading social thinkers were uniting to bring the expertise of the moral sciences to bear upon the same issues. This close linkage between the state, social interests, and the moral sciences would be a recurring theme in the latter's ensuing history. It shows the ineluctable ties between the sciences of society and the social, political, and institutional contexts in which they are embedded.

The affiliation between social and physical science so assiduously promoted by Condorcet and his nineteenth-century successors has been subsequently reexamined and often repudiated. Exponents of the new "interpretive" social science have been the latest to reject these linkages and in their place have stressed the common intellectual and method-ological bonds that unite social science to the humanities.[3] Proponents of the interpretive school are more likely to seek inspiration in the me-thods of literary critics than the theorems and experimental processes of physicists. The consequent change in sources of influence has led to another reconceptualization in identity and objective of the social sciences. This shift in emphasis from laws to letters is but the latest episode in a history that has demonstrated the essential mutability and cultural contingency of social scientific boundaries and disciplinary defi-nitions.

It is not surprising, then, that social scientists have consistently turned to historical exegesis in order to understand and chart the chang-ing contours of their disciplines. This urge to historicism has been a characteristic of such early systematists as Saint-Simon and Comte through to contemporary disciplinary practitioners. Many methodolog-ical and epistemological battles within the social scientific community have been waged either on historical grounds or by using historical evidence. The debate between the Boasians and neoevolutionists in re-cent American anthropology serves as a case in point.[4]

Within the historical community, there has been a parallel and growing interest in the history of the social sciences. Among American historians, important and path-breaking studies of social scientific thought have come from the pens of scholars such as H. Stuart Hughes, Merle Curti, and Richard Hofstadter. Their younger contemporaries include, among others, Dorothy Ross, Thomas Haskell, and Mary Furner.[5] Attention to the history of the social sciences also has expanded to include the work of social and institutional historians concerned with the development of the professions and the application of social scientific expertise in behalf of the commonweal.

A similar trend has become evident within the ranks of historians of science. The history of the social sciences has traditionally been a marginal study field within the history of science. However, within the last several years scholars have focused an increasing amount of serious scholarly attention on this hitherto neglected research area. The subject was generally overlooked in Clagett's *Critical Problems in the History of Science*.[6] Almost a decade later, Robert Young acknowledged the con-tinuing neglect of the subject by science historians.[7] Young saw only a few rays of light that had recently improved a rather dismal picture. However, when Hamilton Cravens subsequently reviewed the state of the field, he found much more reason for guarded optimism.[8]

Craven's confidence was well founded. In the twenty years since Young's overview, a significant corpus of secondary material on the history of the social sciences had accumulated.[9] Some of the better and broader-ranging studies originated from historians who identified themselves with American intellectual and social history. Additional contributions came from historians trained within the history of science. A few scholars, with Charles Rosenberg being the most notable example, produced papers and monographs that were claimed by both fields. The combined result has been a great enrichment of our knowledge of the intellectual and disciplinary development of social scientific thought and of its social context and influences.

Study of the history of the social sciences from within the history of science was slow to develop largely because of the effects of some of the intellectual baggage carried by that discipline. Important among these were the lingering effects of an implicit positivism among a whole generation of disciplinary practitioners. Science was viewed as a high endeavor that unraveled the secrets of nature and accumulated a store of positive, enduring knowledge of natural forces and phenomena.[10] Inasmuch as cultural and behavioral phenomena did not seem to be lawful, they did not fall within the realm of hard science and its disciplinary chronicler, the history of science. The latter recorded the intellectual accomplishments of savants of the natural order. The work of social scientists was of a different nature, the study of which fit more properly within the borders of cultural and intellectual history.

This attitude began to change in the 1960s for a number of reasons. Important among them were intellectual and demographic changes within the discipline itself, including a greater emphasis on doing social and institutional history, as opposed to traditional "internalist" intellectual history; recruitment of more disciplinary members from the social sciences and humanities, as opposed to the hard sciences; and a greater relativism in the historiographic and methodological perspectives of science historians. The relativistic nature and cultural basis of social scientific knowledge had long been appreciated. The understanding that cultural bias was present in some degree in all science helped erase the boundaries hitherto in force between the hard and soft scientific disciplines.

A consequence of these changes has been the production of an increasing amount of ever more sophisticated studies of the social sciences from within the history of science. Much of this development has been discussed by Cravens, and we need not repeat his observations here. However, some of the major contributors to the body of social scientific scholarship within history of science include George Stocking, Henrika Kuklick, and Hinsley Curtis in the history of anthropology; Michael Sokal, Robert Richards, David Leary, William Richards, and Mitchell

Ash in psychology; Daniel Kevles, Hamilton Cravens, and Kenneth Ludmerer in eugenics; Kuklick in sociology; Victor Hilts and Ted Porter in statistics. Several essayists within this volume have themselves contributed substantially to the ongoing study of social science history.

Although some recent monographs have made overarching analyses of several social scientific disciplines, such as Cravens's *The Triumph of Evolution,* the majority of studies have focused on episodes within single fields of study.[11] The discipline has remained the focus of attention within the history of science. Broader issues such as professionalization, institutionalization, and the application of expertise to policy needs are sometimes viewed from wider perspectives. However, these issues generally have been treated within specific disciplinary contexts. Thematic concerns, as opposed to disciplinary analyses, have been more characteristic of studies emanating from American and European social and intellectual history. With a couple of exceptions, the essays in this volume are written from a disciplinary perspective.

Parallel to the growth in the depth of historical investigation there also has been an increase in the breadth of topics analyzed. The study of the development of social scientific theory as an intellectual corpus has now been augmented by investigations of the negotiation of disciplinary boundaries, the organization of institutional settings, the popularization of social science knowledge and debates over inclusion and exclusion within disciplinary communities, and the application of social scientific knowledge and expertise to the construction of social programs and policy formats. Within intellectual history, analyses have become increasingly more sophisticated, focusing not on the broad reach of theory but on the uses and meanings of concepts and theories within specific social and intellectual settings. This has included studies of the changing sense and usage of important terms or doctrines and of their significance to the functioning of disciplines, the influence of important methodological innovations on disciplinary development and practices, the transferral across disciplines of particular theoretical perspectives and methodologies, and the analysis of language itself to see how it reflects the social and professional interests and needs of those who wield it.

Much of the above is similarly true for historians practicing within history departments. For the latter, the social sciences have usually functioned either as auxiliary resources for methodological inspiration or as subject material for monographs in intellectual history. Just as historians of science in recent years have broadened their methods to include social and cultural analysis, historians have ceased to view the history of the social sciences as a specialty within intellectual history and have begun to emphasize the interplay among ideas, institutions, biography, method, technology, and politics. This broadened understanding of the history of the social sciences is the result both of a general historiographic trend toward contextualization and synthesis and of the specific influences of two related kinds of inquiry on this field: the sociology of knowledge and the history of the professions. Both approaches have led historians of the social sciences toward a disciplined eclecticism that will not be satisfied by simple narratives or intellectual genealogies. This approach acknowledges both genius and politics, both intellectual evolution and social-cultural structure.

None of us can write about the history of the social sciences in the United States and claim to be doing something entirely new; however, the 1986 Summer Institute at the Center for Advanced Study brought together for intensive study and discussion twenty people from eight disciplines to compare notes on their separate histories. What the participants learned was that the epistemology of each social-scientific discipline figured into the logic of each history: the history of psychology took certain behavioral principles as given in historical explanation; the history of economics took certain economic behaviors as given; the history of geography took certain geographical principles as given. In retrospect, this outcome might have been predicted, but it surprised the group to find that the pattern of logical assumption, the structures of argument, the standards of evidence, and the metaphors of discourse for these separate histories all bore a similar relation to their subject matter: they were in a sense subject to it.

Psychologists, for example, who are interested in their own history (understandably) may care not at all for the larger social, cultural, intellectual, or economic setting in which their intellectual forebears worked, as these other sorts of explanation may challenge the primacy of psychological explanation within this historical context, challenging the autonomy of the self, or of psychology, and subverting the truth-value and universality of the discipline itself. Conversely, it may be precisely this revolution from within that some critical practitioners have in mind in writing their histories.

Disciplinary histories, then, are subject to their own subject matter in the sense that when undertaken as part of an intellectual-genealogical effort, there are internal epistemological incentives for dramatizing the goodness and practicality of the discipline under historical study (or the badness and impracticality) rather than the goodness and practicality of the discipline of history, which historical-types have ultimately in mind, for guild historians are also subject to their own subject matter and place time itself ahead of all other analytic principles.[12] What evidence and logic are taken as given and what are taken as residual becomes all-important.

The history of the social sciences, therefore, if it is to be seen as a field of historical inquiry of some inherent cohesion, will also be, at least potentially, subversive to the professional practice of history, in the sense that it will challenge the positive truth-value of historical understanding as against other forms of social knowledge. However, with a constructive and relativist view toward the disciplines, the historian begins to take seriously both their goodness and practicality. The former, narrow clarity of the historical method gives way to social-scientific eclecticism or even sheer confusion. In this sense, then, is the historical study of the social sciences subversive to the practice of history as we know it.

We would like to suggest, however, that such subversion comes at a season when historians should welcome it. It challenges them to articulate what is good and practical in the study and production of history; to articulate why history, both the past and the discipline, matters, not above all other analyses but indispensably to them all. Furthermore, in the history of neighboring disciplines there lies an opportunity for historians to learn other languages and thereby restructure their relationships to other forms of social scientific inquiry and to their public.[13] At present, few practitioners of historical writing are fluent in psychology, political economy, sociology, anthropology, or literary theory, yet they continually borrow phrases and key words from these languages with little concern for their idiomatic use.[14] Historians may find insight in the terms, but they also risk completely misunderstanding them.

The recent rage among historians for deconstruction is a case in point. It would do historians well to learn more about the historical social context of the theories of language that are so much the fashion now, not in order to be fashionable but to critically examine whether some of these theories help them to appreciate the depths and limits of historical evidence and interpretation. Language is what historical evidence is usually made of. However, if historians borrow merely the vocabulary of deconstruction or of other schools of linguistic and social thought and fail to learn both grammar and etymology (i.e., linguistic history), they will set themselves up to be captured, unwittingly, by the logic of another discipline and make themselves subject to its intellectual assumptions and political priorities without even recognizing them. It is far better that they should know that they are making choices not just of language but of perspective and of tradition; when they borrow terminology they are making political choices.

The history of modernization theory is another case in point: It is forgotten but not gone. Historians in the 1950s and 1960s became intrigued with what seemed a fresh way of conceiving progress and patterns of social change—fresh especially to American historians, because modernization theory took the "underdeveloped" Third World as its subject—and wrote entire books explaining how well this theory worked in the case of colonial North America or nineteenth–century United States.[15] Little did they know that while they were so busy trying on these secondhand theoretical garments, the political scientists who originated them were already exploring dependency theories and world-systems analyses having roots in indigenous political resistance to empire. Worst of all, had historians known more about the origins of modernization theory they would have recognized that it was made out of American-colonial historical evidence mixed with Victorian anthropology, which the political scientists had borrowed in their equally naive fashion from textbook historiography, already superseded, and colonial rationalizations, already disintegrating.

Deconstruction and modernization theory, to focus on just two recent imports adopted by historians, generally have not been treated as historically created cultural systems, as languages in the fullest sense of the term. Historians have too often borrowed terms like "discourse," "modernization," "traditional," "representation," "deconstruction" ahistorically, out of their political-cultural contexts and without due appreciation for the cultural baggage that accompanies these terms.[16] To put this problem bluntly, historians too often have left their historical principles at home when they went borrowing. The point here, however, is not to adopt an intellectual xenophobia but to recognize that linguistic meaning is systematic and not immanent to the word. It is, fundamentally, historical, all the more reason for historians to take care in borrowing terms.

If we had more and better histories of the social sciences, of linguistics, of anthropology, of political science, which included in retrospect the stories of their emergence from the moral sciences, an understanding of how these various modern disciplines have related to one another intellectually, socially, politically, geographically, economically, linguistically, culturally, symbolically, then historians would have an easier time choosing when, whether, and what to borrow. They would understand somewhat better when the different emphasis that a foreign term places on our expression is valuable insight and when it is mere affectation.

There are a lot of people writing now in the history of the separate social sciences, and no one wishes to prescribe that they all become promiscuous comparativists. We wish to suggest that those who work on intellectual biography or on the history of distinct disciplines lift their heads up from their manuscripts more often, read more broadly across the borders of their subject disciplines, and see one another as part of an inchoate professional community who may find a more useful kind of knowledge together than alone. Such a cooperative effort would have to be based on improved communication across the boundaries of disciplines, a relaxation of tensions, increased trade, increased funding for the training of "translators," more scholarly exchanges between academic "countries." We have lived with these interdisciplinary tensions for so long that we are afraid to take the risks of cross-border cooperation.

This doesn't mean that historians should all stop doing history in order to learn all of these other discipline languages, any more than we give up English when we learn Russian. In practice, when the social sciences are studied together, rather than as wholly distinct disciplines with entirely unique and separate histories, it quickly becomes apparent that there are grammatical similarities, cognate terms, practice effects, and even certain economics of scale that operate: Catharine Beecher the educator is also Catharine Beecher the health reformer and the feminist; Francis Galton the eugenicist is also Francis Galton the criminologist; Karl Pearson the statistician is also Karl Pearson the sexual liberal; John Dewey the pragmatic philosopher is also John Dewey the educator; Margaret Sanger the feminist is also Margaret Sanger the eugenicist. Similarly, at an institutional level, funding agencies, museums, universities, and state bureaucracies have multiple, overlapping fields of influence throughout the social sciences and related enterprises. The same "efficiencies" obtain for geographically centered analysis, or for language-centered analysis, and so on.

Our current situation recapitulates the seemingly contradictory impulses in late nineteenth–century social inquiry: rampant specialization and social fragmentation, cloaked in unifying but vague language. Historians recognize that their own specialization and fragmentation have impinged upon their traditional appeal as a universal discipline amenable to commonsensical apprehension. The editors of this volume are hardly the first to call attention to this malaise, but we all might have something to learn from earlier attempts to solve very similar problems. For American historians, there are some useful historical lessons in modern intellectual history.

This would entail a reexamination of the insights of the Chicago circle of pragmatic thinkers, particularly John Dewey, George Herbert Mead, Jane Adams, and Ella Flagg Young, who, long before the deconstructionists came along, were talking and writing about language, politically, socially, psychologically, anthropologically, historically. The centerpiece of this work is Mead's contention in *Mind, Self, and Society*[17] (the obverse of most psychological theory) that the self is socially constructed through communication. The amalgamated meanings of communications between the individual and other people are what Mead calls the "generalized other." It is this abstracted other that, in Mead's view, gives rise to mind.[18] It is not difficult to see the connection between this and Peirce's view of truth as consensus, or between both of these views and John Dewey's dogged insistence on a "scientific attitude" based on, as David Hollinger observes, "a principled openness toward . . . new and temporarily valid knowledge in a universe of constant change."[19] This persistent skepticism and eclecticism was the pragmatic bastion against the narrow pursuit of consensus that leads to intellectual and political orthodoxy.

What the authors of this volume hope for is not a social science Annales school, not an undifferentiated "total social science," but a recognition that in spite of highly developed distinctions among the disciplines in terms of subject matter, method, language, institutions, economics, and politics there are also continuities in each respect. Both the distinctions and the continuities are worth comprehending for the sake of each discipline as well as for the sake of our particular effort here in the history and historiography of the social sciences. The differences and commonalities, moreover, are important to the collective health of the disciplines within liberal arts communities, because an academy divided into tiny fiefdoms is one in which the collective wealth of all is easily and wastefully dissipated. A solution, however, is not to give up specialization but to reclaim its importance as part of a larger collective intellectual enterprise in which both academic "guild" members and a broader public share. We hope that this volume may serve as a step in this direction.

The Essays

The contributors to this volume represent a variety of disciplinary backgrounds and interests. They include economists, historians, historians of science, psychologists, a geographer, a political scientist, and a sociologist. Together, their essays represent a concerted effort to provide a collective vision of important developments and issues in the history of modern social science. All the issues discussed in this collection were the subject of extended debate at the Center for Advanced Study in the Behavioral Sciences. The resulting studies thus represent common concerns but are nonetheless unique and representative offerings of the individual scholars concerned. Historiographical and methodological frameworks are also unique, although in each case they owe much to the revivification of social and intellectual history that occurred in the 1960s through 1980s. It was during the latter part of this period that the scholars represented here received their graduate training.

James Farr's essay is an example of classic intellectual history applied to the study of social scientific disciplines. Farr explores the origin and application of political science's vocabulary in order to recalculate that discipline's intellectual genealogy. He focuses, in particular, on the concept and use of the term *state*—a concept full of potency in American political studies. He urges that scholars examine the history of the language of state in order to make better use of its hermeneutic power. The author explores the history of the vocabulary of political science in order to refute what he argues is its undue attribution to German origins. More importantly, however, Farr argues that in this historiographic pursuit we find several moments in the history of political science that mark its transformation "from discourse to discipline." In the mapping of this transformation, the boundaries between political science and the other estates of social knowledge are surveyed and their historical relationships considered.

Andrew Kirby writes from the unusual perspective of membership in a discipline that acknowledges its own endangerment within the academy. Beginning with Turner's historiographic classic and taking in recent European and American historiography, Kirby argues that the much-lamented antihistoricism of U.S. popular culture is inextricably linked to our concurrent marginalization of geographical thought. Through his history of geography as a discipline, Kirby reconstructs the conceptual interrelation between time and space that the institutional disjuncture of the disciplines, history and geography, has largely obliterated. Kirby emphasizes the interplay between the imaginative aspects of popular culture—popular images of landscape and history—and the academic institutions that house a discipline, in this case geography. Like the essays of Farr, Brown, and Gilkeson, this essay concerns the subtler interactions of popular and professional culture.

David K. van Keuren writes of the history of British anthropology from its imperious inception as an enterprise concerned with no less than the "natural history of man" to its narrower mandate as the "social study of savage people." In examining anthropologists' struggle for disciplinary preeminence at Oxford, van Keuren clearly describes the political and institutional tensions arising with theoretical change. The compelling power of evolutionary theory gave rise to great ambitions among some British anthropologists, who met with adamant resistance from scholars in adjacent disciplines. Van Keuren examines through a concise institutional history of anthropology at Oxford the interplay between the discipline's engagement with general theories of the history of civilization and its organization as a discipline in a particular location and time. He attempts to demonstrate how specific institutional constraints, and the negotiations accompanying them, caused a recasting and narrowing of anthropology's self-described subject purview.

The essay by Margaret Schabas focuses on political economy at a critical point in its intellectual and professional development. Schabas examines the circumstances surrounding the Marginal Revolution of the early 1870s in an attempt to understand the adoption of mathematics as an explanatory and methodological tool by Stanley Jevons and his associates. She concludes that mathematics was appropriated by political economists for reasons that were entirely independent of the processes of disciplinary professionalization currently under way within economics and other scientific and professional fields. Rather, the author argues that there was a natural intellectual fit between mathematics and the subject matter of economists. Mathematics was called in to help Jevons and his associates manipulate economic data and provide the methodological and substantive basis for the new political economics then under construction. The reasons for the adoption of mathematics were consequently intellectual rather than social and professional.

By giving priority to intellectual factors in the mathematization of economics, Schabas takes a contrary position to that espoused by many social and institutional historians. The latter view major methodological innovations, such as quantification, as at least implicitly serving professional ends. The introduction of new methodologies can serve as means of limiting access to what were formerly commonly held bodies of knowledge, a sort of intellectual enclosure movement. Disciplinary actors can and do use such means to gain greater control over their subject area and make it a reservation for a limited and accredited elite. Schabas argues that in the case in question this was not the case: Jevons was moved by purely intellectual reasons to mathematicize economic theory. Professional enclosure resulted as an unintended secondary effect. Thus, Schabas makes an argument for the primacy of intellectual factors in this episode of the history of economics and, by extension, in the broader reaches of the history of the social sciences as a whole.

Jeff Biddle writes on the "instrumental presentism" of the American pragmatic economist John R. Commons. Biddle considers the reflexive relations between Commons's economic theory and his understanding of historical method. The resulting inquiries into the history of economic thought that Commons pursued, Biddle argues, account for the distinction of his theoretical work. Moreover, the engagement that Commons sought between economic history and economic theory holds promise for contemporary theorists as well as for historians of social inquiry. Economists may find in past debates the critical interlocutors that cannot be found among their contemporaries. Significantly, Commons employed an economic metaphor crucial to the dilemmas of his day—the metaphor of collective bargaining—to describe this engagement with the past.

Jill Morawski and Gail Hornstein's study owes much to both the history of professionalization and studies of scientific popularization. The authors are concerned with delineating the dynamics of scientific popularization, as exemplified by psychology. However, they also wish to explore the ways in which such popularization creates challenges to the professional prerogatives of psychologists and how psychologists, in turn, respond to the incursions of amateurs into their domain. To do this, they turn their sights on early attempts of psychologists to establish monopoly over the expertise of mental life.

The process of scientific popularization, Morawski and Hornstein argue, does not straightforwardly channel consensual scientific knowledge to popular audiences. Rather, the social and professional interests of the popularizers transform the processed knowledge. In consequence, popularization is a much more complicated and problematic matter than historians and disciplinary practitioners have generally recognized. Morawski and Hornstein present two case studies in which they explore the significance and impact of this dynamic process. Their case examples include the changing public response of psychologists to psychoanalysis and the rebellion of one psychologist popularizer against the boundaries established by the psychological community to mark the divide between the professional and the popular.

JoAnne Brown, like Hornstein and Morawski, takes up the issue of professionalization and expertise within modern American psychology but explains it from a different and unique perspective. She examines the rhetorical claims to expertise by psychologists, based on an evaluation of their use of language and metaphor. Brown asserts that psychologists borrowed the syntactical methods and language of Progressive era engineers and physicians in an attempt to draw on the public prestige of the latter. Psychologists hoped to draw on the great reservoir of public esteem for physicians and engineers in their own attempt to establish a claim to expertise in the areas of mental testing and evaluation. The public face of professional expertise in Progressive America reflected a common use of language and rhetorical style that stressed scientific objectivity, efficiency, and service in the public good. By borrowing the syntactic structure of professional claims to public power, psychologists hoped to legitimize themselves and the scientific basis of psychology itself. Brown draws on recent studies in the public use of rhetoric, professionalization studies, and intellectual history to explore the public face which psychologists presented to an often credulous public.

While van Keuren has investigated the intrainstitutional negotiations that established British anthropology's subject matter and disciplinary boundaries, Gilkeson explores how a core research concept and methodology was used to redefine American anthropology. He goes on to show how this redefinition served as a basis for disciplinary organization and was subsequently adopted into other social scientific disciplines and popular culture. Franz Boas and his students seized on the idea of culture as an object of analysis peculiarly suited to the professional needs and aspirations of anthropology. The evolutionary overtones of the Victorian use of the term were eliminated, as were its associations with belletristic accomplishment. Culture became an object sui generis, separate from race and an adjunct to behavior. The culture concept was then borrowed by other social scientists and scientific popularizers. Americanists in particular found the idea fruitful as they sought to isolate and explicate what was unique about the American experience. Thus, Gilkeson combines aspects of intellectual, social, and institutional history to analyze the context and social uses of anthropological theory in the twentieth century. In so doing, he is able to shed light on the dynamics of disciplinary professionalization, popularization, and the intellectual relations between the social sciences during this century.

Robert Proctor singles out eugenics for his analysis, the sole example within this volume of a field that is no longer recognized as a constituent member of the social sciences. However, as Proctor points out, eugenics flourished when the boundaries and subject matters of most social sciences were still in flux. Eugenicists often viewed their discipline as a science of society par excellence or, indeed, as an Ur-discipline which within its subject matter comprehended all other social sciences. Inasmuch as eugenicists believed human nature was based on genetic constitution and disposition, it followed that a study of natural inheritance would allow one to ultimately predict and control behavior. This combination of biology and social theory was a potent intellectual force within the first four decades of this century and still has its followers. Social scientists responded varyingly to what was viewed either as the threat or promise of eugenics. In Germany, anthropology became almost subsumed within eugenics while sociology rejected its tenets and went into eclipse until the postwar era. Proctor develops an American-German comparison to show how disparate intellectual and social contexts helped shape the differential development of eugenics in these countries. He also makes adept use of insights gleaned from the history and sociology of science to demonstrate how much our understanding of what comprises a social science is culturally based and to demonstrate the large influence of political factors on the constitution of science as a whole.

Walter Jackson chooses as his topic the social and political context of Gunnar Myrdal's drafting of *An American Dilemma*. Jackson clearly demonstrates how Myrdal's wartime experiences served as a prism through which he viewed the dynamic of American race relations. It was these experiences, constantly reinterpreted as Myrdal shuttled back and forth between the United States and Sweden, that became the template for the *Dilemma* and the basis of the author's stirring manifesto urging moral resistance to injustice and tyranny everywhere. Jackson uses the great breadth of his research in and understanding of Myrdal's career to add a new dimension to our understanding of the origins and drafting of Myrdal's magnum opus. His essay is a fine example of how social and political exegesis can be used to add new depth and vigor to intellectual history and to contextualize social science history.

The final essay in this volume is a comment on historic ethnocentrism within the social sciences themselves. Rubén Martinez turns the tables on social scientists as he, both a trained sociologist and a member of an ethnic minority, observes the observer while commenting on the status of minorities within the social scientific community. It is Martinez's contention that perceptions of minorities as portrayed within social scientific literature display misconceptions and stereotypes that have become ingrained within the viewpoint of the white male academic establishment. Although the social sciences try to eschew the cultural biases peculiar to specific times, settings, or social elites, Martinez asserts that portrayals of minorities in the United States are hopelessly so tainted. The solution is the accretion of social scientific knowledge of minorities by minority scholars themselves. However, there are institutional barriers to participation of minority scholars within the academic establishment. Martinez details these obstacles and suggests what participation by minority scholars in the social scientific enterprise might look like. The author uses the methods of social science to critique the social science status quo and draws on history to provide evidence in support of his thesis.

Notes

1. Marie Jean Antoine Nicholas de Caritat, marquis de Condorcet, "Discours pronounce dans l'Académie Française, le jeudi 21 février 1782, á la réception de M. le marquis de Condorcet," in A. Condorcet O'Connor and M. F. Arago, *Oeuvres de Condorcet* (Paris: Didot Frères, 1847–1849; reprinted by Friedrich Frommann Verlag, Stuttgart–Bad Cannstatt, 1968) 1: 389–415.
2. For a study of Condorcet's participation in the society, see Keith Michael Baker, *Condorcet: From Natural Philosophy to Social Mathematics* (Chicago: University of Chicago Press, 1982).
3. For example, see Clifford Geertz, "Blurred Genres: The Refiguration of Social Thought," in *Local Knowledge: Further Essays in Interpretive Anthropology* (New York: Basic Books, 1983), pp. 19–36.
4. Marvin Harris, *The Rise of Anthropological Theory: A History of Theories of Culture* (New York: Thomas Y. Crowell Co., 1969) is an extended example of the use of historical evidence to argue a methodological point. Harris, an ardent cultural evolutionist, contends that the antinomotheticism of Boas and his students and their capture of the discipline in the United States set back theoretical development in anthropology by several decades. Harris's arguments ignited a fiery debate among anthropologists, who brought historical evidence to bear on both sides of the issue.
5. H. Stuart Hughes, *Consciousness and Society* (New York: Knopf, 1958); Merle Curti, *Human Nature in American Thought: A History* (Madison: University of Wisconsin Press, 1980); Richard Hofstadter, *Social Darwinism in American Thought* (Boston: Beacon Press, 1955); Dorothy Ross, *The Origins of American Social Science* (Cambridge: Cambridge University Press, 1990); Thomas Haskell, *The Emergence of Professional Social Science: The American Social Science Association and the Nineteenth-Century Crisis of Authority* (Urbana: University of Illinois Press, 1977); Mary O. Furner, *Advocacy and Objectivity: A Crisis in the Professionalization of American Social Science, 1865-1905* (Lexington: University Press of Kentucky, 1975).
6. Marshall Clagett, ed., *Critical Problems in the History of Science* (Madison: University of Wisconsin Press, 1959).
7. Robert M. Young, "Scholarship and the History of the Behavioral Sciences," *History of Science* 5 (1966): 1–51.
8. Hamilton Cravens, "History of the Social Sciences," in Sally Gregory Kohlstedt and Margaret W. Rossiter, eds., *Historical Writing on American Science*, Osiris 8 (1985): 183–207.
9. For a comprehensive review of this scholarship, see ibid.
10. See Arnold Thackray, "History of Science," in Paul T. Durbin, ed., *A Guide to the Culture of Science, Technology, and Medicine* (New York: Free Press, 1980), pp. 3–69, for a good overview of historiographic trends and disputes within the history of science.
11. Hamilton Cravens, *The Triumph of Evolution: American Scientists and the Heredity-Environment Controversy, 1900-1941* (Philadelphia: University of Pennsylvania Press, 1978).

12. We use the term *guild* historians here to distinguish those trained in history from scholars with affiliations in other disciplines who practice historical inquiry yet were not trained within the historical discipline or do not publish and teach under its rubric.

13. On problems of language and politics, see Murray Edelman, especially *Political Language: Words That Succeed and Policies That Fail* (New York: Academic Press, 1977), and David Hollinger, "Historians and the Discourse of Intellectuals," in John Higham and Paul Conkin, eds., *New Directions in American Intellectual History* (Baltimore: Johns Hopkins University Press, 1977).

14. We are recasting in linguistic terms the central motive in Robert F. Berkhofer's book *A Behavioral Approach to Historical Analysis* (New York: Free Press, 1969).

15. Richard D. Brown, *Modernization: The Transformation of American Life 1600–1865* (New York: Hill and Wang, 1976).

16. Some examples include Kenneth Lockridge's use of modernization theory, Herbert Gutman's more subtle use of modernization categories, and Eugene Genovese and Elizabeth Fox Genovese's use of deconstruction. Many of these debates are not performed in writing but in seminars and meetings, where debate is fluid.

17. George Herbert Mead, *Mind, Self and Society* (Chicago: University of Chicago Press, 1934, 1940).

18. Ibid., pp. 140, 154, 156, 160–6, 74n.

19. David Hollinger, "The Problem of Pragmatism in American History," *Journal of American History* 67, no. 1 (June 1980): 88–107, 94. See also Carl Degler, review of Peter Novick, *That Noble Dream: The "Objectivity Question" and the American Historical Profession, Journal of American History* 76, no. 3 (December 1989): 892–9.

The Estate
of Social Knowledge

■ 1 THE ESTATE OF POLITICAL KNOWLEDGE

Political Science and the State

JAMES FARR

A new political science is needed for a world itself
quite new.
—ALEXIS DE TOCQUEVILLE

The most perfect example of the modern state is
North America.
—KARL MARX

The national popular state alone furnishes the objective
reality upon which political science can rest in the
construction of a truly scientific political system.
—JOHN W. BURGESS

Much remains to be done—and undone—in the study of the history
of political science. This is a simple consequence of the fact that political
science remembers so little of its own history, and what history it does
remember is often dismissed as dead wrong, or simply dead. In this way,
when it does not forget its past altogether, political science engages in
that "enormous condescension of posterity."[1] Thanks to some recent
labors, however, this posture of forgetfulness or condescension is beginning to give way to a more sympathetic and accurate historical stance,
at least with respect to the twentieth (and the late nineteenth) century,
when political science became a professional academic discipline, and
with respect to certain of its concepts, like voting, public opinion, and
political change.[2] But much remains to be done with respect to the
predisciplinary history of political science, and much remains to be undone with respect to the concept of the state.

On the eve of discipline, political science was conceived of *as* the

1

science of the state. The estate of political knowledge was the "state."[3] Twelve years after the Civil War, at a time when political science was becoming a professionally recognized field of higher education, Theodore Dwight Woolsey could publish his presidential lectures at Yale quite simply as *Political Science, or the State Theoretically and Practically Considered* (1877). The closing years of the century witnessed a profusion of books about the state, and the majority of their most influential authors (like John W. Burgess, W. W. Willoughby, William Dunning, and Woodrow Wilson, among others) were identified as academic political scientists. German scholars for some time had been contributing to the view that political science was the science of the state by conceiving of it as *Staatswissenschaft*. After the American Political Science Association was formed in 1903, the state continued to command the attention of professional political scientists, especially those of Progressive leanings who sought to reform its administrative structure. Well into the New Deal, political scientists cast their works on government, parties, and policy in terms of the state. However, as revolutionary regimes spread and another world war approached, many political scientists, increasingly identified with one or another strain of liberalism, soon came to find the very idea of the state suspiciously socialist or reactionary or both.[4] Harold Lasswell made dark references to the "garrison state."[5] Yet so strong was the identification of political science with the study of the state that it would become a principal object of attack as late as the 1950s during the opening skirmishes of the behavioral revolution.[6] Even now, as one historian of political science regretfully acknowledges, there is "a resurrection of an older concept, that of the state" as a principal locus for the discipline of political science.[7]

This much of the story of political science and the state appears to enjoy agreement among the few historians of political science. On other aspects of the story, however, there appears to be less agreement. Indeed, it is one of the burdens of this essay to make certain disagreements clear. At issue are questions about the predisciplinary identity and ideology of political science; the origin of its concept of the state; and the credibility and coherence of its efforts to theorize about it. It has been alleged, for example, that before the 1870s there was a "sense of statelessness" in American political thought and culture largely because of the intellectual heritage of Lockean liberalism.[8] Political science, we are told, came to be identified as the science of the state only *after* the administrative and bureaucratic revolution that created the "new American state."[9] Even then, however, the state, both in theory and in practice, was to appear "alien to American experience and institutions."[10] The concept of the state, this account continues, was a German import.

Under German influence, the analysis of the state—"the least American of our political words"—proved to be narrowly legalistic, not to mention "perilously figurative," "abstract and convoluted."[11] "Far removed from the everyday talk of the people, political science even reified the state into an entity higher than the people." Consequently, political science proved to be an academic discipline whose "counterrevolution in political rhetoric" abandoned the principles of the American Revolution as it sought to "wrest political argument out of the hands of the people."[12]

In this essay, I wish to counter these particular claims and try to undo such influence they might have. By tracing the changing concepts of political science and the state amidst the ebbing tradition of republican political discourse, we may see that Americans had a sense of the state going back to the earliest years of the Republic. The language of the state was a broadly European and, then, an American one which had pervaded political discussion well before the Civil War and certainly before a number of young academics went off to Germany in the latter decades of the century in pursuit of *Staatswissenschaft*. Though abstract in the way that most complex theoretical terms are, the state provided self-styled political scientists with a framework for analyzing the organizational and ethical complexities of American political life, especially the Constitution, law, liberty, parties, public opinion, popular sovereignty, and republican government. There was, of course, considerable debate about the meaning of all this, but the concept of the state provided unity of attention amid diversity of detail and speculation. Furthermore, the self-styled political scientists of the nineteenth century thought of their pedagogic task as a directly political one: to educate nascent citizens in the public virtues long associated with the republican tradition.

Though critical of the views mentioned above, my intent in this essay is principally both complimentary and complementary because I agree with so much else these authors have taught us about the history of political science and its connection with the American state. In what follows, then, I propose to contribute to their efforts by paying close or closer attention to how political science and the state were expressly and jointly conceptualized and reconceptualized in American political discourse during the nineteenth century. The constitutional founders, Francis Lieber, and a number of late nineteenth–century professionals are singled out for particular attention in this conceptual approach to the history of political science. Their views help constitute three moments in the history of political science, the movement of which we might characterize as the development *from discourse to discipline*. That is to say, in the course of its first century, American political science was transformed from a political discourse in the service of republican principles to a professional discipline in the service of the administrative state. This transformation remains to be elaborated more fully. My efforts here attempt a beginning.

Historiographically speaking, a conceptual approach to the history of political science (or to any science) is admittedly selective and partial. But it has its reasons, especially against the suspicions or prejudices of those historians who incline toward the material, the sociological, or the psychoanalytic.[13] It may be understood as a subset of the broader study of the language of science, which itself ranges from theories to metaphors to rhetoric to the codes of invisible colleges.[14] The concepts which are of principal concern to the historian of science are of two sorts. There are those that define or pick out (differently at different times) the theoretical domain or objects of a science. In political science, these concepts have included law, sovereignty, voting, public opinion, and many others, as well as the state. Here the attention is on the conceptualization of the world "outside" of science, as it were. And then there are those concepts that define or pick out (the nature or the methods of) the science in question. For political science, one might include statistics, interpretation, surveys, and models, among others, as well as the scope and missions of political science when it is explicitly invoked as on object of reflection. Here the attention is on the self-conceptualization of the world "inside" the science, as it were. There is no world "in itself," whether in or out of science. Conceptualization forms the appropriate arena for the conceptual historian of science.

The history of political science, then, will attend to the two sorts of concepts and to the worlds they conceptualize. This is an essential task in that the very identification of political science is itself at stake. Political science, like any human practice, is at least partly constituted by the concepts its practitioners hold or once held about it and its domain. On pain of misunderstanding the past—and especially the *pre*-disciplinary past—the historian of political science must attempt to recover these concepts as well as to trace their change over time. Finer distinctions thereby become important, say between political science and political economy in the eighteenth century or between political science and social science in the nineteenth century. The historian should not collapse these various distinctions in order to create a contextless meta-discourse or metadiscipline, an activity in which historians of (especially political) "ideas" frequently and unfortunately engage.[15] As for their sites, concepts do not exist "in the head," as David Hume once put it, but in words and texts. For it is in words and texts that we find such signs as we can have of what past political scientists thought, intended, or sensed. So it is to them that the conceptual historian turns.[16]

There are evident affinities here to hermeneutics, to internal history, and to historicism.[17] But at least as regards the last of these, almost every historical study of science serves at least some presentist concerns; and certainly the few recent studies in the history of political science reveal a number of different and competing present-day motivations.[18] This essay's conceptual history of political science and the state hopes to lay the historical groundwork for an argument about the lingering republican identity and the requisite methodological pluralism of a discipline designed to educate citizens. It also admits to taking its point of departure from the efforts of political scientists and sociologists who are presently "bringing the state back in."[19] Let us, then, bring back in to the picture those statists who have populated American political science from the very beginning of the Republic.

The concept of the science of politics enters American political discourse in the late eighteenth century, and never more prominently than in the debates over the Constitution. While most of the founders were retrospectively generous about the long history of ancient and modern contributors to this science (this "divine science of politics," as John Adams sermonized even before the Revolution), the most important and immediate influences were themselves eighteenth–century figures, especially those northern Britons credited with having ushered in a Scottish Enlightenment.[20] Like the Scots, the American founders explicitly and repeatedly used the very terms to pick out this nascent science. Thereafter, these terms—*science of politics, political science, science of government, science of legislation,* and their kin—would help reshape American political discourse and indeed the very institutions and practices of American political life.

During the Revolution, but especially during the debates over the ratification of the Constitution, the rhetoric of science was crucial. Science spoke for all sides. Understandably, however, the methodological identity of this science was never fully specified by the various rhetoricians amid the more pressing struggles. Indeed, in the writings of the late 1780s and early 1790s, the science of politics (and its kindred sciences) seemed to range without careful methodological distinction between the rules and practical maxims which inhered naturally in American citizen-statesmen, and those laws, principles, and axioms of politics which formally resembled the generalizations of Newtonian mechanics.[21] The one drew inspiration from history and ordinary experience; the other from physics and controlled observation. But whatever its particular methods, and well over half a century would pass before this became a topic of sustained and independent investigation in American political science, there was a shared sense, as Alexander Hamilton pointed out, that "the science of politics, like most other sciences, has received great improvement." There were "wholly new discoveries" and even "progress towards perfection."[22] David Ramsay thought America itself had played a role in this, for the new nation had placed "the science of politics on a footing with the other sciences, by opening it to improvements from experience, and the discoveries of the future."[23] Yet political science or the "science of government," as James Madison chimed in, had not answered all questions previously raised, especially in the matter of "the privileges and powers of the different legislative branches."[24] The American scientists of politics were there to remedy this defect.

To remedy this scientific defect was to remedy yet other defects, especially those political ones attending the postrevolutionary constitutional arrangements. In this remedial task, political science took (or, rather, was rhetorically made to take) very different sides. At stake (again, especially between Federalists and Antifederalists) was the nature of republicanism in general and in particular the republican arrangements thought to be necessary to an increasingly commercial society in a large territory of the new world. Indeed, the concept of political science (and its kindred sciences) should be understood as a relatively late addition to republican political discourse. Its introduction coincides with (and was conceptually party to) the demise of classical republicanism and the emergence of a new republican discourse more attuned to commerce, the balance of interests, and the institutionalization of virtue.[25] It bears underscoring that neither Federalists nor Antifederalists can or must bear the burden of liberal categories which have been placed upon them by later nineteenth- and twentieth-century interpreters who thought liberalism was somehow "given" in America.[26] Nor, I would suggest, should the identity of political science be understood as an unproblematically liberal one, not only in the founding period but throughout the course of the nineteenth century and perhaps beyond.[27] Well into our century, political science bears the marks of its republican birth.

State was a term that came naturally to these American republicans, as indeed it had to most Western political writers of the previous two centuries upon whom the Americans readily drew.[28] Machiavelli, Bodin, Calvin, and Hobbes are particularly prominent theorists in this stretch of early modern intellectual history who helped give voice to the transformation of the earlier idea of the ruler "maintaining his estate." In its place there developed the idea that there is a separate legal and constitutional order, that of the State, which the ruler has a duty to maintain. One effect of this transformation was that the power of the State, not that of the ruler, came to be envisaged as the basis of government. And this in turn enabled the State to be conceptualized in distinctly modern terms—as the sole source of law and legitimate force within its own territory, and as the sole appropriate object of its citizens' allegiances.[29]

After the American Revolution the now-liberated colonies were conceptualized not only as republics but as states. The leaders of the new American nation were known not only as republicans but as statesmen. Such uses of the term *state* and its cognates were then, as now, so ordinary and taken for granted that citizens and historians then, as now, often overlooked them. However, the Articles of Confederation fully recognized what was at stake with this appellation. They insured the sovereignty of the thirteen new states. Of course, the Articles proved insufficient as an instrument of government, which was one of the few points of agreement of the Constitutional Convention and the ratification debates which followed. But another point of agreement, at least conceptually, regarded the state.

Though Federalists and Antifederalists would disagree about whether sovereignty could be divided and about where the state(s) did or should reside (in the thirteen subnational territories or across the geographical fullness of America), the language of the state was not itself at issue. All agreed that they were discussing the supreme power which acted through government over a sovereign territory and to which citizens and leaders owed their allegiance. Antifederalists meant quite literally—and without the solecism of dual sovereignty—that the thirteen states were sovereign states in the full-bodied European sense.[30] The Federalists denied this particular claim, but only to secure a statist identity for the nation as a whole. Repeatedly and naturally, Federalists spoke about the state or the civil state, including its "supreme powers," "reasons," "pride," "real interests," and "domestic police."[31] Hume, Montesquieu, and de Mably were all explicitly cited in the *Federalist* as appropriate European authorities on the state whose lessons were generally relevant (if not always directly applicable) to New World politics. This point was reinforced (and more authorities cited and criticized in light of the American experiment) by Nathaniel Chipman in 1793 when he repeatedly and naturally invoked the language of the state to discuss Americans' constitutionally guaranteed rights, powers, and liberties.[32]

All parties to the debates, in short, agreed on the basic contours of the concept. The state was the collective political agency given voice by a written constitution and laws and expressing popular sovereignty, whatever governmental, administrative, or federal structure it assumed. Political parties were not seen as creatures of the state, for they fanned the flames of faction rather than channeled the competition of interests. But whatever its place or form and whatever its legal or federal novelties, a state it was. As should be obvious, Publius never had a dream (or Brutus a nightmare) of a Bismarckian state of the sort to emerge on the Continent within a century. But their language fully attests to their sense of stateness, not statelessness. Such was the statist discourse of the republican scientists of politics.

Despite all the conceptual connections it forged and the theoretical possibilities it thereby created, this initial episode in the history of political science in America produced no sustained treatises on the state or any on the scope and methods of political science itself. And no one then explicitly conceptualized political science as the science of the state. While political science and the state would continue to animate American political discourse throughout the early nineteenth century,[33] including making some tentative entries into the moral philosophy and moral science curriculum,[34] it would take Francis Lieber, a Prussian émigré of republican and nationalist commitments, to produce the first systematic treatises on these subjects. In the quarter-century before the Civil War, a time during which Karl Marx thought that America was already perfecting the modern state,[35] Lieber produced a number of works which succeeded in raising the level of theoretical discourse about political science and the state, as well as securing him a chair at Columbia in 1857 as professor of history and political science, the very first of its kind in America. The title was Lieber's own creation and a point of pride he communicated to Alexis de Tocqueville, whose studies of American penitentiaries Lieber had assisted and translated.[36] Lieber himself hoped to provide for America that new political science which Tocqueville foresaw as necessary for a world itself quite new.

As early as the 1830s, the outlines of Lieber's political science were sufficiently well established, particularly in the *Manual of Political Ethics* (1838), *Legal and Political Hermeneutics* (1837), and a *Memorial Relative to Proposals for a Work on the Statistics of the United States* (1836). Later works fleshed these out, principal among them *Civil Liberty and Self-Government* (1857), *History and Political Science: Necessary Studies in a Free Country* (1858), and *The Ancient and Modern Teacher of Politics: An Introductory Discourse to a Course of Lectures on the State* (1860). Collectively, these works bore the marks of his German education under Niebuhr, Savigny, Humboldt, and Schleiermacher, especially the attention to philology and hermeneutics, not to mention history, law, and the state. But Lieber's works also bore the marks of his political naturalization, having lived in America since 1827 and having contributed to its first major literary effort in the New World, the *Encyclopedia Americana*. The *Encyclopedia*, and indeed all Lieber's works from the 1830s on, displayed a genuine integration of European and American sources. On its pages, Montesquieu and Jefferson, Hume and Madison, Humboldt and Calhoun, Haller and Story, Schleiermacher and Kent, Whewell and Hamilton, including the more ancient and venerable figures like Plato, Hobbes, and Pufendorf, in whose number Lieber immodestly counted himself, intermingled and provided authority for a heady brew.[37] Much of this was a show of scholarship, of course, but much of it genuinely provided Lieber with the intellectual sources to take a new look at political science, republicanism, and the state in America.

In contrast to those who preceded him, Lieber wrote more, and more self-consciously, about the methods, objects, and educational objectives of political science. He proved to be a methodological pluralist who thought that statistics, causal generalizations, and hermeneutics all went into that "scientific treatment of politics" that "deals with man as a jural being. . . . [that is,] as a citizen."[38] Hermeneutics was helpful here, for citizens as well as for political scientists, because it was "that branch of science which establishes the principles of interpretation and construction," especially for those jural texts, like the Constitution, which (literally) helped constitute American political life.[39] History was also methodologically important for political science because it provided, among other things, a wealth of facts; and Lieber himself was more historical and factual than any of his predecessors had been. In his inaugural address at Columbia, he put the point this way: "History is continuous Statistik; Statistik, history arrested at a given time."[40] In his earlier *Memorial for Statistics* (which was read into the congressional record from the Senate floor by John C. Calhoun), he had called for "a careful collection of detailed facts, and the endeavor to arrive at general results by a comprehensive view and judicious combination of them."[41] Statistics, in short, were "state-istics"—facts and generalizations useful for enlightened citizens and republican statesmen.[42]

Political science was conceptually connected to the state in two further ways beyond the methodological tie of statistics. Both may be appreciated by pondering the title of an important public address given in 1859 by Columbia's professor of political science: *The Ancient and Modern Teacher of Politics: An Introductory Discourse to a Course of Lectures on the State* (published in 1860). First, Lieber was a pioneer in transforming political science into an independent course of study in higher education (a task he began as early as the late 1830s, when he assumed his first and only other academic post at South Carolina College). While it was still part of the rhetorical armory of American orators and writers through the end of the century, political science was now increasingly identified with college and university. But this was not (yet) a purely academic confinement, at least in that "the teaching of the publicist may become an element of living statesmanship."[43] Lieber was among the first self-styled political scientists to conceive of the task of higher education in political science as instilling public virtues into (potential) citizens, those "sons of republicans," who were otherwise allured by the corruptions of the age, especially perhaps its "fanatical idolatry of success."[44] Justice, fortitude, patriotism, duty, and moderation headed a long list of public virtues for republican self-governance. And a more disinterested, general education was required for this pedagogical task of political proportions: "The future citizen, or active member of the state, is then to be included in the objects of education."[45] Thus our professor of history and political science could praise his newly minted efforts as "the very science of nascent citizens of a republic."[46]

Second, political science was to make the state its principal object of investigation. Lieber first makes this clear well before the Civil War in the *Manual of Political Ethics*. This two-volume work, first published in 1838, should be read as the first systematic treatise on the state in American political science and perhaps in American political literature as such. In dealing with "man as a jural being," political science dealt with the state, for he conceptualized the state as a "jural society," one founded on the "relations of right" between its citizens.[47] The state, he went on, flowed from the "sovereignty of the people," which manifested itself not only in the law but in the governmental institutionalities of power, which best functioned when checking and balancing each other.[48] All this was best realized within a republican framework.

This much had been familiar to Americans for over half a century. But there was also some conceptual change here as well, including the very coining of the term *jural*. In calling the state a "jural *society*" he wanted to distinguish it from a mere association and thereby loosen the holds of contractarian thinking which had been influential at the founding (though not in the minds of a number of the founders' most important intellectual predecessors, in particular the enlightened Scots like Hume). This was one of the natural consequences of the historical and factual thinking with which Lieber sought to infuse political science. "Man cannot divest himself of the state," as he said in his Columbia inaugural address. "Government was never voted into existence."[49] In contrast to the Federalists, he reunited sovereignty, thinking it incoherent to speak of a dual sovereignty. But, in contrast to the Antifederalists, he placed it in the nation as a whole over which the government ruled. In contrast to both, and in full recognition of the de facto rise and institutionalization of the American party system, Lieber confessed that "I know of no instance of a free state without parties."[50] He heightened the theoretical importance of public opinion by making it a direct expression of popular sovereignty. These changes in the concept (or conceptual domain) of the state, once accepted, were to prove important in the subsequent history of American political science, including its veritable preoccupation with law, parties, and public opinion.

None of this, I submit, merits characterization as counterrevolutionary.[51] The evident nationalist sentiments are consistent with that greater half of the country preparing to fight to maintain the Union.[52] Furthermore, none of this is incoherent or overly abstract, at least not any more so than any other complex concept which does double duty in public discourse and academic treatise. This is as true of a concept like rights, which some take to be paradigmatically American and liberal, as it is of the state. In light of the nineteenth- and twentieth-century tomes and the gyrations which they put rights through, Bentham's celebrated words are worth recalling: "Rights, nonsense; Natural and imprescriptible rights, nonsense on stilts." But yet such nonsense, if nonsense it ever was, comprised the very soul of American rhetoric. And this is as true of the state as it is of rights. In the mid-nineteenth century, the state did not sound to American ears as a Teutonic invasion against good sense, at least if we can trust the sentiments which informed the reception of the *Manual of Political Ethics* by Supreme Court Justice Joseph Story in 1838:

> It contains by far the fullest and most correct development of the true theory of what constitutes the State that I have ever seen. . . . To me many of the thoughts are new, and as striking as they are new. . . . [In] addressing itself to the wise and virtuous of all countries, it solves the question what government is best by the answer, illustrated in a thousand ways, that it is that which best promotes the substantial interests of the whole people of the nation on which it acts. Such a work is peculiarly important in these times, when so many false theories are afloat and so many disturbing doctrines are promulgated.[53]

Nullification, states' rights, and secession were indeed on the scene to disturb and frighten the new American statists who understandably had the law and the Constitution uppermost in their minds. Such were the specters haunting political science and the American state.

Between the Civil War and the century's end, the varied efforts of the sort which consumed Lieber's energies came to fruition as political science moved toward discipline. Political science became increasingly self-conscious about its professional identity as a science.[54] It continued to find its site in higher education and its pedagogical purpose in fostering public virtues for nascent republican citizens.[55] This period could well be called the triumph of the state, both in fact,[56] as well as in the self-conceptualization of the most important political scientists of the time.[57] This is made abundantly clear in American works like Theodore Dwight Woolsey's *Political Science, or the State Theoretically and Practically Considered*, W. W. Willoughby's *The Nature of the State*, John W. Burgess's *Political Science and Constitutional Law*, and future president Woodrow Wilson's *The State: Elements of Historical and Practical Politics*. These works were to set the agenda for a generation of American political scientists, including those who became increasingly interested and actually involved in public administration.[58] In theory, political scientists captured the state; in practice, the state captured them.

The late nineteenth century political scientists were increasingly methodological, if not always in actual practice, then certainly in self-presentation. The already much-used rhetoric of science and method continued to exert its pull over the American imagination. In *Political Science and Constitutional Law*, John W. Burgess, Lieber's successor at Columbia and founder of its School of Political Science in 1880, singled out his contribution to the discipline in this way: "If my book has any peculiarity, it is its method. It is a comparative study. It is an attempt to apply the method, which has been found so productive in the domain of Natural Science, to Political Science and Jurisprudence."[59] The natural scientific overtones had indeed been on the minds of self-styled political scientists for well over a century,[60] and they would show no signs of abating well into the next.[61] The methodological invocation of hermeneutics had not (yet) been silenced, as is understandable for a science concerned (for good historical and political reasons) with law, constitutional arrangements, and jural behavior.[62] This was enough to temper the scientism that invariably attends the wish to make political science a natural science of politics. Beyond the scientism, however, it is true and worth underscoring that Burgess and Wilson and many of their peers were indeed more historical; thereby, they were more factual and statistical in their analyses of the state since, for them, history was a great repository of facts and events. And they were genuinely comparative in their focus, providing more or less systematic studies of American, British, French, and German institutions, practices, and laws.

This methodologically self-conscious science was to continue to conceptualize the state as its principal domain. This, too, would continue into the second quarter of the twentieth century, despite (or maybe because of) the Progressive reformers. Most of the late-nineteenth-century political scientists were conscious of the venerable conceptual materials with which they dealt, but also of the scientific novelty which they brought to bear upon them. All gave theoretical expression, as it were, to the Union victory in the Civil War. The modern constitutional state was that law-governed and liberty-protecting organization of the political community whose governmental apparatus was centered and increasingly centralized in Washington, D.C., and whose "principle of popular sovereignty" spread over the still-advancing political geography of America.[63] Indeed, since the subnational governments were not sovereign, "it is no longer proper to call them States at all. It is in fact only a title of honor, without any corresponding substance."[64] Geography notwithstanding, the state was not (as Daniel Rodgers has recently argued) conceived of as an antonym to the people.[65] If anything, it was a synonym, at least if we can trust Burgess's view that "the state is the people in ultimate organization" or Willoughby's view that the state was in essence "a community of people socially united."[66] Thereby the late-nineteenth-century political scientists entered into a century-old American political conversation whose terms were familiar, despite the changing theories which incorporated them and which contributed to their change of meaning. Neither abstract nor convoluted (or, at any rate, no more so than the other key words of American political thought), the state had been and would remain, as Woolsey pointed out, "a fixed political term . . . in our language."[67]

Yet these increasingly professional academics displayed considerable diversity in their theories of the state. Thus we should appreciate that the concept of the state provided them more with an intellectual framework for theoretical debate rather than some universally accepted foundation for a disputation-free science. But this was nonetheless sufficient unity amid diversity. Woolsey began to work away at some distinctions (later to be refined by Goodnow) between the political basis and the practical administration of the state.[68] Willoughby transformed American federal principles into the language of the "composite state" and quibbled about the finer points of popular sovereignty.[69] Burgess looked for "the state made objective in institutions and laws," especially in parties and public opinion. He also pried apart a distinction between state and government, a distinction which (like the modern constitution, individual liberty, and federalism) he thought had reached its greatest clarity in fact and in theory in America.

> In America we have a great advantage in regard to this subject. With us the government is not the sovereign organization of the state. Back of the government lies the constitution; and back of the constitution the original sovereign state, which ordains the constitution both of government and liberty. We have the distinction [between state and government] already in objective reality; . . . This is the point in which the public law of the United States has reached a far higher development than that of any state of Europe.[70]

Germany had hosted Burgess's postgraduate education,[71] but his vision of the "objective reality" upon which political science rested was his own homegrown American state and its republican institutions of government. And there was nothing particularly novel or overly Germanic about this. From the constitutional founders, from Lieber, from countless American publicists and orators, Burgess simply took over the concept of the state as an integral component of American political discourse. And the discipline of political science was in the process of transforming the state, both in theory and practice. Soon enough Progressive political scientists would man the administration, and soon enough an American-educated statist of this period whose principal academic work would sell in Germany in translation as *Der Staat* would become president of the United States. For good or ill, the statists of American political science would see their country's highest office go to one of their number.

Having the state as the object of one's science did not require any particular partisan stance. Indeed, among the late-nineteenth-century political scientists there was considerable diversity in ideological orientation, though none came out explicitly against the people. Many statists were racialists and imperialists; many others were not.[72] "Conservative" is not an altogether unfair description of Burgess, at least given some of his policy recommendations and given our contemporary terminology.[73] The hints of elitism are not unnoticeable (nor had they been in classical republicanism, for that matter), and these hints would be transformed into the ideology of technocratic expertise among the Progressives and statist administrators. Yet the concern with general welfare was shared by most of the nineteenth-century political scientists, and some of them thought this liberal and called it so. At least the author of the *Principia of Political Science* made this clear in his subtitle, *Upon a Reverent, Moral, Liberal and Progressive Foundation*.[74] A student of Burgess's,

Frank S. Hoffman, went further still. A socialist and a Christian, he thought that the state had "not only the right but the duty . . . to abolish all private possession" and to "better promote the well-being of the people."[75] No hegemony of political judgments, in short, followed with iron-clad logic from the American political scientists' concept of the state, whatever the iron chancellor was preparing for Germany.

In conclusion, the late nineteenth century proved to be a period of vitality and fertility for an American science of politics which proclaimed its unity and identity as the science of the state. In the process of educating citizens while theorizing as scientists, the discipline became more professional and thoroughly academic. Soon enough this identity, as professionals and academics, would eclipse or fundamentally transform the republican convictions which had helped to bring it about in the first place. The movement from discourse to discipline would be all but complete.

Notes

In their different capacities, I would like to thank Kristin Bumiller, Raymond Duvall, John G. Gunnell, Lawrence Jacobs, Dorothy Ross, and the editors.

Epigraphs: Alexis de Tocqueville, *Democracy in America* (Garden City, N.Y.: Anchor Books, 1969), p. 12; Karl Marx, *German Ideology* (New York: International, 1970), p. 80; John W. Burgess, *Political Science and Constitutional Law* (Boston: Ginn and Co., 1893), 1: 58.

1. Stefan Collini, Donald Winch, and John Burrow, *That Noble Science of Politics: A Study in Nineteenth-Century Intellectual History* (Cambridge: Cambridge University Press, 1983), p. 377.

2. David Ricci, *The Tragedy of Political Science: Politics, Scholarship, and Democracy* (New Haven: Yale University Press, 1984); Raymond Seidelman (with the assistance of Edward J. Harpham), *Disenchanted Realists: Political Science and the American Crisis, 1884–1984* (Albany: State University of New York Press, 1985); Peter B. Natchez, *Images of Voting/Visions of Democracy* (New York: Basic Books, 1985); Andrew C. Janos, *Politics and Paradigms: Changing Theories of Change in the Social Sciences* (Stanford: Stanford University Press, 1986). It also deserves notice that the American Political Science Association has an oral history project under way consisting principally of interviews with the elder statesmen of the discipline.

3. Besides the fact that the state figured as the distinct intellectual property—the estate—of political science, there is an important etymological and theoretical legacy which links estate to state. See, in particular, Quentin Skinner, *The Foundations of Modern Political Thought*, 2 vols. (Cambridge: Cambridge University Press, 1978).

4. John G. Gunnell, "American Political Science, Liberalism, and the Invention of Political Theory," *American Political Science Review* 82 (1988): 71–87.

5. Harold Lasswell, "The Garrison State and Specialists on Violence," *American Journal of Sociology* 46 (1941): 455–68. An earlier rendition of this thesis was published in 1937.

6. See, especially, David Easton, *The Political System: An Inquiry into the State of Political Science* (Chicago: University of Chicago Press, 1953).

7. David Easton, "The Political System Besieged by the State," *Political Theory* 9 (1981): 303; cf Easton, "Political Science in the United States: Past and Present," *International Political Science Review* 6 (1985): 133–52.

8. Steven Skowronek, *Building a New American State: The Expansion of National Administrative Capacities, 1877–1920* (New York: Cambridge University Press, 1982), p. 5. Skowronek's principal concern is to address the institutional and administrative developments which constituted the process of centralized state building in the latter decades of the nineteenth century. However, he begins with an eye to theories and concepts of the state, especially those of Tocqueville, Hegel, and Marx, when he suggests that there was an "absence of a sense of the state in early America" (p. 5). It is this claim which concerns me here. For a critique of those who, somewhat analogously, think that Americans have a sense of placelessness (or, more particularly, that they are a "people without geography"), see Andrew Kirby, "The Great Desert of the American Mind: Concepts of Space and Time and Their Historiographic Implications," in this volume.

9. Skowronek, *Building a New American State*, passim.

10. Bernard Crick, *The American Science of Politics: Its Origins and Conditions* (Berkeley: University of California Press, 1959), p. 96. Also see his remark that the United States was, late into the century, "a nation which had no sense of the state" (p. 99).

11. Daniel Rodgers, *Contested Truths: Keywords in American Politics since Independence* (New York: Basic Books, 1987), pp. 14, 166, 171. Political scientists, it is further claimed, "acquired the term State" from Germany because of their education there in the late nineteenth century (p. 167).

12. Rodgers, *Contested Truths*, pp. 14, 145, 175. Also see Easton, *The Political System*, passim, for similar assessments.

13. This volume alone contains many different approaches to the history of the social sciences.

14. For some examples, see Mary Hesse, *Models and Analogies in Science* (Notre Dame: University of Notre Dame Press, 1966), esp. pp. 157–77; Michel Foucault, *The Order of Things* (New York: Pantheon, 1970); JoAnne Brown, "Professional Language: Words that Succeed," *Radical History Review* 34 (1986): 33–51; Donald McCloskey, *The Rhetoric of Economics* (Madison: University of Wisconsin Press, 1985); Diana Crane, *Invisible Colleges* (Chicago, University of Chicago Press, 1972).

15. For a still-powerful critique of this activity, see Quentin Skinner, "Meaning and Understanding in the History of Ideas," *History and Theory* 8 (1969): 3–53.

16. For some elaboration, see James Farr, "Understanding Conceptual Change Politically," in Terence Ball, James Farr, and Russell L. Hanson, eds., *Political Innovation and Conceptual Change* (New York: Cambridge University Press, 1989), chap. 2.

17. I use *historicism* not in the sense of Karl Popper, *The Poverty of Historicism* (London: Routledge and Kegan Paul, 1957), but in the sense of George W. Stocking, Jr., "On the Limits of 'Presentism' and 'Historicism' in the Historiography of the Behavioral Sciences," *Journal of the History of the Behavioral Sciences* 1 (1965): 211–218.

18. As observed in James Farr, "The History of Political Science," *American Journal of Political Science* 32 (1988): 1175–95. Also see John S. Dryzek and Stephen T. Leonard, "History and Discipline in Political Science," *American Political Science Review* 82 (1988): 1245–60.

19. Peter Evans, Dietrich Rueschemeyer, and Theda Skocpol, eds., *Bringing the State Back In* (New York: Cambridge University Press, 1985).

20. For discussion of the methodological and political intentions of the Scottish Enlighteners, see James Farr, "Political Science and the Enlightenment of Enthusiasm," *American Political Science Review* 82 (1988): 51–69.

21. See, for example, Alexander Hamilton, James Madison, and John Jay, *Federalist* (New York: New American Library, 1961; originally 1787–88), esp. nos. 9, 31, 37, 47. For Antifederalists, see Herbert J. Storing, ed., *The Complete Antifederalist* (Chicago: University of Chicago Press, 1981), esp. vol. 2 (in the writings of "Brutus" and "The Federal Farmer"). Also see Nathaniel Chipman, *Principles of Government* (Burlington, Vt.: Edward Smith, 1833; originally 1793), pp. 3–4, 15, 45, 130, 219–20 on the science of government and the nature of its rules, maxims, and principles. Also notice the scientific tone of Chipman's discussion of the "experiment . . . first made in these United States" when he avers that "it is true, this form of government is a novelty in the political world, it cannot, it does not, appeal to history for proof of its excellence; but to present facts" (p. 152a).

22. *Federalist*, no. 9.

23. In *The American Revolution*, as quoted in Gordon S. Wood, *The Creation of the American Republic, 1776–1787* (Chapel Hill: University of North Carolina Press, 1969), p. 613.

24. *Federalist*, no. 37.

25. See J. G. A. Pocock, *The Machiavellian Moment: Florentine Political Thought and the Atlantic Republican Tradition* (Princeton: Princeton University Press, 1975), esp. chap. 14–15. Also see Bernard Bailyn, *The Ideological Origins of the American Revolution* (Cambridge, Mass.: Harvard University Press, 1967); Russell L. Hanson, *The Democratic Imagination in America* (Princeton: Princeton University Press, 1985), esp. chap. 2–3; Wood, *The Creation of the American Republic*, esp. chap. 1; and David W. Noble, *The End of American History* (Minneapolis: University of Minnesota Press, 1985).

26. See, paradigmatically, Louis Hartz, *The Liberal Tradition in America* (New York: Harcourt, Brace and World, 1955). Also see the works of Daniel Boorstin.

27. Wood suggests as much, as early as the end of the eighteenth century, in *The Creation of the American Republic*, esp. chap. 15. Crick even takes the methodological ideals of American political science as expressing liberal political principles in *The American Science of Politics*, p. xv. Seidelman and Harpham tell a tale of disenchanted liberals in political science (in *Disenchanted Realists*, p. 2),

but they also point to a variety of other traditions in political science, including the remnants of classical republicanism.

28. For the general background, see Quentin Skinner, "The State," in Ball, Farr, and Hanson, eds., *Political Innovation and Conceptual Change*, as well as his studies of Machiavelli and Hobbes. For the American founding period, see J. G. A. Pocock, "States, Republics, and Empires: The American Founding in Early Modern Perspective," in Terence Ball and J. G. A. Pocock, eds., *Conceptual Change and the Constitution* (Lawrence: University Press of Kansas, 1989), pp. 55–77.

29. Skinner, *Foundations of Modern Political Thought*, p. x.

30. Herbert J. Storing, ed., as abridged by Murray Dry, *The Antifederalist* (Chicago: University of Chicago Press, 1985), pp. 38, 281.

31. *Federalist*, nos. 4, 6, 8, 15, 17, 34, 51.

32. Chipman, *Principles of Government*, esp. pp. 56, 60, 119, 123–26, 137, 145, 176a, 171–79, 180–85. Hobbes, Pufendorf, Grotius, Locke, Vattell, Beccaria, Kames, Smith, Montesquieu, Blackstone, and (especially) Paley all come in for discussion and criticism during the course of Chipman's remarkable treatise.

33. Consider, for example, the *American Review of History and Politics*, which characterized itself at its inception in 1811 as a "general repository of literature and State papers" and which promised to present the best writers in the "science of government." Quoted in Crick, *The American Science of Politics*, p. 5n.

34. See Anna Haddow, *Political Science in American Colleges and Universities, 1636–1900* (New York: 1939). Of particular importance in this literature is Francis Wayland, *The Elements of Moral Science* (New York: 1835).

35. Marx, *German Ideology*, p. 80. Also see his judgment that "the abstraction of the *state as such* belongs only to modern times," in *Collected Works* (New York: International, 1975), 3: 325.

36. Frank Freidel, *Francis Lieber: Nineteenth Century Liberal* (Baton Rouge: Louisiana State University Press, 1947), pp. 89–90, chap. 13.

37. "I know that my work belongs to the list which begins with Aristotle, and in which we find the names of Thomas More, Hobbes, Hugo Grotius, Pufendorf." Quoted in ibid., pp. 164–65.

38. *Miscellaneous Writings* (Philadelphia: J. B. Lippincott, 1880), 1: 351.

39. *Legal and Political Hermeneutics* (Boston: Little, Brown, 1839), second edition, p. 64. A textual and contextual analysis of this neglected work can be found in James Farr, "Francis Lieber and the Interpretation of American Political Science," *Journal of Politics* 52 (1990): 1027–49.

40. *Miscellaneous Writings*, 1: 337.

41. *Memorial Relative to Proposals for a Work on the Statistics of the United States*, Senate Documents 314, 24th Cong., 1st sess. 1836. Serial set 282, p. 1.

42. Rodgers, *Contested Truths*, p. 188.

43. *The Ancient and Modern Teacher of Politics: An Introductory Discourse to a Course of Lectures on the State* (New York: Columbia College Board of Trustees, 1860), p. 10.

44. *Miscellaneous Writings*, 1: 28, 183.

45. Among other places, see *Manual of Political Ethics*, 1: 401, 2: 109. In a more popular though less theoretical way, Andrew W. Young wrote with these ends

in mind as well, especially in *Introduction to the Science of Government* (Rochester, N.Y.: 1842; originally 1839) and in *The Citizen's Manual of Government and Law* (New York: Derby and Miller, 1864). The former work (on pp. 3–4) singled out the massive and increasing number of immigrants as a problem, for their "education does not embrace even the first principles of political science." But common schools can remedy this and so help new and young Americans "assume the duties of citizens" of a republic increasingly the scene of "the collision of contending interests."

46. *Miscellaneous Writings*, 1: 343.

47. *Manual of Political Ethics*, p. 152.

48. Ibid., p. 207.

49. *Miscellaneous Writings*, 1: 351.

50. *Manual of Political Ethics*, p. 253.

51. See n. 12 above.

52. Lieber helped in this task during the Civil War by writing, at President Lincoln's and General Halleck's request, a pamphlet on *Guerilla Parties* and a set of *General Instructions for the Government of the Armies of the United States in the Field*. This latter work was later dubbed "Lieber's Code of War," and it became the explicit model for the documents which emerged from the Hague and Geneva conventions years later.

53. Printed in the second, revised edition of *Manual of Political Ethics*, ed. Theodore Dwight Woolsey (Philadelphia: J. B. Lippincott and Co., 1876).

54. There is a large and important literature on this aspect of political science, and the social sciences more generally, during the last quarter of the nineteenth century. For beginnings, see Burton Bledstein, *The Culture of Professionalism* (New York: Norton, 1976); Thomas L. Haskell, *The Emergence of Professional Social Science* (Urbana: University of Illinois Press, 1977); Mary O. Furner, *Advocacy and Objectivity: A Crisis in the Professionalization of American Social Science, 1865–1905* (Lexington: University Press of Kentucky, 1975); and Dorothy Ross, "The Development of the Social Sciences," in Alexandra Oleson and John Voss, eds., *The Organization of Knowledge in Modern America, 1860–1920* (Baltimore: Johns Hopkins University Press, 1979), pp. 107–38.

55. Besides those to be discussed below, see Joseph Alden, *The Science of Government in Connection with American Institutions* (New York: Sheldon and Co., 1867), whose opening line reads: "The object of this book is to aid the young in acquiring the knowledge necessary for the discharge of their duties as citizens of the United States." The locus of higher education during this period is an important theme of both Crick, *The American Science of Politics*, and Ricci, *The Tragedy of Political Science*. In *Disenchanted Realists*, Seidelman traces political science's mission of civic education well into the twentieth century. By then, however, much of the rest of republican political discourse had lost its vitality and place in American political life, what with its interested commercial energies and its imperial ambitions. But such lingering of republican identity that there was in late nineteenth- and twentieth-century America was (and has been) in good part due to the continuing tradition of civic education.

56. Skowronek's *Building a New American State* is particularly helpful in documenting the centralizing administrative revolution in the American state during this

time period—even if, as I have argued, the Americans had long had a "sense of the state." One might even say that the *state* (and its cognates) provided ready-made terminology for the new theories in political science which were emerging to help citizens and legislators understand and even justify national developments under way since the Civil War. This pattern of political innovation amid terminological stability can be seen in the case of the fourth estate in England as well. See J.A.W. Gunn, *Beyond Liberty and Property: The Process of Self-Recognition in Eighteenth Century Political Thought* (Kingston and Montreal: McGill-Queen's University Press, 1983), esp. pp. 57, 95.

57. This is true in America, as discussed in the text, but also in Britain. Consider the view of the professor of jurisprudence at University College, London, that "the most central notion in political science is that of the *State*." Sheldon Amos, *The Science of Politics*, 3d ed. (New York: Appleton, 1897), p. 63. This is also the era of Bradley, Bosanquet, and T. H. Green.

58. In *Disenchanted Realists*, Seidelman is particularly helpful on this later statist episode in political science.

59. *Political Science and Constitutional Law* (Boston: Ginn and Co., 1893), 1: v.

60. If only to judge by the Newtonian aspirations of the Scottish founders of political science. See Farr, "Political Science and the Enlightenment of Enthusiasm," p. 56.

61. Ricci, *The Tragedy of Political Science*, chap. 3.

62. Burgess, *Political Science and Constitutional Law*, 1: 108.

63. Ibid., 1: 81.

64. John W. Burgess, "The American Commonwealth," *Political Science Quarterly* 1 (1886), quoted in Charles Merriam, *The History of American Political Theories* (New York: Macmillan, 1924), pp. 301–2.

65. Rodgers, *Contested Truths*, p. 146. Also see the claim about the state being reified into an "entity higher than man" (p. 175).

66. Burgess, *Political Science and Constitutional Law*, 1: 88; W. W. Willoughby, *The Nature of the State* (New York: Macmillan, 1896), p. 4. Willoughby also criticized those who would "speak of the State as . . . an entity independent of man" (p. 33).

67. Theodore Dwight Woolsey, *Political Science, or the State Theoretically and Practically Considered* (New York: Scribner, Armstrong, and Company, 1877), 1: 140.

68. Ibid., passim; Frank Goodnow, *Politics and Administration: A Study in Government* (New York: Macmillan, 1900).

69. Willoughby, *The Nature of the State*, esp. chap. 10, 11.

70. *Political Science and Constitutional Law*, 1: 57, 63. Also note Burgess's judgment that "America has yet to develop . . . her own literature of political science. Down to this time, the two names which stand highest in our American literature of political science are Francis Lieber and Theodore D. Woolsey" (p. 70).

71. Given the weight that some historians have placed upon the influences of the German university and of German theories of the state, it bears noting that, of the other notable American political scientists of the state during this period, Woolsey (the erstwhile cleric) studied at Yale, Wilson took his advanced degree from Johns Hopkins, Dunning took all his degrees from Columbia, and Willoughby began and ended his academic career at Johns Hopkins. Some of their

teachers or distant mentors, like Daniel Gilman and Andrew White, had studied in Germany, but most of them had not. Of the former, those (like Burgess) who had studied in Germany often did so with Johann Bluntschli and found in his very influential work, *The Theory of the State*, frequent citation and praise for Francis Lieber. Gilman collected Lieber's papers (now at the University of California at Berkeley). Much more needs to be done on this feature of the intellectual influences on American political science and its conceptualization of the state. But, given the above, I would suggest endorsing Daniel Rodgers's subjunctive clause while maintaining a healthy skepticism about his summary conclusion: "If none of Burgess's fellow political scientists were as deeply smitten by Germany as he, the stamp of German learning on their professional talk was deep and unmistakable" (*Contested Truths*, p. 167).

72. The racialist intimations, especially given the German connection in the case of Burgess and a few others, deserve further study. For a somewhat later period, and in a broader field than political science, see Robert N. Proctor, "Eugenics Among the Social Sciences: Hereditarian Thought in Germany and the United States" in this volume.

73. For this judgment, see Bernard Edward Brown, *American Conservatives: The Political Thought of Francis Lieber and John W. Burgess* (New York: Columbia University Press, 1951). Crick rightly complains of historians "reading back subsequent prejudices into a previous era" and goes on to say that "in his day Burgess was among the leading ranks of 'progress,' a conservative-liberal perhaps, but in no sense himself a conservative" (*The American Science of Politics*, p. 27).

74. R. J. Wright, *Principles of Political Science* (Philadelphia: R. J. Wright, 1876).

75. Frank S. Hoffman, *The Sphere of the State; or the People as a Body-Politic* (New York: G. P. Putnam's Sons, 1894), p. 7. Quoted in Rodgers, *Contested Truths*, p. 165. On the socialist and radical character of many of the late nineteenth-century social scientists, see Furner, *Advocacy and Objectivity*, and Ross, "The Development of the Social Sciences."

■ 2 THE GREAT DESERT OF THE AMERICAN MIND

Concepts of Space and Time and Their Historiographic Implications

ANDREW KIRBY

It was customary, in the mid-nineteenth century, to identify the region between Iowa in the east and the Rocky Mountains to the west as the Great American Desert. Indeed, it was normal at that time to use the Great American Desert label on maps of the region in the manner that medieval cartographers had written resignedly, "here be dragons." Romantic historians of the Plains maintained the existence of the Desert to the end of the century and beyond, and in marginalizing the agricultural potential of the region, they in consequence glamorized the achievements of those who had settled it: Frank W. Blackmar wrote in 1906 that "the region's desert conditions are gradually disappearing through the efforts of the man who digs and toils and subdues nature."[1]

This essentially pessimistic view of the Prairie environment was replaced in the early twentieth century by the views of Frederick Jackson Turner, who mentioned in his writings the Great American Desert only once. For Turner, the frontier was—in at least strictly geographical terms—an abstraction that paid little attention to the realities of nature. And so powerful was his influence upon academic opinion that past examples of drought and farm closure in the Plains region were reinterpreted as products of the ineptitude of farmers rather than a product of the environmental conditions. Turner's views on the frontier provided the lens through which the Plains were viewed for several decades, and his rejection of the Great Desert dominated thinking until events—in the form of the dustbowl disasters of the Depression era—intruded.

Although Turner's broader notions of the frontier survived, the contemporary reality forced reappraisal of the region and its past in the form of Walter Prescott Webb's reevaluation and subsequent reconstruction of the Great American Desert.

The definitional problems that surround the Great Plains remain unresolved.[2] As some astute commentators have noted, the discussion of the Prairie region is bedeviled by the tendency to "generalize images either from the part to the whole, or the other way around."[3] In short, the Great Plains mythology is an excellent example of the ways in which we pay scant attention to the geographical complexity of reality. In consequence, my purpose in beginning with this example, and the broader goal of this essay, is to indicate the tenuous hold that geography in its most basic sense has upon the collective consciousness of this country. The existence of the Great American Desert is indeed of less importance than something that I will call, with deliberate irony, the Great Desert of the American Mind; that is, the lack of understanding of places and spatial concepts that permeates both the everyday and, by logical extension, the academy. In this essay, I explore the reasons for this lacuna, the way in which the discipline of geography is marginalized within the academy, and the implications that this situation has for the pursuit of understanding and the design of the dominant discourse within American social science.[4]

Blurred Genres

In making a claim for the existence of "blurred genres," anthropologist Clifford Geertz observes that "we wait only for quantum theory in verse or biography in algebra."[5] In keeping with these observations, it is a reasonable task to question to what extent there has been a real rapprochement between fields of knowledge and to what length world views can be integrated. In recent years, we have seen some common cause between historical sociology and social history;[6] between ecological history and cultural geography,[7] and between urban history, urban geography, and urban politics.[8] Yet with these important exceptions, one would be hard pressed to see any real integrations within the broad endeavors of the social sciences. Certainly, there exist shared concerns for rigid methodologies and a focus upon the atomistic worlds of the behaviorist, which tend to turn the pages of, say, the *American Sociological Review*, the *American Political Science Review*, and the *Social Science Quarterly* into virtually generic products. The only thing that allows us to differentiate their contents is the chosen disciplinary focus; for, after all, to employ that term in the sense that it is used by Foucault, the discipline must become an obligation, and if it cannot be an obligation of method, then it must be one of subject matter.[9]

This insight exposes one of the basic impediments to Geertz's optimism. If each discipline has a focus (economy, politics, society, personality, culture), then it is likely that intercourse and collaboration will only take place in those settings where a shared object (cities, the environment, the development process) makes them possible. In other cases, disciplinary turf battles are more usual.[10] This is certainly the case in those instances where disciplines lack a clear object or where disciplines are synthetic and not analytic. This would be true of geography and also of communication, peace studies, and a number of other integrative enterprises. Within the framework being established here, such subjects exist precariously, insofar as they compete explicitly for intellectual territory.[11] This struggle is compounded if the process of synthesis rests upon a specific methodology that is in some manner different from the prevailing and predominant form of inquiry. This would not be the case with the communication discipline that employs, *inter alia*, standard behaviorist methods. It would, though, most certainly apply to geography, which for long periods has invoked an explicitly exceptionalist stance that has placed it at the margins of intellectual life in the United States.

A People without Geography

Geography in the United States is to be understood within the same chronology as other social sciences. Departments were established in the early years of the twentieth century (Chicago in 1903, for instance), and geography faced the same problems of establishing a clear turf as did, for example, sociology.[12] As Hayes (a sociologist) noted in his essay on the relations between geography and sociology published in 1909, it was hard for the former to justify a place in the academy, for if one accepted that "geography is a description of geographic phenomena in their relations with all other phenomena of which the geographic phenomena are conditions," then the discipline had a low-level cataloging function. Put differently, geography was under this rubric a centrifugal science, identifying the factors that condition other phenomena. As Hayes concluded, "all the work of the centrifugal science will be duplication."[13]

Unsurprisingly, geographers viewed their contributions somewhat higher; indeed, as we will see in greater detail below, it was normal to claim some primacy for geography as an "Ur-discipline." Hayes, for example, quotes from a Chicago geographer who argued as follows:

the matter of the largest interest in modern geography is the interaction between man and his physical environment. But the physical environment itself is the fundamental part of the field. My analysis would be 1. physiography . . . 2. meteorology and oceanography . . . 3. biogeography. . . . 4. economic geography. . . . The fifth term in this series passes beyond geography, is the field for which geography should be the conscious and purposeful preparation, economics, and sociology, yes, and history too. I like to think of sociology as the flower of geographic study.[14]

This emphasis upon the disciplinary terrain was hardly unusual.[15] Unlike other disciplines, however, geography lacked a clear fiefdom and in consequence sought for alternative ways to achieve legitimation. An obvious one was the search for illustrious forebears, notably among German intellectuals—Immanuel Kant was pressed into service, for example.[16] One unlooked-for outcome of this process was a fossilization that froze the means and manner of geographic inquiry in the ways in which it was laid down by individuals like Kant, von Humboldt, Ritter, and their followers. David Stoddart, a disciplinary historian, observes:

such inductive history [was] markedly internalist. Written from the perspectives of the present, such studies identify a continuous series of men [sic] and ideas, linked together in chronology and content. Thus Hartshorne and subsequently many others have traced a development within geography. . . it is not surprising that the names of Darwin, Marx and Freud are absent. . . that they give little or no attention to philosophical or epistemological issues; and that the history traced remains unrelated to social, economic and political conditions.[17]

The key word here is undoubtedly "internalist." Geography was, to its practitioners at least, to be evaluated only in terms of deviations from these historical norms and not in terms of its contributions to social scientific inquiry. As far as other disciplines were concerned, however, this claim to exceptionalist status was unconvincing, a fact that was underlined by the refusal to permit geographers representation within the Social Science Research Council.[18]

It was thus unsurprising that when autocriticism emerged within geography in the late-1950s, it would constitute an explicit attack on the closed world of Kantian geography. By announcing self-consciously a paradigm change, a new generation of geographers tried to make contact with the developments occurring elsewhere within social science, which were being codified at that time by Thomas Kuhn. Their focus remained demonstrably internalist, however, and the outcome of this struggle was little more than a face lift within the discipline. The calls for greater scientism altered only the manner in which research was undertaken; they altered nothing with respect to the content of the discipline, which remained intellectually suspect.[19] Despite the first steps toward change that began in the 1950s, this was also the beginning of the period of departmental closure in the United States.

This brief overview of geography has been designed to give a flavor of the subject's recent past and the problems that it faces within the U.S. Those problems continue to mount: in recent years, departments have closed at the University of Chicago, at Columbia, and at Northwestern.[20] The next section of this essay places the subject back within a wider context of understanding and relates what has happened to geography to what has gone on within other disciplines in the social sciences.

Self-images and Folk Images

In attempting to make sense of an intellectual history, it is possible to cast about for a number of insights.[21] This argument will focus on three very different approaches: first, what has been termed the "social construction of reality"; second, the institutions that comprise the discipline; and third, the epistemological development of the latter.[22] My task is not to "test" these constructs for their ability to "explain" the position of geography; my aim is to create a plausible history that will be informed by these approaches. In addition, it should be noted that there are hints of infinite regress in this exercise. Just as a historian is likely to turn automatically to the historical method (or one version thereof), so the geographer is concerned for the varied contexts of reality. That is to say, this analysis of geography is inevitably informed by a geographical training, which may suggest some important insights for this type of exercise.

I want to begin with the discipline, for it is the "Mertonian paradigm" that constitutes the most frequent point of departure for examinations of the behavioral sciences.[23] However, an important point of difference is immediately manifest when examining geography—notably, that there is no single discipline but rather a fragmented arrangement. In Europe, the U.S.S.R., Canada, Australia, and Japan, geography is a prominent high school subject and is represented within nearly all universities, a situation which does not obtain in the United States. This disjuncture raises some interesting issues about how to address academic effort. Following Foucault in thinking about the disciplines as organizations with both subjects and objects (that is to say, practitioners and those who in some way accept the disciplinary "message") may pose some problems in the case of geography: It has practitioners in the U.S., but there are few settings in which the message is wholeheartedly accepted.[24] Clearly, there are a number of ways in which this is to be understood, but they point in the main to the need for a contextual analysis; this means that the understanding of geography is to be found less by internalist critique than by study of the interface between it and the different social milieus within which it is found.

Attempting, in the first instance, to explain the variation in geography's impact brings us to a restatement of the problem of American exceptionalism.[25] In this instance, we need to address the different social formations extant within many European nations and the United States and in turn the interface between these societies, their ideologies, and the roles that different types of knowledge play therein. Such an analysis, echoing the social construction of reality identified by Berger and Luckmann, reveals some interesting insights about geographical inquiry.[26] Most simply, geography performed a powerful role in nations committed to overseas exploration, scientific development, and colonial expansion. In countries like France, Germany, and Great Britain, the creation of both formal and informal empires was predicated upon the collection and manipulation of formal knowledge about the world. In Britain, the Royal Geographical Society was founded in 1830 and played a central role in organizing exploration, scientific missions, and data collection. The RGS itself took the initiative in the creation of various university departments of geography and was instrumental in developing the department at Cambridge, for example.[27] However, the subject was not reserved solely for undergraduates, for even small children did not escape the net of imperialism. Osbert Sitwell, writing of his childhood in the last decade of the nineteenth century, remembered that

> there were some lessons that I came near to enjoying: English history, with
> its crowned and bearded kings striding with their long legs from legendary
> mists towards the beacon of present progress inaugurated by Queen Vic-
> toria; or geography—so long as it was not represented, in a frenetic attempt
> to "make it attractive" to children, by arrangements of flags, barred and
> striped and starred in the most hideous manner; a sort of foretaste, I can
> see now of those horrible little flags, stuck on pins and dug into war maps,
> that seem to have haunted the whole span of my life so far.[28]

The situation is, however, noticeably different in the United States. Despite early expressions of a Manifest Destiny, the creation of an extensive formal empire, and subsequently a massive impact upon the world economy, Americans have disclaimed an interest in being a global actor with an explicit, normative agenda. According to political theorists, this is to be understood in terms of the importance of communalist ideals within American society, an idealism that is expressed in a strong tradition of localism.[29] The roots of this tradition are not hard to find. The American Republic emerged from highly disparate colonies; indeed, the first Continental Congress of 1774 was, in Albion Small's words, an early effort to find a "common consciousness."[30] This reflected the singularity of the communities that comprised the country, a tension that was to continue through the forging of the Republic and beyond. While united within "Nature's nation," no single locality could transcend the divergences between agricultural and urban interests, between North and South, between East Coast and West Coast.[31] In consequence, the creation of the modern state was a slow and complex affair; as one political scientist argued, it was a process of "patching" that had to overcome local resistance and extended long into the modern era.[32]

The consequences of this tradition are still manifested strongly. Individual knowledge of the spatial integration of the U.S. and, by extension, of the globe is minute; awareness of or concern for that lack of knowledge is even smaller.[33] Rather, there is an emphasis upon the local community, its traditions, its discourses, and the role of the locality within the nation's political system. From this perspective, it is unsurprising that political science (rather than geography or some other discipline) has a pivotal role within the American schoolroom, for it performs the key ideological function of transcending these locational differences and emphasizing encompassing republican values.

At the most general level of argument, then, we can suggest that there is no absolute necessity for geographical study to exist within American society in the way that, for instance, some form of political science is necessary.[34] However, that could also be said of many other disciplines, from anthropology to zoology. To comprehend the performance of a discipline of this type, we need to shift our level of analysis somewhat in order to place the discipline among its counterparts.

There are a number of functions that practitioners of geography undertake: These include the teaching of cartography, the manipulation of remotely sensed imagery, the provision of information on urbanism, the environment, and climate, and other general integrative topics that are rarely covered by other disciplines. This notwithstanding, and despite these niches, geography has not proved its indispensability. I shall argue that this problem has not lain in the identification of a particular turf; after all, geography deals with a basic material dimension, namely space, and is thus no more or less remarkable than history and the latter's responsibility for examining time. The problem has been one of language, of method, and of communication; expressed another way, geography has consistently shown itself to be out of step with other disciplinary activities.

We can trace this problem historically, identifying in the first instance what has been termed the "unity myth"; that is, the establishment in the later decades of the nineteenth century of the fundamental principle that geography was, alongside history, one of the Ur-disciplines.[35] As noted above, this logic was derived from Kant, who argued that chorology and chronology constituted the fundamental axes of knowledge. Strictly interpreted, such a rubric left all contemporary (nonhistorical) study to the geographer. Moreover, Kant was also interpreted to argue that such investigations were not subject to the normal practices of scientific inquiry: the so-called principle of exceptionalism.[36]

The fatal allure of the unity myth cannot be overstated. Employing Kantian logic, geographers in the Victorian era lay claim to be engaged in the ultimate act of synthesis, an activity that placed geography at the core of human knowledge. As long as they undertook extensive fieldwork, visited exotic locations, and (one hoped) returned with systematic information on the regions they had visited, geographers could perhaps be seen to be—literally—mapping out the intellectual terrain for others to follow. It was less easy to make such claims in the post-imperial eras, although this was the period when we see the unity myth being reified. Figure 1, for instance, a graphic representation offered in a presidential address to the Association of American Geographers in 1919, shows quite clearly the way the discipline was to marshal the preliminary research of others. Contemporaneously, an attempt was made at Clark University to phase out a number of graduate programs and replace them with a single "Geographical Institute."[37] As noted above, this immodesty was not convincing to other disciplines, which were engaged in the same period in establishing their own turf: As Hayes observed, a "centrifugal" discipline could be assumed to have a fairly low-level function within the academy.[38]

It may be useful at this point to digress somewhat with respect to the undertaking of fieldwork. As suggested, the latter possessed some mystique in societies where imperialism dictated the exploration and management of distant lands. It possessed, though, little kudos in an America which accepted Turner's arguments that the frontier had, by the early part of the twentieth century, disappeared. For the geographer, however, fieldwork remained a worthy activity; indeed, it became almost an end in itself, a principle that was enshrined by the 1950s as a cornerstone of geographical method: "the principal training of the geographer should come, wherever possible, by doing fieldwork."[39] To some, this remains a self-evident principle, and criticism thereof produces the

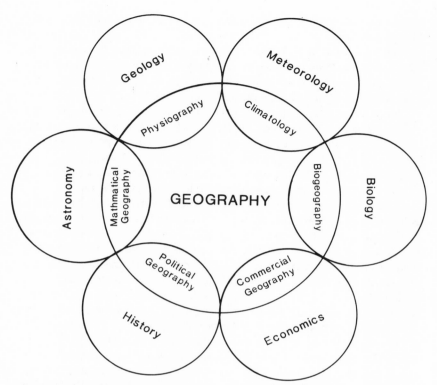

Figure 1. The centrality of geography, from a Presidential Address presented to the Association of American Geographers, 1918. For a discussion of physiography, see note 14.
Source: After Fenneman[37]

response of the noble backwoodsman [*sic*] to the cynical proddings of the effete urban intellectual.[40]

If fieldwork lingers, anachronistic yet important, in the era of remote sensing, so too does the role of synthesis. It is intriguing to compare, for instance, Figure 1, produced at the end of the First World War, with Figure 2, produced at the height of the Vietnam War. Taken from a volume that proclaimed the end of traditional geography and the self-conscious emergence of a new paradigm of inquiry, we see a more sophisticated presentation (employing set theory) that demonstrates nonetheless the same unity myth.[41] Indeed, one of the more intriguing ironies of geographical development is the way in which change has proceeded at a dizzying rate, although nothing has actually altered. As geographer and historian Thomas Glick points out with admirable parsimony, "A particularly unsavory aspect of the unity myth is that it has encouraged the avoidance of epistemological and conceptual issues. As the rolling program brings new explanatory modes to the top of the heap, those that have suffered loss of prestige are suppressed at the conceptual level even though the processes that they describe continue to be studied. Indeed, nothing that geographers have ever done can be wholly discarded without doing violence to the myth."[42]

Any assumption of disciplinary centrality must produce boundary conflicts with other disciplines. These are likely to be bloody when any discipline claims another's turf: If that discipline is also employing special claims to "exceptional" epistemological status, then we can expect compounded problems. And such has been the case with geography in the United States. As noted, the discipline had no automatic claims to a place within the academic community; it had laid claims to a different

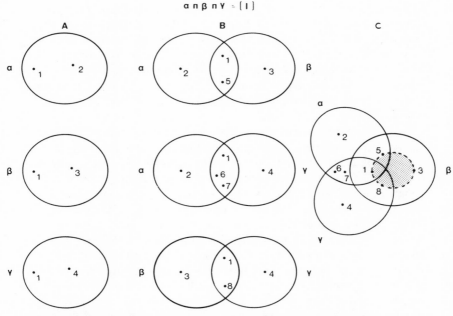

Figure 2. The centrality of geography, 1965. The key to understanding the Venn diagram is as follows: 1, geography; 2, geology; 3, demography; 4, topology; 5, human ecology; 6, geomorphology; 7, surveying; 8, locational analysis

Source: After Haggett and Chorley[41]

modus. Most ironically, when efforts were made in the 1960s to retool the discipline, new problems were created. As shown, the so-called quantitative revolution, with its self-conscious evocation of Kuhn's terms to ward off the specters of idiographic research, was hardly based on an entirely new set of premises. Most importantly, these changes drove a wedge between the new, shiny self-image of the discipline and what Glick calls its folk-image. The generic view of a geographer is of an individual who can adroitly reel off the capitals of the world's countries. What the changes of the "new geography" of the 1960s produced was a subject suddenly adept in the mathematical transformation of space, the modeling of spatial behavior, and an emphasis more upon geo-metry than geo-graphy.[43] Despite a massive amount of intellectual effort, there is little question that this quantification had almost no impact upon other social sciences. A number of reasons can be produced to explain this. The first is a simplistic one: Those in other disciplines could see no point to this mathematization; why was it necessary to go to these lengths to undertake research that had little purpose? Why was it of interest to measure the connectivity indices of Latin American rail networks? Taxi flows across the City of London? Shortest distance solutions to traveling salesman problems? And so on. Although much of the early work in "spatial science" was trivial, this is no longer true today: work in disease contagion, migration, regional economics, and electoral dynamics is sophisticated and important.[44] The current problem (to employ a spatial metaphor) is the lack of diffusion of ideas from geography to its counterparts.

More important, and more subtle, is the disjuncture that remains between the discourse of geography and that employed elsewhere within the behavioral sciences. At its most basic, geography is about chaos and complexity. Its entire history has revolved about the study of areal differentiation, an activity that does not lend itself to parsimony. Even in its self-styled "positivistic" phase, the emphasis was upon quantitative description of the complexity of reality, be it the movement of phenomena between locations or the comparison of data values for different regions. Now this type of research is very different from that which goes on elsewhere in the behavioral sciences, indeed, this very term provides a clue to the problem, for while disciplines like political science, psychology, and economics were focusing upon general facets of behavior(ism), geography was focusing upon individual actors only insofar as they gave clues about aggregates of individuals in specific locations. To reiterate, then, while the behavioral sciences sought laws of behavior, geography acknowledged complexity and difference.

In turn, the language of geography has moved farther and farther from this mainstream. At one time, the discipline talked of maps, of projections, of regions, of places. Suddenly, the discourse was transformed and terminologies were altered: geographical was replaced by spatial, places by regions 1–n, simple maps became complex cartograms involving topological transforms, geographical space became social space, places became nodes or stations, journeys became vectors, and geographers became surly if asked to give advice to the State Department concerning conditions in remote locations. Even when efforts have been made to move closer to a supposedly "scientific" position, such efforts have run counter to the norms of the academy. For instance, the most powerful efforts to scientize geography have revolved around models that describe spatial behavior and that employ a specialized terminology; more to the point, these efforts lie on the interface of cartography and topology and are as such employing specialized languages—map transforms—that are not penetrated readily by other (social) scientists.

To summarize, this section has provided an illustration of a number of enmeshed ways in which geography has, in the United States, maintained a marginal position within the academy. To reiterate, the discipline has sought exceptionalist status, has employed nonconforming forms of language and analysis and has lacked a central ideological function. It is possible of course that my emphasis and interpretations are incorrect; my essential argument, which revolves around marginality, is not.

Geography among Its Peers

An inattention to places has allowed social science several luxuries it does not deserve, namely, a lack of reflexive consideration concerning its own practice and an inattention to detail that encourages hopelessly broad generalization. There is a link between the weakness of geographical study and the manner in which American social science has resolved itself. This is not to argue for any form of causality here; that is to say, we cannot assume that these problems are a direct product of geography's weaknesses. However, we certainly can argue that the discipline's marginality permits this situation to continue.

In the first instance, we must face up to the premise that inquiry is shaped by its own settings: On the one hand, an atomistic American social science reflects the possessive-individualistic society that it studies. European social science, on the other hand, is much more driven by structural analysis, which in turn reflects its class-based settings. A greater sensitivity to this basic difference would lead us to realize that there are no "timeless questions and answers," to quote Skinner.[45] For the behavioral scientist, however, these are simply noise factors that can be reduced to an error term within the linear model of explanation. Mention of the linear model is intentional, for it is the principle of regression that has driven much of the progress made in sociology, political science, and other quantitative studies in recent decades. In other words, it is the reduction of a spread of data to some mean characteristics that has characterized the process of inference. The methods of regression (or, indeed, of any parsimonious manipulation) destroy some of the implications of our data. The most important element within a data set may be its diversity, a richness that is destroyed in the creation of mean values. Once more, the opposition of terms like richness and meanness is intentional and apposite.

The practice of much American behavioral science is in contrast to other older and more subtle research procedures that are able to confront the variation extant with reality and that do not descend into triviality; such analysis is not necessarily nonquantitative. Such research deals with the details and the larger picture and in so doing finds material that is highly charged with significance. The most obvious example in this case is the work of the French Annales school, of which the writings of Fernand Braudel are perhaps the best known beyond the discipline of history.[46] The creativity of Braudel's insights relate to the manner in which he juggles both time and space. His analysis is ever conscious of the ways in which the general processes of capitalism were resolved in a multitude of different ways in different localities at different moments. This is of some importance, of course, because it is the manner in which general processes resolve themselves in specific cases that in turn accounts for further processes of change. To take a particular example: mercantile capitalism established itself in very different ways throughout India in the sixteenth and seventeenth centuries. There emerged something akin to a mosaic, with some localities maintaining and others relinquishing their traditional economic and social practices. It was this mosaic that was then the setting for the uneven unrest of the Indian Mutiny of 1857, which ultimately failed because it was in turn unable to spread ubiquitously throughout the subcontinent. In such an instance, it would be inadequate to write of a simple struggle between colonialism and feudalism or some such general statement; the Indian Mutiny was, despite its name, a highly localized instance of collective action.[47]

This kind of perspective may not at first pass appear to offer major challenges to contemporary research practice; it does, however, take us to the heart of a complex methodological problem. Of importance in the views of Braudel (and others) is the recognition of a relationship between the extremes of structure and agency. All would argue that it is not possible to force this dualism apart and to privilege one above the other. That is to say, structure determines the ways in which human agents act; but those agents are responsible for recreating the structure, and they do this task in subtly different ways. As a result, they frequently change the structure in some manner. An obvious example here is that of music; we inherit its structure and as listeners operate within certain conformities, but in recreating it, individuals change the terms and shades of the musical forms, such that each generation is presented with a changed text from that which went before. In consequence, it is now seen to be not possible to break apart the "big picture" and the small details; resorting to our previous example, human agents recreate capitalism in specific ways, and in so doing they create tensions that have impacts upon the system as a whole. Specific localities inherit the blueprints of a structure like industrialism in different ways; agents impose upon it particular cultural meanings, particular priorities, with the result that there emerge different types of labor relations, different forms of legal practice, and different social relations. Nor do these exist in isolation, for all parts of a complex economic system have then in turn some impact upon the whole; capital and labor are both mobile and may move to take advantage of such variations. Once more, the whole is continually reinterpreted and changed by individual and, in consequence, local action.

The identification of the specifics of a particular narrative is thus of theoretical importance, because without knowledge of such instances, realistically we cannot understand the creation and recreation of the whole. Analysis of the constituents is crucial to the recreation of structures—a process variously termed structuring or structuration.[48] Such a view will necessarily pay attention to moments of time and the variations of place. Many are aware of the historical dimension but, as this essay has argued, are much less conscious of the spatial dimension. The assumption that society is a monolithic structure, undifferentiated from locality to locality, ignores, though, the reality of the ways in which social practices have been resolved and continue to resolve themselves. During much of human history, behavior has been confined to particular localities. This reflected, in some measure, the problems of interaction across long distances and the way in which power was rooted in locally specific phenomena such as cities and land. That is why for Braudel the "structures of everyday life" are so important, because it was the realities of diet and lodging, not the ideologies of capitalism or religion, that determined often the trajectories of political quiescence or rebellion. It is only in relatively recent periods that the fragmentation of collective existence has diminished as the power of the state has increased.[49]

However, the rise of the state apparatus does not imply that localities and the styles of life that exist within them are now of little importance. As Foucault observes, this progressive coalescence of the fragmented bases of human organization has posed particular problems for the political organization of society. This, which he relates to the spatiality of society, is fundamentally a question of integrating complex styles of life (typically, though not exclusively, manifest in different locales) within the grip of the state. Time and space are, once more, central to this concern, for it is the diminution of the importance of these material bases that permits the state to override the localized practices of its internal units. Spatial integration can be achieved, *inter alia*, via transportation change and other forms of technological innovation, while the standardization of localized measures of time took place via changed economic practices and the creation of uniform measures of clock time. The alteration of conceptions of time and space is indeed a key component of the movement toward the modern state; as sociologist Anthony Giddens notes, the breaking down of temporal and spatial barriers is instrumental in the creation of state institutions that can now intrude virtually instantaneously into every home, meeting, and educational establishment.[50] Equally, this shift has been manifested throughout society; as Kern has shown in some detail, changing views of time and space have occurred in the spheres of art, religion, architecture, and politics,[51] and others have argued that a shift in conceptions of space was even a prerequisite for the scientific revolution of the seventeenth century.[52]

In short, it is possible to show that a social science that lacks any sense of geography, of space as a fundamental material dimension, is trapped in certain forms of inquiry, an important point that will be taken up again toward the end of this essay. As the example of the Annales school and analogous discourse indicates, a close consideration of these material dimensions opens up very different vistas, in which the richness of human action is revealed quite openly and distinctly.

Toward an Alternative

This essay, in contributing to some project to "bring geography back in," suggests two broad implications for American social science. First, it emphasizes an explicit contextual understanding; that is, an analysis of the way in which social relations are expressed in particular settings, be they the family, the neighborhood, the city, the region, the nation-state, or the world economy. And in so emphasizing one material dimension, that of space, it must in addition invoke the other and call for a historical interpretation, for the study of context must be anchored in both time and space. Quite clearly, this approach to knowledge invokes a specific set of luminaries: Unsurprisingly, it excludes Parsons, Marx, and Weber *per se*; it draws more heavily on a generation of theorists such as Abrams, Bhaskar, Braudel, Castells, Foucault, Geertz, Giddens, Katzenelson, Thompson, Tilly, Urry, and Zunz. These theorists (most of whom are European) are attentive to the complexity of reality. Implicit in such an innocent statement is a number of additional insights, listed below with no particular priority. First, if we move away from some basic assumption of order and simplicity in the world, it becomes a little easier to accept that particular perspectives may have some analytical value in particular circumstances. In other words, a move away from a single mode of explanation permits other, currently marginal forms of discourse to appear: The obvious example here is feminism, although it would also be true of various forms of phenomenology. In turn, then, several other things also present themselves for consideration. The most important of these is that structuralism—of the narrow Althusserian variety—is rejected and replaced implicitly by a willingness to consider the roles of individuals—as women, gays, blacks, or production workers—and of collectivities—tenants, prochoice activists, or moral minorities. In short, people enter into the analytic equation on much more human and necessarily diverse terms. From there, it may then in turn be a short step toward a world of postmodernism (and, reflecting it, a postmodern social science) in which nearly all the familiar rules dissolve. It becomes impossible to deal in totalizing discourses, and we must search for new ways to reconstruct understanding. The analysis of individuals to some dictates existential ethnography rather than participant observation.[53] And most crucially, there appears a sharp discontinuity with the past, such that for the critical theorist Fredric Jameson, "our relationship with the past is now a spatial one." He continues:

> One privileged language in modernism, Proust or Thomas Mann for example, always uses temporal description. That notion of "deep time" . . . seems radically irrelevant to our contemporary experience, which is one of perpetual spatial present. Our theoretical categories also become spatial: structural analyses with graphs of synchronic multiplicities of spatially related things (as opposed to, say, the dialectic and its temporal moments), and languages like Foucault's with its empty rhetoric of cutting, sorting, and modifying, a kind of spatial language in which you organize data like a great bloc to be chopped up in various ways.[54]

Clearly we are far away from the postmodern challenge overthrowing the norms of contemporary social science, not least because it challenges not only the mainstream but most forms of Marxism too. Nonetheless, it is pleasant for a geographer to daydream, albeit briefly, about a system of thought in which spatial concepts have replaced temporal ones as a matter of course.[55]

At this point, we may return usefully to our opening example of the Great American Desert and appraise the new scholarship on the American West. To an important degree, this reappraisal is—in its call for "local knowledge"—entirely consistent with the views sketched out here. Historian Patricia Nelson Limerick, for instance, argues that "Turner's frontier was a process, not a place . . . in rethinking Western history, we gain the freedom to think of the West as a place—as many complex environments occupied by natives who considered their home-lands to be the center, not the edge."[56] As her book indicates, "conceive of the West as a place . . . and Western American history has a new look"; take context seriously, and the familiar cast of characters of the Hollywood West is deconstructed to reappear in very different guises— women, native Americans, blacks, European immigrants with a fondness for littering the landscape with tin cans, people and groups with as-pirations, strategies, and even some dignity. Importantly, this is not local history for the sake of it (not that the latter is inherently a bad thing, of course). Limerick goes on to show that once we have taken places and settings seriously, once we have moved away from the West as a myth,[57] so too it is possible to move toward some form of integration: She writes, "an exciting trend in modern scholarship leads toward com-parative history—toward Western American history as one chapter in the global story of Europe's expansion. Studies in 'comparative con-quests' promise to help knit the fragmented history of the planet back together," a conclusion with which Fernand Braudel, for one, would have agreed.[58]

Summary and Conclusions

Geography in the United States has been described as middle-class, midwestern, and middle brow.[59] While the first two of these epithets may be sound, the third is particularly apposite. This essay has argued that the discipline has been, in comparison with its namesakes in other countries, extremely ineffective in presenting a vision of the "geograph-ical imagination" to the rest of the academy and to the American people. Of course, there are some mitigating circumstances. Geography does not possess the same advantages (notably a specific intellectual niche) within the social formation that are possessed by other disciplines in the U.S. and by geography itself elsewhere. The imperial past has been a curious one within this country and has not depended upon the tools of geographers. The centrality of communalism—the importance of the locality within day-to-day existence—has not encouraged the study of the ways in which the world hangs together, the ways in which different places are in and of themselves of common interest. This dearth of geographical understanding has, as we have seen, resulted in the ultimate paradox. A society that is locally focused has developed an academic discourse that is committed to generality and a recreated, existential world that lacks both time and space as essential anchors. We are familiar with the abstractions of the median voter, the worker, the immigrant, and so on, as if these collectivities existed without due regard for the specifics of particular locations. To reiterate, a geographical imagination emphasizes the importance of contexts, the ways in which practices have been laid down over time in localities, to create, both by design and by accident, certain styles of life, certain coping mechanisms, and certain daily practices. By reintroducing a newly shaped and accented geography, we can enrich the practice of social science and in particular unite the investigation of the basic material dimensions, space and time.

Notes

My interest in this topic was kindled during a period spent at the Center for Advanced Study in the Behavioral Sciences, Stanford. I would like to thank my colleagues in that enterprise, and in particular JoAnne Brown and Jim Farr, for encouragement. An earlier version of the paper was presented to the Association of American Historians in 1987 and benefitted greatly from comments by Gordon Clark, Tom Glick, Stephen Kern, Dorothy Ross, Penny Waterstone, and John Wiener, although they are covered, if they wish, by the usual disclaimers. Parts of this research have been supported by a grant from the University of Colorado.

1. This discussion of the Great American Desert is taken from Martin Bowden, "The Great American Desert in the American Mind: The Historiography of a Geographical Notion," in D. Lowenthal and M. Bowden, eds., *Geography of the Mind* (New York: Oxford University Press, 1976), pp. 119–47; and E. Dick, *Conquering the Great American Desert* (Lincoln: Nebraska State Historical Society, 1975).
2. William Riebsame, "The Dust Bowl: Historical Image, Psychological Anchor, and Ecological Taboo," *Great Plains Quarterly* 6, no. 2 (1986): 127–36.
3. A. H. Clark, "The Great Plains: Perception by Any Name," in B. W. Blouet and M. P. Lawson, eds., *Images of the Plains* (Lincoln: University of Nebraska Press, 1975), p. xi.
4. In this essay I shall use the term *social science* with the explicit intention of including "the humanities" but differentiating discourse associated with "science"—laboratory investigation and so forth—although, as I argue, "blurred genres" make such a distinction a heroic one.

5. Clifford Geertz, *Local Knowledge: Further Essays in Interpretive Anthropology* (New York: Basic Books, 1983), pp. 19–35.

6. W. G. Roy, "Time, Place, and People in History and Sociology: Boundary Definitions and the Logic of Inquiry," *Social Science History* 11, no. 1 (1987): 53–62.

7. William Cronon, *Changes in the Land* (New York: Hill and Wang, 1983).

8. See, for instance, Susan Clarke and Andrew Kirby, "In Search of the Corpse: The Mysterious Case of Local Politics," *Urban Affairs Quarterly* 25, no. 3 (1990).

9. Joshua Goldstein, "Foucault among the Sociologists: The Disciplines in the History of the Professions," *History and Theory* 23, no. 2 (1984): 170–92.

10. Henrika Kuklick, "Boundary Maintenance in American Sociology: Limitations to Academic 'Professionalization,'" *Journal of the History of the Behavioral Sciences* 16 (1980): 201–19.

11. This conflict in resources is a real one insofar as it takes place within funding agencies and within universities and high schools and not across some abstract intellectual territory.

12. L. Ward, "The Place of Sociology among the Sciences," *American Journal of Sociology* 1 (1895): 16–27.

13. E. C. Hayes, "Sociology, Psychology, Geography," *American Journal of Sociology* 14 (1909): 371–403; quotation, pp. 390–1.

14. Ibid., p. 395. Physiography has as a term an interesting history, as Stoddart has shown. Originally developed by Huxley as a didactic device, it rapidly became a sprawling history of all geomorphology and geology, with the predictable result that the field splintered and ultimately disappeared; see David Stoddart, *On Geography* (Oxford: Basil Blackwell, 1986).

15. See Kuklick, "Boundary Maintenance in American Sociology."

16. Paul Richards, "Kant's Geography and Mental Maps," *Transactions of the Institute of British Geographers* 61, no. 1 (1973): 1–16. Kant was claimed as a geographical authority on the basis of a class that he taught from 1757 to 1793 in Königsberg. His text, entitled *Physische Geographie*, was, however, only a later collection of his lecture notes and did not constitute a major statement of philosophy. This process of claimstaking has, unsurprisingly, taken on rather ludicrous overtones: The most outlandish attempt to rewrite a Whig history of geography is the claim for the medieval monk, the Venerable Bede, to be included "on our side." For more thoughts on the "history of geographography," see J. K. Wright, "A Plea for the History of Geography," *Isis* (1926): 477–491.

17. Stoddart, *On Geography*, p. 2. Richard Hartshorne produced a major history of the discipline in 1939. Its production represents an interesting light on the paucity of intellectual thought in geography during the early decades of the century. Hartshorne was incensed by some comments published by John Leighly in 1938, in which he criticized the slavish dependence upon German intellectual thought and reinterpreted some aspects of the latter. Hartshorne, attempting to undertake fieldwork in Germany on the eve of the second war, found himself confined to library work. In responding to Leighly's arguments, he produced a paper which ran to over 450 pages of the American Geographers' *Annals*. This historical survey, subsequently republished in book form, remained the last word on the right and wrong ways of doing geography for some thirty years (material on

Hartshorne from Kirby, unpublished manuscript to appear in Neil Smith and Anne Godlewska, eds., *Geography and Empire* [Oxford: Basil Blackwell, 1991]; see also Neil Smith, "Geography as Museum: Private History and Conservative Idealism in *The Nature of Geography,*" Occasional Publications of the Association of American Geographers (1989): 89–120.

18. Isaiah Bowman, president of Johns Hopkins during the 1950s, was one of the few geographers who achieved national prominence, a position from which he contributed to the closure of the geography department at Harvard, see Neil Smith, "Academic Warfare over the Field of Geography," *Annals of the Association of American Geographers* 77, no. 2 (1987): 155–172. His book, *Geography in Relation to the Social Sciences* (New York: Scribners), was written in 1934 at the behest of the AHA and the SSRC and made the case that the discipline had a role to play within the academy. The Social Science Research Council, for one, never did agree; see Peter Gould, "Geography 1957–77: The Augean Period," *Annals of the Association of American Geographers* 69, no. 1 (1979): 139–50.

19. Tudor David, "Against Geography," *Universities Quarterly* 12 (1957): 261–73.

20. Colleagues have suggested to me that these departments deserved to be closed and that we should not infer anything from their demise. This may in itself be true, but it leaves some issues unresolved, not least of which is the fact that there are many poor departments in other fields which are resuscitated because the discipline in question is too important to be allowed to die. The example of sociology at Harvard, which for a time was augmented by a Department of Social Relations, is a case in point.

21. Ronald J. Johnston, *Geography and Geographers* (London: Edward Arnold, 1979).

22. Little attention will be given here to institutional analysis, although there is little question that this is of great importance. Departments, for instance, can mold the way in which a discipline evolves, a point developed at length by Diner in his exhaustive study of the Department of Sociology at the University of Chicago. Equally (and more to the point in this discussion), the demise of a department can hurt a discipline, as occurred when Harvard dispensed with geography with the retirement of Derwent Whittlesey in 1955. While the study of departments is thus entirely consistent with the contextual position emphasized here (and even a structurationist perspective), there is also a danger of examining the department in isolation and overemphasizing the roles of individuals. In this chapter, I have in consequence opted for the wider social settings within which geography is to be understood; see S. J. Diner, "Department and Discipline: The Department of Sociology at the University of Chicago 1892–1920," *Minerva* 13, no. 4 (1975): 515–53; Smith, "Geography as Museum."

23. See, for instance, Robert Merton, *The Sociology of Science* (Chicago: University of Chicago Press, 1973).

24. See Goldstein, "Foucault."

25. As generations of researchers have observed, the evolution of American society has taken a different path from that demonstrated in many European countries, particularly with respect to the absence of socialism. This dissimilarity has invited a number of explanations, ranging from the importance of apple pie to the pivotal role of the western frontier. Although these individual studies are important, they

are of course miscast: There is little reason to expect that social evolution will follow predictable paths from nation to nation.

26. Peter Berger and Thomas Luckmann, *The Social Construction of Reality* (New York: Doubleday, 1966).

27. Stoddart, *On Geography*.

28. Osbert Sitwell, *The Scarlet Tree* (London: Macmillan, 1946), p. 92.

29. Peter Steinberger, *Ideology and the Urban Crisis* (Albany: State University of New York Press, 1985). I discuss the implications of this logic in greater detail in, among others, Andrew Kirby, "Context, Common Sense, and the Reality of Place," *Journal for the Theory of Social Behavior* 18, no. 2 (1988): 239–50.

30. Albion Small, "The Beginnings of American Nationality," *Johns Hopkins University Studies in Historical and Political Science* 8 (1890): 1–77.

31. The phrase is Perry Miller's, quoted by Dorothy Ross, "Historical Consciousness in Nineteenth Century America," *American Historical Review* 89, no. 24 (1984): 913. In this paper, she places a very different construction on these issues from the one used by the author. She argues, for instance, for the late emergence of historicism within the U.S. and notes that "Americans . . . could relegate history to the past while they acted out their destiny in the realm of nature. They could develop in space rather than in time." Implicit in this perspective is, in my view, the assumption that the frontier represented more than a symbol and was, rather, part of a geographical consciousness. As I argue in this chapter, the frontier was at worst a myth and at best a process rather than a place. This emerges with even greater force in her arguments concerning political history, where we can trace a principle of universal republican values, an early emphasis upon the state rather than the individual and the community. This underlines a discontinuity between a fragmented political reality and academic discourse, which was in consequence unprepared for the Civil War. It was thus only at the close of the nineteenth century that historians such as John Burgess could confront the fact that the Civil War had shredded the myth of the universal state *in the past*, although this reinterpretation was of course taking place as the United States entered a gilded age in which state institutions began to be consolidated for the future.

32. Stephen Skowronek, *Building a New American State* (Cambridge: Cambridge University Press, 1982). These arguments are spelled out more fully in Andrew Kirby, "State, Local State, Context and Spatiality: A Re-appraisal of State Theory," in J. Caporaso, ed., *The Elusive State* (Newbury Park, Calif.: Sage, 1989), pp. 204–26.

33. The statistics are repeated, with variations, at frequent intervals: It is to be generally assumed, for example, that within a freshman college class, only half will be able to identify the outline of the U.S. on a world map; see, for instance, Edward Tenner, "Harvard, Bring Back Geography!" *Harvard Magazine* (May–June 1988): 27–30.

34. Without descending into teleological speculation, we can argue that the creation of the school and college curriculum is an important part of the development of the state apparatus. In Britain, geography had as part of its role the portrayal of the magnificence of the Empire, a role which can still be seen in texts produced in the 1950s. Geography was taught in schools in the U.S. as long as westward

expansion was under way but languished during subsequent periods of settlement at home and supposed isolationism abroad. At the same time, political science developed as a discipline with an important ideological function, namely, to teach about the centrality of the Constitution within American society. As my colleague Penny Waterstone reminds me, history begins this task in high school; political science continues it at the college level.

35. A. Reynaud, *La Géographie entre la myth et la science* (Reims: Travaux de l'Institut de Géographie, 1974).
36. See Fred Schaefer, "Exceptionalism in Geography," *Annals of the Association of American Geographers* 43 (1953): 226-49.
37. Neville Fennemann, "The Circumference of Geography," *Annals of the Association of American Geographers* 9 (1919): 3-11; W. A. Koelsch, "Wallace Atwood's Great Geographical Institute," *Annals of the American Association of American Geographers* 10, no. 4 (1980): 567-82.
38. Hayes, "Sociology."
39. Carl Sauer, "The Education of a Geographer," *Annals of the Association of American Geographers* 46 (1956): 287-99, 295.
40. Allan Pred, who has done much to import social theory into contemporary geography, has written that "the distinction between fieldwork and other more everyday observations and experiences is but one manifestation of a general unwillingness to accept the fact that our professional lives are not in dichotomous opposition to one another, but dialectically interrelated"; Allan Pred, "From Here and Now to There and Then," in M. Billinge, D. Gregory, and R. L. Martin, eds., *Recollections of a Revolution* (London: Macmillan, 1984), pp. 86-103. To Stoddart, a voyager "in a great tradition," this becomes a recognition that "here is not there, yesterday cannot be tomorrow, and if you are doing one thing you cannot be doing another," an insight which has "been apprehended by the fieldworkers among us for some time. Certainly the life-paths of most explorers would have been abruptly terminated in short order without this knowledge. I am glad to think that the insights of physical geography are in general somewhat more profound"; Stoddard, *On Geography*, p. 147, n. 21.
41. Peter Haggett and Richard Chorley, *Frontiers in Geographical Teaching* (London: Arnold, 1965).
42. Thomas Glick, "In Search of Geography," *Isis* 74, no. 1 (1983): 92-9, 96.
43. William Bunge, *Theoretical Geography* (Lund: Gleerup, 1963).
44. Gary Gaile and Cort Wilmott, *Geography in America* (Boston: Bobbs-Merrill, 1989).
45. Quentin Skinner, "Meaning and Understanding in the History of Ideas," *History and Theory* 8 (1969): 3-53.
46. Alan R. H. Baker, "Reflections on the Relation of Historical Geography and the *Annales* School of History," in A. R. H. Baker and D. Gregory, eds., *Explorations in Historical Geography: Interpretative Essays* (Cambridge: Cambridge University Press, 1984), pp. 1-27.
47. Fernand Braudel, *Civilization and Capital*, 3 vols. (New York: Harper and Row, 1981, 1984).
48. Philip Abrams, *Historical Sociology* (Ithaca, N.Y.: Cornell University Press, 1982); Anthony Giddens, *A Contemporary Critique of Historical Materialism*

(Berkeley and Los Angeles: University of California Press, 1979).

49. Anthony Giddens, *The Nation State and Violence: A Contemporary Critique of Historical Materialism, vol. 2* (Berkeley and Los Angeles: University of California Press, 1985).

50. Ibid.

51. Stephen Kern, *The Culture of Time and Space 1880-1918* (Cambridge, Mass.: Harvard University Press, 1983).

52. P. A. Heelan, *Space-perception and the Philosophy of Science* (Berkeley and Los Angeles: University of California Press, 1983).

53. N. K. Denzin, "Review Symposium on Field Methods," *Journal of Contemporary Ethnography* 17 (1988).

54. A. Stephanson, "Regarding Postmodernism—A Conversation with Fredric Jameson," *Social Text* 17 (1987): 29–54.

55. Readers may not be amused by this flight of fancy, although the marginalization of history should appear no more barbarous than the exclusion of geography in other circumstances. For a contemporary example of a geographer making such an imperialistic claim for the discipline, see Michael Dear, "The Postmodern Challenge," *Transactions of the Institute of British Geographers* 13 (1988): 262–74. For a fuller exploration of space, social theory, and postmodernism, see Edward Soja, *Postmodern Geographies* (London: Verso, 1989).

56. Patricia Nelson Limerick, *The Legacy of Conquest: The Unbroken Past of the American West* (New York: Norton, 1987), p. 26.

57. V. E. Mattson, "West as Myth," *Journal of the History of the Behavioral Sciences* 24, no. 1 (1988): 9–12.

58. Limerick, *Legacy of Conquest*, pp. 26–27.

59. Glick, "In Search of Geography."

■ 3 FROM NATURAL HISTORY TO SOCIAL SCIENCE

Disciplinary Development and Redefinition in British Anthropology, 1860–1910

DAVID K. VAN KEUREN

In 1922, four years after the end of the Great War and not quite two decades since its own founding, the (British) Sociological Society decided it was once again time to host public discussions over the question of the mutual intellectual and disciplinary interrelations of the social sciences. In particular, the society's members were intent on analyzing the relations between sociology and such "specialisms" as economics, human biology, and anthropology.[1] The Sociological Society had been organized in 1904 with just such a purpose in mind, and in subsequent papers and debates its members had repeatedly wrangled over questions of heuristics, methodology, and how the social sciences knit together to form a common fabric of theory and praxis.[2] However, the society had not held such discussions since the prewar years. It now seemed appropriate to do so at Oxford, where the correlation of modern subjects in the new "Greats School" was being actively debated.[3] Oxford was also a peculiarly congenial place to bring together the various economists, anthropologists, historians, geographers, psychologists, biologists, and general sociologists whose professional interests were concerned.

One of the hosts of the conference was R. R. Marett, reader in social anthropology, secretary of the Committee for Anthropology, and a former examiner of the School of *Literae Humaniores* at Oxford. Marett had studied at Balliol and then Exeter College in Oxford, winning the Green Moral Philosophy Prize for his essay "The Ethics of Savage

Races" in 1893.[4] He stayed on as a tutor and examiner at Exeter, eventually serving as the spiritual successor to Edward Burnett Tylor when the latter retired in 1909. Besides representing Oxford University as a whole, Marett also stood as a spokesman for the attending anthropologists. It was in this latter role that Marett participated in the dialogue on how to establish a working correlation between social scientific specializations.

Marett prefaced his conference remarks by suggesting that it was not necessary at a sociological conference to insist on the theoretical continuity of the cultural history of man. Nevertheless, he confessed that "anyone who calls himself an anthropologist will be prepared to admit that his science is scarcely able to live up to its name. Whereas, its titular authority extends over the whole subject of Man, its interest is effectively restricted to the primitive, or rudimentary, forms of human culture. This was virtually unoccupied territory until the anthropologist acquired squatter's rights over it."[5] On the other hand, had he claimed to interpret what Lecky calls "the European epoch of the human mind" a host of rivals, representatives of the old-established humanities, would have denounced him as an upstart. Prudently, then, the anthropologist has tended to resign to others the study of civilized society.[6]

Being perforce an expert on primitive culture, Marett argued, it was only from the outside that the anthropologist could attempt to understand how the history of the highest cultures could be brought in phase with studies of the development of the lowest. The efforts of students of civilized societies, including economists, sociologists, and historians, needed to be added to that of anthropologists to give complete pictures of cultural development.[7] The anthropologist was a social scientific specialist whose professional domain ended where that of the student of modern industrialized societies began.

The Oxford conference, under the aegis of the Sociological Society, was promoting sociology as the covering manifold for all social scientific research while recognizing the internal integrity of "specialisms," or specific areas of social analysis. The latter included anthropology, comparative jurisprudence, comparative religion, psychology, economics, and history.[8] Sociology, as defined by L. T. Hobhouse, holder of the Martin White Chair of Sociology at the University of London and an important conference participant, was a synthesis of the social sciences which offered a means of achieving a holistic view of the whole spectrum of social life. Its problem was "the investigation of the general character of the social relations and the nature and determining conditions of social development."[9] Anthropology's role within this synthesis, according to Marett, was that of elucidating the various coexistent forms of primitive culture through consideration of the economics, politics, law, religion, art, etc. of a culture complex.[10]

Marett's delineation of anthropology's boundaries and objectives differed markedly from that of Edward Burnett Tylor, his predecessor in social anthropology at Oxford.[11] Tylor had come to Oxford as keeper of the University Museum in 1883, was made reader in anthropology in 1884, and then professor twelve years later. Tylor's original appointment was a consequence of negotiations between university science men and Augustus Pitt-Rivers over the bringing of Pitt-Rivers's ethnological collection to the university.[12] The science men wanted the collection for its educational and research potential in the history of cultural evolution. Pitt-Rivers required the university to build a museum and hire a curator to arrange and oversee the collection. Tylor, who had received a D.C.L. from the university in 1875 and was well known to its small scientific community, was appointed keeper of the broader university science museum as a compromise.

Tylorian anthropology, primarily delineated through the author's *Researches into the Early History of Mankind* and *Primitive Culture*, had boldly defined itself as a comprehensive study of mankind which elaborated the "synopsis of man's bodily and mental nature, and the theory of his whole course of life and action from his first appearance on earth."[13] Its purported topic was the whole history of human development and the rise of civilization. Tylor's textbook review of his field, *Anthropology, an Introduction to the Study of Man and Civilization*, started off with a study of man, ancient and modern; moved to the study of man's relationship to other animals; then to analysis of the origin, interrelationship, and nature of human races; and on through language, writing, material culture and social life, the history of religious and mythological belief, and social organization.[14] Tylor described anthropology itself as the "natural history of mankind," which, in the general classification of knowledge, stood "as the highest section of zoology . . . itself the highest section of biology or the science of living beings."[15]

This dramatic redefinition of disciplinary scope and emphasis was effected within one generation. Approximately twenty-five years separated the appointments of Tylor and Marett at Oxford, yet within that time the science of man in Britain had effectively been transformed from Tylor's "natural history of man" and the history of civilization into Marett's social studies of savage peoples. This shift in emphasis from natural to social science is a pivotal passage in the development of modern anthropology. Its origins have much to do with changing intellectual perspectives and methodologies, but even more with the changing nature of the anthropological community and the institutional settings within which it pursued its work. The remainder of this paper will attempt to explore in outline form the nature and impact of these disciplinary and institutional changes, from the 1870s through the Edwardian period.[16]

Generational Change and Disciplinary Redefinition

By the early 1870s, British anthropology had achieved a measure of organizational stability and scientific respectability after a decade of intellectual and institutional strife. Two previously competitive anthropological societies had resolved their differences and merged to form the Anthropological Institute of Great Britain and Ireland in 1871.[17] The new society was intellectually and socially eclectic but was dominated by a circle of scientific naturalists who had followed John Lubbock into the Ethnological Society of London, a component of the new Institute, on his election to the society presidency in 1863. The circle which formed around Lubbock included T. H. Huxley, George Busk, Alfred Russel Wallace, William Spottiswoode, Joseph Hooker, Francis Galton, George Rolleston, and, to a lesser extent, Augustus W. Franks and E. B. Tylor.[18] Young, ambitious, and intellectually aggressive, the Lubbock Circle members played critical organizational roles in Victorian science and were central participants in efforts to win professional status and social respectability for it. Moreover, they were all committed Darwinians who often had been personally involved in the intellectual revolution of the 1850s and early 1860s that challenged and shattered the accepted notions regarding the permanence of species and the antiquity of humanity.

As a group, Lubbock and his colleagues were intent on extending the analysis of evolution to the human physical and cultural spheres. With some assistance from institute philologists and antiquarians (the core of traditionalist ethnology), they helped construct an anthropological synthesis which united ethnography, ethnology, antiquarianism, comparative philology, and comparative anatomy—all well established by the 1860s—with prehistorical archaeology, comparative religion, folklore, evolution-based analyses of culture, and developmental biology. Building on an intellectual base that used comparative philology in the pursuit of ethnological taxonomy, the new anthropologists adopted the use of the comparative-historical method for the elucidation of the evolution of man and society.[19] Although evolutionary studies of culture, including language, religion, and social organization, antedated Darwinian theory, it was the intense debate over human evolution that stimulated a comprehensive approach to progressionist analyses of human physical and cultural change.[20] The new synthetic evolutionary anthropology aspired to create a natural science which chronicled the developmental record of man's physical and cultural history. It was to be one of several new or reconstituted sciences which their proponents hoped would change the face of Victorian society.[21]

The analytic tool by which Victorian anthropologists hoped to achieve their ends was the comparative-historical method. The method, which as its name suggests was both comparative and historical in nature, had its roots in the comparative history of civilizations pursued by the *philosophes* of the French and Scottish Enlightenment. The Victorians revivified and reconceptualized the theory, turning it into a rigorous tool for analyzing and comparing the material culture and institutions of both primitive and advanced societies. As the method itself has been extensively analyzed by historians elsewhere, I will simply summarize it here.[22] The principle underlying evolutionary thought was that human culture and physical form developed according to ascertainable laws which the careful observer could isolate and describe. The general and specific characteristics of culture and social organization were not the result of chance but were due to the "uniform action" of "uniform causes." Cultural change was a lawful process proceeding in the same fashion from one culture to another, although the rate of development varied. Change, furthermore, using Herbert Spencer's terminology, proceeded from the less complex to the more complex and from the homogeneous to heterogeneous.[23] Cultures were roughly classifiable into the categories of savage, barbaric, and civilized, although the scale of development itself was unitary, linear, and continuous, from the least to the most civilized. Not all the stages of development were represented by contemporary primitives, so both present and prehistoric cultures needed to be compared and assorted to isolate the path of upward cultural change. Consequently, the comparative-historical method was based on extensive use of the data of both ethnography and prehistory.[24]

Within the framework of evolution theory, then, there was an implicit research program. It consisted of ordering ethnographic data into the probable sequence of cultural development. The result of the developmental process—contemporary Victorian culture—was known and the beginning could be surmised. What remained was to collect data on primitive contemporary and prehistoric cultures, develop ethnographic descriptions which fully described the cultural attributes of as many cultural systems as possible, and order them according to their relative occurrence on the developmental ladder.[25] Once the outlines were known, research became a puzzle-solving activity, where details could be filled in as data became available. This was the task set in motion by the evolutionary anthropologists of the 1860s and 1870s.

The intellectual tone of the Anthropological Institute and the anthropological section of the British Association (Section H) was set by the leading members of the Lubbock Circle in the 1860s and 1870s. Lubbock, along with Huxley, was one of the chief scientific popularizers of the age. A strong supporter of Darwin, he published several articles in the early 1860s on European prehistory.[26] Lubbock's writings used archaeological and paleontological evidence to convincingly argue for an extended age for humans in Europe. His succeeding 1865 monograph, *Prehistoric Times, as Illustrated by Ancient Remains and the Manners and Customs of Modern Savages,* is a classic application of the comparative-historical method and caused a popular sensation at publication through its unblinking proclamation of a vastly extended human antiquity based on the recent discovery of Pleistocene human remains.

While Lubbock extended the time scale for human history, Huxley effectively argued for the existence of human evolutionary links with the higher apes. His *Zoological Evidences as to Man's Place in Nature* (1863) carried on from where Darwin had left off in *The Origin of Species.*[27] Huxley used skillful scientific observation and reasoning to compare and contrast human and ape anatomy, breaking down in the process the various anatomical barriers which previous naturalists and controversialists had erected to divide and differentiate them. The zoological evidence, as read by Huxley, went far to demonstrate common ancestral linkages for *Homo sapiens* and the apes.[28] Any future attempt to trace the origins of the human form and its varieties would need to take developmentalist biological theory into account. Indeed, Alfred Russel Wallace would subsequently declare that evolutionary theory conclusively resolved the old debate between monogenists and polygenists regarding whether human races were taxonomic varieties or distinct species.[29]

Similarly, Francis Galton was moved by his reading of *The Origin of Species* to undertake a lifetime study of human heredity.[30] Starting from an ethnological inquiry in the 1860s into the mental peculiarities of different races, Galton subsequently attempted to develop a system for discriminating between different physical characteristics and determining the manner in which they were passed from one generation to another.[31] Inasmuch as a race was ultimately dependent upon and characterizable by its constituent family lines, Galton set as his goal the measurement of the physical and mental characters of those component lines and their comparison within and across racial types. The history and charting of human inheritance was thus identified as being a major objective of anthropological science.

The comparative evolutionary interests of Lubbock, Huxley, Galton, and their compeers was quickly adopted by new conscripts to the central circle of the Anthropological Institute and became characteristic of the society as a whole. Augustus (Lane-Fox) Pitt-Rivers, Lubbock's father-in-law, was a collector of prehistoric and contemporary artifacts. His collections became famous for their broad-ranging demonstration of evolution within material culture.[32] E. B. Tylor applied the comparative-historical method to extensive studies into the evolution of culture and institutions. William Henry Flower, who eventually became director of the Natural History Museum, was an expert on comparative anatomy and became a leading exponent of evolution within the museum setting.[33] Like both Lubbock and Huxley, Flower was able to pass easily from biology to human prehistory and ethnology.

Other theorists, such as Herbert Spencer, Henry Sumner Maine, and John McLennan, who played little or no role in the institutional life of British anthropology, took theoretical stances similar to their contemporaries within the Anthropological Institute and the British Association.[34] The common defining element in their research and writing was application of the comparative-historical method to the history of human institutions and a broad concern with evolutionary development from prehistoric times to the present.

The anthropological synthesis constructed from the work of the Lubbock Circle members and their successors combined distinct research specialties integrated by a common methodology and research assumptions. At the level of the object of analysis, however, anthropology still remained a federation of distinct study fields. The research interests of members of the Anthropological Institute separated along specific subdisciplinary lines whose major components included somatology or physical anthropology, prehistory and archaeology, ethnology, ethnography, antiquarianism, and cultural studies, which included philology and research on comparative religion and material culture.[35] Thus, the new anthropology of the 1870s was by design embracive and inclusive. Any aspect of human culture or any factor that bore on human culture, such as race and comparative racial development and anatomy, was felt to be an integral part of the science of man. This breadth and freedom of research scope was reflected in the definitional boundaries which anthropologists placed on their science.

Anthropologists generally agreed that the study of mankind *in extenso* was a vast enterprise which required the cooperation of specialists. Francis Galton, for example, emphasized the importance of specialization within a broadly defined anthropology. A thoroughly pursued human science, he argued, needed intense concentration on all its subareas, a task which only specialists could attain to:

> The object of the Anthropologist is plain. He seeks to learn what mankind really are in body and mind, how they came to be what they are, and whither their races are tending; but the methods by which this definite inquiry has to be pursued are extremely diverse. Those of the geologist, the antiquarian, the jurist, the historian, the philologist, the traveller, the artist, and the statistician are all employed, and the Science of Man progresses through the help of specialists.[36]

Similarly, E. B. Brabrook, active within both the Anthropological Institute and the British Association, described anthropology as a collaboration of research interests, including physical anthropology, prehistoric archaeology, linguistics, psychology, ethnography, ethnology, and sociology, the last of which applied "the learning accumulated in all the other branches of anthropology to man's relations to his fellows."[37] Anthropology was in effect a synthesis of subspecialties, unifying them in just such a fashion as Comtian *sociologie* unified scientific analysis of man and nature.

This breadth of definition received its ultimate codification in 1875 when E. B. Tylor summarily described his science as the "natural history of mankind."[38] Tylorian anthropology took as its major task the tracing of the evolutionary course of man's progress from savagery to civilization. Culture or civilization was defined by Tylor to be the "complex whole which includes knowledge, belief, art, morals, law, custom, and any other capabilities and habits acquired by man as a member of society."[39] The relative condition of culture among human societies, insofar as it was capable of being investigated on general principles, was the domain of anthropological investigation. To this was added study of previous human societies through prehistory and archaeology and the development of the human form and races through somatology. Indeed, Tylor suggested that anthropology served as a comprehensive science of humanity to which more specialized studies contributed.[40] Thus, Tylor's anthropology ultimately strove to be just such a synthesis of human cultural and physical studies that Hobhousian sociology would later claim to be for the social sciences as a whole.

Beginning with the 1890s but particularly becoming more pronounced in the early years of the twentieth century, a new generation of men came to positions of relative dominance in anthropology. Born in the 1850s and 1860s, educated in the 1870s and 1880s, they were too young to have experienced the debate over Darwinism, evolution, and the antiquity of man. In contrast to many leading lights of the Lubbock Circle, such as Lubbock or Tylor, they had attended one of the national universities (generally Oxford or Cambridge) and had specific academic training in the arts or sciences to bring to bear on anthropology. It was men such as A. C. Haddon, C. H. Read, R. R. Marett, Henry Balfour, and William Ridgeway who helped direct the course of anthropology when the older generation began to lose its sway due to age and infirmity. As a whole, they occupied professional positions in anthropology or related fields and held its highest elected offices in the Anthropological Institute and British Association from the late 1890s on.[41]

The change in both the educational and professional backgrounds of the leading members of the anthropological community between the 1870s and 1910 is striking. A comparison of the officers of the Anthropological Institute reveals an important shift from a council whose members had limited academic backgrounds and professional ties to anthropology to one where a significant majority had a baccalaureate education at minimum and whose primary professional responsibilities were tied to anthropological research or teaching within university or museum settings.[42] Thus, while only about 17 percent of the officers within the Anthropological Institute had an undergraduate university education in 1883, 67 percent had the equivalent level of education in 1910. Similarly, while only a very small proportion (about 7 percent) of the officers had a postgraduate degree in 1883, almost two-fifths (39 percent) had achieved that level of education by 1910. Even more importantly, only a quarter (24 percent) of the officers of the institute held professional positions in anthropology in universities or museums in 1883, but better than two-thirds (70 percent) held them by 1910. Thus, the generational shift in leadership had important repercussions for the discipline as a whole.

The research interests of the new generation tended to be more narrow in scope than that of their older colleagues. Each had professional responsibilities in universities or museums which focused their interests. Thus, Ridgeway emphasized classical studies related to his specialization in Bronze Age Greece. Balfour stressed the material culture of contemporary savage peoples, a logical outgrowth of his curatorship of the Pitt-Rivers Museum at Oxford. C. H. Read wrote on Bronze Age and medieval antiquities. Marett and J. G. Frazer, who both had backgrounds in the classics, researched the development of religious and mythological beliefs and the concomitant evolution of ethical and philosophical systems. Haddon, who had the broadest range of interests, had his research shaped by his early expeditions to the Torres Straits in 1888 and 1898–

99. Thereafter, he specialized in ethnographic and cultural studies of contemporary savages, particularly those of Melanesia. In conjunction with this greater degree of specialization within anthropology, the younger generation of anthropologists narrowed the disciplinary boundaries which they ascribed to their science.

R. R. Marett's work is exemplary of the changes that were affecting anthropology at the beginning of this century. In ideal terms, Marett continued to espouse a scope for anthropology which allowed it to treat man in his entirety. Anthropology, for him, was the whole history of man pervaded by the idea of evolutionary advance.

> Man in evolution—that is the subject in its full reach. Anthropology studies man as he occurs at all known times. It studies him as he occurs in all known parts of the world. It studies him body and soul together. . . . Having an eye to such conditions from first to last, it seeks to plot out the general series of the changes, bodily and mental together, undergone by man in the course of his history.[43]

Anthropology was concerned not only with the savage but with the history of the whole species in general.[44] Savagery was taken as a starting point from which to explain the origins of civilization:

> Hitherto, anthropology has devoted most of its attention to the peoples of rude—that is to say, of simple—culture, who are vulgarly known to us as "savages." But, although it has always up to now pursued the line of least resistance, anthropology does not abate one jot or tittle of its claim to be the whole science, in the sense of the whole history, of man. . . . We anthropologists are out to secure this: that there shall not be one kind of history for savages and another for ourselves, but the same kind of history, with the same evolutionary principle running right through it, for all men, civilized and savage, present and past.[45]

In Marett's eyes, anthropology lay "clearly among the liberal studies, the humanities" and its function was "first and foremost, to enlarge the mind."[46] With a fuller experience of the wide content of human intelligence, men would tend to become more tolerant of diversity and more inclined to widen their tastes.[47] As such, anthropology played a role traditionally ascribed to the *Literae Humaniores* at Oxford. It disciplined the mind while inducing catholicity of taste. Nevertheless, for reasons of practical expediency, within the context of university debates over the nature and breadth of anthropological teaching, Marett effectively acted to help limit the sphere of anthropological studies.

The cause for the contradiction between Marett's rhetoric and actions must be sought within the internal politics of his university.

Marett's predecessor, E. B. Tylor, had made an attempt in 1895 to include anthropology as one of the subjects of the Finals School in Natural Science. Medical and other degree students as a result would have been able to take it as an honors subject. However, although the statute garnered strong support among representatives of the medical and natural science schools, opponents from the theological and arts schools—referred to by Tylor as members of the "non-placet society"—had united to defeat the measure.[48]

The 1895 defeat was only the latest of a string of disappointments for Tylor and other proponents of anthropological teaching within the university. A proposal by the Board of Natural Science Studies in 1882 had first recommended inclusion of anthropology as one of the subjects offered at the Final Honours Exam. The accompanying anthropological syllabus was extensive, including surveys of physical anthropology, ethnology, archaeology, and cultural studies.[49] Human and comparative anatomy and physiology, anthropometry, man's relation to the apes, the description and analysis of the origin of the human races, evolution of culture, philology, social organization, and archaeology were all considered necessary elements of the proposed study area. Indeed, the breadth of the proposed science dwarfed that of the long-established classical languages and literature and trespassed on the curricular prerogatives of the Literae Humaniores, theology, and developing studies in law and history. As a consequence, perhaps, the board's proposal disappeared from sight and never reached a vote in the university Convocation.[50]

Similar attempts to add anthropology to the Final Honours Exam in 1885 and 1890 failed due to the resistance aroused by the extensive nature of the proposed study. This was the background to Tylor's renewed attempt in 1894–95 to bring anthropology within the Final Honours School. Careful and cautious lobbying for the effort brought initial success to the measure when it was brought before the university's Hebdomadal Council and then Congregation (the university's resident deliberative body).[51] However, the final vote before Convocation (the deliberative body of all resident and nonresident M.A.s) was lost.[52] The measure had the support of the representatives of the university's developing science side and the votes of the more liberal members in law, arts, and theology. However, the ensuing debate roused the opposition of the majority of the representatives of the Literae Humaniores and theology, resulting in a narrow no vote. In Tylor's own summary of the proceedings, "incautious utterances by defenders put first the classical men and then the theologians on their guard and they whipped up the surrounding curates."[53] This coalition against the inclusion of new subjects into the university curriculum and testing structures was well established by the 1880s.[54] Anthropology was just one of its targets.

However, the vote against anthropology was not simply one more rejection of another new study area by university traditionalists. In a real sense, the encompassing nature of Tylorian anthropology was viewed as posing a real threat to more established study fields. Thus, Tylor commented to Henry W. Acland after the vote that "the plan of his opponents is to make Anthropology one of the special subjects in the Greats School, while allowing any particular research in it to qualify for a Research Degree. This was more or less said by the opposition in Convocation last week, but I hardly took it as more than the trash of debate. You now see that we are face to face with an organized attempt to place Oxford under the rule of the Classics and Philosophy."[55] Inasmuch as anthropology took human history, arts, religion, social customs, and philosophy as part of its own subject matter, it was bound to produce confrontations with both long-established and new-born study areas which claimed the same subject matter. Stanley Gardiner, professor of classical archaeology and art, would representatively argue a few years later that anthropology and archaeology stood at the base of historic studies and needed to be investigated jointly with ancient and modern history, not with biology and the kindred studies to which it had been wrongly conjoined.[56] Certainly, it was the sentiment of Tylor's adversaries within the university that the study of culture as such rightly belonged within the Greats School and not tied to natural science. This implicit disagreement over the status of cultural studies helped doom Tylor's efforts to advance the cause of anthropology within his university.[57]

It was within this historical context that Marett later took heed of Tylor's defeat and made important compromises on his science's subject and boundary claims. While continuing to pay lip service to the Tylorian ideal of an inclusive, holistic science of man which included the development of human culture, Marett in effect compromised these claims away. Thus, in negotiations over the syllabus for the anthropological diploma program at Oxford in 1905–06, he sided with men from the arts school who believed anthropology should limit itself, within the university at least, to the study of "past and present savagery."[58]

Marett reluctantly agreed with the assertion of Lewis Farnell, lecturer in classical archaeology, that "it would . . . be desirable to indicate more clearly that Anthropology is to be understood as the study of *primitive* man; and that therefore 'Comparative Religion' as a branch of it means only the comparative study of primitive religions; for the phrase 'Comparative Religion' in itself properly applies to the comparative study of Christianity, Buddhism and the other higher religions of the world; and such a vast study cannot be regarded as a special subject of primitive Anthropology."[59] Comparative religion, Marett's own particular forte, under these terms was accordingly reduced to "Savage Religion, Magic, and Folklore."

John Linton Myres, who also participated in the debate over establishment of an anthropological diploma program, later confirmed that anthropology had by force of circumstances been gradually excluded from fields of investigation it considered rightfully its own. In a retrospective view of anthropological science, he declared:

> From the circumstances that the older and more academic studies which have preoccupied so much of the anthropological field were interested in the behavior and achievements of people akin to ourselves, and in periods of their history for which there was literary record, Anthropology, gleaning in unreaped corners of that field, found itself concentrating its attention on the more remote and less civilized peoples, and on aspects of the present age which illustrate rather the infancy and adolescence than the maturity of mankind. . . . Thus, when this Cinderella among the sciences began, rather late, to be conscious of its own existence and of a special programme, it found large parts of that field of knowledge—the study of mankind in general—which theoretically belonged to it, already preoccupied by more special and more departmental studies, already fairly well established.[60]

Myres bemoaned the fact that the scope of the science had been thus limited but accepted the practical expediency of the reality. From his own position as a classical archaeologist, professor of ancient history, and examiner in the Final Classical School, in geography and in modern languages, Myres was well aware of the jealously erected boundaries dividing fields of study at the universities and of the increasing specialization that characterized academic studies. Anthropology needed to adapt itself to such conditions.

Similarly, at Cambridge, James George Frazer played a collateral role in the intellectual redefinition of anthropology's subject matter. Frazer held a Trinity College fellowship at Cambridge and occupied the chair of social anthropology at the University of Liverpool after 1907. A classicist who became well known through his several editions of *The Golden Bough*, Frazer had specific research commitments to the study of comparative religion and mythology. Skillfully utilizing the comparative historical method, he wove well-crafted analyses of the development of basic themes in the religious belief systems of ancient and savage peoples.

Frazer was in general agreement with L. T. Hobhouse over the interrelationship of sociology and the other social sciences. While sociology dealt with the study of human society in its entirety, Frazer wished to limit the sphere of social anthropology to the "crude beginnings, the rudimentary development of human society."[61] Anthropology did not, Frazer argued, "include the maturer phases of the complex growth of human society," still less did it "embrace the practical problems [with] which . . . modern statesmen and lawgivers are called upon to deal. The study might accordingly be described as the embryology of human thought and institutions, or, to be more precise, as that enquiry which seeks to ascertain, first, the beliefs and customs of savages, and, second, the relics of these beliefs and customs which have survived like fossils among peoples of higher culture."[62]

Social, or what Frazer later termed mental, anthropology set as its task the study of the evolution of the human mind which had accompanied the evolution of the human body. Inasmuch as the later stages of that evolution had been long studied by other sciences, it was only fair that the new science should confine itself to those earlier stages of which the older science had hardly taken account.[63]

This redefinition of anthropology's scope by Frazer, Marett, Myres, and other younger anthropologists was a readjustment to existing realities at the end of the Edwardian era in Britain. There were too many other competing and expanding fields of study directing their attention to the topic of human cultural and psychological development to allow for anthropology's monopolization of the field. Similarly, the increasing demands for professionalization among university lecturers and researchers forced them to narrow and refine their research topics.[64]

The formulations of the Lubbock Circle had reflected the synthetic nature of evolutionary thought in the 1870s. Its members had tied together biological evolution with the reanalysis of man in society and the development of material and social culture. The Lubbock Circle, often men from biological backgrounds or with strong biological interests, had sought to build a unified science of man directed by the theory of evolution and building on the application of the comparative-historical method. Darwinian evolution had similarly rejuvenated and united the various strands of natural history into a newborn biological science in the 1860s.

Where Tylor had spoken of the science of culture and subsumed the study of the evolution of civilization under the broader purview of the natural history of mankind, his successors spoke in narrower terms and assigned to anthropology the task of analyzing the development of culture among the simpler or savage peoples.[65] The intellectual linkages which Tylor and the Lubbock Circle as a whole had drawn between natural law and cultural process were deemphasized, and culture was again reified as an object of study sui generis. In the new order, anthropology became only one of many cultural studies, and, in effect, the attention of anthropologists soon turned to social relations among primitive peoples. Cultural behavior became a construct of social relations rather than an inherent growth defined by natural law.

The new generation of anthropologists, often men with classical or other humanistic backgrounds (Marett, Myres, and Frazer, for example, were all trained classicists), were no longer concerned with legitimizing the science of anthropology and were facing institutional and professional pressures which their predecessors did not have to bear. They were not overtly interested in integrating physical and cultural anthropology, partly because physical anthropology was following a separate pattern of institutionalization tied in to comparative anatomy, human biology, and medicine.[66] The task which they faced was that of realigning disciplinary parameters and pretensions in accordance with institutional realities and professional needs. The shift from a federation of research interests united by a shared methodology within a common scientific forum, such as the Anthropological Institute, to a teaching and research specialization embedded within highly competitive and departmentalized university structures was a significant one. It in turn had significant causal consequences.

By the time of the 1922 Oxford conference, the transformation of anthropology from a comprehensive science of man to the social studies of primitive peoples was relatively complete. Durkheimian sociology, as espoused by Hobhouse and his followers and pursued within the new Department of Sociology at the University of London, had taken anthropology's place as the synthetic science of man.[67] Anthropology in its new and more modest estate fit well into the university curriculum, alongside comparative law, classical history, and the new area studies then proliferating within the universities. Physical anthropology had been divided off into the natural science faculties and was following a discrete process of professionalization among the biological sciences. Social anthropology had joined psychology, political science, and economics among the specialist disciplines within the social sciences.

This paper does not wish to argue that changing interpretations of anthropological data, new research methodologies, and different intellectual climates are (or were) insignificant to the process of disciplinary definition and change within the social sciences. The social sciences are, after all, bodies of theory subject to the processes and norms of intellection within both elites and society at large. Neither do I wish to argue against the grounding of social theory within the social and economic contexts of particular times and places. However, I do wish to suggest that institutional contexts, and the sociopolitical debate and negotiations that go on within them, are important and often critical for understanding both theoretical and disciplinary change. As the anthropological estate was crystallized and formalized within distinct institutional contexts, its disciplinary parameters were redrawn as a compromise between the needs and aspirations of its practitioners and the demands of its new patrons—in this case the Edwardian university. In the resulting compromise worked out between human science and humane letters, the consequence was a social study that combined parts of both into a new whole.

Notes

1. Alexander Farquharson, "The Oxford Conference on the Correlation of the Social Sciences: An Appreciation of the Discussions. . . with Abstracts of the Papers Read," *Sociological Review* 15 (1923): 48–64. For background on the Sociological Society, see Phillip Abrams, *The Origins of British Sociology, 1834–1914* (Chicago: University of Chicago Press, 1968), esp. pp. 102 ff., and Stefan Collini, *Liberalism and Sociology: L. T. Hobhouse and Political Argument in England, 1880–1914* (Cambridge: Cambridge University Press, 1979).
2. V. Branford, "A Note on the Conference," in Farquharson, "The Oxford Conference," p. 64.
3. The establishment of an Honour School in philosophy, politics, and economics was approved in 1920. The subject of the new study area was the philosophical, political, and economic principles of modern society and also included extensive study in modern British history. The supervising board of studies included representatives of the boards of the faculties of Literae Humaniores and modern history and of the Committee for Economics and Political Science. The first examination was scheduled for the academic year of 1923-24. See the *Oxford University Gazette*, 20 October 1920, p. 76, 17 November 1920, p. 192, 1 December 1920, pp. 233–34. The Honour School was strenuously opposed by the remnants of the old non-placet society. See Sir Charles Oman, *Memories of Victorian Oxford and of Some Early Years* (London: Methuen, 1942). Oman declares that "of all the more recently-established Honour Schools the one which most provoked my disapproval is that which the Gods call *Philosophia Politica et Economica* . . . but men 'Modern Greats,' to use a Homeric form of diction. . . . Around the whole school we may detect an atmosphere permeated with twentieth-century slogans concerning 'social science,' and 'the broadening of mind'—procured by narrowing knowledge of things which do not fit in to the scheme" (p. 240).
4. See Robert Ranulph Marett, *A Jerseyman at Oxford* (London: Oxford University Press, 1941), and L. H. Dudley, "R. R. Marett," in *Custom Is King: Essays Presented to R. R. Marett on His Seventieth Birthday, June 13, 1936*, ed. L. H.

Buxton, (London: Hutchison's, 1936), pp. 3–8. Marett served on the council of the Royal Anthropological Institute in 1910–11, as president of Section H (Anthropology) of the British Association for the Advancement of Science in 1916. He was the principal founder of the Oxford University Anthropological Society in 1909.

5. R. R. Marett, "Anthropology," in Farquharson, "The Oxford Conference," p. 57.

6. Ibid.

7. Marett's remarks appear to be an implicit bow toward the new Board of Studies of Philosophy, Politics, and Economics at Oxford, which was composed of members of the Literae Humaniores, historians, and representatives of economics and political science. The Honour School was just such a working collaboration as Marett was recommending to his auditors at the Sociological Society meeting.

8. Farquharson, "The Oxford Conference."

9. Lionel Trelevyan Hobhouse, "Sociology," in *Encyclopaedia of Religion and Ethics*, ed. James Hastings (New York: Charles Scribner's, 1921), 11: 655. See also "Sociology as a Method of Correlation," in Farquharson, "The Oxford Conference, pp. 62–63. For a good study of Hobhouse's thought and career, see Collini, *Liberalism and Sociology*.

10. Marett, "Anthropology," p. 58.

11. There is an extensive secondary literature on Tylor. For the best analysis of Tylor's thought, see selected essays in George W. Stocking, *Race, Culture, and Evolution: Essays in the History of Anthropology* (Chicago: University of Chicago Press, 1982); also G. W. Stocking, *Victorian Anthropology* (New York: Free Press, 1987); J. W. Burrow, *Evolution and Society: A Study in Victorian Social Theory* (Cambridge: Cambridge University Press, 1966); and Joan Leopold, *Culture in Comparative and Evolutionary Perspective: E. B. Tylor and the Making of Primitive Culture* (Berlin: Dietrich Reiner, 1980). For Tylor's professional role in Victorian anthropology, see Stocking, *Victorian Anthropology*, and David van Keuren, "Human Science in Victorian Britain: Anthropology in Institutional and Disciplinary Formation, 1863–1908," Ph.D. diss., University of Pennsylvania, 1982.

12. Van Keuren, "Human Science," esp. pp. 216–218.

13. Edward Burnett Tylor, *Researches into the Early History of Mankind and the Development of Civilization* (London: J. Murray, 1865) and *Primitive Culture: Researches into the Development of Mythology, Philosophy, Religion, Language, Art and Custom* (London: J. Murray, 1871). Quotation is from "Anthropology," in *Encyclopaedia Britannica* (Edinburgh: Adams and Charles Black, 1875), 2: 107.

14. E. B. Tylor, *Anthropology, an Introduction to the Study of Man and Civilization* (New York: D. Appleton, 1891; first published by J. Murray in 1881).

15. Ibid., p. 107.

16. Changes in anthropological theory during the last third of the century have been well analyzed by several historians; see, for example, Stocking, Burrow, and Leopold. The relationship of institutions and disciplinary formation to theory, however, is little explored; see van Keuren, "Human Science."

17. See George Stocking, "What's in a Name? The Origins of the Royal Anthropological Institute (1837–71)," *Man, The Journal of the Royal Anthropological Institute* n.s. 6 (1971): 369–90; Ronald Rainger, "Race, Politics, and Science: The

Anthropological Society of London in the 1860s," *Victorian Studies* 22 (1979–80): 52–70; J. W. Burrow, "Evolution and Anthropology in the 1860s: The Anthropological Society of London, 1863–71," *Victorian Studies* 7 (1963–64): 137–54; van Keuren, "Human Science," pp. 9–88.

18. T. H. Huxley, Busk, and Franks joined the Ethnological Society in 1863, Wallace in 1866, Tylor in 1867, and Hooker in 1868. Rolleston, Galton, and Spottiswoode were already members. Huxley, Busk, Hooker, Lubbock, and Tyndall were all members of the X Club, a scientific dinner club dedicated to the advancement of British science. For background on the X Club, see Ruth Barton, "The X Club: Science, Religion, and Social Change in Victorian England," Ph. D. diss., University of Pennsylvania, 1976; Roy MacLeod, "The X Club: Science, Religion, and Social Change in Victorian England," *Notes Received by the Royal Society of London* 24 (1969): 305–22; J. Vernon Jensen, "The X Club: Fraternity of Victorian Scientists," *British Journal of the History of Science* 5 (1970): 63–72.

19. Van Keuren, "Human Science."

20. See Stocking, "What's in a Name?"; also *Victorian Anthropology* (New York: Free Press, 1987); J. W. Burrow, *Evolution and Society*.

21. The reformist bent of the new sciences is clear in the writings of Huxley, Lubbock, Tylor, and others. Tylor declared of anthropology in particular that it was a "reformer's science", *Primitive Culture*, p. 410. See also Barton and Mario A. Di Gregario, *T. H. Huxley's Place in Natural Science* (New Haven: Yale University Press, 1984).

22. See Stocking, *Victorian Anthropology*; J. W. Burrow, *Evolution and Society*; Henrika Kuklick, "The Sins of the Fathers: British Anthropology and African Colonial Administration," *Research in Sociology of Knowledge, the Sciences, and Art* (November 1977): 93–210; Leopold, *Culture*.

23. See, for example, *First Principles of a New System of Philosophy*, 2d ed. (New York: D. Appleton and Company, 1868), pp. 545–46.

24. The extension of the human time scale established by the prehistorical researches of Henry Christy, John Evans, Boucher De Perthes, and others during the late 1850s and 1860s was critical to the Victorian reformulation of comparative-historical methodology. See Jacob Gruber, "Brixham Cave and the Antiquity of Man," in Regna Darnell, ed., *Readings in the History of Anthropology* (New York: Harper and Row, 1974), pp. 380–406.

25. See David van Keuren, "Museums and Ideology: Augustus Pitt-Rivers, Anthropological Museums, and Social Change in Later Victorian Britain," *Victorian Studies* 28 (1984–85): 171–89; "Cabinets and Culture: Victorian Anthropology and the Museum Context," *Journal of the History of the Behavioral Sciences* (January 1989): 26–39.

26. For example, see "Kjoekkenmoeddings: Recent Geologico-Archaeological Researches in Denmark," *Natural History Review* (1861): 489–504; "On the Ancient Lake-Habitations of Switzerland," *NHR* (1862): 26–52; "On the Evidence of the Antiquity of Man Afforded by the Somme Valley," *NHR* (1862): 244–69; "On the Geologico-Archaeological Discoveries in Denmark, Switzerland and France," *Proceedings of the West Yorkshire Geological Society* 4 (1860–64): 238–73.

27. Charles Darwin, *The Origin of Species by Means of Natural Selection, or the*

Preservation of Favoured Races in the Struggle for Life (London: J. Murray, 1859). Darwin had concluded his book with the carefully guarded statement that future research, based on his theory, would throw light "on the origin of man and his history." He did not directly address human evolution until the publication of *The Descent of Man* in 1871, well after Huxley and others had taken up the question.

28. Huxley's work and thought on this question are extensively chronicled in the historical literature. See, for example, Di Gregario, *T. H. Huxley's Place.*

29. "The Origin of Human Races and the Antiquity of Man Deduced from the Theory of 'Natural Selection,'" *Anthropological Review (and Journal)* 2 (1864): clvii–clxx.

30. Francis Galton, *Memories of My Life* (London: Methuen, 1908), p. 287.

31. *Hereditary Genius: An Inquiry into Its Laws and Consequences* (London: Macmillan, 1869); *Inquiries into Human Faculty and its Development* (London: Macmillan, 1883).

32. See van Keuren, "Museums and Ideology"; William Ryan Chapman, "Arranging Ethnology: A. H. L. F. Pitt-Rivers and the Typological Tradition," in George W. Stocking, Jr., ed., *Objects and Others, Essays on Museum and Material Culture* (Madison: University of Wisconsin Press, 1985), pp. 15–48.

33. See Flower's *Essays on Museums and Other Subjects Connected with Natural History* (Freeport, New York: Books for Libraries Press; repr. of 1898 ed.).

34. For a discussion of the work of Spencer, Maine, and McLennan, see Burrows, "Evolution and Anthropology"; and Stocking, *Victorian Anthropology.*

35. Van Keuren, "Human Science," pp. 89–110.

36. Galton, "Address to Section H," *Report of the British Association for the Advancement of Science* 55 (1885): 1206.

37. E. B. Brabrook, "Address to Section H," *Report of the B.A.A.S.* 68 (1898): 998.

38. Tylor, "Anthropology."

39. Tylor, *Primitive Culture*, p. 1.

40. Tylor, "Anthropology."

41. Haddon was a part-time lecturer in physical anthropology at Cambridge from 1894 to 1898, lecturer in ethnology at the University of London from 1904 to 1909, and reader in ethnology at Cambridge from 1909; he was Institute president in 1901–2. C. H. Read was assistant keeper and then keeper of British and Medieval Antiquities and Ethnography at the British Museum from 1880; he was Institute president from 1899–1901. Henry Balfour was curator of the Pitt-Rivers Museum at Oxford from 1891 and taught courses in technology and prehistoric archaeology from 1907; he served as Institute president in 1903–4. Ridgeway was Disney Professor of Archaeology at Cambridge from 1892 and Brereton Reader in Classics from 1907; he was Institute president in 1909–10.

42. About 10 percent of the 1883 council came from the clergy, law, and medicine; 10 percent came from various branches of the civil service; 18 percent were primarily businessmen, active or retired. For 1910, the corresponding figures were 6 percent, 14 percent, and 6 percent. The figures for the ordinary members of the Institute are less telling, both because less information is available and because the educated and professional elite tended to dominate the society and be best represented in the elected leadership positions. The above data are drawn from

a collective biography of the Institute from 1873 to 1920. Of twenty-nine officers in 1883, information was available for twenty-four of them; for 1910, information was available for thirty-four of thirty-six. The selection year 1883 was chosen because a full membership list was published for that year. For more complete figures, see van Keuren, "Human Science."

43. R. R. Marett, *Anthropology* (New York: Henry Holt and Company, 1912), pp. 7–8.

44. R. R. Marett, *Man in the Making: An Introduction to Anthropology* (Garden City, New York: Doubleday, Doran and Co., 1928), p. 2.

45. Marett, *Anthropology*, pp. 11–12.

46. Marett, *Man in the Making*, p. 4.

47. Ibid, p. 6.

48. The term *non-placet* refers to a no or "it does not please" vote in Congregation and Convocation. Arthur Engel describes the society as an alliance between younger dons, who entered the university during the hard times of the great agricultural depression of the last third of the century, and nonacademic members of Congregation. They combined their forces to oppose reforms of which they disapproved. In particular, they opposed any university expansions which would likely further siphon off funds from the already depleted university chest. See A. J. Engel, *From Clergyman to Don: The Rise of the Academic Profession in Nineteenth Century Oxford* (Oxford: Clarendon Press, 1983), esp. pp. 202 ff. Sir Charles Oman, self-proclaimed member of the society, described the motivations of its members in his *Memoirs of Victorian Oxford* as follows: "There was a considerable body of us who thought it wise to maintain the University, as far as possible, on its old system of cultural education, and believed that the classical basis was the best. . . . The phrase about 'broadening academic studies' was one which we met with grave mistrust. . . . We thought that we were not bound to provide instruction in very specialized lines of study, for which there would never be any appreciable body of students. . . . We thought it ill-judged to create professorships for subjects where the professor would never be able to collect a class, and which lay quite outside the normal University curriculum. And perhaps most of all, we considered that it was a misguided policy to institute 'Final Honour Schools,' with all their apparatus of First, Second, and Third Classes, for studies in which the examiners were not unfrequently more numerous than the examined" (pp. 233–34). See also A. T. S. Goodrick, "Congregation and Convocation," *Macmillan's Magazine* 90 (1904): 223–32. Opponents of the non-placet society united in what Lewis Farnell described as a "militant dining club" composed of reformers within the humane letters and new study areas and scientific dons of the "Museum" set. See *An Oxonian Looks Back* (London: Martin Farnell, 1934), pp. 270–71.

49. Board of Natural Science Studies, Report to the Vice-Chancellor, 13 May 1882, Hebdomadal Council Papers, 1882, Oxford University Archives. The study schedule for the new subjects, including anthropology, was drawn up by Henry Mosely and Henry Wentworth Acland. No copy of the original schedule survives; however, its outline is clearly visible in a comment draft returned to the drafters by Pitt-Rivers. See Letter to W. Hatchett Jackson, 10 May 1882, in the Acland Papers, Bodleian Library, Oxford University.

50. A renewed attempt to revise the Final Honours Exam in natural science was made in the spring of 1883. Several new subjects were prepared as additions to the examination list; however, anthropology was not one of them.

51. The Natural Science Board, at Tylor's recommendation, voted for the addition of anthropology to the subjects of the Final Honours School in natural science in December of 1894. Congregation voted initial approval of the measure by a vote of 25 to 16 in May of 1895. A second vote in Congregation was subsequently also gained. The weight of support from the medical and natural science schools and of more reform-minded members in theology, law, and humane letters was sufficient to carry the day over the objections of opponents. It is clear from surviving correspondence that Tylor had carefully marshaled support for the measure from friends both within and without the university. See, for example, correspondence to Francis Galton on 20 May and 7 June in the Francis Galton Papers, University College Library, London.

52. The final vote was 68 to 60. Convocation was traditionally the arena where conservatives, and the non-placet society in particular, were strongest. Nonresident M.A.s were brought into Oxford from the surrounding countryside and, depending on the importance of the issues, London and elsewhere to vote. Many of the most important debates over issues of science and university reform were eventually settled in Convocation. For a discussion of Convocation debates, see Goodrick, "Congregation and Convocation."

53. Tylor, Letter to Francis Galton, 18 June 1895, Galton papers.

54. See Engel, *From Clergyman to Don*, pp. 207 ff.; Oman, *Memoirs of Victorian Oxford*, 232 ff.

55. Tylor, Letter to Acland, 27 June 1895, Acland Papers. Tylor made similar remarks to Pitt-Rivers and others. In a letter to the former he wrote that "the main motive of the successful opposition to Anthropology having an examination in the Science Faculty where it belongs, was that it might be captured thus by the Classical School"; 23 September 1895, Pitt-Rivers Papers, Blackmore Museum, Salisbury.

56. *Oxford at the Cross Roads: A Criticism of the Course of Literae Humaniores in the University* (London: Adam and Charles Black, 1903), p. 80.

57. Cambridge was more amenable to the inclusion of new science studies, and the intemperance of the Oxford debates was not repeated there. However, instruction in ethnography was not initiated by Alfred Cort Haddon until 1895. From 1892, lectures on physical anthropology were available from S. J. Hickson of Downing College. Alexander Macalister also gave instruction in physical anthropology as a branch of historical anatomy. Anthropology thus made its appearance at Cambridge through comparative anatomy, a well-established university study and research area. An ethnological lectureship was not established until 1900. The controversy aroused by anthropology as a "science" of "culture" never developed at Cambridge. However, Cambridge never considered itself to be the bastion of established culture and cultural studies that Oxford did. For a study of science within Cambridge University during the last half of the nineteenth century, see Gerald L. Geison, *Michael Foster and the Cambridge School of Physiology: The Scientific Enterprise in Late Victorian Society* (Princeton: Princeton University Press, 1978). For a broad study of academic reform at Victorian Cambridge, see

Sheldon Rothblatt, *The Revolution of the Dons: Cambridge and Society in Victorian England* (London: Faber and Faber, 1968).

58. R. R. Marett, Letter to the Committee for Anthropology, 12 February 1905, Original Documents, Committee for Anthropology, Oxford University Archives.

59. Lewis Farnell, Letter to the Committee for Anthropology, 15 February 1905, Original Documents, Committee for Anthropology, Oxford University Archives. Farnell's comments were made in regard to the proposed syllabus for the new anthropological diploma program then under discussion. See van Keuren, "Human Science," pp. 230–41.

60. J. L. Myres, "The Science of Man in the Service of the State," *Journal of the Royal Anthropological Institute* 59 (1929): 27. Earlier, in a letter to R. W. Macan, the junior proctor, during the debate over the establishment of the diploma program, Myres had exasperatedly asked Macan whether he could "correct a mere apprehension which I gather from a member of the Lit. Hum. Board is prevalent that either Tylor or his immediate supporters mediated anything like a division of Humanities between Lit. Hum. and anthropology. Certain teachers in Arts have personally been anxious that Anthropology should limit itself to savage man." 21 May 1905, Original Documents, Committee for Anthropology.

61. J. G. Frazer, "The Scope of Social Anthropology," in *Psyche's Task: A Discourse concerning the Influence of Superstition on the Growth of Institutions* (London: Macmillan, 1920), p. 161.

62. Ibid.

63. J. G. Frazer, "The Scope and Method of Mental Anthropology," in *Garnered Sheaves: Essays, Addresses, and Reviews* (London: Macmillan, 1931), p. 241.

64. For a more detailed and general study of the effects of professionalization on the university and university faculty, see Engel, *From Clergyman to Don*; and Rothblatt, *Revolution of the Dons*. See also Geison, *Michael Foster*, for a study of professionalization in scientific Cambridge at this same time.

65. Tylor uses the term *science of culture* widely in his work. See particularly his article on anthropology in the *Encyclopaedia Britannica* and *Primitive Culture*, where it serves as the title for chapter 1.

66. By the end of the nineteenth century, the increasingly specialized and technical nature of human biology and medicine tended to make physical anthropology a distinct and independent subspecialty within British anthropology, with diminishing intellectual linkages to the discipline as a whole. Academic physical anthropologists tended to teach comparative anatomy and to be segregated into the biological and medical faculties. Archaeologists and cultural anthropologists, on the other hand, were primarily educated in the classics and history and were located within the arts.

67. The department was established by J. Martin White in 1907, and both Hobhouse and Edward Westermarck were appointed to professorships. London traditionally was more amenable to new subject areas than the older universities. The creation of the department by fiat also helped avoid lengthy negotiation and intramural resistance. Nevertheless, London was the exception, and sociology was very slow in breaching the academic walls of British universities, possibly because of its extremely broad subject claims.

■ 4 MATHEMATICS AND THE ECONOMICS PROFESSION IN LATE VICTORIAN ENGLAND

MARGARET SCHABAS

Arguably the most critical juncture in the history of economics, the Marginal Revolution of the early 1870s transformed the core of economic theory from a literary into a mathematical pursuit. The most effective uprooting took place in Britain. There, the doctrines of David Ricardo, Thomas Robert Malthus, and John Stuart Mill came under attack in the late 1860s and were boldly repudiated by William Stanley Jevons, whose *Theory of Political Economy* (1871) laid the foundations for the neoclassical paradigm. Controversy ensued, but by the mid-1880s the Jevonian program was widely endorsed. The main landmark came in 1890, with the publication of Alfred Marshall's *Principles of Economics*. As the leading text of the period and the first definitive overview of the subject since Mill's *Principles of Political Economy* (1848), it exemplified a balanced use of prose and mathematics in the service of economic analysis. Much reinforcement was offered on methodological issues with the publication in the same year of John Neville Keynes's *Scope and Method of Political Economy*.[1]

The most active economists of the 1880s and 1890s were all academics. Jevons held the chair at University College, London, and was succeeded in 1881 by Herbert Somerton Foxwell. Alfred Marshall dominated the program at Cambridge but was ably assisted by Neville Keynes, Henry Sidgwick, William Cunningham, and Foxwell. Francis Ysidro Edgeworth, at Marshall's recommendation, acquired the Drummond Chair at Oxford in 1888, and Philip Henry Wicksteed began lecturing in the extension of the University of London at much the same time. This group also took steps to establish a professional association and journal with the clear objective of settling any remaining controversy. After several years of planning, they formed the British Economic Association (BEA) and its mouthpiece, the *Economic Journal*, in 1891. Viscount Goschen, chancellor of the exchequer, was the founding president and Edgeworth the founding editor of the journal, a position he held until 1926. The London School of Economics opened in 1895 and the Cambridge tripos in economics, after years of lobbying by Marshall, was set up in 1903.

It seems almost too obvious for words that late Victorian economists embraced mathematics in order to strengthen their professional identity. Once armed with a set of mathematical tools, economists could certainly exercise greater control over the entry into their discipline and thereby better maintain the sort of scientific standards they held dear. And yet, it is not clear that the prime movers at the same time sought to equate membership in the profession with mathematical dexterity. Or, to put it another way, they seemed anxious to keep the doors open to interested parties regardless of an ability to contribute to the cutting edge of the discipline. One must bear in mind a critical trait about economics: As a source of knowledge for sound policy, it must appeal to both statesmen and the general public. Mathematics is thus a double-edged sword. It may serve to differentiate the expert from the amateur, but it also tends to leave behind the very group the economist seeks to influence, for economists then as now sought to change the world. As Foxwell remarked in 1885, "No study is more inspired by a practical object than Economics. Its end is preeminently Action."[2]

I shall argue here that mathematics took hold primarily for reasons that were independent of professional aspirations per se. For one, the move to strengthen the identity of the economics community was part of a more widespread movement to transform the English universities into breeding grounds for research scientists. For another, the adoption of mathematical techniques had little effect on economic policy until the period after World War One. If anything, the appeal of mathematics stemmed from new insights in logic and the philosophy of science. As we will see, the move to professionalize and the move to mathematize, while carried out by the same individuals, proceeded along parallel, but distinct, trajectories.

Since the middle of the eighteenth century, political economy was placed among the moral sciences. By the early 1800s it was commonplace for the prefaces to texts on political economy to proclaim the subject a science in the tradition of Newton. This usually took the form of appeals to what we would now call the hypothetico-deductive method. Certain generalizations on the properties of bodies were proposed and accepted if their observable consequences were borne out. Just as one inferred the inverse-square law of gravitational attraction by its effects on falling bodies or pendula, so too one inferred laws of human nature and market forces by their effects on prices and quantities exchanged.

Such lip service to the Newtonian edifice was common practice among most philosophers and should not be taken as a sign of insecurity on the part of economists. Quite the contrary, political economy had attained considerable respectability by the early nineteenth century. Two of the leading spokesmen for science at the time, John Herschel and William Whewell, acknowledged its importance in their celebrated books on scientific inquiry, and Charles Babbage, one of the founders of the British Association for the Advancement of Science (BAAS, founded in 1831), secured a place—Section F—for statistics and, implicitly, political economy, in 1833. Statesmen and theorists mingled regularly at the Political Economy Club (founded in 1821) and thrashed out controversies on trade, coinage, and taxation. While there was no publication devoted exclusively to the subject, this was true of most other branches of knowledge at the time. Political economy had a strong profile in the leading periodicals of the day, the *Edinburgh Review*, the *Quarterly Review*, *Blackwood's*, and the *Westminster Review*. George Stigler has located some 1,190 articles on economics in these journals in the years 1802 to 1853.[3] Hardly a case of neglect or underrepresentation.

By mid-century, economists took much of the credit for Britain's transformation into the workshop of the world. As Nassau Senior remarked to a foreign visitor at the Great Exhibition of 1851, "It is a triumph of theory. We are governed by philosophers and political economists." Somewhat later, Walter Bagehot credited the *Wealth of Nations* with the fact that "the life of almost every one in England—perhaps every one—is different and better in consequence of it."[4] Clearly, few other sciences could claim such practical benefits or such striking confirmations.

By the standards of early Victorian science, political economy was as bona fide as chemistry or geology.[5] It was not yet a profession, but, then, neither were other branches of science. But some ground had been broken. Malthus had held the first professorship in the subject, at Haileybury College (1805), and Senior the first chair at Oxford (1825). By the 1830s, virtually every university in the British Isles had established a chair in political economy. Whewell had played an active role in promoting it at Cambridge and established the tripos in the moral sciences along with the tripos in the natural sciences in 1838. Adam Smith was heralded as the Newton of his day and David Ricardo as one of the most brilliant minds since antiquity. His *Principles of Political Economy and Taxation* (1817) was deemed to have the rigor and completeness of Euclidean geometry and thus to have rendered political economy into a full-blown deductive science. Numerous "Principles" texts of the 1820s and 1830s served to consolidate the theoretical core with its set of laws and methods for advancing the subject. Classical political economy reached its apogee with Mill's *Principles*, both for its range and maturity of thought.

To be sure, political economy came under attack in the period up to Mill. Thomas Carlyle cast aspersions on the subject as the "dismal science" and Richard Jones discredited its pretensions to universality. But on average there was about as much consensus and respectful give and take as one finds in other branches of science at the time. It is worth recollecting just how remarkable the achievements of Smith, Malthus, and Quetelet were for discerning regularity in the social realm.[6] People marveled at the fact that the actions of individuals in the aggregate would follow paths as constant as the planets. We in a more secular age may have lost sight of a primary source for motivating a belief in the existence and operation of social laws, but for our eighteenth- and nineteenth-century counterparts, such orderliness resonated with their belief in a world created and governed by the deity.

Nineteenth-century England experienced a marked growth in higher education. The main bursts of expansion transpired in the 1820s and 1830s and in the last three decades of the century, during which, for example, the number of chairs in the natural sciences literally doubled.[7] Many more students attended lectures on economics, although few universities offered it as a specialized field for a degree until the beginning of the twentieth century. Nevertheless, it was taught extensively as a branch of moral philosophy, history, and law, thereby giving rise to a sizable pool of statesmen and businessmen capable of following informed debates. In the mid-1880s, Cambridge housed six lecturers on the subject and Oxford at least three. In contrast to the French-speaking world or the United States, where the mathematically gifted economists Léon Walras and Irving Fisher found themselves in a veritable vacuum, in England there was a sizable number of capable economists: for example, Joseph Shield Nicholson, Robert Giffen, and Edwin Cannan. As Schumpeter noted, English economics thrived in the period 1870 to 1914 in part because of the "quality of the 'second line.'"[8]

It was also more and more likely that a university student would be versed in both mathematics and the moral sciences. As has been well documented, an extreme reverence for the Newtonian emphasis on synthetic or geometric modes of reasoning hindered the development of mathematical inquiry in England during the eighteenth and early nineteenth centuries. The reason for the longevity of this tradition was the belief that one studies mathematics (at Cambridge at least) to acquire a liberal education. It was not so important that one learned the differential calculus as that one acquired an appreciation for the nature of truth and the art of demonstration.[9]

Only in the latter part of the nineteenth century did things begin to change. The calculus had hitherto developed in tandem with problems in mechanics such that the notion of pure analysis was quite foreign to the leading expositors. Several independent developments, non-Euclidean geometry, number theory, and the rigorous formulation of the concept of a limit aided the clarification of the distinction between pure and applied mathematics. The early neoclassical economists, among others, reaped the benefits of these shifts in the scope and epistemological standing of mathematics. There now existed equally viable consistent schemes rather than one single path to certainty. Mathematics was just a language, a tool to aid inquiry, not the exclusive property of those engaged in physics and astronomy.

In the first half of the nineteenth century, the university was often peripheral to the pursuit of science. The BAAS and related scientific societies were much more fruitful forums for the exchange of ideas. Some of the newer universities, such as Owens College at Manchester (founded in 1851), began to introduce the German model of the research laboratory and to develop science degrees with the aim of training professional scientists. Several individuals, such as Henry Enfield Roscoe at Owens, began to lobby for government support. By the 1870s, the university became a much more hospitable place for the pursuit of science. The number of chairs expanded significantly, and the founding of the Cavendish Laboratory at Cambridge in 1872, under the directorship of James Clerk Maxwell, signified that research scientists had found their proper niche.[10]

Jevons's campaign to overhaul the subject began at a propitious moment. As has been well documented, economic theory had tended to stagnate after the publication of Mill's *Principles*. This was due partly to the lack of gifted minds and partly to the fact that Mill had himself declared certain theoretical topics, the labor theory of value and iron law of wages, a closed book. But he was sorely mistaken. By the 1860s, it became clear that several tenets of the classical theory were invalid. In response to severe criticism, Mill issued his famous recantation of the wages fund theorem. Other classical doctrines also came under attack. As Terence Hutchison has remarked, "in the space of a few years in the late sixties and early seventies the Ricardo-Mill system of theory underwent a remarkably sudden and rapid collapse of credibility and confidence, considering how long and authoritative had been its dominance in Britain."[11]

Jevons's insistence that "economics, if it is to be a science at all, must be a mathematical science"[12] steered things on a new course. It was not that he was the first to use mathematics. Indeed, his own researches unearthed close to a hundred predecessors. But he was the first to argue at length that the subject was inherently quantitative and thus mathematical and to provide an extensive analysis of the epistemological status of mathematics and the laws of nature.

For all his books and essays on economics, Jevons considered his *Principles of Science* (1874) to be his main achievement. As a treatise on logic and scientific method, it stands out in its generation and in the century as a whole. Most importantly, it signaled the shift away from Enlightenment predilections for complete certainty. Its thorough treatment of problems of explanation and measurement in the natural sciences served to elucidate the many doubts and difficulties that beset even the most revered branches of science. Jevons's methodological insights are a world apart from the apodictic tenor of Mill's *System of Logic* (1844). Even a brief perusal reveals a grasp of many of the problems that still engage contemporary philosophers of science: the theory-ladenness of facts, the so-called Duhem-Quine problem, and the problems of representation and theory choice. His emphasis on the limitations of knowledge rings loud and clear: "In truth men never can solve the problems fulfilling the complex circumstances of nature. All laws and explanations are in a certain sense hypothetical, and apply exactly to nothing which we can know to exist. . . . When we probe the matter to the bottom physical astronomy is as hypothetical as Euclid's elements."[13]

Jevons also took stock of recent developments in thermodynamics and evolutionary biology and thus the advent of probabilistic modes of thinking. Based on his criteria of theory appraisal, he bestowed much praise on the new trends in biology: "Judging from the immense numbers of diverse facts which they harmonise and explain, I venture to look upon the theories of evolution and natural selection in their main features as two of the most probable hypotheses ever proposed."[14] He still advocated emulation of the physical sciences, but not with the same single-mindedness of previous economists and moral theorists. Marshall also recognized that economists deal with mere likelihoods and tendencies and proposed that they look to the biological sciences as their Mecca. The phenomena of the moral realm were more akin to those of the organic world than the inorganic.[15] That the two leading advocates of mathematical economics favored biological analogies and probabilistic laws suggests a program that was anything but a simplistic attempt to imitate physics.

Jevons's treatise also made contributions to mathematical logic, building on the innovations of George Boole and Augustus De Morgan. Starting in the 1840s, their reforms of Aristotelian logic led to the formulation of sentential logic and systems of symbols devised to highlight the analogies between algebraic and logical inference. Jevons came to grasp the fact that logic and algebra were one and the same, the recognition of similarity or identity. He developed a system of symbols for logic and interpretations of the main sentence connectives that survived several generations of students.

Jevons also advanced a version of logicism by which mathematics was to be reduced to logic via the concept of number. As he put it, "the mathematician is only strong and true as long as he is logical, and if number rules the world, it is logic which rules number."[16] His system of logic attempted to explicate the concept of number as the discernment of quantity above and beyond quality. The laws of the mind could thus be channeled into mathematics or logic but insofar as they dealt with quantities, called for mathematical treatment. The most explicit example of this was the determination of the final degree of utility. As Jevons argued:

> I should not think of claiming for the mind any accurate power of measuring and adding and subtracting feelings, so as to get an exact balance. . . . The theory turns upon those critical points where pleasures are nearly, if not quite, equal. I never attempt to estimate the whole pleasure gained by purchasing a commodity; the theory merely expresses that, when a man has purchased enough, he would derive equal pleasure from the possession of a small quantity more as he would from the money price of it.[17]

Prices are clearly quantitive, but so are the deliberations that engender them. Hence, "all economic writers must be mathematical so far as they are scientific at all, because they treat of economic quantities, . . . and all quantities and relations of quantities come within the scope of mathematics."[18]

Marshall reinforced these links, particularly the need for the calculus:

> Our observations of nature, in the moral as in the physical world, relate not so much to aggregate quantities, as to increments of quantities, and that in particular the demand for a thing is a continuous function, of which the "marginal" increment is, in stable equilibrium, balanced against the

corresponding increment of its cost of production. It is not easy to get a clear full view of continuity in this aspect without the aid either of mathematical symbols or of diagrams.[19]

He also shared Jevons's belief that mathematics was constitutive of market deliberations: "Economic theory supplies a machinery to aid us in reasoning about those motives of human action which are measurable." Mathematics was thus deeply woven into the neoclassical analysis of market exchange.

Others were in complete agreement with this. Wicksteed maintained that Jevons "was right in declaring that certain fundamental relations and conceptions in the theory of political economy are essentially mathematical."[20] Foxwell, one of Jevons's most ardent supporters, included the mathematical theory in his lectures and examinations at London. And Edgeworth's first and only book, *Mathematical Psychics* (1881), gave a more detailed account of the psychological dimensions of the new mathematical economics than any other treatise at the time. His many subsequent articles for the *Economic Journal* also attest to his allegiances to the new approach.

These insights did not blind the early neoclassicists to the limitations of mathematics. Quite the contrary, they seemed overly cautious about the possibility that the use of mathematics would give the false impression that economics had become more certain or exact. Both were a matter of the degree of fit between theory and fact, a task for the statistician and historian. Applications of mathematical methods, then, were always to be subordinated to the pursuit of economic realism. This was reiterated time and again by Jevons, Edgeworth, Wicksteed, and, above all, Marshall. His oft-quoted letter to Arthur Bowley recommends that the economist burn his mathematical explorations if he is unable to illustrate them with examples drawn from the real world.[21]

At the same time, it became clear that mathematics provided an engine for discovery. Jevons had delineated the dimensions of economic theory for the first time and articulated some of the key notions of marginalism. Wicksteed ironed out some of the various wrinkles left in the Jevonian account. Edgeworth discovered the analytical virtues of indifference curves and secured a place for the calculus of variations and Lagrangian multipliers. Marshall found rigorous ways to formulate consumer surplus and the price elasticity of demand.

Whereas the classical theorists had focused on supply, particularly labor, as the mainspring of economic activity, the early neoclassicists emphasized the importance of demand. Value was to be determined subjectively and prices, whether of goods or factors of production, were determined at the margin, in terms of the utility of the last unit consumed or produced. The set of problems associated with defining absolute or natural value that had weighed so heavily on the minds of the classical economists evaporated into thin air.

The utility theory of value also served to strengthen the conviction that economics could be reduced to psychology and thus grounded on a more realistic conception of man. One need only juxtapose Mill's assertion that no "political economist was ever so absurd as to suppose that mankind are really thus constituted [to act solely from the desire of wealth]" with Marshall's assertion of 1890 that economists "deal with man as he is: not with an abstract 'economic' man; but with a man of flesh and blood."[22] For Marshall, we are each said to be engaged in producing and consuming utility, a stuff of sufficient versatility to incorporate our basic material needs as well as those of more cultivated tastes. One could consider the trade-off between bacon and ballet in the same moment. Various classical distinctions, such as the one between productive and unproductive labor, were discarded. It no longer mattered that ship building created a concrete object whereas opera singing left just a set of memories. Insofar as both yielded utility to some consumer or other, they constituted productive labor.

The early neoclassicists were quite explicit about the psychological foundations of their discipline. As Wicksteed remarked, "The laws of political economy then, being ultimately laws of human conduct, are psychical and not physical; and therefore psychology enters into political economy on something more than equal terms with physical science and technology."[23] But both Jevons and Edgeworth believed that the calculus of pleasure and pain could in principle be reduced to physical states of the mind and body and therefore welcomed insights on the reception and processing of stimuli worked out by Helmholtz, Wundt, and Fechner.

Much of this, however, was mere lip service. By and large *Homo economicus* had not evolved since Bentham's servant to pleasure and pain. If anything, evolutionary biology served to restore the Benthamite equation of pushpin and poetry that Mill had so vehemently opposed. While Jevons acknowledged more refined moral sentiments, they were taken to differ only in degree, not in kind, from the sensations of pleasure and pain. As he quipped, he preferred to "hold to the dry old Jeremy" on this matter.[24]

Indeed, while Bentham and Smith wrote at much the same time, the Utilitarian program remained quite separate from the theoretical core of classical political economy until the time of Jevons. Smith had acknowledged the primary goal of a happy populace but lacked the means by which to aggregate from the individual to the group. By linking the utility calculus to market phenomena and adopting a more unidimensional image of humanity, Jevons and his successors found the means by which later economists, such as Arthur C. Pigou, could define social justice in economic terms.

Somewhat ironically, this was viewed as a move to make economics more in tune with ethics. The leading contributor was Henry Sidgwick, a self-proclaimed Jevonian and major exponent of Utilitarianism. He and his contemporaries sought to accommodate economic distribution to working-class interests without sacrificing the status quo. As Foxwell noted in 1887, the political economy of the mid-century period of free trade was "unmoral," insofar as the poor were told to follow the dictates of the market. Due to the influence of Jevons, Sidgwick, and Henry George, the questions of poverty could no longer be dismissed:

> It is the mechanical, unmoral economics, even more than the policy of *laissez faire*, which the new school has banished to Saturn. . . . The new school hold, what is quite as important, that a man must act as honorably in his industrial capacity as he would in his private relations. They will not allow him, by pleading "the state of the market," to excuse himself from the ordinary obligations of humanity. With the old school, the worst scandals were calmly referred to "demand and supply," as though such a reference were final. With the new school, if the conditions of the market are such as to lead to injustice or to swell the mass of social wreckage, these conditions must be overhauled, and as far as may be rectified. It is their decided conviction that, if competition is to remain the basis of economic relations, society must see that it is so held in check that it shall not violate the older and deeper principles of justice and humanity.[25]

Thus not only the methods but the scope of economics was transformed. Both Smith and Mill had granted the global applicability of the methods of economic analysis but resisted universalizing their model of economic man. If anything, they emphasized the institutional relativity of their analyses. Mill, somewhat in jest, claimed that his behavioral assumptions would have to be modified if his theory was to be applied to the French. With the neoclassicists, we find the sincere belief that all human beings maximize utility, the Australian aborigine as much as the housekeeper in London. Ethnological differences appeared to count for naught.

Furthermore, the core of economic theory was cast in ahistorical terms. For Jevons, the economic theorist's task is quite simple: "Given, a certain population, with various needs and powers of production, in possession of certain lands and other sources of material: required, the mode of employing their labour which will maximize the utility of the produce."[26] Note that no system of government, technology, or monetary medium is specified. Put this way, one could apply the theory to almost any place or period.

While the new theory, by contrast with the old, was remarkably ahistorical, the pursuit of economic history as a subdiscipline was heartily welcomed as a source of empirical support. The economic historians that surfaced in the 1870s, led by T. E. Cliffe Leslie and John Kells Ingram, were not particularly enamored with mathematics, but they came to respect its integrity and to adapt their historical approach to the mainstream. At Oxford, followers of Arnold Toynbee also developed the study of economic history. Somewhat ironically, they were more favorably disposed toward Jevons than either Ricardo or Mill, socialist allegiances notwithstanding. It seems that they admired the radical spirit of Jevons, in addition to his writings, and regarded the classical economic theory as more antithetical to working-class interests. Two members of this group, Edwin Cannan and William Hewins, went on to the London School of Economics, where they helped to develop a well-rounded curriculum.[27]

At the same time, the relationship between theory and policy was redefined. Senior and Mill had drawn the distinction between the art and the science of political economy. The former served as a guide to the statesman but always called for additional knowledge drawn from history or moral philosophy. The latter was the contemplative search for the laws that govern the wealth of nations. Senior and Mill tried to keep the two distinct but inevitably succumbed to the temptation of crediting England's economic hegemony with the establishment of free trade. Only in the 1860s did they begin to resist such appeals. John Elliott Cairnes, Mill's leading disciple, and Walter Bagehot, editor of *The Economist*, both insisted that the science of political economy had nothing to do with laissez-faire doctrines. As Cairnes put it, that would be analogous to assessing the laws of mechanics by the state of the railways.[28]

Jevons and Marshall took this one step further by dropping the adjective "political" from the title of the subject. Economics had a normative component, but its theoretical core was understood to be politically neutral. Jevons advocated partitioning the burgeoning field of economics:

> The present chaotic state of Economics arises from the confusing together of several branches of knowledge. Subdivision is the remedy. We must distinguish the empirical element from the abstract theory, from the applied theory, and from the more detailed art of finance and administration. Thus

will arise various sciences, such as commercial statistics, the mathematical
theory of economics, systematic and descriptive economics, economic sociology, and fiscal science.[29]

And while he insisted that there was no science of legislation, his proposal of a fiscal science would be a close approximation in practice.

As has often been noted, Marshall avoided political controversy. In
fact, he worried that his students might detect some policy preferences
in his lectures.[30] Jevons wrote more extensively on policy issues, but it
is difficult to trace any consistent doctrinal line. Later commentators
remarked that they had no clue as to how he had voted. Whereas Jevons
favored the development of public housing and education, he opposed
a government-owned rail service. He showed much concern for the lot
of the working class, as did Marshall, and sought out their company
and audience as a lecturer. Trade unions, however, ought to restrict their
influence to nonpecuniary improvements. Wages were best settled by
market forces.[31]

Both Jevons and Marshall had studied political economy after a
thorough grounding in mathematics and the natural sciences and were
attracted to it primarily by a desire to better the world. Both had, on
their own initiative, taken extensive walking tours of the poorest districts
of London and been moved by the terrible conditions they observed.
Edgeworth, having risen from Irish gentry, was not so moved. But he
endeared himself to those of a more socialist bent by demonstrating in
1897 that the principles of marginal utility entailed a system of progressive taxation. Wicksteed, a minister by training, turned to political economy after reading Henry George and always considered himself to be
a socialist.

By no stretch of the imagination, however, could Jevons or Marshall
be called socialists, let alone Marxists. Jevons died without knowing
about Marx (though their paths may have crossed at the reading room
of the British Museum in the 1860s), but Marshall happened upon Marx
early on and showed some appreciation. As he reminisced: "I owe much
to him [Marx]. I read his book in 1870, and his excerpts from English
blue-books—garbled though many of them are—were of great service
to me. Now everyone knows about the state of factory labour early in
the century; in 1870 few people had given their attention to it."[32]

Marshall did not take the trouble to read volumes two and three
of *Das Kapital*, since he did not find the analyses in volume one particularly enlightening. But he also never seemed worried by Marxian
economics. Wicksteed had seen to it, in a well-publicized confrontation
with George Bernard Shaw, that the Jevonian theory of value outwitted

that of Marx and the classical theorists.[33] Indeed, so successful was Wicksteed in promoting the use of mathematics and the utility theory of value that he succeeded in converting Shaw.

Shaw and Sidney Webb then made a point of attending a reading group, composed of Wicksteed, Edgeworth, Foxwell, Palgrave, and Marshall, among others, to study in depth recent works in economics, including Jevons. This so-called Economic Circle made a point of avoiding political questions. As Shaw remarked, "the work kept on abstract scientific questions" and "the conditions were practically university conditions." The group met at the home of a London stockbroker named Henry Beeton starting in 1886 or 1887. By 1889, Marshall proposed the formation of a more official Economic Club, which then developed into the BEA of 1891.[34]

The leading instigators were Foxwell, Henry Palgrave, John Neville Keynes, and Henry Higgs, though Marshall, Shaw, and Edgeworth pulled many strings from backstage. Foxwell had proposed that the society serve many functions: "it would aim at the advancement of theory, at the consolidation of economic opinion, at the encouragement of historical research, and at the criticism and direction of industrial and financial policy."[35] He also urged it to compile a dictionary and bibliographic aids, undertake translations and reprints, and publish its own journal, all of which came to pass.

There were efforts made to differentiate the new association from the Political Economy Club, which had come to resemble the smoking room more than the academy, and from Section F of the BAAS, the meetings of which had acquired the reputation of degenerating into political quarrels. The London Statistical Society and, to a lesser extent, the American Economic Association (AEA, founded in 1885) offered better models to emulate. But they too had their shortcomings. The first tended to be too narrow in focus and the latter had been plagued with political controversy since its founding. By comparison to the British, the American economists were much more up in arms over the questions of Social Darwinism and the tenets of socialism.[36]

Perhaps the most striking aspect of the newly founded BEA was its open admission. Anyone could join provided he paid the one-pound annual fee. This was partly due to the need for funds to support the journal and partly because Marshall sought the support of statesmen and men of commerce. Of the approximately seven hundred founding members, only some one hundred were educators. Many more were in businesses such as banking, insurance, or accounting.

The exchange between Marshall and Shaw on the appointment of Goschen as president is worth noting. Shaw had hoped for less overt partisanship in the leading appointments. Marshall replied that, while not a supporter of Goschen politically, "since we cannot have an economist who has no political opinions at all, we could not have a better President than Mr. Goschen."[37] The point was vividly reinforced by the concentration of statesmen on the original council. In addition to Goschen, the four initial vice-presidents—A. J. Balfour, H.C.E. Childers, Leonard Courtney, and John Morley—were all members of Parliament. Nonacademic members continued to fill some of these slots for several decades. In fact, the first academic president was not appointed until 1928, although attempts had been made to recruit Marshall on his retirement in 1906. It was as though Marshall intended to give the appearance that statesmen governed the academic economists, the triumph of praxis over theory.

Marshall gave the inaugural address, however, and subsequent addresses were also more often drawn from the academic ranks. Marshall emphasized the need for civility and the avoidance of unhealthy controversy. Obviously, he wished to avoid bitter political debates that had beset the early years of the AEA and were still being waged in the 1890s. Professor Coats has interpreted this, as well as the large number of businessmen in the association, to signify a lack of professional self-confidence at the time and of the level of dissension within the subject. This was also manifest in the fact that there were few persons at the time trained explicitly as economists. Even Sidgwick claimed not to be an economist in the academic sense.

But one could view Marshall's unquestioned authority and call for dispassionate debate as a sign of the level of maturity achieved by that point. Had political economists been insecure or terrified of falling into the same traps as the Americans, they would have struck a different charter for membership. As it was, the inner core of members was completely devoid of "quacks" and the nonacademic council members seemed fully aware that their status was mostly honorary. Balfour, Goschen, and Higgs all deferred to the judgment of Foxwell, Marshall, and Edgeworth. It was clear who was contributing to the field and who was not, and thus who should make the major annual address.

By far the most important point to bear in mind is that political economy had undergone a fair degree of depoliticization in the mid-century, first with Mill and then with Cairnes and Jevons. The leading economists had never espoused crude laissez-faire doctrines and had long advocated government support for education and poor relief. In sum, debates had never been as polarized as they were in the United States, between all or no government intervention. Marginalism and mathematics could mesh with Fabianism precisely because both Marshall and Shaw were past the stage of dogmatism.

As we have seen, the mathematization of economic theory went hand in hand with a distinct stage in the ascent of the professional economist. But both sprang from separate currents that ran long and deep. The first grew from modes of expression already found in Ricardo and was spurred on by new developments in logic and the philosophy of science. Economists came to realize that there was something in the nature of the subject matter itself that lent itself to mathematical reasoning. The second development arose out of a more general growth in higher education as well as a concern on the part of the leading economists of the day to encourage the wider application of their findings. Possibly in the post–World War Two era, these two have taken on a different, more intimate, relationship. But our findings indicate that there was little in the late Victorian period to support the assumption that mathematics was adopted primarily to enhance the goals of professionalization.

Notes

The author thanks Mary S. Morgan and A. W. Coats for several helpful suggestions.

1. Scholars have generally underestimated the extent to which Marshall and Jevons advocated the same major changes to economic theory, primarily because of Marshall's refusal to label himself as a follower of Jevons. But I have argued that the links were much stronger, both methodologically and conceptually. See my "Alfred Marshall, W. Stanley Jevons, and the Mathematization of Economics," *Isis* 80 (March 1989): 60–73.

2. Quoted in Alon Kadish, *The Oxford Economists in the Late Nineteenth Century* (Oxford: Oxford University Press, 1982), p. 133.

3. George J. Stigler, "Statistical Studies in the History of Economic Thought," in *Essays in the History of Economics* (Chicago: University of Chicago Press, 1965), p. 41.

4. Senior quote from T. W. Hutchison, *On Revolutions and Progress in Economic Knowledge* (Cambridge: Cambridge University Press, 1978), p. 58; Walter Bagehot, "The Postulates of Political Economy," in R. Holt Hutton, ed., *Economic Studies*, 2d ed. (London: 1895), p. 1.

5. See Robert Bud and Gerrylynn K. Roberts, *Science versus Practice: Chemistry in Victorian Britain* (Manchester: Manchester University Press, 1984); and Salim Rashid, "Political Economy and Geology in the Early Nineteenth Century: Similarities and Contrasts," *History of Political Economy* 13 (1981): 726–744.

6. See Theodore M. Porter, *The Rise of Statistical Thinking, 1820–1900* (Princeton: Princeton University Press, 1986).

7. T. W. Heyck, *The Transformation of Intellectual Life in Victorian England* (Chicago: Lyceum, 1982), chaps. 3–6.

8. Joseph A. Schumpeter, *A History of Economic Analysis* (New York: Oxford University Press, 1954), p. 757.

9. Harvey Becher, "William Whewell and Cambridge Mathematics," *Historical Studies in the Physical Sciences* 2 (1980): 1–48.

10. R. Sviedrys, "The Rise of Physical Science at Victorian Cambridge," *Historical Studies in the Physical Sciences* 2 (1970): 127–145.

11. Terence W. Hutchison, "The 'Marginal Revolution' and the Decline and Fall of English Classical Political Economy," *History of Political Economy* 4 (1972): 442–68, esp. pp. 450–51.

12. William Stanley Jevons, *The Theory of Political Economy*, 5th ed. (London: Macmillan, 1957; repr. New York: Augustus M. Kelly, 1965), p. 3.

13. William Stanley Jevons, *The Principles of Science*, 2d ed. (London: Macmillan, 1877), p. 458.

14. Ibid., p. 762.

15. See H. Scott Gordon, "Alfred Marshall and the Development of Economics as a Science," in *Foundations of Scientific Method: The Nineteenth Century*, ed. Ronald Giere and R. S. Westfall (Bloomington: Indiana University Press, 1973), pp. 234–58.

16. Jevons, *Principles*, p. 154.

17. Jevons, *Theory*, p. 13.

18. Ibid., p. xxi.

19. Alfred Marshall, *Principles of Economics*, 8th ed. (London: Macmillan, 1920), pp. vii–ix.

20. Philip Henry Wicksteed, *The Common Sense of Political Economy and Selected Papers*, ed. Lionel Robbins, 2 vols. (London: Routledge, 1935), 2: 811.

21. A. C. Pigou, *Memorials of Alfred Marshall* (London: Macmillan, 1925), p. 427.

22. John Stuart Mill, "On the Definition of Political Economy; and on the Method of Investigation Proper to It," in J. M. Robson, ed., *Collected Works of John Stuart Mill*, 4, *Essays on Economics and Society* (Toronto: University of Toronto Press, 1967), p. 322; and Marshall, *Principles*, p. 22.

23. Philip Henry Wicksteed, *The Common Sense of Political Economy* (London: Routledge, 1933) 2: 767.

24. See Jevons, *Theory*, pp. 26–27 and his essay "Utilitarianism," reprinted in *Pure Logic and Other Minor Works*, ed. Robert Adamson and H. A. Jevons (London: Macmillan, 1890).

25. Herbert Somerton Foxwell, "The Economic Movement in England," *Quarterly Journal of Economics* 2 (1888): 84–103, esp. p. 102.

26. Jevons, *Theory*, p. 267.

27. See Kadish, *Oxford Economists*.

28. John Elliott Cairnes, *The Character and Logical Method of Political Economy* (London: Macmillan, 1875), p. 253.

29. Jevons, *Theory*, pp. xvi–xvii (preface to 1879 edition).

30. John Maloney, *Marshall, Orthodoxy and the Professionalisation of Economics* (Cambridge: Cambridge University Press, 1985), p. 227.

31. See R.D.C. Black, "W. S. Jevons, 1835–1882," in D. P. O'Brien and John R. Presley, eds., *Pioneers of Modern Economics in Britain* (London: Macmillan, 1981);

and T. W. Hutchison, "The Politics and Philosophy in Jevons's Political Economy," *Manchester School* 50 (December 1982): 366–78.

32. Cited in Maloney, *Marshall*, p. 49.

33. This appeared in the socialist journal *To-Day* (January 1885). Reprinted in Wicksteed, *Common Sense*, 2: 724–30.

34. For more details on this interesting episode, see A. W. Coats, "The Origins and Early Development of the Royal Economic Society," *Economic Journal* 78 (June 1968): 349–71.

35. Foxwell, "Economic Movement," p. 103.

36. See Thomas L. Haskell, *The Emergence of Professional Social Science* (Urbana: University of Illinois Press, 1977), chap. 8; and A. W. Coats, "The First Two Decades of the AEA," *American Economic Review* 50 (September 1960): 555–72.

37. Quoted in Coats, "Royal Economic Society," p. 357.

■ 5   THE IDEAS OF THE PAST
AS TOOLS FOR THE PRESENT

The Instrumental Presentism
of John R. Commons

JEFF E. BIDDLE

> I do not see that there is anything new in this analysis.
> Everything herein can be found in the work of outstanding
> economists for two hundred years. The things that have
> changed are the interpretations, the emphasis, the weights
> assigned to different ones of the thousands of factors which
> make up the world-wide economic process.
> —JOHN R. COMMONS, *Institutional Economics*, chap. I

Politically, John R. Commons was a progressive. Philosophically, he was a pragmatist. Economically, he was an institutionalist. However, Commons's work in each of these traditions was characteristically idiosyncratic. In keeping with a lifelong skepticism of conventional wisdom and an incessant desire to see and decide things for himself, Commons fashioned his own brand of progressivism and developed his pragmatism independently of James and Dewey on the basis of his reading of C. S. Peirce. His "Wisconsin-style" institutionalism was distinct from the institutionalist tradition in economics founded by Thorstein Veblen.[1]

That a progressive reformer hoped to establish a science of political economy based on a foundation of pragmatic theory and method should not be surprising. James Kloppenberg's book *Uncertain Victory* has made clear the connection between progressive political theory and pragmatism, and although Kloppenberg does not specifically deal with Commons, Commons's activities and the development of his ideas fit well within the broader picture painted by Kloppenberg of developments in political theory and philosophy between 1870 and 1920.

Kloppenberg points out that along with an acceptance of pragmatism comes a "historical sensibility," a belief that humanity's experience, laid out in the historical record, is the most useful guide for those hoping to resolve social problems in the present.[2] Commons's historical sensibility is reflected in the relationship between his work as a labor historian and the labor legislation he advocated. His understanding of how economic institutions and class relations had evolved in the past in response to changing situations informed his efforts to design reform measures that would prove workable and beneficial in his own day.[3]

This essay is concerned with a different aspect of Commons's historical sensibility. Commons sought inspiration for his work not only in the history of events but also in the history of ideas; more specifically, the history of economic doctrines. His theoretical works are filled with assessments and interpretations of the ideas of the past, many of which are extremely idiosyncratic and rather far from textbook versions of the history of economics. I will argue that Commons's interest in and interpretation of ideas of past economists reflect his epistemological and methodological beliefs and that his efforts as an intellectual historian can be seen as the result of his consistent application of a particular historiographic method. An implication of this argument is that there is a two-way relationship between Commons's own theories and his interpretations of the theories of others. A. W. Coats has pointed out that many of Commons's assessments of the ideas of other economists are only intelligible when viewed in the light of his own ideas.[4] A reverse statement is also true, in that one's understanding of Commons's ideas is enriched by a careful study of Commons's writings on Smith, Malthus, Ricardo, and others. It is my belief that an appreciation of this two-way relationship and of the logic of Commons's historiographic method is of value to those interested in understanding Commons's writings. Further, an examination of Commons's approach to historiography suggests lessons for both historians and practitioners of the social sciences.

Commons's career spanned a rather unsettled time in the history of economics. The classical school of political economy, which had reached its peak in the first half of the nineteenth century, was clearly in decline by the 1870s. Over the next several decades, proponents of alternative approaches to economics—Marxists, socialists, historicists, marginalists, and others—worked to further undermine the authority of the classical school and establish their own set of doctrines as the true science of economics.[5] Commons began his graduate study in economics at Johns Hopkins University in 1888 amid this chorus of competing voices. Like so many others of his generation, Commons was persuaded by the writings of Henry George that social reform and the study of political economy could go hand in hand. At Johns Hopkins, this conviction was strengthened by Commons's association with Richard T. Ely, a disciple of the German historical economists and an opponent of the laissez-faire doctrines propounded by the rank-and-file followers of the classical school.

Commons left graduate school in 1889 committed to social reform and an academic career. Over the next ten years he held three teaching positions and associated himself with Christian Socialism and the trade union movement. His activism cost him his position at Syracuse University in 1899, and he spent the next five years as an advisor to the U.S. Industrial Commission, the Department of Labor, and various private-sector reform groups, including the National Civic Federation. In 1904 Ely asked Commons to come to the University of Wisconsin, where he soon became an advisor to Robert LaFollette. Commons remained at Wisconsin for the rest of his career and compiled an impressive record as a mediator, arbitrator, government advisor, and designer, defender, and administrator of reform legislation.[6]

Though Commons in his day was exposed to a wide range of alternative approaches to understanding economic activity, no single one seemed to him to adequately address the social issues that concerned him. His first book, *The Distribution of Wealth* (1893), was an attempt to blend Austrian marginalism with German historicism. It was poorly received and Commons considered it a failure.[7] Over the years, Commons's continuing involvement in practical economic affairs reinforced his opinion that existing economic theories could not make sense of his own experiences or provide adequate guidance for solving the problems that confronted him. He began constructing a conceptual framework of his own, combining aspects of various economic theories with ideas culled from such disparate fields as legal theory, social psychology, and philosophy. By the end of his career, Commons had a vision of a new political economy: an evolutionary social science that would unite the study of law, economics, and ethics to facilitate constructive solutions to social problems.

Commons's blueprint for a new political economy can be found in three books: *The Legal Foundations of Capitalism*, published in 1924 when Commons was sixty-two; *Institutional Economics*, published ten years later; and *The Economics of Collective Action*, published in 1950, five years after his death.[8] These books contain the outline of Commons's conceptual system along with detailed descriptions of its components and examples from history and Commons's own life to illustrate its application. It is also in these books, especially *Institutional Economics* (hereafter cited as *IE*), that Commons presented his interpretation of the history of economic thought.

Commons discussed the history of economic thought in a decidedly presentistic manner, examining the ideas of his predecessors from the point of view provided by his own knowledge and experience and assessing the contributions of those writing decades before him on the basis of what he believed to be correct economic theory. However, a wider reading of Commons suggests that his adoption of a presentistic approach to studying the history of economics was a logical step, given his ideas on how the human mind should and did pursue knowledge about any subject.

Commons's epistemology resembles what Kloppenberg has called the "voluntary theory of action" found in the works of the pragmatists and other like-minded philosophers.[9] It centers around the concept of the "active mind," which Commons contrasted with the image of the mind as a passive receptacle for ideas that were reflections of the outside world. According to Commons, the mind did not merely reflect impressions that impinged upon it from without; instead, it actively sought out impressions in the external world, combined them with impressions existing in the memory, and created from the impressions ideas which were tools for the further investigation of impressions. The seeking, combining, and recombining of impressions were purposeful, guided by the mind and directed toward controlling the future. Thus, the active mind did not acquire knowledge by reflecting an external reality; rather, it created knowledge by interacting with the outside world, and the output of the creative process depended upon the individual's prior experiences and his goals for the future (*IE*, pp. 150 ff.).

Related to the doctrine of the active mind was Commons's description of the problem-solving process. According to Commons, individuals came into any situation with preconceptions based on past experiences and with a desire to advance some purpose. In attempting to assess or respond to a situation that might embody the interactions between hundreds or thousands of elements, the human will had the unique ability to seek out and concentrate upon the "limiting factor," an element or set of elements that seemed to hold the key to resolving the situation in the individual's favor (*IE*, pp. 58, 89–90).[10]

Commons believed that the theory of the active mind was the "psychology of all scientific investigation," so it is not surprising to find that it is consistent with his approach to investigating the history of economic ideas. Commons did not want to passively reflect the ideas of the past but to engage in a dialogue with them, using them as raw material to be blended with his own experiential knowledge and shaped into tools for understanding and solving present-day problems. Commons's presentism was thus an instrumental presentism. And, as Commons's theory of problem solving through focusing on limiting factors would suggest, Commons focused his presentistic analysis only on those ideas of past writers he found most helpful in advancing his own purpose (i.e., in working through his own theoretical problems), leading to an unusual pattern of emphasis in Commons's discussion of past economists.

Evidence consistent with this view of Commons's approach to studying disciplinary history can be found throughout *Institutional Economics*. For example, Commons's first lengthy discussion of Marx comes in a section dealing with the proper use of statistical averages. Here Commons argues that Marx's Social Labor Power was a mental construction, a weighted average, to which Marx had fallaciously attributed a real existence (*IE*, pp. 267–69). Still, Commons found it and the rest of the labor theory of value useful for measuring changes in productive efficiency. This explains Commons's enigmatic assessment of Marx's value theory: "Marx was the first economist to formulate all the factors necessary, and exclude those not necessary, to the modern concept of efficiency." Commons wanted to develop a measure of efficiency and changes in efficiency that would not rely on market-determined values such as prices or wages. As he read Marx he was especially intrigued by discussions of the labor theory of value, in which he saw a basis for developing his efficiency measure. That Commons saw Marx's value theory as a malleable input into his own theoretical production process is apparent in this statement, which follows closely the previous quote: "We proceed to reconstruct Marx's theory into a theory merely of efficiency, as we can observe it coming in as a part of a whole theory of political economy (*IE*, p. 275)."[11]

One can gain further insight into Commons's writings on the history of economic thought by understanding the holistic nature of Commons's method of investigation, recently explained by Yngve Ramstad.[12] Commons's method was to focus on part-whole relationships, beginning with an examination of individual cases or situations (parts) in search of general themes or shared principles that characterized the system from which the cases arose (the whole), with a belief that a study of the general themes of a system and their interrelationships would bring a clearer understanding of each individual case. The method involved a three-part process of thinking: analysis, the process of classifying the parts of a system through comparing similarities and differences across cases; genesis, the investigation of the changing nature of the parts; and insight, through which the fruits of analysis and genesis were synthesized into a picture of an evolving whole.

Ramstad provides an excellent description of how Commons applied this three-part process to his study of the history of economic thought. Political economy and the economic system it described were two interrelated parts of an evolving whole. The various aspects of the economic system had their counterparts in the concepts or theoretical categories devised by economists. Each economist's attempt to construct a theory describing a part of the economic system could in turn be considered a part of a whole theory, as each economist potentially focused on a different aspect of the subject or perceived the subject in a different way. Commons's analysis involved the comparison and classification of past theories on the basis of their treatment or omission of factors he believed to be relevant to his own attempt to understand some aspect of the modern economy, and in the course of the analysis Commons's own theoretical positions were clarified. Genesis is embodied in Commons's description of how theories had been modified over time and required further modification, because earlier versions of the theory were incomplete or because the phenomena they attempted to describe had changed. The insight lay in molding the useful parts of past theories with Commons's own ideas to create a theory that was appropriate for Commons's purposes.[13]

Analysis and genesis are apparent throughout Commons's references to the history of economic thought. One cannot help but notice Commons's penchant for classifying and reclassifying schools of economic thought. Coats has counted over forty different terms used by Commons to describe various schools of economics, with any given writer potentially falling into several classes.[14] This is simply the outcome of the process of analysis. Each classification scheme would arise when Commons seized upon some "factor" important to the understanding of a particular part of the economic process, then grouped economists according to their similarities and differences in dealing with that factor.[15]

For example, Commons's discussion of business cycle theories in *Institutional Economics* begins with the announcement of a basic classification scheme: "Running through the Nineteenth and Twentieth Centuries, from the time of Ricardo and Malthus who split on the issue, are distinguishable the two fundamental but opposing theories of the causes of alternations of prosperity and depression. One we name the Profit-Share theories, the other the Profit-Margin theories." Commons bases his typology on a limiting factor he believes to be of importance in understanding business cycles: "Each is based on the ultimate fact that business men, who have legal control of industry, are the ones who . . . determine whether production shall continue, expand, or stop" (*IE*, p. 526). Then Commons combines analysis and genesis in exploring the development of each of the opposing viewpoints with his discussion of the evolution of the profit-share theories, beginning with another classification system: "Four stages of the Malthusian Profit-share argument we shall distinguish as the Consumption Stage, the Savings Stage, the Dividend-Lag and the Sales-Lag stages of the argument" (*IE*, p. 527).

Over the next eighty-six pages, the discussion of past business cycle theories continues, mainly as a backdrop to the exposition of Commons's own profit-margin theory of the business cycle and his related policy recommendations for dealing with cycles. The entire section is presented in a way that creates the impression that Commons's theory is the result of insight applied to past theories and to the economic events Commons had observed. This mode of presentation is repeated throughout the book.

Commons's purposes in exploring the history of economic thought, the list of "limiting factors" on which he focused in his investigation, and his holistic view of the relationship between his ideas, the ideas of past economists, and the whole of political economy are all explicit or implicit in the brief first chapter of *Institutional Economics* entitled "The Point of View." A part of this chapter bears quoting at length:

> [Institutional Economics] also consists in going back through the writings of economists from John Locke to the Twentieth Century, to discover wherein they have or have not introduced collective action. Collective action, as well as individual action, has always been there, but from Smith to the Twentieth Century it has been excluded or ignored . . . The problem now is not to create a different kind of economics—"institutional" economics—divorced from preceding schools, but how to give collective action, in all its varieties, its due place throughout economic theory.
>
> In my judgment this collective control of individual transactions is the contribution of institutional economics to the whole of a rounded-out theory of Political Economy, which shall include and give a proper place to all the economic theories since John Locke. (*IE*, pp. 5–6)

What does Commons mean by "giving collective action its due place" in economic theory? To understand this and to understand Commons's forays into the history of economic thought, some further discussion of Commons's idea of collective action is required.[16]

For Commons, economic activity was the product of individuals choosing and acting on the basis of perceived opportunities. However, the opportunities available to individuals and their perceptions of those opportunities were restricted and influenced by collective action, manifested in what Commons called the "working rules" of society. Working rules ranged from the customary patterns of behavior learned by the individual in the course of his or her socialization and enforced by society's approval or disapproval, through the standard procedures of economic organizations enforced by economic sanctions, to the laws of the state, enforced ultimately with physical sanctions. By limiting the choices available to individuals, working rules helped to shape the economic process and determine economic outcomes.

Working rules arose because of the fundamental problem of scarcity, which created conflicts of interest between individuals vying for control of scarce resources. While scarcity created conflict between individuals, it also created interdependence between individuals, for cooperative action was more effective than individual action in alleviating scarcity. To survive, a society required working rules to create order: that is, to insure enough forbearance by individuals in the pursuit of their own purposes to allow cooperative endeavors to succeed and group purposes to be advanced. Working rules defined who would control scarce resources, to what uses they could be put, how the benefits of cooperation were to be shared, and so on (cf. *IE*, p. 194).

However, no set of working rules was so complete that it did not allow some discretion for individuals. Within this range of discretion individuals acted, sometimes unreflectingly, sometimes habitually, but always purposefully, with an eye toward achieving some future goal. Looming as potential obstacles or aids to the advancement of an individual's purpose were the purposeful actions of others. To plan one's own future course of action, one had to anticipate what others would do. Expectations regarding the actions of others were stabilized to some extent for the individual by his or her knowledge of working rules, which limited the possible actions of others as well as himself. Still, working rules left to others some discretion in their actions, so the active, purposeful mind of the individual fashioned plans for controlling the actions of others, employing measures of persuasion, coercion, or force permitted by existing working rules and knowing full well that others chose their actions with an eye to their own purposes and assessments of future possibilities.

When Commons declared his intent to establish a "volitional" theory of economics, he meant a theory that recognized the importance of these meetings of partially controlled, partially free human wills. Such meetings ("transactions" in Commons's phraseology) were the essence of economic activity, and their outcomes had economic dimensions.

Properly integrating the meeting of wills into economics would require a new psychology, which Commons called a "negotiational psychology."[17]

Commons's volitional theory of economics required a volitional theory of value, meaning a theory of value in which an individual's valuations of objects or actions were related to his purposes and to his expectations of the future. In a volitional theory of value social or "market" values, as objectified at any point in time in prices, incomes, interest rates, and so on, reflected the collective but subjective expectations of many individuals regarding the future, as well as the prevailing tastes or ethics of society. Since working rules stabilized expectations and gave to different classes of individuals differential access to the scarce resources necessary to advance individual purposes, collective action was instrumental in determining individual and social valuations.[18]

Commons was also concerned with what he felt was a double meaning inherent in the common usages of the word *value*. From one perspective, the value of a good was its ability to satisfy human needs or desires. From another perspective, the value of a good arose not from the good itself but from ownership of the good, which represented the ability of an individual to withhold a good from others who might want it. Value in the first sense increased as the quantity of the good increased, but value in the other sense, which was reflected in the unit price of a good and which Commons called scarcity value, could decrease as the good became more abundant. Often, both aspects of value were represented in a single value concept, although they might not be completely captured or properly distinguished. A rounded-out political economy would differentiate and then correlate the two aspects of value.[19] Institutional economics was particularly concerned with scarcity value, as the rights of ownership that gave rise to scarcity value were created and maintained by collective action (cf. *IE*, p. 5).

The foregoing discussion indicates that from Commons's point of view, an inquiry into the extent to which an economist incorporated collective action into his or her work could entail a focus on several aspects of that work. To what extent was the economist's system based on a recognition of scarcity? Since the need for collective action was created by scarcity, a failure to recognize the problem of scarcity could lead to a neglect of collective action. Did the economist's theory recognize the active, choosing nature of the human will, and was the interaction of discretionary wills with conflicting interests a part of it? If discretion in individual action and confrontations between wills were ignored or assumed away, the role of collective action in limiting but also creating a range for individual discretion was obscured. Did the economist recognize that action and value in the present were influenced by future expectations? If not, another point of entry for collective action into economic theory, as a stabilizer of future expectations, was closed off. Finally, was the economist concerned with the changing nature of economic processes throughout history? Such changes represented or resulted from changes over time in the working rules of collective action.

These questions embody some of the limiting factors to which Commons directed his attention as he studied the history of economic thought. Economists' investigations of scarcity, volition, futurity, or change would lead them to a consideration of collective action, so Commons looked to the past to see where such investigations had been taken up or neglected. Where they had been taken up, Commons explored whether collective action had been ignored, deftly avoided, or incorporated into the analysis. Interspersed throughout and providing clear reference points for these discussions of the theories of the past were Commons's own theories, offered as applications of previously established verities, corrections of others' faulty theoretical formulations, or resolutions to theoretical difficulties faced by previous economists. Because of this, it is possible to read Commons's discussions of the ideas of the past and be left with the impression that they are mostly packaging, an attempt to give his own ideas a pedigree and to portray them as natural developments of and improvements upon the great insights of the past. In this interpretation, Commons's theory existed in final form before he began his excursions into the history of economic thought, and he gave a distorted account of that history in an attempt to give his theory more legitimacy.

However, an alternative interpretation is possible if one takes the position that the process of thinking Commons believed to characterize all investigation was the process he himself employed in attempting to create his institutional economics. In seeking to integrate scarcity, volition, futurity, and change into his theory of collective action, Commons's active mind focused on the elements of his own experience that seemed relevant, but it also sought input in the form of the ideas of other economists.[20] Of course, Commons's initial attitudes toward the ideas of others and his choice of which ideas to focus on were colored by his own preconceptions, as would inevitably be the case for any investigator, if we accept Commons's view of things. As he studied the theories of past economists, he looked for similarities and differences across their ideas and between their ideas and his. And he sought out the reasons for differences in theories, with his epistemological beliefs leading him to focus on differences in the preconceptions, habitual assumptions, or experiences of the theoreticians. This process of analysis was a prelude to the process of insight, in which Commons reformulated, refined, and clarified his own theoretical constructs.[21] (Recall the active mind's combining and recombining of received and retained impressions to create tools for further investigation.) By the end of his study of the history of economic thought, both Commons's ideas and his perceptions of the ideas of the past were changed. What finally appeared in print, Commons's theoretical system intertwined with his interpretation of the history of economics, must be viewed as a whole, because the development of each part was influenced by the development of the other.

This interpretation is consistent with Commons's own statements, both the one quoted at the beginning of this paper and the one that follows it closely in the text: "What I have tried to do is to work out a system of thought that shall give due weight to all economic theories, modified by my own experience" (*IE*, p. 8).

As I asserted earlier, accepting that Commons's descriptions of the active mind in the process of discovery reflect his own way of trying to understand both the economy and the history of economics implies a two-way relationship between Commons's theoretical system and his writings on disciplinary history. It means that Commons's assessments of the ideas of others are only understandable in terms of his own ideas, but also that Commons's writings on the ideas of the past are important sources for those trying to understand Commons's theoretical constructs. Commons's discussions of the history of economic thought touch upon the works of dozens of thinkers and are found throughout the nine hundred–plus pages of *Institutional Economics*, as well as in sections of Commons's other two theoretical books. Rather than attempting a concise overview of all this material, I will attempt to illustrate the two-way relationship by examining Commons's treatment of Adam Smith.[22]

In Commons's opinion, he and Adam Smith approached political economy with the same purpose, that of advising policy makers on how to best proportion inducements to insure that individual actions benefited both the individual and the state.[23] But while Commons's institutional economics involved an investigation of collective action, Smith's writings represented a condemnation of collective action as Smith perceived it: that is, collective action in the form of mercantilistic regulations and monopolistic associations. Smith advanced his argument with the aid of a mental construction he called the "simple system of natural liberty," which served as a benchmark by which to judge the reasonableness of economic outcomes (*IE*, pp. 207-10). Although collective action was almost completely absent from the system of natural liberty, individuals pursuing their self-interest within the system would promote socially beneficial outcomes that were not part of their intention.

Clearly, Smith's system of natural liberty had implications that were completely inconsistent with Commons's way of thinking. For Commons, collective action controlled but also liberated and expanded individual action. Collective action imposed order on the inevitable conflicts of individual interests, an order that provided the security of expectations necessary for economic activity. Collective action created the inducements that directed individuals toward activities deemed socially beneficial and penalties that discouraged socially useless or harmful activities. Collective action liberated individuals by controlling individuals, because one could only be free if he could be reasonably sure that others would not interfere with his actions. For Smith, however, the presence of collective control meant the absence of individual liberty. The removal of collectively created inducements to individual action led to increased prosperity, and in the absence of collective action not a conflict but a harmony of interests emerged. Thus, when examining Smith's work, Commons explored Smith's background, conceptual framework, and assumptions to find explanations for the differences between Smith's attitude toward collective action and his own.

Commons noted that Smith could easily see through the hypocritical arguments advanced to support the regulations and privileges of the mercantilist system, and those regulations were obvious examples of collective action suppressing individual liberty and diminishing prosperity (*IE*, pp. 201–2). Commons felt that Smith's distaste for mercantilism led him to distrust all collective action and to shape his theory into an argument for individualism and against collectivism (*IE*, pp. 167–68). Implicit in Smith's thinking was a belief that the results of individual decision making and individual action were superior, both ethically and economically, to results influenced by collective activity of any sort. Thus, whenever Smith encountered a manifestation of collective action that seemed to lead to undesirable consequences, he recognized it as collective action and analyzed it as such. When he encountered a socially beneficial manifestation of collective action, he could not or did not recognize or classify it as collective action, instead portraying it as the result of some instinct based in the individual or a reflection of divine intention.

For example, Commons found that the elimination of collective action from Smith's system of natural liberty was extensive but not complete. Though voluntary associations were frowned upon and positive action by the sovereign or the legislature was proscribed, the state was responsible for providing national defense and public works and for enforcing individual property rights and voluntary contracts. In Commons's view, the property rights that were the keystone to the system of natural liberty were themselves working rules of collective action, permitting some activities, prohibiting others, and providing the security of expectations necessary to keep society going. They had developed over time in response to changes in historical circumstances and as a result of the purposeful decisions of common-law judges attempting to advance what they perceived as the public interest. But Smith did not treat individual property rights as a form of collective action and did not attempt to explain the origin or evolution of those rights. In place of an explanation he offered a justification, borrowing from John Locke the notion that labor had a natural right to its product. Individual property rights were created through and defined in terms of individual action, and Smith represented them as natural law or part of a divine plan. They were to be contrasted rather than classed with the collectively created privileges of the mercantilist system and the collectively controlled property rights of guilds and other voluntary associations. If Smith accepted a classification like Commons's, in which individual property rights were just another variety of man-made collective action, it would undermine his argument for the superiority of individualism as embodied in his system of natural liberty (*IE*, pp. 162–68, 198–200).

In addition to representing the collective action that did exist in the system of natural liberty as something other than collective action, Smith avoided acknowledging the need for collective control, restraint, or direction of individual action by assuming the existence of mechanisms in the human psyche that performed these functions. As Commons noted, "If collective action is abolished, then the theorist must find in the individual breast a set of instincts that keep society going. These instincts must be placed there by some external power that intended the welfare of mankind" (*IE*, p. 166). Commons found Smith's descriptions of such instincts in both *The Wealth of Nations* and *The Theory of Moral Sentiments*. In the latter volume, Smith argued that each individual had a "sense of propriety," an innate appreciation of virtue in himself and others. Individuals did not consider the public interest when they acted but instinctively avoided acts that were contrary to it, behaving as if an "impartial spectator" were judging their actions (*IE*, pp. 158–59). It would be possible to consider Smith's impartial spectator to be a form of collective action, representing one's socialization or one's awareness of the unorganized social sanctions enforcing customary ethical notions. But Smith avoided letting collective action into his system through this route, as he held that the sense of propriety was designed and implanted in the psyche by a beneficent deity. (*IE*, p. 215).

Smith continued in the same vein in *The Wealth of Nations*. To insure that individuals would engage in productive activities within the "natural" system of property rights, a beneficent creator had endowed them with unlimited wants and a drive to pursue their self-interest. To insure that productivity would be enhanced by the division of labor and specialization, individuals had been created with an "instinct to truck, barter, and exchange." Thus, manmade and collectively enforced rules were not needed to induce individual effort or channel it in the proper directions, because individuals were already instinctively compelled to behave in a manner that was optimally suited to the natural laws of property (*IE*, pp. 159–60).

It was the opinion of some scholars in Commons's day that Smith's emphasis on self-interest in *The Wealth of Nations* contradicted the sense of propriety stressed in his earlier book. Not so, according to Commons, because of a crucial but implicit assumption of Smith's system. Following Locke, Smith had assumed an abundance of resources and opportunities, reflecting the beneficence of the creator. This meant that the pursuit of self-interest by one, within the bounds established by the natural rights of property, could not possibly violate the sense of propriety by harming others (*IE*, p. 161). In Commons's system, it was scarcity that created the conflict of individual interests and gave rise to the need for collective control of the conflicts of individual wills that were the essence of economic activity. Smith's assumption of abundance eliminated the need for collective control. In Commons's opinion, it also focused the attention of Smith and subsequent economists away from the conflict between man and man, which they believed could be eliminated by the removal of the restraints of collective action, and toward the relationship between man and nature, which they saw as the source of property and value (*IE*, p. 172).

It is easy to question many of Commons's assertions concerning Smith. Perhaps Commons overstated Smith's hostility toward collective action and took too literally Smith's references to Providence and natural liberty. Commons's tendency to focus on isolated passages and concepts in Smith's work led him to ignore qualifications and subtleties existing elsewhere.[24] But Commons's interpretation makes more sense when examined in light of his purposes. His theoretical purpose was to integrate a treatment of collective action into an existing body of economic theory that employed many of Smith's ideas. His practical purpose throughout life was to advocate new forms of collective action, often in the face of opposition based on a belief that Smith had conclusively condemned all collective action.

So it is not surprising to follow Commons through Smith and find ourselves being shown all the points where collective action has been shut out by a key assumption, or disguised by a linguistic sleight-of-hand, or simply overlooked. And after having done so, we have a better understanding of Commons's own concept of collective action and of what he has been trying to say about its relationship to scarcity, liberty, conflict, and control.

Herbert Butterfield, in *The Whig Interpretation of History*, wrote of the pitfalls associated with "history written for the sake of the present." Attempts to find in the past analogues of current events or ideas often involved the removal of individual historical episodes from their larger contexts; a desire to find order or a progressive trend in a complex historical record led to the construction of overly simplistic causal sequences linking the ideas and events of the past to the circumstances of the present. In general, when a historical study was organized with reference to the concerns of the present, the result would be a distortion of the historical record and a tendency toward misinterpretation and misrepresentation.[25]

Commons self-consciously let his present concerns guide his investigation of the ideas of the past, and his resulting written account of the history of economic doctrines is marked by many of the flaws Butterfield associated with history written for the sake of the present. Commons tended to subject small parts of an author's work to intense scrutiny while giving little or no attention to those parts that did not seem relevant to his purposes; he then over-generalized on the basis of such uneven treatments. His interpretations were filled with anachronisms and often bore the scars of his penchant for forcing theories and ideas into idiosyncratic categories and systems of historical stages. Commons's assertion that Adam Smith would have wanted to outlaw telephone directories and his reduction of Marx's labor theory of value to an attempt to measure efficiency after the fashion of scientific management are but two examples of this.[26]

In a sense, however, Commons's written history of economic thought is only a by-product of his instrumental presentism. As should by now be clear, Commons's instrumental presentism was more than a method of historiography; it was a component of a broader social science methodology. Thus, in assessing it one should look beyond its somewhat limited value as a tool for the historian and a method of reaching a better understanding of history to its potential worth to the practicing social scientist.

Some observations that are salient to such an assessment can be found in George Stocking, Jr.'s essay "On the Limits of 'Presentism' and 'Historicism' in the Historiography of the Behavioral Sciences."[27] The essay is generally critical of presentism and supportive of Butterfield's position. However, at one point Stocking notes that there may be a place for presentism in the historiography of the behavioral sciences. It is possible for the social science practitioner to find in the history of his and related disciplines neglected or forgotten ideas that could shed light on questions of current interest. Stocking argues that

> because [the behavioral sciences] are pre-paradigmatic, the various competing schools of the present and the past exist in a sense contemporaneously. But because they have on the whole notoriously short historical memories, the behavioral sciences of the present have very little awareness that their predecessors were in many instances asking questions and offering answers about problems which have by no means been closed. And because of the disciplinary fragmentation of approaches which were in the past often much more integrated, there may be fruits of interdisciplinary cooperation which are as easily picked in the past as in the present.[28]

But, Stocking cautions, the social scientist whose interest in the past is motivated by present-day concerns would do well to adopt an enlightened presentism, an approach which is "in practice if not in impulse 'affective' and 'historicist.'" Such an approach would be non-judgmental, sensitive to the historical context of the ideas of the past, and as interested in the reasonableness of ideas to those who held them as in their rationality in light of a modern or absolute standard.

There is much in Stocking's argument to suggest that Commons's instrumental presentism was appropriate for his time and may also be of some value to the modern historian and practitioner of the social sciences. I mentioned earlier the pre-paradigmatic nature of economics during Commons's career; Commons also lived in a time when economics was increasingly distancing itself from other social sciences. In the face of this Commons engaged in his program of "constructive research," borrowing concepts freely from diverse fields of study as well as from past and present schools of economic thought in an attempt to understand and solve the problems of his day.[29] I would also argue that Commons's treatment of the ideas of the past had some of the historicist elements that Stocking suggests should accompany an enlightened presentism.

The historicist elements of Commons's instrumental presentism stem mainly from his conception of what constituted truth or reality in the social sciences. There is a tendency among modern social scientists, economists especially, to see the truth as an objective reality that is slowly being revealed. Each generation builds on the discoveries of the last and thus uncovers more of the truth. Commons's quite different notions of truth and reality, like his concept of the active mind, were based on his reading of C. S. Peirce. Peirce's truth was the opinion "fated to be agreed upon by all those who investigate" and the "object represented in this opinion" was reality. Commons believed Peirce to mean that truth was a social consensus of opinion and that there need be no predetermined uniformity underlying it. The external world was highly complicated, made up of a myriad of interrelated forces and processes. When individuals perceived this external world they did not reflect it but selectively sought out a few impressions from the thousands surrounding them, with the selection being based on their preconceptions and purposes. As a result, individual perceptions were unavoidably subjective. We could never be sure whether our beliefs were the result of predispositions inside us or activities going on outside us. Differences across individuals' purposes and habitual assumptions led to differences in individual beliefs about reality. Meaning at the individual level was always bias (*IE*, pp. 152–56).

The reality or truth that was both the basis and the goal of scientific endeavors was a consensus drawn out of these conflicting individual opinions. The discussions and experiments associated with science were processes through which individual biases were revealed or eliminated and compromise was achieved. This consensual truth was not an absolute truth, however, but a relative truth, relative to the shared preconceptions and purposes that formed the basis of the consensus (*IE*, p. 152, n. 38). It was also an instrumental truth, because it was a truth that the scientific community, and eventually the community at large, could accept and use as a basis for action in the future. This view of truth was behind Commons's description of a fact as a "mental construction expressed in words" that has as a constituent part persuasiveness, or the ability to elicit acceptance from others (*IE*, p. 197).

The relativism of truth was particularly notable in the social sciences, for investigators were studying a system of which they were themselves a part and behaviors in which they themselves engaged.[30] Their day-to-day activities were based on ethical beliefs and assumptions about reality, and beliefs and assumptions that influenced behavior within the system could not be easily excised from more formal theories of the system (*IE*, p. 103).[31] Further contributing to the relativity of truth was the fact that the social system itself was changing over time.

Commons's ideas about reality led him to realize that the validity of his own opinions was limited by his personal biases and that any truth in his beliefs was relative to his times and his experiences. The same was true of the beliefs of economic thinkers of the past and their present-day followers. They were all competent investigators, but they disagreed on many matters, because in trying to make sense of a complex world they had made different choices regarding which factors to emphasize in their theories and which to ignore. Commons's attempt to synthesize his own institutional economics with the ideas of the past in a rounded-out science of political economy was an attempt to create a consensus-based truth out of the biased views of individual investigators. This purpose guided Commons's explorations into the history of economic thought. With an appreciation of the bias in his own point of view, he searched through the arguments of others, savoring the insights that broadened his own understanding and uncovering the assumptions that led them to conclusions different from his own. He was not trying to "debunk" the ideas of the past but to find a compromise between those ideas and his own. To use one of Commons's favorite metaphors, he wanted to engage in collective bargaining with those thinkers, past and present, who disagreed with him in hopes of finding a more reasonable basis upon which economic science could operate in the future.[32]

Commons's view of reality and his desire to identify the habitual assumptions that colored the theories of past economists also made him sensitive to the historical context of each author he studied. As Coats pointed out, Commons's conviction that individuals' perceptions of reality were heavily influenced by their past experiences led him to believe that historical events determined what ideas emerged and were dominant at a given point in time.[33] His discussions of ideas he did not completely agree with often included attempts to explain why those ideas seemed reasonable to their originators and adherents, and he always sought links between the theories of an individual and the historical trends of that individual's day.[34]

Coats wonders whether Commons believed that his own theory was as much a relative part-truth as the theories he examined.[35] The interpretation of Commons advanced here implies that he did, and perhaps the best evidence that he did is found in a section of *The Economics of Collective Action* entitled "The Personal Equation." After defining the personal equation as the bias of the investigator himself, Commons remarks that "I always warn my students to make corrections for my personal equation." Later, he lists the working rules that should guide the investigator. Notably, the first is "skepticism—skepticism of himself and others." The second, "inseparable from skepticism," is tolerance.[36]

Commons's commitment to skepticism and tolerance points to certain elements of his instrumental presentism that the modern historian of the social sciences might do well to embrace. They include a recognition by the historian that his own interpretations are influenced by his preconceptions and thus limited in their validity; a tolerance of and openness toward the interpretations of others; and a belief that there are gains to be made through discussion and attempts at persuasion and compromise.

I also believe there are aspects of Commons's instrumental presentism that are of value to modern social scientists, at least to those practicing in my own discipline of economics. Most economists today work within a research program that is rather ahistorical in nature. To the extent that modern economists think at all about the history of their discipline, they imagine it to be filled with people trying to figure out things they already know or to develop analytical techniques they have already mastered. What is not appreciated is that the history of economics is a record of different perspectives, of different ways of looking at or thinking about economic activity, and of different methods of approaching some of the same problems that vex us today. Instrumental presentism involves a recognition that these alternative visions exist and a belief that they deserve the attention of the investigator. They are worthy of attention because each offers a way of thinking about any given problem that may reveal key aspects of the problem, aspects that go unnoticed when it is viewed from the perspective that currently dominates the discipline. Instrumental presentism also involves an attitude that the investigator can accept the validity of and employ certain elements of alternative approaches to economics without necessarily abandoning modern analytical tools or techniques. In fact, one may discover in a long-neglected approach to economics unexploited but potentially fruitful applications of those tools and techniques.

However, I think that an acceptance by modern economists of this much of instrumental presentism might not be all to the good—and might not even be possible—without a concomitant realization of the limitations inherent in the dominant approach to economics, and I think that a Commons-style treatment of the history of economics could help in bringing about such a realization. One strength of Commons's approach was its commitment to revealing the unspoken and sometimes unrecognized normative and ethical biases that colored the nominally objective theories of his predecessors. We economists have accepted certain theories developed in the past as the foundations for our present theories and investigations, and in doing so we have sometimes unconsciously adopted their ethical and normative underpinnings as well. By pointing out to us the biases of past investigators, a Commons-style analysis could illuminate the way those biases and our own biases limit the usefulness of our theoretical tools and the applicability of our theoretical conclusions. Facing the limitations of our own hard-won part-truths would be a useful first step toward opening ourselves to tolerant discussions of alternative approaches, discussions that might leave us better equipped to grapple with the questions and problems that perplex us.

Notes

The author would like to thank JoAnne Brown, James Farr, David van Keuren, and Warren Samuels for helpful comments on earlier drafts.

1. Literature discussing the nature of Commons's Progressivism includes W. F. Kennedy, "John R. Commons, Conservative Reformer," *Western Economic Journal* 1 (Fall 1962): 29–42; and Lafayette G. Harter, "John R. Commons: Conservative or Liberal?" *Western Economic Journal* 1 (Summer 1963): 226–32. A radical critique of Commons's reformism is Morris Isserman, "'God Bless Our American Institutions': The Labor History of John R. Commons," *Labor History* 17 (Summer 1976): 309–28. On the relationship between Commons's ideas and Dewey's pragmatism, see Allan G. Gruchy, *Modern Economic Thought* (New York: Augustus M. Kelley, 1967 [1947]). The claim that Commons developed his ideas independently of Dewey and James is advanced by Kenneth Parsons, "J. R. Commons' Point of View," reprinted in J. R. Commons, *The Economics of Collective Action* (New York: Macmillan, 1950). Comparisons between Wisconsin-style institutionalism and the Veblen-Ayres institutionalist tradition can be found in Gruchy, *Modern Economic Thought*; David Seckler, *Thorstein Veblen and the Institutionalists* (Boulder: Colorado Associated University Press, 1975); and Malcolm Rutherford, "J. R. Commons's Institutional Economics," *Journal of Economic Issues* 17 (September 1983): 721–44.

2. James T. Kloppenberg, *Uncertain Victory* (New York: Oxford University Press, 1986). On the "historical sensibility," see pp. 107–14.

3. Commons was leader of the project that compiled *A Documentary History of American Industrial Society*, 10 vols. (Cleveland: Arthur H. Clark Co., 1910–1911) and the lead author of *History of Labour in the United States*, 4 vols. (New York: Macmillan, 1918–1935).

4. A. W. Coats, "Commons as a Historian of Economics," *Research in the History of Economic Thought and Methodology* 1 (1983): 147–61.

5. Wesley C. Mitchell, *Types of Economic Theory*, ed. Joseph Dorfman, 2 vols. (New York: Augustus M. Kelley, 1969). Mitchell was a prominent contemporary of Commons, and his book gives not only a good account of various approaches to economics coexisting during Commons's career but also a sense of the prevailing uncertainty regarding which approach, if any, would dominate the future of economics.

6. Accounts of Commons's life and activities can be found in Commons, *Myself*

(New York: Macmillan, 1933) and Lafayette G. Harter, *John R. Commons: His Assault on Laissez-Faire* (Corvallis: Oregon State University Press, 1962).

7. J. R. Commons, *The Distribution of Wealth* (New York: Augustus M. Kelley, 1963 [1943]). Reviews of the book and Commons's reactions to them are discussed in Harter, *John R. Commons*.

8. Complete citations for these works are *The Legal Foundations of Capitalism* (New York: Macmillan, 1924); *Institutional Economics* (Madison: University of Wisconsin Press, 1961 [1934]); and *The Economics of Collective Action*, ed. Kenneth Parsons (New York: Macmillan, 1950).

9. Kloppenberg, *Uncertain Victory*, pp. 79–94.

10. Commons, *Legal Foundations*, pp. 378–79.

11. See also Commons, *Myself*, pp. 152–53.

12. Yngve Ramstad, "A Pragmatist's Quest for Holistic Knowledge: The Scientific Methodology of John R. Commons," *Journal of Economic Issues* 20, 4 (1986).

13. Ibid,. pp. 1091–92. Note the reference in the quote concerning Marx (fn. 13) to bringing in a reconstructed version of Marx's theory as "a part of the whole theory of political economy."

14. Coats, "Commons as a Historian," p. 156.

15. A typical example of classification and reclassification is found in Commons, *Institutional Economics*, pp. 117–21. The method of and reasons for classifying, and the relationship between classification systems and the purpose and assumptions of the classifier, are discussed in Commons, *Legal Foundations*, pp. 342–49.

16. The next six paragraphs sketch out some key features of Commons's system. Details can be found in Jeff Biddle, "Purpose and Evolution in Commons's Institutionalism," *History of Political Economy* 22 (Spring 1990): 19–48; Richard Gonce, "John R. Commons's Legal Economic Theory," *Journal of Economic Issues* 5 (September 1971): 80–95; Gruchy, *Modern Economic Thought*, pp. 135–246; and Rutherford, "J. R. Commons's Institutional Economics."

17. On "negotiational psychology," see Commons, *Institutional Economics*, pp. 90–92, 105–6; and Commons, *Collective Action*, p. 109.

18. This is the reasoning behind Commons's somewhat cryptic assertion that economic causation lies in the future. See Commons, *Institutional Economics*, p. 7.

19. Thus, Commons's particular interest in Marx's labor theory of value noted earlier.

20. As Coats notes, Commons's autobiography is a catalog of illustrations of how Commons's experiences allegedly led to his theoretical concepts. Coats, "Commons as a Historian," p. 154.

21. Cf. this passage from Commons's autobiography, recalling his activities during the summer of 1916: "I took with me the books of several German economists and *studied them, making notes and revising my theories* for two or three hours each morning" (emphasis mine; Commons, *Myself*, p. 182).

22. The two-way relationship can also be seen in Commons's treatment of Malthus, as discussed in Biddle, "Purpose and Evolution."

23. Commons, *Legal Foundations*, pp. 362–63.

24. On some points, such as the thematic unity between *The Wealth of Nations* and *The Theory of Moral Sentiments*, Commons was closer to modern views of Smith

than the interpreters of his day. For a survey of some recent interpretations of Smith's ideas, see Edwin G. West, "Developments in the Literature on Adam Smith: An Evaluative Survey," and Donald Winch, "Commentary," the two of which comprise chapter 2 in *Classical Political Economy: A Survey of Recent Literature*, ed. William O. Thweat (Boston: Kluwer Academic Publishers, 1988).

25. Herbert Butterfield, *The Whig Interpretation of History* (New York: Charles Scribner's Sons, 1951).

26. See Commons, *Institutional Economics*, p. 164. Coats, "Commons as a Historian," offers further examples.

27. George Stocking, Jr., "On the Limits of 'Presentism' and 'Historicism' in the Historiography of the Behavioral Sciences," in his *Race, Culture, and Evolution* (Chicago: University of Chicago Press, 1968).

28. Ibid., p. 10.

29. "Constructive research" is Commons's own term, more fully defined in John R. Commons, *Labor and Administration* (New York: Macmillan, 1913), chap. 2.

30. Commons also believed in the relativism of truth in the physical sciences. See Commons, *Collective Action*, p. 156.

31. See also ibid., p. 202.

32. Commons himself invokes the collective bargaining metaphor in a sense in this passage from the "Point of View" chapter: "My point of view as an experimentalist is therefore quite the same as that of an arbitrator, a legislator, a court, an administrator—endeavoring to decide a dispute where many conflicting interests with conflicting principles, causes, or purposes, must be made to work together peaceably, if possible" (Commons, *Institutional Economics*, p. 9).

33. Coats, "Commons as a Historian," p. 154. See also Commons, *Labor and Administration*, chap. 4, for an evolutionary model of the determination of the ruling ideas of an age by historical circumstances.

34. For one of many examples, see Commons's discussion of John Locke in Commons, *Institutional Economics*, pp. 13 ff, 30 ff.

35. Coats, "Commons as a Historian," p. 155.

36. Commons, *Economics of Collective Action*, pp. 201–2.

■ 6 QUANDARY OF THE QUACKS

The Struggle for Expert Knowledge in American Psychology, 1890-1940

JILL G. MORAWSKI and GAIL A. HORNSTEIN

As a young discipline at the turn of the twentieth century, psychology in the United States had to differentiate its work from that of other disciplines concerned with human nature, especially biology and philosophy. However, disciplinary divisions were not the only boundaries that posed a problem for psychologists; they also had to differentiate their claims of knowledge from those of other avowed experts of mental life and from ordinary actors for whom psychological explanations were a regular part of everyday experience. To do this, psychologists had to try to convince the public that scientific psychology offered an understanding of mental events superior to that of common sense. While psychologists were quick to see that psychics, healers, mystics, and other "quacks" were somewhat dangerous competitors, they were slower to recognize the need to establish their scientific understanding of the mind as truly superior to everyday accounts.

In the early years of the discipline development, from 1885 to 1910, psychologists presented their arguments for superior knowledge primarily in academic settings, training students to appreciate and acquire a scientific attitude toward psychological phenomena. Through such training procedures, the distinctions between valid and invalid, scientific and nonscientific forms of knowledge were painstakingly constructed and refined. In describing the proper scientific mind, textbook writers often contrasted the objectivity and rationality of the experimental scientist with the subjectivity of the layperson. Well-known Cornell psychologist E. B. Titchener, for example, encouraged "long training" to overcome the "ignorance" of the untrained.[1] G. Stanley Hall, an early founder of psychology laboratories and graduate programs, held that research "emancipates the mind from error and superstition" and "gets the mind into independent action so that men became authorities and not echoes."[2] Harvard psychologist Robert Yerkes employed a psycho-dynamic account when contrasting those trained in psychology with the untrained: "Millions of human beings— unfortunate but all unconscious of what they are missing—go through life blind to the psychological world."[3] The ability to "psychologize," the special talent of the properly trained psychologist, was clarified by such contrasts.[4] Thus, to the extent that the trained researcher could be identified by special cognitive skills of observation and reasoning, then the ordinary person was reduced to a poor observer, one deficient in or incapable of rational thinking and the appropriate scientific gaze on mental events.

These two social classes, the scientific psychologist and the layper-son, were obvious enough by 1921 that an author could title his textbook *The Psychology of the Other-One.*[5] Meanwhile, in the development of laboratory practice, researchers established roles for the experimenter and the subject that reflected and maintained such social distinctions. At times, the criteria defining what constituted the proper attitude were even used to discredit other academic psychologists whose work was not seen as sufficiently accurate, precise, or controlled to warrant being called "psychology."[6]

These constitutive arguments regarding the psychologist's advan-tage were extended to address a larger public, typically in the form of popular writings on assorted psychological subjects. Few of the prom-inent early psychologists refrained from describing their "new" science in popular magazines or newspapers. They wrote to clarify the differ-ences between traditional philosophy and their new scientific enterprise as well as to demystify folk thinking about human nature by introducing the scientific attitude, often materialistic and reductionist.[7] Here psy-chologists refined further a rhetoric that set themselves and their ac-counts apart from what the ordinary observer might say about a par-ticular psychological topic. In so doing, psychologists often deliberately presented as opaque and problematic what commonly was held to be self-evident or intuitively clear.

However, popular psychology in the early twentieth century was not restricted to simple translation and transmission of the scientific spirit. Psychologists devoted much of their popular articles, books, and radio talks to explicating the practical uses of psychological knowledge. Il-lustrious figures such as Hugo Münsterberg, John B. Watson, James McKeen Cattell, Joseph Jastrow, and G. Stanley Hall, as well as many lesser-known researchers, extended psychological findings to the explanation of such diverse life situations as marital discord, success, education, thumb sucking, and work efficiency. For instance, between 1916 and 1924, four leading psychologists published utopias in which the perfected worlds were fashioned according to psychological knowledge and managed by psychological experts.[8]

In producing a popular literature on practical psychology, these researchers were not creating an entirely new genre. By the early twentieth century there already existed a corpus of what can be termed human improvement psychology. Historians have examined the rise of popular self-improvement literature that stressed psychological mechanisms, and magazines in general often adopted a rhetoric of personal control. Popular psychology appealed to a culture of readers said to be motivated by a therapeutic ethos of self-help, narcissism, and control.[9]

Given this cultural climate in which everyone was psychologizing to some degree, it would be misleading to try to understand the popularization of psychology through any simple model of united scientists speaking to a naive readership. The dynamics of popular science in general are more complex, especially after World War I, when scientists had to make appeals both for economic support and a respectable self-image. During this postwar period, for instance, physicists sought not only to relay new research advances but also to present their science as democratic, socially responsible, and useful.[10] Organizations such as Science Service were created precisely to organize and control the voices of scientists and the image of science being presented to the public.[11]

While riding the postwar wave of interest in psychological phenomena, a time in which one historian claimed psychology had become a "national mania,"[12] psychologists had to continue their efforts to define and maintain distinctions between their scientific knowledge and the audiences' common-sense reasoning. By the 1920s, their popular rhetoric, which originally had been intended as a way to identify and market a specific form of expert knowledge, actually created a blurring of this boundary. That is, in order to sell scientific psychology to the public, psychologists modified and simplified their accounts, often omitting details of methodology, conceptual analysis, and theory. The resultant discourse was clearly accessible to a large audience of readers; however, it also could be imitated readily by writers who were not formally trained as scientific psychologists. Thus, in the end, popularization served as much to erode the fragile boundaries between common sense and science as to create them, which had been the original intention. As a result, some psychologists attempted to sharpen the distinctions between "common sense" of the layperson and "popular psychology" of the expert. In naming his 1928 textbook *Popular Psychology*, A. A. Roback reminded readers that his book was a psychology of the "scientifically trained person" which had been obtained by "authority," an essential feature "which no amount of common sense or general experience can compensate for."[13] Nevertheless, journalists were to capitalize on this fuzzy boundary, and in writing about psychological subjects they became not simply lay interpreters of psychological knowledge but actual contributors to that knowledge.

The history of popular psychology in the early twentieth century has much in common with recent historical studies of popularization of the physical and biological sciences. These studies have challenged the notions of popular science as a process of simplifying and diffusing scientific knowledge for the purpose of informing laypersons. Popularization has served more than a singular enlightenment function. Its audiences are often highly educated and may even include scientists (for example, Fermi was a regular reader of popular science presented in *Reader's Digest*).[14] Popular accounts do not always represent consensual scientific knowledge that remains unaltered by the simplification process. The knowledge communicated through popularization may actually represent the thinking of a subgroup of scientific practitioners; it may be fashioned to serve and persuade a particular audience; it most certainly is transformed through the processes of redescription and retelling.[15]

This study presents two case studies in the popularization of psychology in the twentieth century. Both cases illustrate the complications of blurred boundaries between psychologists' knowledge and knowledge of psychological processes held by others. The first case traces psychologists' reactions to psychoanalysis, a movement which had captured the public imagination in the first decades of the century. Initially, Freud's work was a subject of critique by academic psychologists who attempted to discredit his enterprise and dissociate it from their own work on the grounds that it was not scientific. However, in spite of these efforts, psychoanalysis became so popular during the 1920s that it threatened psychologists' claims to sole expertise over mental phenomena. In response, psychologists in the 1930s and 1940s began to switch from discrediting psychoanalysis to demonstrating how its concepts could be incorporated into scientific psychology. The second case is an account of the intentional blurring of boundaries by a scientifically trained psychologist who rebelled against the proffering of a practical psychology by fellow psychologists. The rebel, Grace Adams, found such popularizing unbefitting to the scientific attitude and at the same time misleading to the audience of eager readers who sought guidance in their personal lives. Her ventures into a critical popular psychology produced both resentment among psychologists and paradoxes in her own writing.

Thus, both of these cases illuminate some of the general processes involved in establishing and maintaining claims to expert knowledge.

Psychology's Problematic Relations with Psychoanalysis

When experimental psychology emerged as a distinct activity during the last decades of the nineteenth century, it had to effect a differentiation from related disciplines such as philosophy. This was done primarily on the basis of method, with psychologists adopting the experimental approach of the natural sciences. But to ensure that the subject matter of their field was in fact different from philosophy, psychologists had vigilantly to insist that a whole range of phenomena which might otherwise be considered psychology were in fact not part of the discipline as they conceived it.

From a certain purist perspective, this narrowing of focus might have been a successful strategy on which to launch the new discipline were it not for the problem of ensuring sufficient support to carry on its activities. But to attract university positions, research funds, and students, psychology was obliged to demonstrate that its understanding of mental events was superior to that of common sense. The discipline thus found itself in a bind—the more abstruse its formulations and the more esoteric its subject matter, the more scientific and expert it appeared. However, these same qualities also made it seem unresponsive to the concerns of ordinary people, who continued to be interested in such banned phenomena as suggestion, self-improvement, extrasensory perception, dreams, irrationality, and so on.

There were some attempts to persuade the public that scientific psychology was worthy of interest and respect in its own right and that it could be useful in daily life. One striking example is a series of mystery stories published between 1909 and 1911 in which Luther Trant, the brilliant "psychological detective," arrives at amazing solutions to his cases by relying on esoteric findings from current research in experimental psychology.[16] In general, however, scientific psychologists resisted applications of their work and thus risked having their discipline seem irrelevant to the concerns of the public. At best, they asserted that their work would someday have important practical applications, but these could not yet be demonstrated because psychology was such a "young" science.[17]

Meanwhile, a whole host of other "psychological experts" were claiming the attention of the public through their discussions of faith healing, Christian Science, mind cures, and so on, to which scientific psychologists could respond only with disgust. Yet whether psychologists liked it or not, people continued to think that they knew something about their own minds, their behavior, and other people, and they remained interested in any approach, scientific or not, that appeared to concern these issues.[18]

Yet when psychoanalysis first arrived in America via the previously little-used port of Worcester, Massachusetts, psychologists saw little reason to worry that this new, seemingly crackpot theory would provide any competition with their careful scientific work. Appearing to be simply the latest in a string of popular mind cures of the period, psychoanalysis seemed fated to take its place with the Emmanuel Movement, Weir Mitchell's rest cure, faith healing, and the rest as a mere diversion.[19]

And indeed it did take some time for psychoanalysis to attract more attention, either from psychologists or from the general public. There were a few early supporters (mostly psychiatrists), a few early critics (mostly psychologists), and a few popular presentations of the theory. But by the mid-teens, psychoanalysis had "eclipsed all other [mind cures] in the nation's magazines"[20] and had captured the public imagination with such enticing articles as "You Can't Fool Your Other Self," "How We All Reveal Our Soul Secrets," "Speaking of Psychoanalysis: The New Boon for Dinner Table Conversationalists," and so on.[21]

It is hardly surprising that psychoanalysis became so popular. It combined in an almost perfect way the key ingredients of sensationalism—sex, violence, and hidden motives. It appeared to promise a miracle cure for all sorts of ills. It told people what they were *really* like, how they should raise their children, live their lives, and so on. And it appealed to the kind of magical, superstitious thinking characteristic of many people while being couched in the language and authority of science. Thus, people could believe in a mysterious force inside of them that controlled their behavior and still be scientifically *au courant*. In general, psychoanalysis reflected and described precisely that tension in American society created by the repression of sexuality. The conflicts and symptoms this repression caused constituted a major social problem. But complete license was not an acceptable solution for most people. Psychoanalysis both advocated more freedom and yet insisted that it was important to maintain some control (ego) over the dictates of irrational desire (id). It also explained the inconsistencies rampant in Victorian behavior (gentlemen who went to prostitutes, a country that talked constantly of peace but prepared systematically for war, and so on).[22]

The intense popularity of psychoanalysis presented a number of problems for scientific psychology. First, it meant a return, in the guise of science no less, of all those phenomena that psychologists had taken such pains to banish.[23] There were really two problems here: The phenomena themselves were back, and psychology's claim that they were inherently unscientific was being undermined. An even larger problem was that psychology's claim to expertise over mental phenomena was being eroded, thereby endangering large sections of its intellectual turf.

Had psychologists been willing to consign themselves to practicing an esoteric specialty with no particular relation to daily life, they could simply have ignored both these problems and psychoanalysis itself. However, their desire to constitute themselves the arbiters of psychological understanding and to claim expert knowledge over this realm was too strong. Even more nettlesome was the fact that the public confused psychologists with psychoanalysts and thus came to assume that psychology had something to say about dreams, sex, and other personal experiences. Students arrived in introductory psychology courses (and still do) because they wanted to learn about these things and they thought psychology was the place to do it. For all these reasons, there turned out to be no way for psychologists simply to ignore psychoanalysis.

The First Response: Criticize from Outside

Starting around 1915 or so, psychologists began to put forward the argument that psychoanalysis was unscientific and should therefore be discounted on these grounds. A spate of articles of this sort appeared both in psychological journals and in the popular press, varying in tone from careful critique to hysterical outcry. An example of the former is Robert Woodworth's paper in the *Journal of Abnormal Psychology* in 1917, which examines in systematic detail the concept of causality inherent in psychoanalytic thought as a way of showing that conclusions derived from this perspective are not empirically grounded but are based instead on preconceived assumptions.[24] But it was the impassioned attacks in the popular press that received the greatest attention. Christine Ladd Franklin, for example, writing in the *Nation* in 1916, describes psychoanalysis as a product of the "undeveloped" German mind and as an "utterly unscientific" view comparable to witchcraft; she concludes by warning that "unless means can speedily be found to prevent its spread . . , the prognosis for civilization is unfavorable."[25] Unfortunately for psychology, these critiques seemed to fall on deaf ears: The number of popular articles exclaiming the wonders of psychoanalysis increased in the early 1920s,[26] and psychoanalysts themselves seemed uninterested in whether their work was scientific enough to warrant the approbation of psychologists.

The Second Response: Criticize from Within

In the late 1920s and into the 1930s, some psychologists tried a different tack—fighting the enemy from within. For reasons that are not entirely clear and no doubt differed for each individual, a number of experimental psychologists, among them some of the leading lights of the discipline, chose to undergo psychoanalysis themselves, at least in part to find out what the fuss was all about. Some years after they had concluded their analyses, they published accounts of their experiences in a special symposium in the *Journal of Abnormal and Social Psychology* in 1940 entitled "Psychoanalysis as Seen by Analyzed Psychologists."

E. G. Boring's paper, "Was This Analysis a Success?" is particularly revealing of psychologists' mixed feelings. Boring entered analysis because he was depressed and unable to work (to "save face" he told his colleagues that he was investigating the relation between experimental psychology and psychoanalysis). He was critical of the metaphysical assumptions and lack of methodological rigor which in his view characterized psychoanalysis. However, he was also poignantly and painfully trusting in its ability to effect a magical transformation of his personality within the space of ten months. When this appeared not to be forthcoming, he became "desperate" and "distraught." Consoling himself with the belief that this transformation might not emerge until a few months after the end of the analysis, he waited nervously "for a light from heaven, [or] at the very least to be changed from Saul to Paul." Nothing happened. In a plaintive tone, he concluded his paper with the statement, "there is so much about this personality of mine that would be better if different, so much that analysis might have done and did not!" And in the final hope that there might have been some positive outcome that he had overlooked, he persuaded his analyst, Hanns Sachs, to append his own evaluation of the analysis to Boring's paper. Although considerably less naive than Boring, Sachs was no more optimistic about the success of the analysis. As readers, we are supposed to conclude from all of this that experimental psychology was right all along: Psychoanalysis was nothing but a bunch of metaphysical hokum, raising people's hopes only inevitably to disappoint them.[27] But what is also clear is that if psychoanalysis could attract even hard-boiled experimentalists (who appeared drawn to it, almost in spite of themselves), then the public, which didn't care in the slightest whether psychoanalysis was scientific or not, could hardly be blamed for lapping it up.

The Third Response: Co-opt What You Can, Ignore the Rest

It had become clear to psychologists by the 1930s that psychoanalysis was not a passing craze but a serious competitor which threatened the foundations of scientific psychology, at least in the mind of the public. Criticizing it out of hand had not seemed to work. Trying it and then criticizing it hadn't had much effect either. Some other response was needed, and here psychologists took a page from the politician's book and tried the strategy of co-optation. This approach, which continues to be an effective one, involves granting the importance of some of the phenomena psychoanalysts examine while remaining critical of the methods they use to study them. Thus, by the 1930s, we see the beginnings of a movement still in full force today in which psychologists attempt to appropriate for themselves those aspects of such phenomena as emotion, self-awareness, infant experience, psychopathology, and so on that can be made amenable to experimental treatment.

For instance, in an early example of this genre, John B. Watson wrote in 1927 that there *are* certain phenomena corresponding to the realm the psychoanalyst terms the "unconscious" and that these need to be taken seriously by the psychologist. But, Watson argued, this does not mean that one has to resort to the "voodooism" of mental constructs like "conscious" and "unconscious"—these phenomena can be more efficiently examined by the behaviorist strategy of differentiating between the "verbalized" and the "unverbalized."[28]

The main thrust of psychologists' attempts to co-opt psychoanalytic phenomena entailed subjecting these notions to the rigors of quantified experimentation. Thus, starting in the late 1930s and continuing at least into the 1950s, we see a whole host of studies in which such classic psychoanalytic concepts as reaction formation, the Oedipal conflict, the oral character, and so on are brought into the laboratory for careful dissection. The intent of this extensive line of research was to separate the wheat from the chaff: that is, to differentiate those psychoanalytic notions that could be shown to be "scientifically valid" and thus worthy of inclusion in the canon of psychological theory from those that could not and should therefore be discarded."[29] This effort restored psychologists to their rightful role as the arbiters of psychological truth, even if they did at times look a bit silly, as for example, when O. H. Mowrer pronounced reaction formation a meaningful concept because it could be demonstrated to occur in rats.[30]

This strategy of co-optation accomplished several things. First, it demonstrated that scientific psychology was not, in fact, irrelevant to the concerns of ordinary people, that it had something of importance to say about these things. Once psychologists established their expertise over the irrational, psychoanalysts stopped looking as if they had some special claim to their territory. This garnered for psychology some of the public respect that psychoanalysis had generated and enabled psychologists to join analysts in making various public pronouncements about how people should live their lives, bring up their children, run their relationships, and so on. The seemingly limitless market for such statements testifies to the wisdom of this strategy.

But because psychologists took the so-called irrational and subjected it to the rigors of experimental study, they were able to insist that they were not simply aping the analysts but in fact taking over their job and doing it the way it should be done. Thus, the methodological purity which had served as the hallmark of scientific psychology was reasserted and shown to have been right all along.[31] Indeed, if anything, it was strengthened, since if such methods could be used to study even such seemingly metaphysical phenomena as the "self," then this demonstrated the apparent superiority of experimentation as a way of knowing.

The Fourth Response: If All Else Fails, Beat Them at Their Own Game

The strategy of co-opting those psychoanalytic phenomena that could be made amenable to experimental treatment and ignoring or disparaging the rest continues to work well for experimental psychologists. Indeed, it seems to have removed the threat that psychoanalysis once presented to a scientific psychology whose boundaries were diffuse and difficult to maintain. However, experimental psychology now represents but one subarea within a more diverse discipline and, as it turns out, its particular resolution to the problem of psychoanalysis does not hold for other areas of psychology. In particular, the co-optation strategy does not work for the clinicians, who have become the current combatants in the apparently endless struggle between psychology and psychoanalysis.

For reasons that are complex and reflect the ambiguity of clinical psychology's status vis-à-vis psychiatry, an increasing number of clinical psychologists have become interested in receiving psychoanalytic training to expand the range of their professional expertise. However, psychoanalytic training institutes in the United States have insisted since their formation early in the century on restricting admission to only those individuals with a medical degree, that is, psychiatrists.[32] Although Freud himself opposed this policy, and it does not characterize the practice of European institutes, the American Psychoanalytic Association has refused to alter its rules and has for years systematically rejected the applications of psychologists. As a consequence, the American Psychological Association, acting on behalf of its huge clinical constituency, filed a lawsuit several years ago against the American Psychoanalytic Association in an effort to force it to admit psychologists as training candidates. Arguing on the grounds of restraint of trade, the psychologists claimed that the analysts had created a monopoly on psychoanalytic practice and were unfairly limiting competition.[33] In an out-of-court settlement, the psychologists recently won this battle and in so doing have ensured a place for themselves within American psychoanalysis. The irony of this accomplishment, given the earlier history of psychology's hostility to psychoanalysis, hardly needs comment.

The shifting boundaries of American psychology and the difficult task it faced in maintaining its claims to expert knowledge are further illustrated in our second case, that of the rebel popularizer, Grace Adams.

Practical Psychology versus Common Sense

By the 1920s, psychologists had begun to establish arguments for distinguishing their knowledge of human action from that held by the ordinary person. Roback's concept of scientific authority was assumed and the "other-one" was portrayed as deficient in objectivity and rationality. Popularizing psychology afforded a means whereby the laity could begin to understand the superiority of psychologists' knowledge of mental life. They could gain an appreciation of expertise and simultaneously learn the limitations of common sense. Popularization, then, was presumed to be a straightforward process through which scientific knowledge was simplified and presented in a comprehensible form to a lay audience.

At least one psychologist challenged these assumptions about popularization and the laity. Grace Adams employed what was becoming the conventional genre of popularization to disclose some unspoken qualities of the production of scientific psychological knowledge and its implication in popularization. Yet she found popularizing to be a convenient medium, a means to debunk aspects of psychology she had come to disdain. While exposing the hidden life of the popularizing process, she profited by its established presence in American culture. This debunking in turn led her to a rather unusual view, at least for the therapeutic and technocratic ethos of the 1920s and 1930s, that common sense might be the best guide to assessing the mental processes of self and others. As we shall see, her rather radical defense of common sense created a paradox which she seemed unable to remove or transcend.

Without the usual artifacts and imprints of an academic career, there remains little evidence of Grace Adams's professional life. After receiving a B.A. from Randolph-Macon Women's College she did graduate work in psychology under E. B. Titchener at Cornell. Her dissertation research adhered to the Titchenerian experimental tradition: She studied the observer's introspective memory of smells, tastes, colors, sounds, and cutaneous sensations when the usual qualities of the stimulus objects were exchanged for atypical ones (i.e., a rose smelling of lily perfume or a copy of Titchener's *Textbook of Psychology* hollowed out and filled with basswood).[34] Both this research and Adams's popular writing attest to the influence of Titchener on her stance regarding psychology. Although no evidence can be found of Titchener's evaluation of Adams, one observer's opinion was that she stood as a favorite among his "girls."[35] After completing the Ph.D., Adams taught psychology at Goucher College for a year (1923–24) and worked for a year as a psychiatric aide in a private children's home. She then began her popular writing, which stands as both the most concrete marker and the accomplishment of a short career (although there is some evidence that she periodically held positions in public education in the 1950s). These works, appearing between 1928 and 1952, include at least twenty-five articles and five books. Adams died in Spain in 1958. Her career was on the margins of the profession and resembles those of many women psychologists of that generation who could not secure regular positions teaching in universities.[36]

Questioning of Science

During the first six years of her writing (1928 to 1934), Adams's publications were unique among the popular articles on psychology, although she was among a distinguished company of trained psychologists who wrote for the popular press. From the beginning of the century, psychologists had written about the new experimental psychology and especially its practical utility in guiding everyday life. Psychology in all its varieties had the potential to inform self-enlightenment as well as control the social problems that seemed to threaten cultural stability.[37]

Adams's articles contrasted with these exuberant messages of eupsychias.[38] They all contained in varying degrees a chastisement both of psychologists and the reading audience. The negative assessment of American psychology and psychologists was twofold: It included direct accounts of scientific shortcomings and only slightly more subtle critiques of the psychological community itself. The two earliest articles, on animal mentality and human instincts, at first sight appear as fair reviews of research on those subjects. However, both suggest psychologists' slippage from the appropriate scientific standards. American psychology, Adams noted, had "laid its grasp on the human instincts" that were once a subject of biology. In doing so, psychologists had turned away from objective, experimental evidence and instead relied upon logic, and "when the evidence for accepting a group of phenomena into a science is based not on experimental data but on logic, there is no guarantee that this logic will be continually persuasive or that its interpretation will always be the same."[39] To illustrate the frailty of depending on such processes, Adams juxtaposed various psychologists' definitions and enumerations of instincts. Her account not only suggests an arbitrariness in psychological theorizing but more importantly reveals a lack of consensus in the house of psychology.

In later pieces Adams further developed the image of a confused and divided scientific community. In one narrative history, the "decline" of this community is described as a failure to uphold the founding ideals of a rigorous and objective experimental science. After jesting about William James's mysticism, G. S. Hall's religiosity, and John B. Watson's entrepreneurism, the cause of psychology's decline is baldly stated: "What has happened to psychology in America is clear. The objective records of the psychologists themselves tell the tale. Of all the outstanding experimentalists since the science was established here, only one neither deserted his subject nor lowered its standards. And he was never part of America. The mooniness which passes as psychology today is the inevitable result of popularization and neglect."[40]

Adams's twofold strategy was forceful. First, in illustrating the multiple cases where the scientific attitude had been forsaken for fact or popular appeal, credible doubts were cast on the scientific status of an already questionable science. The plethora of contesting theories and the pull of sensationalism apparently weakened the cognitive faculties of even the most objective of psychologists, John B. Watson:

> The most alarming feature of this general trading of psychological terms among the various schools is that it is so contagious that even Dr. Watson is becoming slightly infected whenever he enters the nursery. When he is proclaiming behaviorism from the platform he still denounces the psychoanalysts for the charlatans he has always found them; but when in softer moments he advises young mothers about how to fashion their daughters' nighties and how to powder their sons small behinds, he speaks of inferiority and father fixations as though they were the most respectable of established facts.[41]

Just as objectivity, experimentation, and disinterestedness were found to be substituted by the logic of theorizing, so that logic was infused with metaphysics. Child psychologists had confused understanding with an idealistic worshiping of children: "So instead of casting a cool and disinterested eye upon the brats they found around them, they bestowed upon the 'child soul' all the transcendent virtues of both animals and angels."[42] Once mental hygienists began categorizing neuroses and psychoses they "realized that there was not one door forever locked against their techniques of discovering abnormalities among the seemingly normal."[43] And on Terman's use of school grades as a criterion of his intelligence tests being an "objective measure of intelligence," Adams simply noted that "his brother educators saw nothing paradoxical in using admittedly faulty personal judgment as the final test of the objective tests, themselves."[44] The disregard for scientific methods and experimental procedures was shown to result in psychologists' confusion, a vertigo so serious that it left these scientists less competent on matters of the mind than most laypersons. For instance, in assessing intelligence research Adams concluded that so far the chief result had been to confirm the psychologists' doubts as to the nature of intelligence. "Not only are they not sure what intelligence is; these tests make them uncertain what it is not."[45]

Psychologists' failure to maintain scientific standards supported Adams's reporting of chaos in the scientific household. Identifying fragmentation and even dissent among these scientists probably represented the strongest indictment of American psychology. After all, this portrayal of disorder challenged the common assumption that scientists produce and confirm truths that ultimately are acceptable to their entire community. The argument of a fractured science was enhanced both by Adams's considerable knowledge of the history of psychology and by her rhetorical skill. Through simple but strategical listing of contrasting points of view, nearly every psychological subject that Adams reviewed gave evidence of confused disagreement. Her 1931 book *Psychology: Science or Superstition?* best exemplifies these capabilities with historical narrative. In telling of the rise of an experimental science and its collapse with popularization and the proliferation of ungrounded ideas, Adams interjected the rhetoric of cruel satire. However harsh, her play with history and words was effective:

> Yet from this welter of claims and accusations and denials and even bitterness, one thing seemed permanent: despite all small, internal differences and bickering, there were three distinct and incompatible schools of psychologists: the conscious, the unconscious, and the anticonscious. The pronouncements of any one group must remain forever unintelligible to the other two. There was apparently no hope of compromise or reconciliation.

> Yet the miracle has come to pass. There are today in American universities professors who recognize no conflict between the fundamental positions of the behaviorists, the introspectionists, and the psychoanalysts. They can skip nimbly and agilely from one set of concepts to the other. They can quote Watson in one sentence and Freud in the next as if both gentlemen were talking about identical processes. The only instruments they need are elaborate "restatements" of old theories and a brand new terminology for every book they write.[46]

Whether one's school was conscious or unconscious, it had lost certain analytic skills associated with normal scientific thinking. Adams furnished luring anecdotes to portray this community of confusion. A straightforward listing of the varied papers presented at the 1929 Congress of Psychology created a cacophonous effect beyond that which any carefully honed argument could provide, and her numerical study correlating the rise and fall in popular psychology articles with the stock market before and after the 1929 crash illustrated the profiteering behind American psychology.[47]

Adams's critical stance on practical and popular psychology is consistent with that of her mentor, E. B. Titchener, who had spoken vehemently against the trends toward practical psychology and for retaining rigorous and pure experimental science in the tradition of nineteenth-century German psychology. These claims, along with several efforts to create elite learned societies of experimentalists, earned him a reputation as a purist. Even his rare excursion into popular writing privileges that which is experimental and uninteresting.[48] There is considerable evidence in Adams's early writings that she shared his esteem for pure experimental psychology and a belief in the introspective study of consciousness. However, Titchener is not simply praised but also subjected to her poison pen. Her accounts of Titchener's contributions to experimental science are laced with less praiseworthy character assessments. The failure of the experimental tradition to continue after Titchener's death in 1927 was attributed to his autocratic governing of labs and journals and the consequential absence of competent progeny who could undertake leadership roles.[49] Adams did not hesitate to mention his exploitation of "lady" psychologists and his lifelong allegiance to German rather than American culture.[50] In an article devoted entirely to Titchener's career, his laboratory was likened to both an industrial factory and an empire. Titchener directed his students much like Henry Ford might have instructed assembly line workers: So closely did Titchener identify the men who comprised his department with the subject that he taught them that they seemed to belong to him not only as professional assistants but as human beings.[51] Adams acknowledged Titchener's commitment to psychology but questioned his "quality of affection" for experimental work, noting that "an experimental scientist is a rather different kind of person from a successful executive."[52]

Despite her respect for a particular research tradition, Adams clearly was not an emissary of Titchener's ideology. Even if she had not written so acidly about him, her other major focus of criticism belies any Titchenerian scientific elitism. Embedded in her critiques of contemporary psychology was a critical commentary addressed to the reading audience of nonpsychologists. She found that the failure of the experimental program and the scourge of the practical psychologies was hastened by that "younger generation of college students who, in their high school days, had learned that psychology meant either the personality that helps a salesman sell bonds, or a polite word for smut."[53] Not just students but all participants in the American commercial spirit were implicated:

> Not only were the psychology of business and the psychology of personality popular with students looking for snap courses, but they also find favor with presidents and trustees looking for appropriations. If the graduate students of a university can be put to work discovering the kind of desk kindergarten children prefer, some company manufacturing such desks may be induced to hand over a nice sum to the university.

Or:

> America, to be sure, wanted a science of psychology, and wanted it badly, but Americans reserved the right to construe their own definition of that science. They had no desire to make "impersonal observations"; they had no sympathy with the "disinterested attitude." They asked for results. They demanded of the psychologist that he teach them how to improve their own minds and how to understand and solve their practical psychic problems.[54]

Psychologists' claims to offer a competent technology were, after all, "what the public wanted and what it offered its good dollars for at the bookstores. But eventually it got more than it paid for—and a good headache into the bargain."[55] Given the socioeconomic bases of psychology's popularity, Adams found it quite understandable that Americans' disillusionment with psychology coincided with the Great Depression.

Claims of the public's vulnerability are typically made from an author's distanced position as expert, but Adams rejected such a hierarchical stance. Her accounts of Titchener were in themselves self-indicting, for she herself had been an active member of his autocratic system. Adams's self-reflective gestures went further. In an article on psychiatric care she reported her own professional participation in charlatanism: She wrote candidly of her role in a scam aimed at the rich and through which suffering children were the victims of irresponsible professional practices.[56]

Adams's self-criticism is a clue to the politics undergirding what appears to be simple muckraking. The politics are laid out in the introductory pages of *Psychology: Science or Superstition?* at the point where psychology is differentiated from physical science: "The domain which the psychologist explores is accessible to everyone who realizes that he has a mind."[57] Further, in the 1920s American psychology "had become a popular spectacle of absorbing interest to everyone"; the McDougall-Watson debate captivated the public much like a Dempsey-Firpo fight, and Joseph Jastrow's news columns competed with those of Dorothy Dix.[58] Thus, just as American psychologists (excepting Watson and Titchener) were unwilling to accept the fact that "we are conscious automata,"[59] so the consuming public was unwilling to recognize their role in sensationalizing psychology and especially their potential ability to use their own discerning judgment about mental processes. Between 1928 and 1934 Adams's articles are laced with this two-strand message of reprimand and empowerment. Although she invokes cases where the laity fall prey to psychological jargon, she also intimates their own competency and their ability to be reasonable judges and independent actors.

Reconsidering Common Sense

From 1934 onward Adams's writings reflect a marked change in strategy. The articles and books written between 1934 and 1943 contain rare mention of the technicalities of scientific psychology—its leaders, theories, treatises, or experiments. The writings largely concern practical life problems (although several pieces focus primarily on political and social institutions)[60] and proffer a consistent "theory" for dealing with these problems. Adams continued to castigate experts of the mind and soul along with the laity who blindly rely on them, but the critiques contain a new tactic. The experts over-analyzed human problems and neglected to simply observe real life. As a consequence they imposed ideal and aseptic standards of conduct while failing to appreciate human interaction for the messiness, bumblingness, and spontaneity that make it worthwhile. Parents, it would seem, can barely face their child's simple inquiry into where babies come from. That question "has caused more worry to parents and more needless embarrassment to their offspring, and it has also been responsible for more ponderous books being written and more tedious lectures listened to, than any other five-word sentence that could possibly be fashioned in any language."[61] If people try to explain sexual matters, like obscenity, "in terms of thwarted sex lives, or the emotional strictures of civilization, or some other abstraction invented by the psychologist," they too are "disregarding the facts of common observation." Adams invited readers to imagine a world governed by the utopias implied in psychological theories: "Suppose by some psychological magic not dreamed of, the sexual urge could be so disciplined that human beings would desire and enjoy only its most exalted manifestations and lose all interest in its lowlier ones. Suppose that normal people found no more pleasure in scandal-mongering, or suggestive dancing, or incidental spontaneous love-making. What kind of world would result?"[62] Not only does the experts' advice on how to answer the child's questions about babies result in the child's confusion and reluctance to inquire further, not only does the advice that the mother of adolescent boys should have open, unrepressed conversations on sex encourage those boys to frequent convenient brothels, but these therapeutic guidelines rob life of its mundane if less than noble pleasures.[63]

In these later writings Adams privileged common sense and the common life. Her conception of common life was that children indeed are often selfish, stubborn, and cruel; adolescents are in a murky period of groping and fumbling; and humans are fond of practices such as obscenity. Common sense dictated a method for everyday living, be it mating or parenting: Rather than subscribing to some academic profundity one would be better to take "the more devious path of common human experience."[64] The terms *common sense*, *natural*, and *normal* were reinvested with values they had been denied in recent psychology. In keeping with these prescribed methods Adams's next two books contain only the rarest comment on psychological theory. *Don't Be Afraid*, rather than drawing upon the wealth of research available on fear, actually contains only several such passages; instead it advocates, largely through anecdote, the use of common-sense treatments of fear. Thus, just as one learns through experience to avoid foods that upset the stomach, so one should avoid phobias. Likewise, one ought to confront superstitions and defy them by boldly putting "your cigarette to a match that has already lighted two others." Those banished concepts of "reason" and "conscience" are revised as guides to conduct.[65]

These writings might be interpreted not as advocating common sense and legitimating ordinary judgment processes but rather as unrelenting criticisms of psychology. Adams then might be seen as a Menckenite, an imitator of the period's most famed journalist. Among other things, H. L. Mencken was renowned for pouring "critical acid" on what he viewed as academic pomposity and invented a style of critical journalism that was consumed voraciously by readers and imitated routinely by other writers and editors.[66] Or Adams's invectives might be taken as the reactions of a committed reductionist (like Titchener), a psychologist intolerant of any but a most pure materialist theory.

In her writings on common sense, however, Adams departed substantially from these two figureheads, especially in their denigration of the common man—Mencken through his satire on the "booboisie" and Titchener through dogmatic differentiation between the "trained" and "untrained" observer. Her confidence in the ordinary person's judgment is elucidated in her third book, *Your Child Is Normal*. Like the preceding works, the text criticizes experimental psychologists and other avowed experts on childrearing except that it recognizes those psychologists who rely on natural observation, especially observation of their own children (she argued that physical and mental measurement ignores the complexity and variance of the normal child). Drawing upon the records of these professional-observer parents, Adams developed the thesis that parents' observations are important and can be used to control the child's environment and ultimately influence his/her development. Over and over again, Adams stressed the naturalness of a wide range of behaviors, from displaying lack of special talents to destructiveness and masturbation. She simultaneously reinforced parental judgment in discipline: "Because all children are born into this world innocent of standards of conduct and ignorant of ideals of living, and must, in one way or another, acquire such practical guides from the adults with whom they live most constantly, our influence over them is very real and very potent."[67]

Parents are thus empowered with observational acumen and discerning judgment abilities. Yet, in order to instill these powers, Adams spoke from an empowered position as psychologist and writer, one who can discern good from bad psychological research, natural from unnatural child behaviors, and responsible from nonresponsible parental guidance. Adams both anticipated and challenged the attitude taken by authors of childrearing manuals, the bibles of the post–World War II generation. After all, Benjamin Spock's first book, *The Common Sense Book of Baby and Child Care*, published in 1945, opened with a section entitled "Trust Yourself: Don't Be Afraid to Trust Your Own Common Sense." Yet that command is preceded by another, less confidence-inspiring one: "Bringing up your child won't be a complicated job if you take it easy, trust your own instincts, and follow the directions that your doctor gives you."[68]

Her fourth book, *Workers on Relief*, follows another strategy, for it makes no mention of psychological science. It provides an extensive common-sense analysis of the psychological effects on workers of the

WPA. In keeping with the shift away from formal psychological talk, Adams employed fictional narrative, complete with characters and dialogue. Through the lives of several WPA workers, Adams portrayed the psychological damage rendered by the Depression program intended to increase employment and well-being.[69] Adams's final book was written with her husband, Edward Hutter, in 1942. *The Mad Forties* also is a narrative story, but this time in the form of a loosely fictional history. Through the life story of Mary Gove (Nichols), a nineteenth-century reformer and water-cure physician, Adams and Hutter recounted the medical and psychological fads of the 1840s. The parallels with fads of the twentieth century are hardly disguised. In describing one practitioner of a variation on phrenology, Adams and Hutter compared his work to mental testing: "The aptitude tests, through which the vocational psychologists practice psychometry today, seem merely to complicate and render more mysterious his candid and straightforward technique."[70]

Adams's popular writing, both critiques and advice, resulted in paradox. Despite vitriolic critiques of popular psychology, Adams shifted from criticism to the production of popular psychologies. Her repeated suggestions that readers need not rely on experts to guide their lives but rather might better believe in common sense evolved into something of an expertise of common sense whereby she undertook the authority to pronounce what counted as "normal," "natural," "healthy," and, above all, "common sense experience." In other words, common sense mediates between cultural beliefs and the corpus of formal knowledge, which was becoming known as scientific psychology. Adams appropriated common sense and argued for the empowerment of everyday understanding, yet she did so from the position of expert, the "knower" of scientific psychology and its methods.

Between Common Sense and a Common Science

What can we make of this career in and about the popularization of psychology? Adams's work can and has been taken as simple muckraking, albeit journalism from an enlightened muckraker.[71] Such a classification, however, dismisses a corpus that is at once keenly vested in the hope of a scientific psychology, the eradication of metaphysics, and the protection of human agency and reason. Given this heterodox agenda, it is possible to see Adams's journalistic career as a compromise. Women social scientists of Adams's generation were most likely to find their stellar graduate education leading them to careers at the margins (if anything) of academic life. Their careers meant substantial sacrifices in personal life and in their scientific as well as political, often reformist, beliefs.[72] Adams's writing echoes these dynamics: It combines, but certainly does not blend, the highest ideals of academic science, the politics of individual rights, and the practical attitude of earning one's keep.

Whatever the motivations, the writings of Grace Adams reveal some possibilities and peculiarities in the popularization of psychology. Popularization is not a simple derivative or extension of scientific activity but rather entails transformation of knowledge. Adams herself identified some of these transformative processes and criticized them. Her deconstruction similarly exposed two other suspect assumptions about popularization: that the knowledge being relayed comes from a cohesive, consensual scientific community, and that the relation between scientist-popularizers and audiences is a simple and hierarchical one. Adams revealed tensions, gaps, and contradictions in scientific work and highlighted the interdependence of scientific writers and their readers. One of her chief interests, common sense, underscores a peculiar problem in the popularization of psychology. In order to instill the privilege of their position and the legitimacy of their knowledge, psychologists had to tread the narrow line between denigrating the reader's mental competency and convincing her or him of the cognitive superiority of the psychologists' purchase on social reality. Adams attempted to erase this line only to redraw it, trying to situate common sense (and thus knowledge) somewhere in the middle between expert and layperson. In this regard Adams's work was at the margins: Although challenging the conventions of popular science, she nevertheless was unable to eradicate or transcend the discursive boundaries of this genre of professional writing, boundaries which were constructed upon a privileging of the knowledge transmitted through certain expert voices.

The popularization of psychology, both in its conventional form and in its variations as illustrated by Grace Adams's writings, offers a valuable perspective on the development of scientific psychology. On the surface, such writings reveal scientists' missions that are not included in intellectual histories of science—they represent the public relations of new disciplines. Close analysis of popularization shows how it functions in setting the scientists' status and publicizing their product, at least during the emergence of scientific psychology. Popularization represented a dynamic negotiation about what products psychologists were to manufacture and distribute. To diverge from the formula of scientist as knower, as Adams did, was to invite cultural paradoxes or irony.

The Quandary Continues

The two cases we have examined in this chapter indicate that the boundaries of psychological expertise are intrinsically vulnerable to permeation or transformation and thus have to be negotiated and reclaimed repeatedly. Psychologists' strategies to defend their disciplinary turf have had only limited success: Although a few skirmishes have been won, the war has surely been lost. Indeed, the present situation seems considerably worse than that which existed earlier in the century. Although the expertise of scientific psychology was questioned and sometimes attacked in the 1920s and 1930s, the ideology of the Progressive movement at least ensured that the assertions of psychological "experts" would be taken more seriously than those of the laity. This is hardly the case at present. Almost anyone can write a book, host a TV or radio show, or give a talk which deals with psychological issues, and the public remains hopelessly confused about which of these people are professional psychologists and which are journalists, hucksters, or general self-help advisors. In a vain attempt to stem the tide of ersatz psychologizing, the American Psychological Association decided several years ago to purchase the popular magazine *Psychology Today*. The hope was that if professional psychologists could recapture control over the market for popular psychology, they might be able to upgrade its quality. After losing several million dollars and watching scores of scientific psychologists defect from APA in disgust, the leadership of the organization finally decided to sell the magazine at a considerable loss. Psychologists continue to criticize journalists for misrepresenting their discipline and to debate about the ethics and efficacy of self-help books, but these discussions have done little either to create or maintain a clear boundary between professional and popular psychology.[73]

Why has it been so difficult for psychologists to establish themselves as the arbiters of psychological knowledge? Disciplines ranging from the natural sciences to art history have managed to map out their own unique intellectual terrains and defend them from the intrusions of nonexperts; why haven't psychologists been able to do the same? While no single answer can be given to this broad question, there seems little doubt that part of the problem has to do with the subject matter of psychology. People seem to feel acutely ambivalent about giving the analysis of their private experience over to outsiders, alternately seeking and rejecting the opinions of these "experts." For psychology to succeed in garnering for itself hegemony over the psychological realm, it would have to persuade people that they were entirely incapable of understanding the conduct and meaning of their own lives. That the public resists such attempts is unsurprising. And yet the very complexity of contemporary life makes people aware that they do not in fact know how to cope with many of the situations facing them and, in this sense, they desire advice. The problem for psychologists is that the public is willing to be eclectic, to take any advice that seems to make sense, whether it arises from science, common sense, or divine revelation. Unlike their natural science colleagues, psychologists have failed to establish the scientific way of knowing as clearly superior to other means. However, professional psychology can reassure itself that at least it has succeeded in establishing its claims as no less credible than those of its competitors; in this respect, it has fared better than philosophy.

Notes

1. Edward B. Titchener, *A Text-Book of Psychology* (New York: Macmillan, 1910), p. 350.
2. G. Stanley Hall, "Research, the Vital Spirit of Teaching," *Forum* 17 (1894): 558–70.
3. Robert M. Yerkes, *Introduction to Psychology* (New York: Henry Holt, 1911), p. 13.
4. Carl E. Seashore, *Introduction to Psychology* (New York: Macmillan, 1923), p. viii.
5. M. Meyer, *The Psychology of the Other-One* (Columbia: Missouri Book, 1922). These social distinctions were crucial to early social psychologists. See J. G. Morawski, "Contextual Discipline: The Unmaking and Remaking of Sociality," in *Contextualism and Understanding in Behavioral Science*, ed. Ralph L. Rosnow and Marianthi Georgoudi (New York: Praeger, 1987), pp. 47–66.
6. For historical accounts of the social roles in experimentation, see Kurt Danziger, "A Question of Identity: Who Participated in Psychological Experiments?" in *The Rise of Experimentation in American Psychology*, ed. Jill G. Morawski (New Haven: Yale University Press, 1988), pp. 35–52; Karl E. Scheibe, "Metamorphosis in the Psychologist's Advantage," in ibid., pp. 53–71. For some examples of the "more scientific than thou" attitude between psychologists themselves, see E. W. Scripture, "Accurate Work in Psychology," *American Journal of Psychology* 6 (1894): 427–30; George Trumbull Ladd, "Is Psychology a Science?" *Psychological Review* 1 (1894): 392–95.
7. Ludy T. Benjamin, "Why Don't They Understand Us? A History of Psychology's Public Image," *American Psychologist* 41 (1986): 941–46; John C. Burnham, *How Superstition Won and Science Lost: Popularizing Science and Health in the United States* (New Brunswick: Rutgers University Press, 1987).
8. There is now a growing literature on psychologists' claimmaking. See Michael M. Sokal, "James McKeen Cattell and American Psychology in the 1920s," in *Explorations in the History of Psychology in the United States*, ed. Joseph Brozek (Lewisburg, Pa.: Bucknell University Press, 1984), pp. 273–323; John C. Burn-

ham, "The New Psychology: From Narcissism to Social Control," in *Change and Continuity in Twentieth Century America: The Nineteen Twenties*, ed. J. Braeman, R. H. Bremmer, and D. Brody (Columbus: Ohio State University Press, 1968); Ben Harris, "Give Me a Dozen Healthy Infants: John B. Watson's Popular Advice on Childrearing, Women, and the Family," in *In the Shadow of the Past: Psychology Portrays the Sexes*, ed. Miriam Lewin (New York: Columbia University Press, 1984), pp. 126–54; Ben Harris and Jill Morawski, "John B. Watson's Predictions for 1979," paper presented at the annual meeting of the Eastern Psychological Association, Philadelphia, April 1979; J. G. Morawski, "Assessing Psychology's Moral Heritage through Our Neglected Utopias," *American Psychologist* 37 (1982): 1082–95.

9. John G. Cawelti, *Apostles of the Self-Made Man* (Chicago: University of Chicago Press, 1965); T. J. Jackson Lears, "From Salvation to Self-Realization: Advertising and the Therapeutic Roots of Consumer Culture, 1880–1930" and Christopher P. Wilson, "The Rhetoric of Consumption: Mass-Market Magazines and the Demise of the Gentle Reader," in *The Culture of Consumption 1880–1920: Critical Essays in American History 1880–1980*, ed. Richard W. Fox and T. J. Jackson Lears (New York: Pantheon Books, 1983), pp. 3–38, 41–64; JoAnne Brown, "Professional Language: Words that Succeed," *Radical History Review* 34 (1986): 33–51.

10. D. Kevles, *The Physicists: The History of a Scientific Community in Modern America* (New York: Knopf, 1977).

11. R. C. Tobey, *The American Ideology of National Sciences, 1919–1930* (Pittsburgh, Pa.: University of Pittsburgh Press, 1971); J. G. Morawski, "Psychologists for Society and Society for Psychologists: SPSSI's Place among Professional Organizations," *Journal of Social Issues* 42 (1986): 111–26.

12. W. E. Leuchtenburg, *The Perils of Prosperity, 1914–1932* (Chicago: University of Chicago Press, 1955), p. 164.

13. A. A. Roback, *Popular Psychology* (Cambridge, Mass.: Sci-Arb Publishers, 1928), pp. 17–18.

14. Leona Marshall Libby, *The Uranium People* (New York: Crane Russak, 1979), p. 17.

15. There is a growing literature on the multiple functions of popularizing science and the roles of scientists and audiences. An extensive reanalysis of popularization is undertaken in Terry Shinn and Richard Whitely, eds., *Expository Science: Forms and Functions of Popularization* (Boston: D. Reidel, 1985). See also Dorothy Nelkin, *Selling Science: How the Press Covers Science and Technology* (New York: W. H. Freeman, 1987); Frank M. Turner, "Public Science in Britain, 1880–1919," *Isis* 71 (1980): 589–608; Burnham, *How Superstition Won*.

16. The Luther Trant series was written by E. Balmer and W. B. MacHarg and was published in *Hampton's Broadway Magazine* intermittently from 1909–1911. We are indebted to Michael Sokal for bringing these materials to our attention.

17. See Burnham, *How Superstition Won*, pp. 91, 94.

18. Indeed Burnham notes (ibid., p. 85) that for much of the nineteenth century, knowledge of "psychology" was the property of any educated person.

19. For a detailed discussion of these other forms of psychotherapy popular at the turn of the century, see N. G. Hale, Jr., *Freud and the Americans: The Beginnings*

of Psychoanalysis in the United States, 1876-1917 (New York: Oxford University Press, 1971), esp. chaps. 6 and 9.

20. Ibid., p. 397.

21. For a few examples of such articles, see P. C. Macfarlane, "Diagnosis by Dreams," *Good Housekeeping* 60 (1915): 125-33, 278-86; F. Dell, "Speaking of Psychoanalysis: The New Boon for Dinner Table Conversationalists," *Vanity Fair* 5 (1915): 52-53; J. P. Toohey, "How We All Reveal Our Soul Secrets," *Ladies Home Journal* 34 (1917): 97; B. Barton, "You Can't Fool Your Other Self," *American Magazine* 92 (1921): 11-13, 68. There was also a detective series, reminiscent of the Luther Trant stories, which featured Craig Kennedy solving mysterious crimes through dream analysis and psychoanalytic interpretation. See, for example, A. B. Reeve, "The Dream Doctor," *Cosmopolitan* 55 (1913): 325-34, and "The Psychic Scar," *Cosmopolitan* 64 (1918): 85-89, 128-31.

22. See Hale, *Freud and the Americans*, esp. chaps. 2, 10, and 13; Burnham, *How Superstition Won*; A. Bugbee, "The Popularization of Psychoanalysis," unpublished paper, Department of Psychology, Mount Holyoke College, 1988; P. T. Cominos, "Late Victorian Sexual Respectability and the Social System," *International Review of Social History* 8 (1963): 18-48, 216-50.

23. T. H. Leahey and G. E. Leahey, *Psychology's Occult Doubles: Psychology and the Problem of Pseudoscience* (Chicago: Nelson-Hall, 1983) discuss this general issue in detail. And, consistent with the present analysis, they note (p. 14) that psychology's occult doubles (e.g., phrenology, mesmerism, spiritualism, etc.) can be seen as the "dark, unconscious side of establishment psychology."

24. R. S. Woodworth, "Some Criticisms of the Freudian Psychology," *Journal of Abnormal Psychology* 12 (1917): 174-94.

25. C. L. Franklin, letter to the editor, *Nation*, 19 October 1916, pp. 373-74.

26. Burnham, "The New Psychology"

27. E. G. Boring, "Was This Analysis a Success?" *Journal of Abnormal and Social Psychology* 35 (1940): 9-10; H. Sachs, "Was This Analysis a Success?—Comment," pp. 11-16. The rest of the symposium includes papers by C. Landis, J. F. Brown, R. R. Willoughby, P. M. Symonds, H. A. Murray, E. Frenkel-Brunswick, D. Shakow, R. Alexander, and A. B. Wood. They vary in their conclusions about psychoanalysis, and some of the more clinically minded psychologists are reasonably positive, but it can hardly be said that the symposium as a whole did anything to improve the overall relation of psychology to psychoanalysis.

28. J. B. Watson, "The Myth of the Unconscious," *Harpers Magazine* 155 (1927): 502-3.

29. The key epistemological issue raised by this research and by the general struggle between experimental psychology and psychoanalysis has to do with what will be taken to count as data. Experimental psychologists steadfastly refused (and still do) to consider clinical evidence to be data. It therefore goes without saying that if experimental data constitute the only "real" data, then psychoanalysis is indeed not a data-based theory. That the argument was joined in this way is, however, not surprising, since the primary characteristic that differentiated late nineteenth-century experimental psychologists from the philosophers who were studying many of the same problems was the fact that the former relied

on experimental data. Psychologists have thus been obliged to defend the necessity of such data at all costs or risk the foundation of their whole enterprise. Thus we see Boring in his *History of Experimental Psychology*, 2d ed. (New York: Appleton-Century-Crofts, 1950), p. 713, calling psychoanalysis "prescientific," because "it lacked experiments, having developed no technique for control." He does grant that "psychoanalysis has provided hypotheses galore" which can then be rigorously tested by experimental psychologists. Since, in terms of the ideology of the experimental method, hypotheses arise from "hunches" and other unknown intuitive processes, this is not much of a compliment.

30. O. H. Mowrer, "An Experimental Analogue of 'Regression' with Incidental Observations on 'Reaction Formation,'" *Journal of Abnormal and Social Psychology* 35 (1940): 56–87. Many of these kinds of studies have been assembled in collections which evaluate the general "scientific status" of psychoanalytic theory. See, for example, P. Kline, *Fact and Fantasy in Freudian Theory*, 2d ed. (London: Methuen, 1972); H. J. Eysenck and G. D. Wilson, *The Experimental Study of Freudian Theories* (London: Methuen, 1973).

31. For a detailed history of this methodological ideal, see Gail A. Hornstein, "Quantifying Psychological Phenomena: Debates, Dilemmas, and Implications," in *Rise of Experimentation*, pp. 1–34.

32. For general histories of American psychoanalysis, see C. P. Oberndorf, *A History of Psychoanalysis in America* (New York: Grune and Stratton, 1953); J. C. Burnham, *Psychoanalysis and American Medicine, 1894–1918: Medicine, Science, and Culture* (New York: International Universities Press, 1967); Hale, *Freud and the Americans*; J. M. Quen and E. T. Carlson, eds., *American Psychoanalysis: Origins and Development* (New York: Brunner/Mazel, 1978).

33. See Bryant Welch, Ph.D., et al. against American Psychoanalytic Association et al., memorandum in support of plaintiffs' motion for class certification, 14 October 1987, unpublished legal brief, pp. 4–71; Anonymous, "Psychologists Continue Battle for Recognition in Psychoanalytic Suit" and "Impact from the Psychoanalytic Suit and Other Legal Actions Favors Psychology," *Practitioner* 2 (Winter 1988): 9–10; J. Buie, "Psychoanalysis: Lawsuit Takes Aim on Barriers to Training, Practice for Non-MDs" and "Analysis Plaintiffs Allege Restraint, Economic Harm," *APA Monitor* 19 (February 1988): 1, 14–15; J. Buie, "Psychoanalytic Group Bolstered by Legal Win," *APA Monitor* 19 (December 1988): 21.

34. Grace Kinckle Adams, "An Experimental Study of Memory Color and Related Phenomena," *American Journal of Psychology* 34 (1923): 359–407.

35. Oral history of Cora Friedline, 3 May 1966, pp. 13–14, Archives of the History of American Psychology, Akron, Ohio. In correspondence, Titchener repeatedly referred to Yerkes's "girl" students: "They are good girls, and have worked hard; and once they catch the attitude they ought to psychologize all right." E. B. Titchener to R. M. Yerkes, 5 May 1907, Robert Yerkes Papers, Sterling Library, Yale University, New Haven.

36. There is now a substantial research literature on the careers of women in psychology and related disciplines. These studies report the frequent pattern of professional marginalization: if women could secure employment in universities, it was typically in auxiliary roles. Women researchers often took positions in

applied areas; some left their field entirely. See Penina M. Glazer and Miriam Slater, *Unequal Colleagues: The Entrance of Women into the Professions, 1890–1940* (New Brunswick: Rutgers University Press, 1987); Laurel Furumoto, "Shared Knowledge: The Experimentalists, 1904–1929," in *The Rise of Experimentation*, pp. 94–113; Rosaland Rosenberg, *Beyond Separate Spheres: Intellectual Roots of Modern Feminism* (New Haven: Yale University Press, 1982); Margaret Rossiter, *Women Scientists in America: Struggles and Strategies to 1940* (Baltimore: Johns Hopkins University Press, 1982); Elizabeth Scarborough and Laurel Furumoto, *Untold Lives: The First Generation of American Women Psychologists* (New York: Columbia University Press, 1987).

37. See nn. 8 and 9.

38. Historian Frank Manuel coined the term *eupsychias* to refer to the twentieth-century reliance on psychological thinking in the formulation of utopian plans. For a review of psychologists' formal and informal utopias between 1915 and 1930, see Morawski, "Assessing Psychology's Moral Heritage."

39. "Human Instincts," *American Mercury* 14 (August 1928):456–57; "Animal Mentality," *American Mercury* 15 (October 1928): 196–99.

40. "Decline of Psychology in America," *American Mercury* 15 (December 1928): 453. The "one," of course, was Titchener.

41. "Babel of the Psyche," *American Mercury* 20 (August 1930): 462.

42. "Minds of Children," *American Mercury* 30 (December 1933): 471.

43. "Golden Age of Mental Hygiene," *American Mercury* 23 (May 1931): 95.

44. "Measuring the American Mind," *American Mercury* 17 (June 1929): 194.

45. Ibid., p. 198.

46. *Psychology: Science or Superstition?* (New York: Covici, Friede, 1931), p. 257.

47. Adams frequently referred to the economic forces behind the rise of practical psychology. These claims are most developed in *Psychology: Science or Superstition?* and "The Rise and Fall of Psychology," *Atlantic Monthly* 153 (January 1934): 82–92.

48. See E. B. Titchener, "Recent Advances in Psychology," *International Monthly* 2 (1900): 154–68.

49. See especially "Decline of Psychology," p. 453.

50. Ibid., pp. 450–53.

51. "Titchener at Cornell," *American Mercury* 24 (December 1931): 444.

52. Ibid., p. 446.

53. "Decline of Psychology," p. 453.

54. Ibid., "Titchener at Cornell," p. 442.

55. "Rise and Fall of Psychology," p. 92.

56. "A Few Carefully Selected Children," *American Mercury* 31 (January 1934): 74–82.

57. *Psychology: Science or Superstition?*, p. 16.

58. Ibid., pp. 19–20.

59. Ibid., p. 276.

60. These include "Comrades, Lay Off!" *Harpers* 176 (January 1938): 218–20; "White Collar Clothes," *Harpers* 177 (October 1928): 474–84; *Workers on Relief* (New Haven: Yale University Press, 1939).

61. "Where Do Babies Come From?" *American Mercury* 32 (August 1934): 489.

62. "The Lesser Ways of Love," *American Mercury* 34 (January 1935): 29.

63. "Where Do Babies Come From?"; "Lesser Ways of Love."

64. "Lesser Ways of Love," p. 28.

65. *Don't Be Afraid* (New York: Covici, Friede, 1935), pp. 91, 115, 176–87.

66. Frederick Lewis Allen, *Only Yesterday: An Informal History of the Nineteen-Twenties* (New York: Harper and Brothers, 1931), p. 192. Mencken started and edited the *American Mercury*, to which Adams contributed a number of articles. In the announcement of the magazine in 1924, the editor promised that it would be devoted "pleasantly to exposing the nonsensicality of all such hallucinations (as Marxism, Prohibition), particularly when they show a certain apparent plausibility." Frederick J. Hoffman, *The Twenties: American Writing in the Postwar Decade*, rev. ed. (New York: Free Press, 1955), p. 348.

67. *Your Child Is Normal: The Psychology of Young Childhood* (New York: Covici, Friede, 1934), pp. 236–37.

68. Benjamin Spock, *The Common Sense Book of Baby and Child Care* (New York: Duell, Sloan and Pearce, 1945), p. 3.

69. *Workers on Relief* (New Haven: Yale University Press, 1939), pp. 236–37.

70. Grace Adams and Edward Hutter, *The Mad Forties* (New York: Harper and Brothers, 1942), p. 132.

71. Indeed, Adams's early popularized critiques were considered scandalous among some psychologists. Robert Yerkes reported being distressed and referred to her *Mercury* articles as an "outpouring." Boring claimed to have been so upset that he wrote Mencken and even submitted a "corrective" to one of her articles. Boring as well as others mentioned that Adams left academic work for freelance writing because she had broken "some smoking rules." On the other hand, Boring and Yerkes as well as Hull found her first book to be a refreshing and accurate analysis of the problem besetting American psychology. Yerkes to Boring, 4 December 1931; Boring to Yerkes, 7 December 1931; Yerkes to Boring, 12 December 1931, Robert Yerkes Papers, Sterling Memorial Library, Yale University, New Haven; Clark L. Hull, "The Conflicting Psychologies of Learning—A Way Out," *Psychological Review* 42 (1935): 492.

72. See n. 36. Also see Gail Agronick, "Feminist Psychologists, 1915–1930: Personal, Political, Professional Constraints," B.A. thesis, Wesleyan University, 1988.

73. For a representative critique of journalists' reporting on psychology, see Carol Tavris, "How to Publicize Science: A Case Study," in J. H. Goldstein, ed., *Reporting Science: The Case of Aggression* (Hillsdale, N.J.: Lawrence Erlbaum Associates, 1986), pp. 21–32. For a review of the discussion regarding popular self-help books, see G. M. Rosen, "Self-Help Treatment Books and the Commercialization of Psychotherapy," *American Psychologist* 42 (1987): 46–51; also see commentaries on Rosen's article, *American Psychologist* 43 (1987): 598–600.

■ 7 MENTAL MEASUREMENTS AND THE RHETORICAL FORCE OF NUMBERS

JOANNE BROWN

The familiar "method" of Science, whatever its logical and epistemological virtue, also has tremendous *rhetorical* power. If applied correctly, it has overwhelming persuasive force.
—J. M. ZIMAN, 1968

The Americans, who love to do things big, often publish experiments made on hundreds and even thousands of persons. They believe that the conclusive value of a work is proportional to the number of observations made.
—ALFRED BINET, 1903

The enterprise of measuring intelligence, culminating just before World War I in standardized mental tests, carried into the realm of mental life the quantitative ethos that had come to dominate the older professions of medicine and engineering during the nineteenth century. Psychologists in the United States after 1880 organized their thinking about mental *capacity*, mental *speed*, and mental *hygiene* according to the evolving, increasingly statistical logic of medicine and engineering.[1] By following, analogically, the methods of science as defined in these two better-established professions, scholars in the nascent field of psychology drew upon the prestige of medicine and engineering in ways that are not entirely obvious. Quantitative methods became in psychology a vocabulary with considerable persuasive force.

Professional engineers and physicians during the Progressive era shared a technical rhetorical style, or voice, that reflected and celebrated their considerable theoretical and practical accomplishments. It was an impersonal voice that admitted nothing of politics, family, religion, or personality; this disinterested stance was one of the hallmarks of a bureaucratic Progressivism, a reaction to the perceived corruption and nepotism of traditional American politics. In addition to adopting a psychological vocabulary based on medical and engineering metaphors, psychologists adopted this cool, impersonal technical voice as their own.[2] Their style implied, syntactically, that the research results and policy recommendations growing out of psychological testing were purely scientific, matters of wide consensus, or even facts of nature and unrelated to the political or personal interests of the researchers.

A prominent feature of scientific and professional language is its virtual obliteration of personal opinion stated as such. The passive voice prevails: "The contention here supported is that human efficiency is a variable quantity that [varies] according to law."[3] In instances where the statement does require a personal pronoun, "we" is often substituted for "I," lending a subtle atmosphere of consensus to one author's opinion: "our efforts have too long been directed by 'trial and error' "; "greater efficiency, we are always working for."[4] Members of the opposition do not get the same rhetorical company; in professional discourse, third person is usually singular. Thus one psychologist wrote of the World War I army testing program, "Early experience showed that a soldier's own estimate of his own skill could not be trusted, even when he had the best intentions."[5] This subtle shift in the expression of general or impersonal statements implies that "we" the professional scientists are many; our subject, or potential critic, is alone—even though, in this example, the psychologists were working with more than a million soldiers. In small grammatical and syntactic ways, psychologists allied themselves with an informed and intelligent majority and upheld the public good against (semantically) isolated and ignorant critics, doubters, and subjects.[6]

As the psychologists of the testing movement understood it, science and scientific method, unlike traditional "philosophical" methods, led inevitably to consensus. Scientific method was therefore equally useful in the laboratory and in the political arena. Among the scientists most admired and most often cited by the American psychologists of the testing movement was British statistician Karl Pearson, a student of Sir Francis Galton and his biographer. Pearson is remembered for his statistical invention, Pearson's r. In 1892 Pearson articulated the scientific approach to social polity in *The Grammar of Science*: "It is because the so-called philosophical method does not . . . lead, like the scientific, to practical unanimity of judgment, that science, rather than philosophy, offers the better training for modern citizenship."[7] Conceiving scientific truth as consensus begs the question of whose opinions are to be taken into account. The psychologists of the testing movement were not oblivious to this problem but answered it with reasoning that was tautological, at best. According to Columbia University psychologist E. L. Thorndike, "The rule then is that what the expert in the science of education deems scientific has the greatest probability of being so."[8] Thorndike's student Truman Lee Kelley, a most prominent American statistician of his day, boldly stated that consensus, in order to be scientific, must be a "weighted consensus" among experts. "Where there is disagreement," concluded Kelley, "the minority is in error."[9]

The publication of the numerical results of psychological tests and surveys contributed to the persuasive force of psychology's scientific method. Psychologists joined sociologists and anthropologists during the Progressive years in contributing to the mass of statistical information available on pressing social problems. Social-scientific surveys of the public schools became conspicuous public symbols of a true "progressive" spirit among educators, and psychologists seized these opportunities to publicize the usefulness of their complicated testing methods while aiding the cause of public education. The author of a school survey taken in St. Paul, Minnesota, in 1917 explained that the facts, as elicited by mental tests, spoke for themselves: "The results are given in tables of figures and in graphic representations. They are thus rendered objective and tangible. Any reader may interpret them in any manner he finds possible." Publication in and of itself, the author argued, automatically rendered the data objective. This absolved the reporter of responsibility for the test results: "The writer of this report is as little responsible for the facts of the tables and graphs as he would be for the heights of the men in a regiment of soldiers which he had measured with a meter stick. The facts revealed tell their own story which may be read by any who have learned the language of educational measurement."[10]

The American psychologists held that the large numbers of questions in a given test, and of individuals in a given group tested, were sufficient to factor out any taint of personal opinion that, in the view of test advocates, commonly polluted traditional examinations.[11] The larger the sample of individuals tested and the more questions in each test, the more objective were the results expected.[12] Sheer agglomeration distinguished the new tests from old-fashioned methods. Although the new tests were always standardized against the "known" intelligence of subjects, a knowledge usually based on the opinions of schoolteachers, psychologists claimed on the basis of large numbers of figures that the new tests were superior to "mere" opinion. Edward Thorndike, who spent his career in the company of teachers, attributed the superiority of scientific tests to their plurality. In a 1913 article called "Educational Diagnosis," Thorndike explained science in evangelical tones: "Experiments measuring the effects of school subjects and methods seem pedantic and inhuman beside the spontaneous tact and insight of the gifted teacher. But his personal work is confined by time and space to reach only a few; their results join the free common fund of science which increases the more, the more it is used, and lives forever."[13] Numbers, it seemed, guaranteed not only truth but immortality.

Unlike traditional evaluations, psychologists asserted, the new scientific tests were not compromised by personal, ethnic, or political circumstances. In the context of widely perceived conflict concerning school politics, this neutrality was a powerful asset. Educator Paul Hanus and psychologist Edward Lincoln, both of Harvard University, emphasized this asset in reporting on their survey of twelve Massachusetts Cape towns: "These measuring instruments . . . yield results which are not influenced by friendship, family ties, local patriotism, or any form of prejudice. They are not perfect measuring instruments, but have been found to be much more dependable than the subjective judgments of teachers."[14]

This stance of political neutrality mimicked that of contemporary physicians and engineers. Physicians argued that their profession let them carry the "flag of truce" in all social conflicts. According to Edwin Layton's study of engineering-society presidential addresses, Progressive era engineers saw themselves as logical thinkers, free from personal bias and thus suited to the role of arbiter between classes.[15] Sociologists and historians of the professions have identified this neutrality as a key characteristic of aspiring professional groups.[16]

Professionals seek to achieve political neutrality by exchanging personal opinion for group authority. As historical sociologist Paul Starr observes, "They claim authority not as individuals, but as members of a community that has objectively validated their competence." As Starr explains, "The professional offers advice, not as a personal act based on privately revealed or idiosyncratic criteria, but as a representative of a community of shared standards."[17] Psychologists, like the doctors and engineers who were their models, found two kinds of strength in numbers. Psychologists gathered themselves in large numbers into professional associations, and they gathered volumes of statistics on mental characteristics and their correlates. Thus on both the social and the epistemological level, numbers were a significant aspect of professional power. Because psychologists explicitly defined scientific truth in terms of consensus, their ability to augment their membership and create consensus within their professional community through the use of metaphor and the impersonal scientific voice and their ability to conduct numerous large-scale studies with published, quantitative results were key features of their cultural authority and political success. The psychologists worked during an era characterized by a fondness for large numbers; both their language, which made a small profession appear larger, and their numerical research methods, by which hitherto immeasurable phenomena were gauged and counted, contributed to their professional prestige within this cultural context.[18]

School Surveys: Power in Numbers

Beginning in 1904 with the publication of Edward Thorndike's textbook on mental and social measurements in education, school officials became increasingly enthusiastic about the potential for dramatic policy changes that might result from quantitative investigations of the public schools. These surveys, modeled after the industrial and administrative investigations of efficiency engineers and after public health surveys, were conducted in hundreds of schools between 1909 and 1944. As one historian has put it, "it seems there was hardly a state or local school system in America that was not surveyed."[19] The surveys generally were commissioned by city or state governments with the primary aim of justifying tax expenditures, but they were welcomed by various reform groups who used the resulting statistics to promote specific educational policies.

The prototypical school survey, such as the Gary, Indiana, survey, was an exhaustive study of every imaginable aspect of school administration. Spelling, arithmetic, and geography performance was studied, measured, and recorded alongside classroom lighting, heating, and sanitation; incidence of contagious and congenital "defects" and diseases were also listed. Often surveyors paid special attention to the nativity and socioeconomic status of schoolchildren and teachers, and children were frequently classified and compared according to race and gender. The progressive-scientific attitude, while often denying the importance of such cultural and heritable differences for the practice of social scientific research, paid close, even obsessive attention to such differences among its subjects. Researchers attempted to correlate the school system's expenditures on certain kinds of instruction with children's achievement in the same area. Correlations between the results of medical inspections and classroom performance were particularly common, for they often justified medical programs while excusing or explaining poor educational performance.

By the turn of the century, public health reformers had achieved considerable political success by amassing statistics on the efficiency of one or another public health technique.[20] Municipal governments were gathering similar figures about their various operations to account for the use of tax dollars. As Robert Wiebe aptly observes, "It seemed that the age could only be comprehended in bulk," and everything from sinners to telephones was counted.[21] In his introduction to the Progressive social-policy statement *The Wisconsin Idea* (1912), Theodore Roosevelt argued that "without means of attainment and measures of result an ideal becomes meaningless." Social progress, Roosevelt argued, depended on measurement: "The real idealist is a pragmatist and an economist. He demands measurable results. . . . Only in this way is social progress possible."[22] American psychologists were thus part of a larger historical pattern of quantification as it pertained to social problems.

The Wisconsin Idea, which entailed government utilization of university talents in research, gave a philosophical rationale and institutional structure to the already popular enterprise of counting and measuring.[23] Progressive intellectuals, responding in part to Frederick Jackson Turner's famous frontier thesis, argued that "the test-tube and the microscope, not the axe and rifle," were the necessary tools on the new American frontier of science.[24] An "information fever" pervaded Progressive-era social reform, and it seems inevitable that it should soon infect the vulnerable administrators of the public schools, already weakened by intense public criticism.[25]

Many beleaguered school officials welcomed the school surveys, for in the very welcoming gesture they raised their own professional status.[26] As one educator noted, referring to Salt Lake City's impending school survey, "That the city has asked for a plain statement of actual conditions is an indication of a progressive educational spirit."[27] Frank W. Ballou, Boston's superintendent of schools, saw the movement for educational measurement and school surveys as a boon to "educational efficiency." In 1914, he praised the leaders of the measurement movement: "They have realized that the increased prestige of the educational profession depends on the adoption by the profession of the scientific attitude. The profession demands it, the public demands it, and in this direction lies the opportunity of our profession."[28] Another writer concerned with the status of education hoped that "units and scales of measurement" would "do much toward convincing the honest critics of the schools the real value of the work being done, as well as toward placing teaching more firmly on a professional basis."[29] These writers welcomed almost any measuring device that would help answer critics of the schools' efficiency, and it was in this context that the psychologists introduced their new mental tests into the schools.

Years before psychologists began to speak of "human engineering" and the efficient use of "pupil material," educators themselves were mimicking engineers by adopting the self-consciously "scientific" language of statistics in order to enhance their own professional status and make sense of the problems at hand. The president of the Boise, Idaho, school board praised the results of a quick school survey done in 1913 by some of E. L. Thorndike's students. The president was glad to see that education had "at last reached a stage of development that it is indeed a profession." The Boise survey, he observed, "will certainly compare favorably with expert reports made by engineers etc."[30]

Proponents of the school survey frankly admitted that statistical studies were educators' best defense against critical attack.[31] The first school surveys, done by independent journalists in the late 1890s, relied heavily on traditional tests of school achievement. Most influential among these studies were the investigations of Joseph Mayer Rice, a physician-turned-muckraker. His national study of public schools, printed first in the *Forum* magazine, then as *The Public School System of the United States* in 1893, was a scathing assault on traditional pedagogy. In his 1913 best-seller, *Scientific Management in Education*, Rice applied the Progressive panacea to the ailing schools and earned himself a name in the measurement movement. His status as a physician likely did him no harm; Rice himself had developed standardized achievement tests for spelling and arithmetic as early as 1900.

This kind of achievement testing became the basis for Leonard P. Ayres's famous exposé, *Laggards in Our Schools*, in 1909. Ayres had already written *Medical Inspection of Schools* in 1908 with the physician and health reformer Luther Halsey Gulick. Medical investigations of the health of schoolchildren, like the mental tests they anticipated, served in part to relieve schools and teachers of the blame for educational failure. This is not to say that proponents of school hygiene harbored only base motives but that the pervasive defensiveness among educators in the prewar decade encouraged them to welcome any explanation for deteriorating school conditions and rising costs that would not undermine their own shaky profession.[32] By mounting large-scale investigations of the schools, resulting in pages of statistics, educators made their defense in terms that critics could not easily answer, simply because no school board or city government was likely to commission more than one survey, so great was the expense and so tedious were the methods involved.[33]

By 1917, many major cities already had established bureaus of educational research: Boston, Detroit, Dubuque, Kansas City, Louisville, New York, Oakland, Rochester, and St. Paul all boasted these Progressive institutions. Psychologists thus were able to use the existing framework of the school survey to promote their new mental tests. They argued that achievement tests (the favorite tool of school efficiency engineers) were virtually meaningless unless each pupil's innate capacity for learning was also known. This argument had even greater appeal to teachers than the arguments for achievement testing, for it divided responsibility for performance among the pupils, rather than apportioning to teachers complete responsibility for success or failure.[34] As one surveyor explained, intelligence tests show "the sort of pupil material with which the classroom teacher has to work."[35] Just as, in the school hygiene movement, medical examinations of schoolchildren had succeeded sanitary inspections of the school buildings, intelligence tests succeeded achievement tests. In both cases, the latter development emphasized the innate qualities or chronic condition of the schoolchild rather than the school environment itself.

Authors of school surveys alternated engineering metaphors with medical terms, such that words like "gauge" and "diagnose," "treatment" and "material" lost all metaphorical sense and became standard technical vocabulary. When metaphors thus become part of a technical vocabulary, their larger implications become less obvious, less open to question. In a survey of Portland, Oregon, schools, a Stanford research team that included Lewis Terman on child hygiene advised that children too old for their grades be organized into separate classes, "so that they may receive the treatment that their condition requires."[36] In another survey, a Teachers College research group reported on having "fairly measured" the "products of the St. Paul schools." Peoria surveyors used the Illinois test "for measuring the quality of pupil material."[37] Boston school superintendent Jeremiah Burke requested a school survey to acquire "a body of statistical information relating to the age, retardation, elimination, persistency and salvage of pupils."[38] In a survey of schools in Buffalo, New York, researchers recommended that a permanent department of measurement be established, for "diagnosing problem cases on a scientific basis." Such a "laboratory" or "clinic," the authors recommended, "should not be confined to making routine psychological tests" but should be equipped for "complete mental, physical and social study of the child, for diagnosis of his difficulties, and for recommendation for treatment."[39] As the joint projects of city accountants, school administrators, and psychologists, school survey reports were melting pots for the several vocabularies of their professional authors.

Educators and psychologists were quick to notice that school surveys could accelerate school reform; the surveys themselves, apart from their results, afforded publicity for the problems they investigated. Administrators found that the first result of a survey was a welcome increase in the school budget.[40] Specific reforms, too, profited by the surveys.

The survey results were brought to bear in reform proposals on every-thing from special classes for the feebleminded to school dental clinics. In an article for Goddard's *Training School Bulletin*, one author praised the Salt Lake City survey by observing that "school surveys can do much to emphasize the extent and importance of the problem of feebleminded-ness."[41]

In addition to drawing attention to certain educational problems (and away from others; e.g., low pay for teachers), the school surveys were advertisement for the methods they entailed. Paul Hanus, director of many surveys done by the Harvard Graduate School of Education, frankly admitted that his purpose in using intelligence tests in school surveys was twofold: "(1) to gain information concerning the student body, and (2) to suggest that the perennial use of measurement is an indispensable aid in studying . . . school problems."[42] Such surveys also helped employ the burgeoning numbers of students graduating from the new departments of psychology.

As early as 1914, education researchers for the National Society for the Study of Education proposed that all school surveys include the new Binet Scale of Intelligence as part of their statistical instrumentation.[43] The 1915 Salt Lake City school survey featured a promotion of Terman's forthcoming manual for the Binet test, *The Measurement of Intelligence* (1916).[44] Ellwood P. Cubberley directed the Salt Lake survey, assisted by his newly appointed junior colleague at Stanford, Lewis Terman. Cubberley, like George Strayer, who directed many surveys in eastern and midwestern cities, had trained in statistics at Teachers College, un-der Edward Thorndike.[45] This professional community expanded as school surveys became *de rigueur* for every progressive school system.

Where school surveyors considered mental testing (and nearly all surveys after 1920 did), they invariably judged existing facilities and programs inadequate and recommended expansion. Most surveys in-cluded a recommendation that the school system establish a separate bureau of measurement and strongly implied that schools without such a department labored under pitiable conditions.[46] One psychologist hint-ed that in the absence of a broad program of mental measurement, schools failed to maintain basic American values: "If the junior high school is to be a democratic institution, it will attempt to discover the differences in pupils' special gifts, and train each pupil to be happy and effective in making his particular contribution to human happiness as efficiently as possible."[47] This patriotic appeal, coming on the heels of the Red Scare and the 1919 Palmer raids, anticipated the furor over the tests that arose in 1922 and 1923 through Walter Lippmann's attacks on the army tests in the pages of the *New Republic*. In more restrained tones and without appeal to democratic principles, Thorndike's protégé George Strayer concluded in his 1928 survey of a small New Jersey school system that although "a large mass of material is now available" to aid in the establishment of mass testing programs, the school under survey "in common with the large mass of other schools, has not as yet organized to take advantage of these materials."[48] In Strayer's view this school system wasn't so much a threat to democracy as it was merely backward.

Though it seemed to Strayer that progress in mental testing was slow, by the mid-1920s about four million children were being tested annually by one or another of the commercial mental tests. Most popular were Terman's Group Intelligence Test, the Dearborn General Intelligence Test, and the National Intelligence Scale, the last a version of the army Alpha tests.[49] Terman's group test alone sold over half a million copies in 1923.[50]

The importance of the school survey in institutionalizing testing practices in the schools should not be underestimated; it was these preexisting links between the research universities and the public schools, as much as the army testing program, that produced the great expansion of mental testing after World War I. In many schools, children were first subject to intelligence and achievement tests not as part of an internal school examination program but as part of a school survey conducted by outside "experts." Although many large cities had established bureaus of educational research, New York City alone seems to have used intelligence tests on a wide scale before 1917.[51] This educational progressivism in New York was consistent with pioneering efforts there in school hygiene and in public health generally; New York had been the first American city to institute widescale medical inspection of schools.[52]

After World War I, as a result of popular interpretations of the army test results, the momentum increased to include intelligence tests in school surveys. By 1920, schoolchildren in Detroit were all taking group intelligence tests in the first grade as a basis for homogeneous grouping through their first six years of schooling. A similar plan obtained in the industrial city of Jackson, Michigan.[53] The Terman Group Test was introduced to school officials in Atlanta, Georgia, the same year.[54] In the spring of 1921, Boston schools adopted both the individual Stanford-Binet and the Terman Group Intelligence Tests as an aid to promotion and grading in the city schools.[55]

Even tiny rural schools, if they were conveniently located near universities with education departments, underwent testing in the immediate aftermath of the war. Oconee County in the northwest corner of

South Carolina had a school population of 5,513 in 1920, scattered among fifteen one-room schools and forty-nine schools of two or more teachers. In Oconee County, with an average of nine pupils per school, the assessment of children's intelligence was hardly the large-scale production problem for which tests had been designed. Nonetheless, in June 1923 the children were duly tested with the eighteen-minute Pressey Mental Survey, administered by students of the Clemson Agricultural College Division of Education.[56]

By 1926 Springfield, Massachusetts; Peoria, Illinois; Trenton, New Jersey; and Buffalo, New York were among the many cities that had adopted mass intelligence testing as part of school routine. Springfield students were tested for intelligence upon entering high school. In Peoria, all sixth and eighth graders took the Illinois test. Trenton school-children had their "MAs" (mental ages) recorded alongside their "CAs" (chronological ages) on hospital-style charts. In Buffalo, children in grades four through eight took the Illinois Group Intelligence Test in 1926, and kindergartners were each tested individually every spring thereafter. In Oakland and Berkeley, California, mental testing thrived under the direction of Terman, Cubberley, and their students at Stanford.[57]

Overseas, too, testing spread rapidly after the Great War. In 1921 Terman gave permission for *The Measurement of Intelligence* to be translated into Japanese and, in 1923, Spanish; his earlier book, *The Hygiene of the School Child* (1913), already had been published in Chinese. In 1921 the English psychologist Cyril Burt began work on a British version of the Stanford-Binet. A psychologist from the Psychological Institute in Kristiania, Norway, in 1923 asked Terman's permission to have the army Alpha tests translated for use in the Norwegian navy.[58]

The Shape of Criticism

Although the best-remembered attack on mental tests was that launched in 1922 by Walter Lippmann, scattered criticism of the psychologists' new enterprise emerged very early, a decade before the wartime testing program put psychology on the front page.[59] Interestingly, much of this early criticism was aimed squarely at the metaphors that guided both the testing project and the Progressive era enthusiasm for educational efficiency. Just as psychologists modeled their work after medicine and engineering, educators and others who were critical of the efficiency movement began their critique by shattering those linguistic models.

Among the professional leaders whom scientifically minded psychologists and educators emulated was the engineer and social reformer

Morris Llewellyn Cooke. Cooke, a latecomer to Frederick Taylor's scientific management group, was Taylor's favorite student. Cooke's empiricist slogan, "One Best Way," became a rallying cry for anyone, including school officials, who wanted to show allegiance to scientific method.[60]

Following Morris Cooke's 1911 Carnegie Foundation report on educational and industrial efficiency, Professor Maclaurin of the Massachusetts Institute of Technology wrote a sharp reply in James McKeen Cattell's journal *Science*. Maclaurin began by attacking the metaphorical basis of Cooke's influential report. In education, he wrote, "we are not making shoes or bricks or cloth, but are dealing with material of the utmost complexity and variety." He explained, "Uniformity in the product is not only unattainable, it is not even desirable, and factory methods are entirely out of place." Noting that Cooke was hardly alone in promoting the "snap and vigor" of business methods for education, Maclaurin warned that even without such reports, "there are already forces at work to give sufficient prominence to mechanical conceptions and mechanical tests." He wryly concluded, "the value of snap in the domain of education may very easily be overestimated."[61]

In 1912 an editor of the progressive *Nation* magazine wrote a scathing attack on mental measurement entitled "Measuring the Mind." The entire editorial was a critical appraisal of the analogies on which psychological testing was (and is) based. The author (probably the *Nation*'s editor Harold DeWolf Fuller) focused particularly on the work of psychologist Edward Thorndike and educational surveyor Leonard P. Ayres, author of *Laggards in Our Schools*. The editorial is worth quoting at length, for it demonstrates a striking linguistic sensitivity: "Much of the reasoning urged on behalf of this new system is by analogy. To offset the objection that the personal work of education is not in the domain of exact science, we are reminded that 'mothers do not love their babies less who weigh them.' Yet they would love them less if they thought of them purely in terms of pounds and ounces." Turning his sights on Leonard Ayres's principles of scientific school management, the journalist continued: "'We have ceased exalting the machinery,' says Mr. Ayres, 'and have commenced to examine the product.' And he proceeds to explain what marvels scientific management has wrought in brick laying. But bricks is bricks! . . . If properly wrenched, it is true, any analogy is useful. There is just enough truth in all this propaganda to create a following," the editor concluded; "Our youth are indeed to be pitied if the fad of scientific management ever has full sway in the schools."[62] The logical difficulties of analogic reasoning in general and of technical analogies in particular were as apparent in 1912 as they are today.

Even among psychologists, some found the mechanical engineering metaphor inappropriate. Alfred Binet himself warned that his scale of intelligence was not, "in spite of appearances, an automatic method, comparable to a scale which, when one stands upon it, throws out a ticket on which one's weight is printed." Binet feared that other physicians would apply the tests in institutional settings without proper attention to procedure. Concerning the individually administered test, Binet cautioned, "It is not a mechanical method, and we predict to the busy physician who wishes to apply it in hospitals, that he will meet with disappointments."[63]

Another critic of mental tests, New York Supreme Court justice John W. Goff, refused to admit Binet test results as legal evidence, remarking that "standardizing the mind is as futile as standardizing electricity."[64] Unlike other critics, Goff accepted the electrical engineering metaphor but used it to make an opposing argument. This "coopting" is a common rhetorical tactic; the editor of the *Nation* used the same tactic in criticizing E. L. Thorndike's "baby" metaphor above.[65] When a metaphor takes hold, it orders even the logic of those who would oppose its original implications. Metaphor is so powerful an organizing feature of debate that it seems to demand acknowledgment. This power lies not in the words, however, but in the degree to which they attract consensus, a socially and historically specific phenomenon. In other words, the power of a metaphor to shape even opposing points of view depends on its resonance in a particular political, historical context. This meant that the few critics of mental testing often found themselves addressing the psychologists' medical and engineering metaphors before they could address mental testing as a scientific or educational technique.

One such critic in 1922 argued against the material metaphor that was the basis for engineering analogies. Writing in John Dewey's reformist journal *School and Society,* this author too aimed his criticism at the psychologists' language: "In all the recent discussions of mental measurement we hear such phrases as the 'amount' of intelligence, and the 'quantity' of intelligence, as if intelligence were a substance like matter which could be weighed, or measured as a length or a surface is measured."[66] The "atomistic" theory of mind, the author argued, sees "a more absolute and ultimate reality in the results of analysis than it does in the whole or synthesis which has been analyzed." It is all too easy, he worried, for psychologists and educators under the sway of this concept to forget the qualitative and human properties of the subjects under study.

The same author warned of a further pitfall in the quantitative study of intelligence, namely, the "surrender of . . . concrete effects to the axiomatic symbolism of mathematics." He cautioned that unless fellow psychologists always remembered the great logical distance separating "abstract number-symbols" from the concrete, qualitative behavioral effects of intelligence, they easily committed "the fallacy of fancying that when we are studying intelligence quotients we are necessarily studying intelligence."[67]

John Dewey, to whom much of the efficiency ethos was anathema, argued that the new "scientific" vocabulary in education merely created the illusion of change. In a 1922 article titled "Education as Engineering," Dewey wrote that the so-called new education was the same old stuff, "masquerading in the terminology of science." The new vocabulary made little difference, Dewey thought, "except for advertising purposes."[68] Such advertising, however, is a major item in the budget of professionalization.

The medical metaphor too became a focus of criticism. In 1914, an article in *Living Age* parodied the "Soothing Syrup of Psychology."[69] Walter Lippmann in his *New Republic* series on the army tests adopted the medical vocabulary of the psychologists whom he criticized but called the testers "quacks," not physicians.[70] The medical metaphor was more difficult to criticize than was engineering language, however, because it rang so true, having a stronger literal component. Psychologists practicing during this period nearly always did have some training in physiology; among the older generation, many held medical degrees or had studied medicine before entering psychology.

The language of medicine and engineering and the symbolism of mathematics not only structured the logic of intelligence research but ordered the logic of its critique. So pervasive was this interlocking linguistic system of "scientific" metaphor that the whole enterprise of mental measurement could hardly be discussed without reference to it. And although contemporary critics of mental testing were able to recognize the logical fallacies hidden in metaphorical and numerical symbols, they did not suggest an alternative metaphorical system that matched the considerable persuasive power of medical and engineering language in the context of Progressive era society. Critics of mental testing, until they launched their own quantitative studies of intelligence in the 1940s, had no basis for their criticism except the rhetoric of democratic theory. Since that vocabulary was also employed with some ingenuity by the advocates and practitioners of mental testing, critics were in a weak position to turn it against the tests. Their critiques of medical and engineering metaphors, and of metaphor in general, went only halfway toward upsetting the measurement industry. For by 1922, mental testing was no longer an experimental technique but a commercial enterprise in which many individuals and institutions had a stake. Most criticisms of the tests, and of the analogic reasoning which supported them, came too late in the profession's development to have great effect. Moreover, critics were unable to muster competing metaphors that would have made alternatives to testing plausible. Such competing metaphors would have had to refute the very importance of quantitative research, in which some critics had as much stake as the testers. Thus on the power of words and the force of numbers, mental measurement prevailed and within the span of two decades transformed the empirical basis of public school policy.

Notes

Epigraphs: J. M. Ziman, *Public Knowledge: An Essay Concerning the Social Dimension of Science* (London: Cambridge University Press, 1968), p. 31; Alfred Binet, *L'Etude expérimentale de l'intelligence* (Paris: Costes, 1903; 1922), pp. 297–8, cited in Theta Wolf, *Alfred Binet* (Chicago: University of Chicago Press, 1973), p. 120.

1. See John Harley Warner, *The Therapeutic Perspective* (Cambridge, Mass.: Harvard University Press, 1988).
2. The metaphorical languages of mental testing are considered at length in the author's forthcoming book, *The Semantics of Profession* (Princeton: Princeton University Press, 1991), from which this chapter is largely drawn.
3. Ziman, *Public Knowledge*, p. 34; Walter Dill Scott, *Increasing Human Efficiency in Business* (1911), p. 7.
4. Lewis Terman, *The Measurement of Intelligence* (New York: Houghton Mifflin, 1916), p. 4; Henry Herbert Goddard, *Human Efficiency and Levels of Intelligence* (Princeton: Princeton University Press, 1920), p. vii.
5. Raymond Dodge, "Mental Engineering during the War," *American Review of Reviews* 59 (May 1919):504–8, 506.
6. On the creation of the subject relation in social science, see Michel Foucault, "The Subject and Power." *Critical Inquiry* 8(1982): 777–95.
7. Karl Pearson, *The Grammar of Science* (London: Adam and Charles Black, 1892; 1900), p. 19.
8. Guy Whipple, *Thirty-seventh Yearbook of the National Society for the Study of Education II* (1938), p. 260, citing E. L. Thorndike, *Fifth Yearbook of the NSSE I* (1906), pp. 81–82.
9. Truman Lee Kelley, *Scientific Method: Its Function in Research and in Education* (Columbus: Ohio University Press, 1929), pp. 40, 41.
10. Report of a *Survey of the School System of Saint Paul, Minnesota*, George Strayer, Director (St. Paul: n.p., 1917), p. 262.
11. Joseph Peterson, *Early Conceptions and Tests of Intelligence* (Yonkers-on-Hudson: World Book Company, 1925), p. 157.
12. Marion Trabue and Francis Parker Stockbridge, *Measure Your Mind* (New York: Doubleday, Page and Co., 1922), pp. 13–14.

13. Edward Lee Thorndike, "Educational Diagnosis," *Science*, 24 January 1913, pp. 133–42, 142.

14. *Education in Twelve Cape Towns: A Study for the Cape Cod Chamber of Commerce by Members of the Staff of the Graduate School of Education, Harvard University* (Norwood, Mass.: Ambrose Press, 1927), pp. 7–8.

15. Edwin T. Layton, Jr., *The Revolt of the Engineers* (Cleveland: Press of Case Western Reserve University, 1971), p. 57.

16. See Gerald Gelson, *Professions and Professional Ideologies in America* (Chapel Hill: University of North Carolina Press, 1983), p.3; Roy Lubove, *The Professional Altruist: The Emergence of Social Work as a Career* (Cambridge, Mass.: Harvard University Press, 1965), p. 121; Talcott Parsons, "The Professionals and Social Structure," in *Essays in Sociological Theory* (Glencoe, Ill.: Free Press, 1954); Paul Starr, *The Social Transformation of American Medicine* (New York: Basic Books, 1982), p. 191.

17. Paul Starr, *The Social Transformation of American Medicine* (New York: Basic Books, 1982), p. 12.

18. Robert H. Wiebe, *The Search for Order 1877–1920* (New York: Hill and Wang, 1967), pp. 40–41.

19. Raymond Callahan, *Education and the Cult of Efficiency* (Chicago: University of Chicago Press, 1962), p. 112.

20. James H. Cassedy, *American Medicine and Statistical Thinking 1800–1860* (Cambridge Mass.: Harvard University Press, 1984).

21. Wiebe, *Search for Order, pp. 40–41.*

22. Theodore Roosevelt, *Introduction to Charles McCarthy, The Wisconsin Idea* (New York: Macmillan, 1912), p. viii.

23. Ibid.

24. Ibid., pp. 124–25, citing Frederick Jackson Turner.

25. See Paul S. Boyer, *Urban Masses and Moral Order in America, 1820–1920* (Cambridge, Mass.: Harvard University Press, 1978), on the "quantification of vice" in the white slavery investigations during this period. Clearly, my own figures of speech ("information fever") and alternating voices are subject to the same critique that I am directing at the psychologist.

26. For an extended analysis of this kind of empiricism among twentieth-century intellectuals, see Robert Booth Fowler, *Believing Skeptics: American Political Intellectuals, 1945–1964* (Westport, Conn.: Greenwood Press, 1978). Fowler examines the roots of liberal skepticism in Progressive era political thought.

27. J. Harold Williams, "Backward and Feeble-minded Children in Salt Lake City," *Training School Bulletin* (September 1915): 123–129, 123.

28. Frank W. Ballou, "The Significance of Educational Measurements," *Journal of Education* (16 July 1914), pp. 74–76.

29. John Palmer Garber, *Current Activities and Influences in Education* (Philadelphia: J. B. Lippincott Co., 1913), p. 152.

30. Charles S. Meek, "Report to the National Council," *National Education Association Proceedings* (1913): 376–80, cited in Raymond C. Callahan, *Education and the Cult of Efficiency* (Chicago: University of Chicago Press, 1962), p. 113.

31. Ibid., pp. 112–20.

32. In Portland, Oregon, between 1902 and 1912, average daily school attendance

doubled, while the school budget increased sixfold. See *Report of the Survey of the Public School System of School District No. 1, Multnomah County, Oregon,* Ellwood P. Cubberley, Director (November 1, 1913), p. xv.

33. Jeremiah E. Burke, Superintendent, Boston Public Schools, *Annual Report of the Superintendent,* October 1925 (Boston: Printing Department, 1925), p. 96.

34. See *Report of the Survey of the Schools of Holyoke, Massachusetts,* George Strayer, Director (Holyoke: Unity Press, 1930), pp. 240–41.

35. *Report on a Survey of Certain Aspects of the Lancaster, Pennsylvania City School District,* Paul H. Hanus, Director (Cambridge, Mass.: Graduate School of Education, Harvard University, 1924–25), p. 39.

36. Cubberley, *Report of the Survey (Multnomah),* p. 146.

37. *Survey of the Peoria Public Schools* (Peoria, Ill.: Schwab Print, 1929); see also Hanus, *Report on a Survey,* p. 39.

38. Boston Public Schools, *Annual Report of the Superintendent* (Boston: Printing Department, October 1925), p. 96.

39. *Report of the Buffalo School Survey* (Buffalo, N. Y.: Buffalo Municipal Research Bureau, 1931), pp. 87–88, 129.

40. Callahan, *Education and the Cult of Efficiency,* p. 115.

41. Williams, "Backward and Feeble-minded Children," p. 129. On the particularly successful efforts for school dentistry, see Steve Schlossman, JoAnne Brown, and Michael Sedlak, "The Public School in Children's Dentistry," *Rand Report* (Santa Monica, Calif.: Rand Corporation, 1985).

42. Hanus, *Report on a Survey,* part 2, p. 38; part 3, p. 57.

43. H. L. Smith and Charles H. Juss, eds., *Plans for Organizing School Surveys, Thirteenth Yearbook of the National Society for the Study of Education,* part 2 (Chicago: University of Chicago Press, 1914), p. 31.

44. *Report of the Survey of the Public School System of Salt Lake City, Utah,* Ellwood P. Cubberley, Director (n.p.: June 30, 1915), p. 212.

45. Geraldine Joncich, ed., *Psychology and the Science of Education* (New York: Teachers College Press, 1962), p. 15.

46. See, for example, Cubberley, *Report of the Survey (Multnomah);* Cubberley, *Report of the Survey (Salt Lake City),* pp. 212–14; Strayer, *Report of the Survey (Saint Paul);* Hanus, *Report on a Survey,* pp. 78, 80; *Report of a Survey of the Schools of Lynn, Massachusetts,* George Strayer, Director (1927), p. 199; *Report of the Buffalo School Survey,* pp. 87–88, 98, 129; Strayer, *Report of the Survey (Holyoke, Massachusetts),* p. 298.

47. Marion R. Trabue, "The Uses of Intelligence Tests in Junior High Schools," *Twenty-first Yearbook of the National Society for the Study of Education,* part 2 (1922), pp. 178–79.

48. *Report of the Survey of the Schools of Cloister, New Jersey,* George Strayer, Director (New York: Institute of Educational Research, Division of Field Studies, Teachers College, Columbia University, February 1928), p. 103.

49. U.S. Bureau of Education, "Cities Reporting the Use of Homogeneous Grouping and the Winnetka Technique and the Dalton Plan," School Leaflet 22 (Washington, D.C.: U.S. Government Printing Office, 1926), pp. 1–11; Lewis Terman to Caspar Hodgson, World Book Company, 15 October 1923, Box 20, file 19, Terman Papers, Stanford University Archives; James McKeen Cattell, copy of ad-

dress to the Pacific Division of the American Association for the Advancement of Science, p. 1, Box 85, file "miscellany," Cattell Papers, Library of Congress. Michael Schudson cites a figure ten times higher, based on a 1947 estimate by Douglas Scates, but this figure includes achievement tests, which were administered more than once to each child. See Michael S. Schudson, "Organizing the Meritocracy," *Harvard Educational Review* (February 1972): 34–69, 49; and Douglas E. Scates, "Fifty Years of Objective Measurement and Research in Education," *Journal of Educational Research* 41 (December 1947): 249.

50. Lewis Terman to Caspar Hodgson, 15 October 1923, Terman Papers, Stanford University.

51. Charles B. Barnes, "Feeble-mindedness as a Cause for Homelessness," *Training School Bulletin* (March 1916): 3–15, 10–11.

52. The historiographic use of the terms *progressive* and *Progressivism* should not be understood as endorsement of the policies here described, but as a reference to what contemporaries viewed as the "progressive," technical, social scientific ethic as opposed to traditional nineteenth-century patronage and plutocracy. The self-styled progressives were, as we all are, encumbered by different interests.

53. Warren K. Layton, "The Group Intelligence Testing Program of the Detroit Public Schools," *Twenty-First Yearbook of the NSSE* (1922).

54. Lewis Terman to Mr. E. R. Parker, 9 September 1920, Box 20, file 18, Terman Papers, Stanford University.

55. *Report on Age and Progress of Pupils in the Boston Public Schools: School Document #12-1925* (Boston: Printing Department, 1925), p. 53.

56. *Public School Survey of Oconee County, South Carolina*, Division of Education, Clemson Agricultural College (June 1923).

57. *Report of the Survey of Certain Aspects of the Public School System of Springfield, Massachusetts, School Year 1923–4*, George Strayer, Director, p. 160; *Survey of the Peoria Public Schools*, Charles E. Chadsey, Director (Peoria, Ill.: Schwab Print, 1924), pp. 91–92; memo, Trenton Public Schools, Department of Educational Research and Efficiency, 9 September 1925, Box M935, Vineland Research Laboratory Papers, AHAP, University of Akron; *Report of the Buffalo School Survey*, p. 75; Paul Davis Chapman, "Schools as Sorters," Ph.D. diss., Stanford University, 1980.

58. See correspondence, Box 12, Terman Papers, Stanford University Archives.

59. See Walter Lippmann, "Mental Age of Americans," *New Republic*, 25 October 1922, pp. 213–15; "Mystery of the A-Men," *NR*, 1 November 1922, pp. 246–48; "The Abuse of the Tests," *NR*, 15 November 1922, pp. 297–98; "Future for the Tests," *NR*, 29 November 1922, pp. 9–11; reply from Lewis Terman, *NR*, 27 December 1922, pp. 116–20; discussion, *NR*, 3 January 1922, pp. 145–6; 17 January 1923, pp. 201–2; 7 February 1923; Lippmann's rejoinder, "Judgment of the Tests," *NR*, 16 May 1923, pp. 322–23. See also the correspondence between Robert Yerkes and Walter Lippmann, Yerkes Papers, Yale University, and the correspondence between Terman and his publishers about the debate, Terman Papers, Stanford University.

60. Edwin T. Layton, Jr., *The Revolt of the Engineers* (Cleveland: Press of Case Western Reserve University, 1971), pp. 154–78; David Tyack, *The One Best System* (Cambridge Mass., Harvard University Press, 1974).

61. R. C. Maclaurin, "Educational and Industrial Efficiency," *Science*, 20 January 1911, pp. 101–3.

62. "Measuring the Mind," *Nation*, 16 May 1912, p. 486.

63. Alfred Binet, cited by Clara Harrison Town, Ph.D., "The Binet-Simon Scale and the Psychologist," *Psychological Clinic*, 15 January 1912, pp. 239–44.

64. John W. Goff. *Literary Digest*, 19 August 1916, p. 405, cited in Daniel Kevles, "Testing the Army's Intelligence," *Journal of American History* 55 (1968): 560–81.

65. In a more recent example, during the 1985 federal budget debate in Congress, a Reagan administration spokesman warned Democratic congressmen that "we are shooting real bullets," meaning, "these budget cuts are genuine." A Democrat replied to the effect, "Yes, you're shooting real bullets all right, and real people are going to get hurt!" In another recent congressional debate over Social Security, no sooner did Republicans compare the system to a "safety net" than Democrats pronounced the net "full of holes."

66. Thomas J. McCormack, "A Critique of Mental Measurements," *School and Society*, 24 June 1922, pp. 686–92, 689.

67. Ibid., p. 688.

68. John Dewey, "Education as Engineering," *New Republic*, 20 September 1922, p. 90.

69. "Soothing Syrup of Psychology," *Living Age*, 28 November 1914, pp. 573–75.

70. Walter Lippmann, "The Mental Age of Americans," *New Republic*, 25 October 1922, pp. 213–15, and "Future for the Tests," *New Republic*, 29 November 1922, pp. 9–11.

■ 8　THE DOMESTICATION OF "CULTURE" IN INTERWAR AMERICA, 1919-1941

JOHN S. GILKESON, JR.

In his 1939 book *Knowledge for What? The Place of Social Science in American Culture,* prominent sociologist Robert S. Lynd developed "two seemingly independent lines of thought": the first, "an appraisal of the present characteristics of American culture, with particular attention to elements of strain and disjunction"; the second, "a critique of current focus and methods in social science research." What underwrote Lynd's claim that these two themes "so inescapably do belong together" was his belief that "social science is not a scholarly arcanum, but an organized part of the culture which exists to help man in continually understanding and rebuilding his culture." By "culture" Lynd did not mean "culture in the refined sense of belles lettres and sophisticated learning." Rather, he used the term "in the anthropologist's sense, to refer to all the things that a group of people inhabiting a common geographical area do, the ways they do things and the ways they think and feel about things, their material tools and their values and symbols." Lynd preferred the anthropological idea of culture to the older belletristic conception because it connoted the "wholeness and interrelatedness of a culture." Thus, when Lynd posed to his fellow social scientists "the common task of understanding our American culture," he did so in the belief that "nothing in American life escapes us."[1]

Lynd was far from the only American social scientist between the First and Second World Wars to invoke the anthropological concept of culture. Until the First World War, most educated Americans had thought of culture in terms defined by the Victorian apostle of culture, Matthew Arnold, in his celebrated book *Culture and Anarchy.* Culture,

153

Arnold had written, designated "the best that has been thought and known in the world." Since 1919, however, a small but influential band of cultural anthropologists had popularized a more technical conception of culture, one that emphasized, in Margaret Mead's words, "the learned ways of behavior characteristic of a group."[2]

This essay traces the popularization of the concept of culture as it made its way first from anthropology to the other social sciences and then to the general public. After discussing how Franz Boas reoriented American anthropology away from attempts to formulate general laws of cultural evolution toward the intensive study of cultures in their unique historical settings, it next examines the ways in which Boas's students disseminated the principles of the American historical school of anthropology to several audiences—in the late teens and early twenties to other social scientists intent on establishing the autonomy of their disciplines; in the twenties to middle-class Americans in search of expert advice on how to live their lives; and after 1929 to American intellectuals in quest of an indigenous American culture. If, as Warren Susman contended, Americans between the world wars attempted "to define America as a culture and to create the patterns of a way of life worth understanding," how did they make use of the concept of culture?[3]

The concept of culture, around which American anthropology constituted itself as an academic discipline in the early twentieth century, cannot be understood without a brief look at the career of Franz Boas. Born of secular Jewish parents in 1858, Boas studied physics and geography at Heidelberg, Bonn, and Kiel. A year spent among the Eskimo on Baffin Island in 1883–84, where he went to investigate "the reaction of the human mind to natural environment," changed the course of the young geographer's life, leading Boas away from "his former interests and toward the desire to understand what determines the behavior of human beings." When he realized that he could not "explain human behavior as a result of geographical environment," Boas dedicated himself to the lifelong "study of human cultures," hoping "to discover what is generally human and what is culturally determined." During three months on the Northwest Coast of Canada in 1886, Boas made the acquaintance of the Kwakiutl, his "people," to whom he was to pay twelve more visits, the last in 1931 when he was seventy-two. After immigrating to the United States in 1887, Boas found employment as an editor for *Science* magazine, next lectured on anthropology at Clark University, then organized ethnological collections at the World's Columbian Exposition, before serving as curator of anthropology at Chicago's Field Museum. In 1896, after more than a year of unemployment, Boas joined the American Museum of Natural History as a curator; he also began teaching at Columbia University. Promoted to professor in 1899, Boas headed Columbia's anthropology department until his retirement in 1936. Though hampered by age and a serious heart ailment, he remained professionally active until his death in December 1942.[4]

Almost as soon as he settled in the United States, Boas began to formulate a critique of the evolutionary theories that held sway among American anthropologists. Inspired in part by Charles Darwin's *Origin of Species* (1859), an earlier generation of anthropologists had formulated unilinear schemes of evolution whereby man was thought to evolve from savagery through barbarism to civilization. Equating cultural achievement with mental aptitude, evolutionary anthropologists assigned the races of the world to their respective rungs on a cultural ladder ascending from primitive African and Australian tribes to the acme of evolution, the Northwestern European. Ethnological phenomena, if arranged on a scale of complexity, would reveal the history of man's cultural development. Boas, however, took issue with the evolutionists' comparative method. In an exchange over the arrangement of ethnological collections with Otis T. Mason, curator at the Smithsonian, in the pages of *Science* in 1887, Boas challenged the assumption, on which the comparative method rested, that "in human culture, as in nature elsewhere, like causes produce like effects." Rejecting this "argument from analogy," Boas instead insisted on the "necessity of studying each ethnological phenomenon individually." For, as Boas put it rather awkwardly, "though like causes have like effects, like effects have not like causes." Only "the tribal arrangement of ethnological collections," which he championed, would "show how far each and every civilization is the outcome of its geographical and historical surroundings."[5]

By 1896, Boas had moved from questioning the validity of the comparative method to urging his fellow anthropologists "to renounce the vain endeavor to construct a uniform systematic history of the evolution of culture." In "The Limitations of the Comparative Method of Anthropology," a paper read before the American Association for the Advancement of Science, Boas contrasted his inductive method with the evolutionary anthropologists' comparative approach. Whereas they regarded "the sameness of ethnological phenomena found in diverse regions" as "proof that the human mind obeys the same laws everywhere," Boas considered the same data evidence of the "well known facts of diffusion of culture." Boas went on to spell out the logic of intensive fieldwork, which was to become the disciplinary hallmark of anthropology. Rather than attempt to force "phenomena into the strait-jacket of a theory," the anthropologist should employ the historical method. "Its application," Boas explained, involved "the careful and slow detailed study of local phenomena" within a "well-defined, small geographical territory." The anthropologist might still make comparisons, but only provided that they were "not extended beyond the limits of the cultural area that forms the basis of the study."[6]

Just as important as his critique of evolutionism was Boas's critique of racial formalism, which he developed between 1894 and 1911. In "Human Faculty as Determined by Race," an address given in 1894 before the American Association for the Advancement of Science, Boas took his fellow social scientists to task for confounding "the achievement and the aptitude for an achievement." "Historical events," he declared, "appear to have been much more potent in leading races to civilization than their faculty." As an example, Boas cited "the rapid dissemination of Europeans over the whole world," which "cut short all promising beginnings which had arisen in various regions." Although willing to admit, on the basis of anatomical evidence, that "it is probable that some of these races may not produce as large a proportion of great men as our own race," Boas saw "no reason to suppose that they are unable to reach the level of civilization represented by the bulk of our own people." Indeed, he placed the burden of proof on advocates of white superiority to "prove beyond a doubt that it will be impossible for certain races to attain a higher civilization."[7]

Over the next seventeen years, Boas presented his heterodox views in a variety of forums. At Atlanta University in 1906, he told the graduating class that they should take pride in the impressive industrial and artistic achievements of their African ancestors. "This picture of native Africa will inspire strength," Boas said, "for all the alleged faults of your race that you have to conquer here are certainly not prominent there." In a number of magazine articles, Boas vigorously denied the widely held "belief in a racial inferiority which would unfit an individual of the Negro race to take his part in modern civilization." Instead, he attributed "the inferiority of the status of the race" to the "tearing away from the African soil," to "the dependency of slavery," and to the "disorganization" and "severe economic struggle against heavy odds" that followed emancipation.[8] Boas synthesized his argument against "the permeation of our whole thinking by biological viewpoints" in *The Mind of Primitive Man*, published in 1911. In addition to declaring that "the differences between primitive man and civilized man are in many cases more apparent than real," Boas stated his firm conviction that race, language, and culture—three concepts commonly conflated by social scientists and laymen alike—"are not closely and permanently connected." Indeed, "the belief that race determines mental behavior and culture rests on strong emotional values," not on scientific proof.[9]

More than any other social scientist of his generation, Boas called into question the validity of race as a social science concept. In 1911, he published the results of the more than eighteen thousand anthropometric measurements of immigrants and their children that he had taken for the U.S. Immigration Commission. Boas's discovery that the head forms of the children changed because of environmental influences refuted the presumed stability of bodily form or racial types, suggesting instead the relative "plasticity" of human nature.[10] Concluding that race was a vague concept in which both environmental and hereditary factors were tangled together, Boas challenged eugenicists "to determine empirically and without bias what features are hereditary and what are not." A relentless critic of the "Nordic nonsense" propagated by polemicists like Madison Grant, Boas seized every opportunity to denounce their "dangerous" opinions, which rested on a number of "dogmatic assumptions which cannot endure criticism," notably "the assumption of identity of race and language."[11] Boas also disputed the results of psychological tests administered during the First World War to army recruits that presumably demonstrated the correlation between race and intelligence. After the war, he secured funding from the National Research Council for three of his students, Melville J. Herskovits, Margaret Mead, and Otto Klineberg, whose researches exposed the cultural biases of the tests while demonstrating the role played by such environmental factors as length of residence in America, facility in English, educational background, and social status in determining intelligence.[12] By 1930, the great majority of social scientists, including some of the very psychologists who devised the tests, had repudiated their earlier belief in the genetic or even the apparent inferiority of the Negro. Many no longer considered "race" a meaningful explanation for human differences.[13]

Boas, then, reoriented American anthropology away from armchair speculation toward intensive fieldwork, disentangled culture (and language) from race, and helped discredit race as a valid concept among social scientists. Yet Boas, a methodological "puritan" who "continually warned" his students against "premature generalization," never synthesized his views for a popular audience. Boas's *Anthropology and Modern Life* (1928) might be hailed by reviewers for accomplishing "the annihilation of the bases of almost all the prejudices and passions on which modern society rests," but Boas's students regretted his failure to summarize "the methodology of his science" and distill "his philosophy of culture." As Edward Sapir wrote in his review of *Anthropology and Modern Life,* Boas was "not the man to articulate implications." That burden fell on his students. Indeed, Sapir thought it incumbent on them to do so, for as anthropology became a "popular science" it ran the risk of "its data and its varying interpretations" being "chosen ad libitum to justify every whim and every form of spiritual sloth."[14]

In a series of texts published between 1916 and 1926, Boas's students synthesized the work to date of the American historical school of anthropology.[15] In an extended methodological essay, "Time Perspective in Aboriginal American Culture" (1916), Edward Sapir demonstrated how anthropologists made use of both "direct and documentary evidence" in order to set "the data of American ethnology into chronologic relations"; Sapir's book *Language* (1921) won rave reviews from his colleagues for the "rare felicity" with which it rendered the abstruse subject of philology intelligible to the "interested layman."[16] In *Culture and Ethnology*, which grew out of a series of lectures that he gave at the American Museum of Natural History in 1917, Robert H. Lowie sounded the clarion call of the new anthropology, "Omnis cultura ex cultura": "Culture," he declared, "is a thing sui generis which can be explained only in terms of itself." This meant that the anthropologist "will account for a given cultural fact by merging it in a group of cultural facts or by demonstrating some other cultural fact out of which it has developed." Lowie's next book, *Primitive Society* (1920), subjected the "speculations" and "catchwords" of evolutionary anthropology to withering criticism.[17] In 1922, Alexander Goldenweiser published *Early Civilization*, "the first book by an American anthropologist," as Margaret Mead recalled, "to present cultures briefly as wholes." Ruth Benedict praised A.L. Kroeber's *Anthropology* (1923) for making "available both the raw material and the fundamental point of view of modern American anthropology."[18]

Clark Wissler, however, did more than any other Boas student to disseminate Boasian anthropology among social scientists. From his post on the National Research Council, he served as an intermediary between anthropology and psychology and sociology. Wissler saw no reason why anthropologists should not study contemporary cultures. Confident "in the technique he has developed," Wissler wrote in 1920, the anthropologist's "hands have long been itching for a chance to lay hold of Europeans and their cultures." Wissler proposed that anthropologists investigate the "colony cultures" of the nation's heterogeneous immigrants, a call echoed by Albert Ernest Jenks, who directed an Americanization Training Program at the University of Minnesota.[19] By 1927, however, Wissler thought that "the anthropological approach" would be just as applicable to the study of "well-established communities in our own country." In two books—*Man and Culture* (1923) and *The Relation of Nature to Man in Aboriginal America* (1926)—as well as in articles that appeared in the *American Journal of Sociology* and in essays contributed to symposiums on the social sciences, Wissler elaborated the "culture-area concept," which had been developed at the American Museum in order to classify a mass of ethnological material collected from Indian cultures in the New World. Culture areas consisted of traits that had been diffused from common "culture centers." As they diffused, the traits formed concentric zoned patterns; from the extent of its distribution, the age of a specific trait could be inferred. Wissler recommended the culture-area concept to social scientists as a "research lead" in undertaking "regional studies of a local nature."[20]

The 1920s were an opportune moment for anthropologists to disseminate the concept of culture. Between 1921 and 1927, foundations increased their outlays for "research and advanced education in the social sciences" from less than $200,000 to more than $7.8 million, much of it channeled through the Social Science Research Council, founded in 1923.[21] A spate of symposiums held during the decade, bearing such titles as *The History and Prospects of the Social Sciences* and *The Social Sciences and Their Interrelations,* promoted "cooperation" and "interdisciplinary research" among social scientists.[22] By the end of the decade, not only private foundations but the federal government looked to the social sciences to solve some of the nation's pressing social problems. In 1929 President Herbert Hoover appointed the President's Research Committee on Social Trends "to examine and to report upon recent social trends in the United States with a view to providing such a review as might supply a basis for the formulation of large national policies looking to the next phase in the nation's development." The publication of the committee's two-volume report, *Recent Social Trends in the United States* (1933), and the monumental, fifteen-volume *Encyclopedia of the Social Sciences* (1930–1935) appeared to bear out Robert M. Hutchins's prediction that the social sciences were in 1929 "on the crest of a wave which we hope will be permanent."[23]

Among social scientists, historians and sociologists proved especially receptive to Boasian anthropology. To historians, anthropological research appeared to put the problem of historical development in a new light. Because there was "little evidence for biological and neurological improvement since the time of the appearance of the Cro-Magnon type," Harry Elmer Barnes commented, "human progress has become more and more dependent upon advances in culture and ideas." As John Higham has pointed out, "New Historians" like Barnes embraced the concept of culture as "an all-embracing pattern" that would at once "satisfy [their] desire to comprehend society as a whole" and "reveal a unifying structure and provide a basis for selection."[24] For sociologists like Malcolm Willey, W. I. Thomas, and William Fielding Ogburn, the premise that culture was sui generis and could therefore be explained only in terms of itself appeared to free sociology from biological (and psychological) reductionism. Willey collaborated with his good friend Melville Herskovits in presenting the Boasians' "historical point of view" to both sociologists and psychologists. Thomas, co-author of the classic ethnography *The Polish Peasant in Europe and America* (1918–1920), acknowledged the seminal influence of Boas's work on his own intellectual development. Ogburn drew on anthropologists' distinction between "social evolution" and human nature to formulate his influential concept of cultural lag. Instances of cultural lag occurred whenever the family, institutions, values, and other parts of "adaptive culture" failed to keep pace with material culture, which changed more rapidly because of the cumulative impact of invention and diffusion. The "widespread application of anthropological concepts to sociology" in the past decade, declared Jessie Bernard in 1929, had prompted not a few sociologists to discard the term *evolution* and speak simply of "change."[25]

Yet Boas's students wanted to disseminate what A. L. Kroeber called the "anthropological attitude" to laymen as well as to social scientists. "The important thing about anthropology is not the science but an attitude of mind," Kroeber explained in the *American Mercury* in 1928. "A widespread and growing attitude of detachment from the culture we are in" made possible "the ability to conceive of culture as such." Western culture, as Kroeber pointed out, "happens to have finally reached the abnormal—and possibly pathological—point where it is beginning to be culturally introspective, and can lay itself on the dissecting table alongside a foreign or dead culture." From this perspective, anthropology appeared to be "the organized, codified symptom of a trend of the period," so pervasive that it was almost a "national sentiment"; by the same token, anthropologists were but "the body of experts professionally engaged in applying the sentiment to new situations."[26]

Two years later, the editors of the *Encyclopedia of the Social Sciences* alluded to Kroeber's article when they assessed the impact of "war and reorientation" on the social sciences. In both America and Germany, they contended, postwar disillusionment had produced "an outburst of national introspection which yielded revealing analyses of their respective civilizations." The editors credited anthropologists with having developed a distinctive "way of thinking" that had "entered into the main stream of twentieth century thought." On the one hand, "our own modern institutions are encumbered and entangled with their historic accretions and so self-evident to us that the clear outlines of their nature and purport are blurred." The "primitive community," on the other hand, could be approached as "a sort of laboratory or a vacuum test tube in which we can reduce all extraneous elements to a minimum and keep our eye on the main intent of the chemical reaction." As a result, the anthropologist "views culture with a detachment that comes, not as the scientist seeks to attain it, through a heroic asceticism and effort at concentration, but with a certain slyness and indirection." Indeed, when applied to "our own culture," anthropology brought the reader up short, for "the strangeness of the contrast between our way of life and the savages' surprises the student into a state of detachment."[27]

As experts, as cultural critics, and in many cases as would-be social engineers, Boas's students wrote for a "middlebrow" audience whose numbers swelled during the interwar period. The vast expansion of secondary and higher education that occurred after 1900, when combined with a proliferation of white-collar jobs and a substantial increase in both leisure time and discretionary income (if only in the form of consumer credit) for many Americans, created a large audience for Sinclair Lewis's novels, H.G. Wells's *Outline of History,* Will Durant's *Story of Philosophy,* J. Arthur Thomson's *Outline of Science,* and Albert J. Beveridge's biography of Lincoln. Eager for useful knowledge yet unsure of their own critical judgment, lay readers turned to social scientists for advice on how to raise their children, come to terms with changing sexual mores, and shore up the beleaguered American family.[28]

In writing for this audience, Boas's students mined a rich vein of cultural criticism. Two decades earlier, in *The Theory of the Leisure Class* (1899), iconoclastic economist and social critic Thorstein Veblen had demonstrated the uses to which a cross-cultural perspective could be put in confuting the hedonistic assumptions of orthodox economics, exposing the cultural determinants of consumer behavior, and satirizing the pretensions of America's nouveaux riches. He also defamiliarized the familiar, rendering the wearing of a corset, the keeping of a front lawn, and other customs exotic and meaningful. Like Veblen, who as a second-generation Norwegian American felt "marginal," Boas's students were perhaps predisposed to cultural criticism by their status as immigrants, Jews, and women.[29] Most joined in the "revolt against a decaying culture" that extended from Greenwich Village to the Left Bank in Paris. All benefited from the cult of the primitive, which manifested itself in slumming at Harlem nightclubs, and, if Sinclair Lewis's character George F. Babbitt was representative, in reading "racy" ethnographies about "customs in the South Seas."[30]

At a time when "scientific and factual authority and sanctions" were largely replacing "biblical authority and religious sanctions" in the nation's magazines, Boas's students wrote as scientific experts on such topical concerns as science and civilization in the United States, the revolution in manners and morals, the problem of the younger generation, and the new status of women. Vienna-born Robert H. Lowie, who reviewed books for the *Dial,* the *Freeman,* and the *New Republic,* assessed the state of American science in one of the decade's most famous symposiums, *Civilization in the United States* (1922). "American science," Lowie declared, was maladjusted: "Notwithstanding its notable achievements," it was "not an organic product of our soil" but a "hothouse growth." With "at best only a nascent class of cultivated laymen who relish scientific books requiring concentrated thought or supplying large bodies of fact," America did not support sustained scientific research. Yet, only three years later, Lowie defended American civilization against charges of "smugness, illiteracy, puritanism, and hypocrisy." Writing in *Century* magazine, Lowie warned those American intellectuals who were thinking of fleeing to Europe in quest of "respect for the individual" that they were in "for a rude awakening." In Europe, "cultivated individualities" were just as rare as in the United States. What was more, expatriates would encounter "a spirit of snobbishness and a servility bred by ages of forced hallelujahs to the upper classes." America, Lowie concluded, was not "so bad, after all."[31]

Boas's students also joined in the discussion about changing sexual mores, a postwar preoccupation. In his contribution to the symposium *Sex and Civilization* (1929), Alexander Goldenweiser, who introduced housewives and businessmen to anthropology at the New School for Social Research, pointed out that masturbation was "neither as dangerous to health nor as rare or exceptional as was once supposed" and that, among certain tribes in the American Northwest and Siberia, "homosexual men and women" were "culture heroes." Edward Sapir, however, attempted to disabuse lay readers of their belief that "sex freedom is the norm for primitive societies." In "The Discipline of Sex," published in the *American Mercury* in 1929, Sapir argued that the "anti-Puritan revolt" had gone too far, investing "sex with a factitious value as a romantic and glorious thing in itself." American youth, he suggested, were in revolt less against "sex repression" than against "everything that is hard, narrow, and intolerant in the old American life."[32]

Like many other intellectuals in postwar America, Sapir thought long and hard about the "fundamental conflict between the traditional ideal of culture and the actual conditions of life in America" and about "the need of a specifically American revision of our ideal of culture." In "Culture, Genuine and Spurious," published in the *American Journal of Sociology* in 1924, Sapir brought together earlier essays on culture that had appeared in the *Dial* and the *Dalhousie Review.* Advancing a definition of a "genuine" culture, Sapir took the measure of America's machine-age civilization and found it wanting. By genuine, Sapir had in mind a culture that was "not of necessity either high or low" but "merely inherently harmonious, balanced, self-satisfactory." It was, "ideally speaking, a culture in which nothing is spiritually meaningless, in which no important part of the general functioning brings with it a sense of frustration, of misdirected or unsympathetic element." If judged by those standards, contemporary American culture was "spurious." Sapir deplored its "spiritual disharmony, which the more sensitive individuals feel eventually as a fundamental lack of culture." Far better, he thought, were the cultures of uncontaminated American Indian tribes. To Sapir, "the Indian's salmon-spearing," however technologically primitive, was "a culturally higher type of activity than that of telephone girl or mill hand." The Indian derived from his activity "a sense of inner satisfaction, a feeling of spiritual mastery" that was sorely missing "in the higher levels of civilization." For, as Sapir concluded, there was "no necessary correlation between the development of civilization and the relative genuineness of the culture which forms its spiritual essence."[33]

Through three best-selling books published between 1928 and 1935 and articles published in such popular magazines as the *Parents' Magazine* and the *Delineator,* Margaret Mead quickly established herself as representative American anthropologist and modern career woman. Dispatched by Boas to study adolescence in Samoa in 1925, she returned home to announce that Samoan adolescents experienced none of the storm and stress so common among their American counterparts. Ironically, Mead's picture of adolescent sexual experimentation in Samoa reinforced the very stereotype of primitive promiscuity that Sapir hoped to dispel. Mead, however, was less concerned with advocating sexual freedom than with encouraging Americans to reexamine their own customs. At the prompting of her publisher, she added two chapters in which she discussed American adolescence in the light of her Samoan research. Her theme, which she reiterated in her magazine articles, was the high emotional and psychological price that Americans paid for the "possibility of choice, the recognition of many possible ways of life" offered by their "heterogeneous, rapidly changing civilisation."[34]

Emboldened by the popular success of *Coming of Age in Samoa,* Mead next did fieldwork in New Guinea. Her second book, *Growing Up in New Guinea* (1930), portrayed the Manus, whose serious, hardworking, competitive manner bore an uncanny resemblance to Americans' Puritan ancestors, a frequent target of criticism during the 1920s. But, as in her previous book, Mead's aim was less cultural criticism than social engineering. In part two of *Growing Up in New Guinea,* entitled "Reflections on the Educational Problems of To-Day in the Light of Manus Experience," Mead put then fashionable progressive theories of education "to the test." To those educators who believed "that there is something called Human Nature which would blossom in beauty were it not distorted by the limited points of view of the adults," Mead retorted that it was "a more tenable attitude to regard human nature as the rawest, most undifferentiated of raw material"; unless "moulded into shape by its society," such material would "have no form worthy of recognition." Regrettably, Manus parents, like their American counterparts, gave "their children little to respect and so [did] not equip them to grow up graciously."[35]

Mead pushed her argument about the role played by cultural tradition in the formation of adult character to its logical conclusion in her third book written for a popular audience, *Sex and Temperament in Three Primitive Societies* (1935). After comparing gender roles among the Arapesh, the Mundugumor, and the Tchambuli peoples of New Guinea, Mead concluded that gender was an "artificial" distinction, or a cultural construct. Extensive fieldwork in the South Seas had convinced her "that many, if not all, of the personality traits which we have called masculine or feminine are as lightly linked to sex as are the clothing, the manners, and the form of the head-dress that a society at a given period assigns to either sex." For Mead, then, anthropological data could be marshaled toward the end of social engineering. If existing customs were culturally and not biologically determined, they were amenable to change.[36]

The publication of Robert S. and Helen Merrell Lynd's *Middletown: A Study in Modern American Culture* in 1929 marked the first time that anthropological methods, devised for the study of primitive cultures, were applied on a large scale to America's complex machine-age civilization. Supported by the Institute of Social and Religious Research, which had commissioned a survey of the spiritual life of the Protestant church, the Lynds spent fifteen months in 1924 and 1925 doing fieldwork among the natives of Muncie, Indiana. Muncie, whose 38,000 inhabitants numbered few immigrants or blacks, provided an ideal locale in which to study the impact of "cultural change" unencumbered by racial change; the city was also compact enough to be studied as a functional, interdependent whole. It is not surprising that Clark Wissler, himself an Indiana native, hailed the book as a "pioneer attempt to deal with a sample American community after the manner of social anthropology." The Lynds traced the spread of new tools, like the automobile, and of new habits, like birth control, from "strong centers of cultural diffusion" to Middletown by means of advertising, mass-circulation magazines, the radio, the movies, and other national media. Because life in America's machine-age civilization functioned as an interdependent whole, change in one area compelled readjustment in other areas. Failure to change produced numerous instances of cultural lag. "Middletown's life," the Lynds wrote, echoing W. F. Ogburn, "exhibits at almost every point either some change or some stress arising from failure to change." Its residents, they concluded, were "learning new ways of behaving towards material things more rapidly than new habits addressed to persons and non-material institutions."[37]

The Lynds' book also exploited anthropology's potential for cultural criticism. H. L. Mencken, the irreverent editor of the *American Mercury*, praised *Middletown* as "one of the richest and most valuable documents ever concocted by American sociologists." The Lynds, who went to Muncie as naive observers with "no thesis to prove," documented "in cold-blooded, scientific terms" the "almost unbelievable stupidities" of "the normal Americano." Indeed, their evidence revealed just "how far short of libel Sinclair Lewis fell" in his unflattering fictional portraits of midwestern life in *Main Street* (1920) and *Babbitt* (1922).[38]

Middletown also provided ammunition for Stuart Chase's critique of machine-age civilization in *Mexico: A Study of Two Americas* (1931). To Chase, life in Middletown had "neither dignity nor unity"; it existed "only as a cell in a vast interdependent industrial structure." Machine-age men, as typified by Middletowners, were lashed by the clock, "perhaps the most tyrannical engine ever invented," and haunted, particularly after the stock market crash of 1929, by the specter of technological unemployment. By contrast, "the handicraft economy of Mexico" was "economically stable and self-sufficient," and its "machineless men," who were "governed not by clocks but by the sun and the seasons," were unable "to produce the humblest thing without form and design." To lend weight to his own impressions of Mexican life, Chase referred frequently to Robert Redfield's community study *Tepoztlan, a Mexican Village* (1930). Redfield's concept of the "folk-culture continuum," which he developed to explain how, owing to the "spread of city ways," "the rustic becomes the urbanite," served as a context for subsequent discussions of America's emergent mass culture.[39]

It is probably too much to claim, as Margaret Mead did twenty-five years later, that Ruth Benedict's *Patterns of Culture* (1934) made culture, as the Boasians defined the term, a household word. But the immense success of Benedict's book, which had by 1959 sold more than 800,000 copies, did much to acquaint lay readers with such Boasian themes as the totality of cultures, cultural integration or the lack thereof, and, above all, cultural relativism. In the book, Benedict rejected the trait-distribution approach that Wissler championed and that she herself had used in her dissertation: "Cultures," she explained, "are more than the sum of their traits." Rather, she preferred to see them as "articulated wholes" or "configurations that pattern existence and condition the thoughts and emotions of the individuals who participate in those cultures." Benedict took issue with the commonly held view that America represented "an extreme example of lack of integration." Like any other culture, American culture was integrated. What she objected to were its dominant cultural patterns, which stigmatized as "abnormal" those individuals "whose congenial responses fall in that arc of behavior which is not capitalized by their culture." In an eloquent appeal for tolerance, Benedict reminded her readers that "the persons who are put outside the pale of society with contempt are not those who would be placed there by another culture."[40]

Patterns of Culture, however, consisted of more than exhortations to tolerance. Benedict's homilies in the introductory and concluding chapters bracketed her biting criticism of American culture. She drew an explicit parallel between the intensely suspicious, treacherous, and above all prudish Dobu and "our Puritan ancestors." To be sure, Dobuan prudery took a different form from that of the Puritans, just as the potlatch, the characteristic "contest of prestige" among the Kwakiutl, differed in form but not in spirit from "the obsessive rivalry of *Middletown* where houses are built and clothing bought and entertainments attended that each family may prove that it has not been left out of the game." The ceremonious, gentle Zuni civilization, "one small but long-established cultural island in North America" whose "way of life" Benedict celebrated as "the way of measure and of sobriety," stood in dramatic contrast to the machine-age civilization of Middletown, where "the fear of being different is the dominating motivation." If, as Benedict maintained, most neuroses and even psychoses had cultural rather than psychological origins, then "America at the present time" clearly required an "educational program" that would foster "tolerance in society and a kind of self-respect and independence that is foreign to Middletown and our urban traditions."[41]

Within five years of the publication of *Patterns of Culture,* the concept of culture had begun to spill over from the academic social sciences into a more popular realm, affecting the ways in which Americans, responding to economic crisis at home and political crisis abroad, attempted, in Alfred Kazin's words, "to chart America and to possess it."[42] The concept of culture thus sanctioned Constance Rourke's path-breaking exploration of such "folk" or vernacular sources as comic almanacs, jokebooks, songsheets, and tall tales on which she had embarked in

American Humor (1931). In her posthumous essay "The Roots of American Culture" (1942), Rourke quoted Ruth Benedict in support of her contention that "it is the whole configuration in the particular period which is important."[43]

For the historians and social scientists who assembled at the annual meeting of the American Historical Association in 1939 to discuss the "cultural approach to history," the concept of culture offered a new holistic "frame of reference." As Caroline Ware explained, "the concept of culture implies that any given society is an integral—though not necessarily a completely integrated—whole, in which basic processes of living and characteristic social relationships constitute a pattern of social behavior." Through the use of such "neglected" sources as folklore, documentary photography, and regional dialects, historians would be able to illuminate the "relationship" of ideas "to other social phenomena," explore the "history of the nondominant cultural groups of the industrial city," and eventually "write American history from the bottom up."[44] Robert Lynd agreed with Ware that the concept of culture provided a new frame of reference. In *Knowledge for What?*, he argued that "explicit use of the concept 'culture' compels overt recognition of the fact that all the jumbled details of living in these United States—automotive assembly lines, Wall Street, share-croppers, Supreme Court, Hollywood, and the Holy Rollers—are interacting parts in a single whole."[45]

After war broke out in Europe in 1939, the concept of culture also became an important component of what Philip Gleason has called the "democratic revival." As John Dewey argued in *Freedom and Culture* (1939), "the problem of freedom and of democratic institutions is tied up with the question of what kind of culture exists." If "free political institutions" presupposed "free culture," then the "problem" became "to know what kind of culture is so free in itself that it conceives and begets political freedom as its accompaniment and consequence." Could American culture, Dewey asked, be made "a servant and an evolving manifestation of democratic ideals"? Following Pearl Harbor, Dewey's challenge was taken up by a host of American intellectuals who proceeded to define American culture as normative.[46]

Between the world wars, Franz Boas and his students popularized an alternative to the belletristic conception of culture that had prevailed since the middle of the nineteenth century. Where the older conception was hierarchical and normative, the anthropological concept of culture was pluralistic and relativistic. Cultures, as pictured by Boas, consisted of elements, either independently invented or borrowed, which cohered into integrated wholes conditioned by the genius of their peoples. To be apprehended as articulated wholes, they had to be studied in their unique historical and environmental settings; thus the necessity of intensive fieldwork. Furthermore, cultures were neither higher nor lower (though some were admittedly more technologically advanced than others); indeed, as Ruth Benedict asserted in *Patterns of Culture,* they were "incommensurable." Finally, the concept of culture denoted learned, not hereditary, behavior. As Robert Lowie had maintained, culture was sui generis. It could be explained only in terms of itself. Culture was therefore not coterminous with race. Indeed, so convincing was the evidence that Boas and his student marshaled against race, and so compelling was their argument for cultural determinism, that in 1948 Stuart Chase could announce that the concept of culture was "coming to be regarded as the foundation stone of the social sciences."[47]

Between the world wars, a conjunction of circumstances allowed Boas and his students to disseminate the concept of culture to other social scientists and to educated laymen. They found receptive audiences among sociologists intent on freeing their discipline from biological and psychological reductionism and among historians intent on finding an inclusive yet meaningful frame of reference. The Boasians also wrote for a popular audience. As "public moralists," detached observers who were given credit for having overcome the ethnocentric bias of Western civilization, they molded middle-class opinion on such topical issues as the American family in transition, the storm and stress of adolescence, and the sexual revolution.[48] As cosmopolitan intellectuals rebelling against what they regarded as a decaying culture, Boas's students exploited anthropology's ability to shock, or at least surprise, through stripping familiar institutions of their historic accretions and calling their self-evident nature into question.[49] In addition, as would-be social engineers, Boas's students endeavored to make Americans more self-conscious about their customs. "Whereas change has hitherto been blind, at the mercy of unconscious patternings," Ruth Benedict wrote in 1929, perhaps it might become possible, "in so far as we become genuinely culture-conscious, that it shall be guided by intelligence."[50]

Finally, the concept of culture opened up new approaches to American culture. Inspired by Clark Wissler, Robert and Helen Lynd adopted a trait-distribution approach to the study of modern American culture. Americans, as the Lynds demonstrated in *Middletown,* did have a culture, and this culture could be apprehended by means of fieldwork in "typical" American communities. By 1929, however, Boas's students were already turning away from the diffusion of cultural traits to what Margaret Mead described as "the set of problems that linked the development of individuals to what was distinctive in the culture in which they were reared."[51] A key work in this shift was Ruth Benedict's *Pat-*

terns of Culture. Benedict conceived of cultures as articulated wholes shaped by the genius of their peoples rather than as accretions of elements. Her elegant depiction of the holism and unity of cultures proved enormously influential among intellectuals interested in charting and possessing America, inspiring Constance Rourke and Caroline Ware to explore vernacular sources, Robert Lynd to adopt an inclusive frame of reference whereby the social sciences were both shaped by and in turn shaped American culture, and John Dewey to invest democracy with a cultural dimension.

Notes

The author acknowledges the support of the National Endowment for the Humanities and the Woodrow Wilson International Center for Scholars, Washington, D.C.

1. Robert S. Lynd, *Knowledge for What? The Place of Social Science in American Culture* (1939; repr. Princeton: Princeton University Press, 1970), pp. ix, 19, 20.
2. Arnold quoted in Lawrence W. Levine, *Highbrow/Lowbrow: The Emergence of Cultural Hierarchy in America* (Cambridge, Mass.: Harvard University Press, 1988), p. 223; Margaret Mead, *An Anthropologist at Work: Writings of Ruth Benedict* (Boston: Houghton Mifflin, 1959), p. 12. On the etymology of *culture,* see Raymond Williams, *Keywords: A Vocabulary of Culture and Society* (New York: Oxford University Press, 1976), pp. 76–82.
3. Warren I. Susman, "The Culture of the Thirties," in his *Culture as History: The Transformation of American Society in the Twentieth Century* (New York: Pantheon Books, 1984), p. 157.
4. Franz Boas, "An Anthropologist's Credo," *Nation,* 27 August 1938, pp. 201–4; reprinted in *I Believe: The Personal Philosophies of Certain Eminent Men and Women of Our Time,* ed. Clifton Fadiman (New York: Simon and Schuster, 1939), pp. 19–29, quotations pp. 20–21, 23; Margaret Mead, *Blackberry Winter: My Earlier Years* (New York: Simon and Schuster, 1972), p. 124. My discussion of Boas's contributions to American anthropology relies on the work of George W. Stocking, Jr., particularly his *Race, Culture, and Evolution: Essays in the History of Anthropology* (1968; repr. Chicago: University of Chicago Press, 1982); and "Introduction: The Basic Assumptions of Boasian Anthropology," in *A Franz Boas Reader: The Shaping of American Anthropology, 1883–1911,* ed. George W. Stocking (Chicago: University of Chicago Press, 1982), pp. 1–20.
5. Franz Boas, "The Occurrence of Similar Inventions in Areas Widely Apart," *Science,* 20 May 1887, p. 485; and "Museums of Ethnology and Their Classification," *Science,* 17 June 1887, pp. 588–89.
6. Franz Boas, "The Limitations of the Comparative Method of Anthropology," *Science* 4 (1896): 901–8; reprinted in Franz Boas, *Race, Language and Culture* (1940; repr. New York: Free Press, 1966), pp. 270–80, quotations pp. 280, 273, 278, 277.
7. Franz Boas, "Human Faculty as Determined by Race," American Association for the Advancement of Science, *Proceedings* 43 (1894): 301–27; reprinted in *A*

Franz Boas Reader, pp. 221–42, quotations pp. 222, 227, 226, 242, 234.

8. Franz Boas, "The Outlook for the American Negro," *Commencement Address at Atlanta University, May 31, 1906,* Atlanta University Leaflet, No. 19; reprinted in *A Franz Boas Reader,* pp. 310–16, quotation p. 313; Boas, "The Negro and the Demands of Modern Life," *Charities,* 7 October 1905, p. 87; Edward H. Beardsley, "The American Scientist as Social Activist: Franz Boas, Burt G. Wilder, and the Cause of Racial Justice, 1900–1915," *Isis* 64 (March 1973): 50–66.

9. Franz Boas, *The Mind of Primitive Man,* rev. ed. (1938; repr. New York: Free Press, 1965), pp. 130, 40, 138, 39.

10. Franz Boas, *Changes in Bodily Form of Descendants of Immigrants,* Senate Document 208, 1911, 61st Cong., 2d sess. (Washington, D.C.: U.S. Government Printing Office, 1911); summarized in *American Anthropologist* 14 (July–September 1912): 530–62.

11. Franz Boas, "Eugenics," *Scientific Monthly* 3 (November 1916): 472; Boas, "Inventing a Great Race," *New Republic,* 13 January 1917, p. 305; Boas, "This Nordic Nonsense," *Forum* 74 (October 1925): 502–11.

12. Melville J. Herskovits, "Brains and the Immigrant," *Nation,* 11 February 1925, pp. 139–41; Margaret Mead, "The Methodology of Racial Testing: Its Significance for Psychology," *American Journal of Sociology* 31 (March 1926): 657–67; Otto Klineberg, *An Experimental Study of Speed and Other Factors in "Racial" Differences,* Archives of Psychology No. 93, January 1928; George W. Stocking, Jr., "Anthropology as Kulturkampf: Science and Politics in the Career of Franz Boas," in *The Uses of Anthropology,* ed. Walter Goldschmidt (Washington, D.C.: American Anthropological Association, 1979), p.42.

13. Thomas F. Gossett, *Race: The History of an Idea in America* (Dallas: Southern Methodist University Press, 1963), chap. 16; Stanley Coben, "The Assault on Victorianism in the Twentieth Century," in *Victorian America,* ed. Daniel Walker Howe (Philadelphia: University of Pennsylvania Press, 1976), pp. 166–70.

14. Margaret Mead, "Apprenticeship under Boas," in *The Anthropology of Franz Boas: Essays on the Centennial of His Birth,* ed. Walter Goldschmidt (Menasha, Wis.: American Anthropological Association, 1959), p. 39; Freda Kirchwey, "Franz Boas," *Nation,* 19 December 1928, p. 689; Edward Sapir, "Franz Boas," *New Republic,* 23 January 1929, pp. 278–79.

15. Regna Darnell, "The Emergence of Edward Sapir's Mature Thought," in *New Perspectives on Edward Sapir in Language, Culture, and Personality,* ed. William Cowan et al. (Amsterdam: John Benjamins, 1986), pp. 556–57. My account of the work of Boas's students in the 1920s and 1930s draws on George W. Stocking, Jr., "Ideas and Institutions in American Anthropology: Toward a History of the Interwar Period," in *Selected Papers from the American Anthropologist, 1921-1945,* ed. George W. Stocking (Washington, D.C.: American Anthropological Association, 1976), pp. 1–50.

16. Edward Sapir, "Time Perspective in Aboriginal American Culture: A Study in Method," in *Selected Writings of Edward Sapir in Language, Culture, and Personality,* ed. David G. Mandelbaum (Berkeley: University of California Press, 1985), p. 394; A. L. Kroeber, "A Study of Language," *Dial* 72 (March 1922): 317.

17. Robert H. Lowie, *Culture and Ethnology* (1917; repr. New York: Basic Books, 1966), p. 66; Lowie, *Primitive Society* (1920; repr. New York: Liveright, 1970), pp. 147, 255.

18. Mead, *An Anthropologist at Work,* p. 8; Ruth Benedict, "Nature and Nurture," *Nation,* 30 January 1924, p. 118.

19. Clark Wissler, "Opportunities for Coordination in Anthropological and Psychological Research," *American Anthropologist* 22 (January–March 1920): 4, 10; Albert Ernest Jenks, "The Relation of Anthropology to Americanization," *Scientific Monthly* 12 (March 1921): 240–45.

20. Clark Wissler, "The Culture-Area Concept in Social Anthropology," *American Journal of Sociology* 32 (May 1927): 885; Wissler, "The Culture Area Concept as a Research Lead," *American Journal of Sociology* 33 (May 1928): 895. See also Clark Wissler, "Recent Developments in Anthropology," in *Recent Developments in the Social Sciences,* ed. Edward Cary Hayes (Philadelphia: Lippincott, 1927), pp. 50–96.

21. Dorothy Ross, "The Development of the Social Sciences," in *The Organization of Knowledge in Modern America, 1860-1920,* ed. Alexandra Oleson and John Voss (Baltimore: Johns Hopkins University Press, 1979), p. 125; John Higham, *History: Professional Scholarship in America* (1965; repr. New York: Harper, 1973), pp. 117–18.

22. Harry Elmer Barnes, ed., *The History and Prospects of the Social Sciences* (New York: Knopf, 1925); William Fielding Ogburn and Alexander Goldenweiser, eds., *The Social Sciences and Their Interrelations* (Boston: Houghton Mifflin, 1927).

23. President's Research Committee on Social Trends, *Recent Social Trends in the United States,* 2 vols. (New York: McGraw-Hill, 1933), 1: xi; Robert Maynard Hutchins, "Address of Dedication," in *The New Social Science,* ed. Leonard D. White (Chicago: University of Chicago Press, 1930), p. 2.

24. Harry Elmer Barnes, "Recent Developments in History," in *Recent Developments in the Social Sciences,* p. 364; Higham, *History,* p. 119.

25. Melville J. Herskovits and Malcolm M. Willey, "The Cultural Approach to Sociology," *American Journal of Sociology* 29 (September 1923): 188–99; Malcolm M. Willey and Melville J. Herskovits, "Psychology and Culture," *Psychological Bulletin* 24 (May 1927): 253–83; Hamilton Cravens, *The Triumph of Evolution: American Scientists and the Heredity-Environment Controversy, 1900-1941* (Philadelphia: University of Pennsylvania Press, 1978), pp. 146–47, 151; William Fielding Ogburn, *Social Change with Respect to Culture and Original Nature* (New York: Huebsch, 1922), pp. 200–1; Jessie Bernard, "The History and Prospects of Sociology in the United States," in *Trends in American Sociology,* ed. George A. Lundberg, Read Bain, and Nels Anderson (New York: Harper, 1929), p. 68.

26. A. L. Kroeber, "The Anthropological Attitude," *American Mercury* 13 (April 1928): 490–91.

27. "War and Reorientation," *Encyclopedia of the Social Sciences,* 15 vols. (New York: Macmillan, 1930), 1: 193, 203.

28. James Steel Smith, "The Day of the Popularizers: The 1920s," *South Atlantic Quarterly* 62 (Spring 1963): 297–309; Higham, *History,* pp. 73–76; Joan Shelley Rubin, "'Information Please!': Culture and Expertise in the Interwar Period," *American Quarterly* 35 (Winter 1983): 499–517; Rubin, "Self, Culture, and Self-

Culture in Modern America: The Early History of the Book-of-the-Month Club," *Journal of American History* 71 (March 1985): 782-806. On how social scientists shaped attitudes toward adolescence and the family, see Paula S. Fass, *The Damned and the Beautiful: American Youth in the 1920's* (New York: Oxford University Press, 1977), pp. 95-118; Christopher Lasch, *Haven in a Heartless World: The Family Besieged* (New York: Basic Books, 1977), pp. 22-43, 62-75.

29. Thorstein Veblen, "The Intellectual Pre-Eminence of Jews in Modern Europe," *Political Science Quarterly* 34 (March 1919): 33-42; George E. Marcus and Michael M. J. Fischer, *Anthropology as Cultural Critique: An Experimental Moment in the Human Sciences* (Chicago: University of Chicago Press, 1986), chap. 6. See also James Clifford, *The Predicament of Culture: Twentieth-Century Ethnography, Literature, and Art* (Cambridge: Harvard University Press, 1988).

30. V. F. Calverton and Samuel D. Schmalhausen, Preface to *Sex in Civilization,* ed. Calverton and Schmalhausen (Garden City, N.Y.: Macaulay, 1929), p. 12; Sinclair Lewis, *Babbitt* (New York: Harcourt, Brace, 1922), p. 117. See also F. H. Matthews, "The Revolt against Americanism: Cultural Pluralism and Cultural Relativism as an Ideology of Liberation," *Canadian Review of American Studies* 1 (Spring 1970): 4-31; and George W. Stocking, Jr., "Essays on Culture and Personality," in *Malinowski, Rivers, Benedict and Others: Essays on Culture and Personality,* ed. George W. Stocking (Madison: University of Wisconsin Press, 1986), pp. 3-12.

31. Hornell Hart, "Changing Social Attitudes and Interests," in *Recent Social Trends in the United States,* 1: 390; Robert H. Lowie, "Science," in *Civilization in the United States: An Inquiry by Thirty Americans,* ed. Harold E. Stearns (1922; repr. Westport, Conn.: Greenwood Press, 1971), p. 155; Lowie, "Is America So Bad, after All?" *Century* 109 (April 1925): 723, 728-29.

32. William E. Leuchtenburg, *The Perils of Prosperity, 1914-32* (Chicago: University of Chicago Press, 1958), pp. 167-70; Alexander Goldenweiser, "Sex and Primitive Society," in *Sex and Civilization,* pp. 53-66; Edward Sapir, "The Discipline of Sex," *American Mercury* 16 (April 1929): 414, 416. An earlier version of Sapir's article had appeared as "Observations on the Sex Problem in America," *American Journal of Psychiatry* 8 (November 1928): 519-34.

33. Edward Sapir, "Culture in the Melting-Pot," *Nation,* 21 December 1916, p.1; Sapir, "Culture, Genuine and Spurious," *American Journal of Sociology* 29 (January 1924): 401-29; reprinted in *Selected Writings of Edward Sapir,* pp. 308-31, quotations pp. 314, 315, 318, 316, 323. See also Richard Handler, "The Dainty and the Hungry Man: Literature and Anthropology in the Work of Edward Sapir," in *Observers Observed: Essays on Ethnographic Fieldwork,* ed. George W. Stocking, Jr. (Madison: University of Wisconsin Press, 1983), pp. 208-31.

34. Margaret Mead, *Coming of Age in Samoa: A Psychological Study of Primitive Youth for Western Civilisation* (1928; repr. New York: Morrow Quill paperback, 1971), p. 247. See also Margaret Mead, "Adolescence in Primitive and Modern Society," in *The New Generation: The Intimate Problems of Modern Parents and Children,* ed. V. F. Calverton and Samuel D. Schmalhausen (New York: Macaulay, 1930), pp. 169-88; Mead, "Standardized America vs. Romantic South Seas," *Scribner's* 90 (November 1931): 486-91; Mead, "Growing Up in the South Seas," *Forum and Century* 87 (May 1932): 285-88.

35. Margaret Mead, *Growing Up in New Guinea: A Comparative Study of Primitive Education* (1930; repr. New York: Morrow Quill paperback, 1975), pp. 211-12, 259.

36. Margaret Mead, *Sex and Temperament in Three Primitive Societies* (1935; repr. New York: Morrow Quill paperback, 1963), pp. 322, ix, 280. See also Mead's retrospective essay, "1925-1939," in *From the South Seas: Studies of Adolescence and Sex in Primitive Societies* (New York: Morrow, 1939), pp. ix-xxxi; and Rosalind Rosenberg, *Beyond Separate Spheres: Intellectual Roots of Modern Feminism* (New Haven: Yale University Press, 1982), chap. 8.

37. Robert S. Lynd and Helen Merrell Lynd, *Middletown: A Study in Modern American Culture* (1929; repr. New York: Harcourt, Brace and World, 1956), pp. vi, 3-5, 7-8, 496-99. See also the fine essay by Richard Wightman Fox, "Epitaph for Middletown: Robert S. Lynd and the Analysis of Consumer Culture," in *The Culture of Consumption: Critical Essays in American History, 1880-1980*, ed. Richard Wightman Fox and T. J. Jackson Lears (New York: Pantheon, 1983), pp. 101-41.

38. H.L. Mencken, "A City in Moronia," *American Mercury* 16 (March 1929): 379, 381.

39. Stuart Chase, with Marian Tyler, *Mexico: A Study of Two Americas* (New York: Macmillan, 1931), pp. 154, 15, 130, 310, 170; Robert Redfield, *Tepoztlan, a Mexican Village: A Study of Folk Life* (Chicago: University of Chicago Press, 1930), pp. 13-14; Reuel Denney, "The Discovery of the Popular Culture," in *American Perspectives: The National Self-Image in the Twentieth Century*, ed. Robert E. Spiller and Eric Larrabee (Cambridge: Harvard University Press, 1961), pp. 170-72.

40. Ruth Benedict, *Patterns of Culture* (1934; repr. Boston: Houghton Mifflin, 1961), pp. vii, xvi-xvii, 47-48, 55, 229, 258-59. See also Judith Schachter Modell, *Ruth Benedict: Patterns of a Life* (Philadelphia: University of Pennsylvania Press, 1983), chap. 7.

41. Benedict, *Patterns of Culture*, pp. 167, 211, 247, 129, 273, 274. See also Clifford Geertz, "Us/Not-Us: Benedict's Travels," in his *Works and Lives: The Anthropologist as Author* (Stanford: Stanford University Press, 1988), pp. 102-28.

42. Alfred Kazin, *On Native Grounds* (1942; abridged ed., Garden City, N.Y.: Doubleday, 1956), p. 378. See also William Stott, *Documentary Expression and Thirties America* (1973; repr. Chicago: University of Chicago Press, 1986).

43. Constance Rourke, *The Roots of American Culture and Other Essays*, ed. Van Wyck Brooks (New York: Harcourt, Brace, 1942), pp. 49-50. See also Joan Shelley Rubin, *Constance Rourke and American Culture* (Chapel Hill: University of North Carolina Press, 1980), chap. 3.

44. Caroline F. Ware, ed., *The Cultural Approach to History* (1940; repr. New York: Gordon Press, 1974), pp. 10-11, 73; "Educating Clio," *American Historical Review* 45 (April 1940): 505, 507, 516-17.

45. Lynd, *Knowledge for What?*, p. 50.

46. John Dewey, *Freedom and Culture* (New York: Putnam's, 1939), pp. 13, 6, 175; Philip Gleason, "Americans All: World War II and the Shaping of American Identity," *Review of Politics* 43 (October 1981): 483-518; Gleason, "World War II and the Development of American Studies," *American Quarterly* 36 (Bibli-

ography 1984): 343–58; Edward A. Purcell, Jr., *The Crisis of Democratic Theory: Scientific Naturalism and the Problem of Value* (Lexington: University Press of Kentucky, 1973), pp. 197–217, 235–72.

47. Benedict, *Patterns of Culture,* p. 223; Stuart Chase, *The Proper Study of Mankind* (New York: Harper, 1948), p. 59.

48. I owe the term *public moralists* to David Hollinger.

49. David Hollinger, "Ethnic Diversity, Cosmopolitanism, and the Emergence of the American Liberal Intelligentsia," in his *In the American Province: Studies in the History and Historiography of Ideas* (Bloomington: Indiana University Press, 1985), pp. 56–73.

50. Ruth Benedict, "The Science of Custom," *Century* 117 (April 1929): 641–49; reprinted in *The Making of Man: An Outline of Anthropology,* ed. V. F. Calverton (New York: Random House, 1931), pp. 805–17, quotation p. 817.

51. Mead, *Blackberry Winter,* p. 126. See also Franz Boas, "The Methods of Ethnology," *American Anthropologist* 22 (1920): 311–22; reprinted in Boas, *Race, Language and Culture,* pp. 281–89.

■ 9   EUGENICS AMONG THE SOCIAL SCIENCES

Hereditarian Thought in Germany and the United States

ROBERT N. PROCTOR

What a galaxy of genius might we not create! We might introduce prophets and high priests of civilization into the world, as surely as we can propagate idiots by mating crétins.
—FRANCIS GALTON, 1865

Eugenics is not a panacea that will cure human ills; it is rather a dangerous sword that may turn its edge against those who rely on its strength.
—FRANZ BOAS, 1928

The Question of Historiography

Eugenics, both American and European, has become the object of intense historical scrutiny in recent years. Why? First and foremost, historians have recognized the importance of studying the social context of science, both in terms of its origins and its application. As part of this, we have seen the growth of efforts to explore the political involvement of science and of scientists. How is science transformed by political movement? How are political movements informed by science? How and why do scientists come to support or resist a particular movement? Eugenics presents a dramatic example of how political priorities can structure scientific priorities.

Fueling historical research in this area has also been the concern that we are in the midst of a revival of eugenics sentiments. The explosive growth of sociobiology and behavioral genetics; the spread of genetic counseling and genetic screening; the revival of biological determinism in discussions of IQ, criminality, alcoholism, schizophrenia, women's mathematical ability, and so forth—these have all evoked comparisons with similar movements in the 1930s. As prospects of an artificial womb and the widespread use of genetic fingerprinting or even gene therapy loom on the horizon, comparisons with historical efforts to breed a better human become of special interest. Many of the concerns surrounding today's biotechnology resonate with events of the past: Soon we may be able to do what eugenicists never dreamed about; perhaps something can be learned from the promises and pitfalls of the 1930s.

Historians, in other words, do not ply their trade in a vacuum. For feminists, eugenics has become of interest because of the centrality of pronatalist ideologies in early twentieth-century eugenics.[1] Antiabortionists hope that comparisons can be drawn between the experience of the Nazis and today's supposed "holocaust" of abortions, and critics of psychiatry try to link the Nazi destruction of "lives not worth living" (administered largely by psychiatrists) to modern psychiatric practice.[2] The recent emergence of a strong disabled rights movement has directed attention onto abuses in this field: Witness the book by Ernst Klee on the extermination of the mentally ill and handicapped in the final years of the Third Reich; witness also the efforts to show that the "final solutions" to the Jewish and Gypsy "problems" were modeled on the extermination of the mentally or physically handicapped.[3] Geneticists, too, have thrown their hats into the ring, recognizing that their disciplinary forebears were among the intellectual vanguard helping to plan the "elimination of defectives" for which the Nazi regime has become notorious.[4]

In the past decade, German scholars have produced an astonishing mass of literature, little known on this side of the Atlantic, devoted to exploring the place of science and medicine under fascism.[5] The timing is not coincidental. Much of the silence that surrounded this topic until the 1970s can be traced to the fact that many of those involved in the construction of Nazi policy maintained positions of power long after the war.[6] (As late as 1982, the head of the West Berlin Medical Chamber was a former SA colonel; even today the head of the Bavarian Medical Chamber is a former SS officer.) For many years, German scientists and physicians were understandably reluctant to explore the Nazi past; even today, much of the pioneering research in this area has been done by persons outside the academic community: Ernst Klee is a journalist; Götz Aly's provocative and ground-breaking *Beiträge* volumes are published by Rotbuch Verlag, a small left-wing press in Berlin.[7]

In both Germany and the United States, historical interpretation has been complicated by the fact that the history of eugenics is a sensitive subject. (When I was gathering photos for my book on *Racial Hygiene,* more than one West German librarian agreed to facilitate my investigations only on the condition that I agreed *not* to thank them for their help!) Historians have been faced with two separate obstacles. On the one hand, there has been the assumption that eugenics is something entirely separate from genetics. Eugenics, in this view, was either a perversion of genetics or else the product of a marginal band of renegades from academic science. Geneticists after the Second World War were often embarrassed by the recent history of their discipline: A. H. Sturtevant, in his 1965 *History of Genetics*, informed his readers that abuses had been committed but also stated that it was better not to name names because "*racism* is a dirty word."[8] Benno Müller-Hill summarizes the problem in stronger and more honest terms: "The rise of genetics is characterized by a gigantic process of repression of its history."[9] Such repression fit rather well with the popular view of science as cumulative and progressive: Eugenics eventually disappeared, so could it ever really have been supported by genuine scientists?

The radical separation of genetics and eugenics (or science and pseudo-science) has been one obstacle. Historians are also faced, however, with the quite different assumption (especially among historians in the United States) that eugenics is indissolubly linked with the crimes of the Nazis. Eugenics, in this view, culminates in Auschwitz, and any effort to detract from this is an insult to those who died there. (A related kind of thinking brands any and all subsequent efforts to foster or improve human genetic health—amniocentesis, genetic counseling, and so forth—as "Nazi.") Holocaust historians have been justifiably concerned about efforts to make Nazi theory or practice look "respectable." Yet in looking at only one outcome of the eugenics movement—the final solution—they have (ironically) tended to adopt the view of science put forward by those who would rather ignore entirely the history of this period, namely, the view that genuine science could in no way have been involved in Nazi programs of genocide.

Ironically, the premise upon which both of these perspectives are based—that science cannot flourish in or contribute to totalitarian rule—has a history not unconnected with efforts to suppress the Nazi past. West German historian Christian Pross has recently shown that postwar American prosecutors at the Nuremberg "doctors' trial" (1946–47) were involved not only in tracking down the guilty but also in recruiting for American military research.[10] American military authorities wanted to discover whether anything of value might be gleaned from the concentration camp experiments conducted by Sigmund Rascher and others; what better way to disguise such efforts than to claim (as one American prosecutor put it) that such experiments were "a ghastly failure, as well as a hideous crime"?[11] The postwar assumption that the Nazi period produced nothing in the way of "genuine science"—and conversely, that genuine scientists could not have participated in the madness of Nazi politics—may therefore be seen as part of an effort to hide the fact that postwar military authorities (especially in America) were in fact quite interested in whatever scientific results might have been produced under the Nazis.

In recent years, historians have recognized that neither of these accounts—that eugenics was entirely separate from genetics, or that eugenics was linked only with the Nazis—is faithful to the historical record. I have already cited German scholarship in this area (see note 5). In the United States, Mark Haller, Kenneth Ludmerer, and Donald Pickens began the modern historiography of eugenics in a series of works in the 1960s and early 1970s; since this time we have seen the publication of Daniel Kevles's comprehensive *In the Name of Eugenics* and a number of other works tracing the rise and fall of eugenics.[12] Loren Graham and Diane Paul have shown that eugenics meant very different things to different people and that it is not possible to shackle a single political ideology to efforts to "breed a better human."[13] Garland Allen, Allan Chase, and Barry Mehler have shown that eugenics concerns were important in immigration restriction legislation and persisted in altered forms long after the war.[14] While interpretations still differ on how and to what extent American eugenicists supported the Nazis, we do have a fairly good sense of the problems and priorities that led to the establishment and demise of the movement.

The purpose of this paper is to provide an overview of the eugenics movement, concentrating on transatlantic links and on the place of eugenics among the social sciences, especially sociology and anthropology. Eugenics, we must recall, was many different things. It was a political movement, providing counsel to governments on questions ranging from immigration, abortion, and racial mixing to penal reform, psychiatric policy, and birth control. Eugenics was "preventive medicine," designed to put a halt to human genetic illness before it could spread. It was a social as well as a biological science, one whose appeal lay in its simplicity, its claim to trace social success or deviance to one's genetic constitution. It was popular science, but it was also science that met with resistance. Eugenics, at least in its early racist and hereditarian form, was ultimately rejected by most leading scientists, but not before the experience of Nazi genocide cast a shadow over the movement that advertised itself as "applied human genetics."

But first a few words on the origins of and early support for the movement.

Early Movements

In 1883 Francis Galton, cousin of Charles Darwin and inventor of the system of identification by fingerprints, coined the term *eugenics* to designate "the study of the agencies under social control that may improve or impair the racial qualities of future generations, either physically or mentally."[15] Twelve years later, German physician Alfred Ploetz published his *Die Tüchtigkeit unsrer Rasse und der Schutz der Schwachen*, coining the term *racial hygiene* (*Rassenhygiene*) to designate the study of "the optimal conditions for the maintenance and development of the race."[16]

Implicit in both Galton's eugenics and Ploetz's racial hygiene was a set of concerns that extended to the human race *as a whole*. Many in the early eugenics movement were not in fact "racists" in the sense we commonly think of that term today.[17] Early eugenicists were often more concerned about the indiscriminate distribution of birth control (neo-Malthusianism) or medical care for the weak and inferior than they were about German-Jewish miscegenation or any of the other views we associate with modern anti-Semitism; there were, in fact, a number of Jews in the early movement.[18] Eugenicists worried that modern civilization had stifled the struggle for existence and that the competitive struggle for existence was in need of repair. Eugenicists warned that socialism, feminism, and other social movements were threatening to impose a false egalitarianism on the natural hierarchies in society.

Interestingly, German Social Darwinians differed from their English or American colleagues in their stress upon a role for the state in correcting these dangers.[19] Among Germans, there was less a sense of "letting nature take its course" than among Spencerian Social Darwinists. German Social Darwinists at the end of the nineteenth century tended to reject the optimistic, laissez-faire liberalism popular in England and America, stressing instead the need for state intervention to stop what they saw as the "degeneration" of the human species caused by the more rapid breeding of inferiors and the growth of medical care for the weak.[20]

With its intellectual foundations laid in the final decades of the nineteenth century, the eugenics movement gained institutional support in the early years of the twentieth. In Germany, the Krupp Prize Essay contest was announced in 1900;[21] this was followed by the establishment of the *Archiv für Rassen- und Gesellschaftsbiologie* in 1904 and the Deutsche Gesellschaft für Rassenhygiene in 1905.[22] Supported by landed Junker and industrialist groups and united against the common threat of democracy, socialized medicine, and Marxist "environmental-ism," racial hygienists advocated a program of state-supported "selection" to counter a perceived tendency of the criminal, the insane, and the working poor to reproduce at faster rates than the more "gifted" military, industrial, and intellectual elites.

In America, too, the institutional foundations for eugenics were laid in the first decade of the century. In 1904, the Carnegie Institution provided funds for the establishment of an Experimental Station for the Study of Evolution at Cold Spring Harbor with zoologist Charles Davenport as its director. In 1910, Davenport managed to persuade Mrs. E. H. Harriman, widow of the railroad magnate, to fund the establishment of an ambitious Eugenics Record Office; between 1910 and 1918 Harriman provided more than $500,000 to the office, located not far from the Experimental Station at Cold Spring Harbor. With additional funds from John D. Rockefeller, Jr., Davenport became the most powerful advocate of eugenics in the United States—the Harvard-trained eugenicist looked forward to the day when a woman would no more marry a man "without knowing his biologico-genealogical history" than a breeder of cattle would take "a sire for his colts or calves . . . without a pedigree."[23] Eugenics journals were founded, including (in America) *Eugenical News* (1916–1953), the *Eugenics Record Office Bulletin* (1911–1933), and *Eugenics, a Journal of Race Betterment,* and (in England) the *Eugenics Review* (1909–1968), published by the Eugenics Education Society, and the *Annals of Eugenics* (1925–1954), published by the Galton Laboratory of London.[24]

As Kevles, Allen, and others have shown, eugenics in both England and America was a popular movement.[25] Parents spoke of "eugenic babies"; young women hoped for "eugenic marriages." Local eugenics societies sprang up all over the United States and in several major cities in England: eugenics meetings, according to one British observer, brought out "all the neo-Malthusians, anti-vaccinationists, antivivisectionists, Christian Scientists, Theosophists, Mullerites . . . vegetarians, and the rest!"[26] Proposals for the new social therapy ranged far and wide, from the castration of criminals to prize awards for "fitter families." Caleb Saleeby, the first to distinguish *positive eugenics* (aiming at increasing superiors) from *negative eugenics* (aiming at eliminating defectives), sought to fuse eugenics demands with the antialcohol movement.[27] A popular handbook on eugenics warned against tight-fitting clothing and self-abuse, illustrating this message with graphic drawings of "injuries caused by the corset" and testicles "wasted by masturbation."[28] Roswell Johnson protested in 1914 that eugenics appeared to embrace anything having to do with the "science of sex" or the "science of health"—he cited ads boasting of "eugenic milk" and even a eugenic "ice station";

he also reported having attended a meeting where the speaker announced that "as the hour is late, we must adjourn for lunch now, to be eugenic."[29]

With institutional support and popular appeal, eugenics quickly found its way into university curricula. By the end of the Weimar period, eugenics was taught in the medical facilities of most German universities; in America, eugenics teaching was even more widespread, with 376 college courses devoted to this topic in 1928.[30] Racial hygiene was advertised as a logical step in the development of medicine. Especially in Germany, racial hygiene was considered one of the three prongs of responsible medical care: *Personal* hygiene was the sphere of traditional medicine, focusing on the individual; *social* hygiene was the sphere of public health, focusing on occupational safety, housing, and clean air and water; and *racial* hygiene was the sphere of care for human genetic health, focusing on future generations. Racial hygiene was preventive rather than curative medicine; racial hygiene would provide tools for the long-term management of the human germ plasm.

Eugenics and the Social Sciences

Eugenics movements emerged in both Europe and America at a time when the goals and institutional structure of most social sciences were not yet firmly fixed. In Germany, the Deutsche Gesellschaft für Soziologie was not founded until 1910 (its first meeting was held in 1911); sociological professorships were not established in Germany until after the First World War. The American Sociological Society was founded in 1906; twelve years earlier, when the *American Journal of Sociology* first appeared, American sociology was (in Albion Small's words) nothing more than a "wistful advertisement of a hiatus in knowledge."[31]

In this fluid environment, eugenicists sought to direct the focus of professional social science societies in directions favorable to their movement. Consider first the case of sociology. By the end of the nineteenth century, Social Darwinism had become an important part of sociological discourse in both Europe and America. Spencer and Sumner are among the better known but in Germany, too, figures such as Ludwig Gumplowicz, Albert Schäffle, and Paul von Lilienfeld sought to construct a sociology based on a synthesis of the organic metaphors of Comte or Spencer and the natural selection of Darwin.[32] German sociologists considered English eugenics of considerable interest for their own work: When Sir Francis Galton founded the London Sociological Society in 1904, Ferdinand Tönnies devoted considerable space in *Schmollers Jahrbuch* to an analysis of the new movement.[33] In 1910, Galton's *He-*

reditary Genius was published in German translation *(Genie und Ver-erbung)*—the translators were the young sociologist Otto Neurath and his wife, Anna Schapire-Neurath.

German sociologists were divided, however, over whether and/or how biology—especially natural selection, the doctrine of descent, and racial theory—was relevant to the social sciences. Debate along these lines occupied much of the attention of sociologists in the years prior to the First World War. At the first meeting of the Deutsche Gesellschaft für Soziologie at Frankfurt in 1910, fully one-third of the entire session was devoted to racial hygiene, which Alfred Ploetz wanted to establish as the centerpiece of the new science of sociology.[34] Tönnies and Leopold von Wiese supported the new Darwinian sociology. Max Weber, however, rejected Ploetz's program as an illegitimate intrusion of the natural sciences into the social sciences,[35] and, at least for a time, Weber's position held sway. At the second meeting of the society (Berlin, 1912), where racial hygiene was again a major topic of discussion, Weber made clear his belief that Ploetz's "confused racial mysticism" could not be taken seriously ("mit der unklaren Rassenmystik nichts anzufangen ist"). Germany's foremost sociologist rejected as "totally unproven" Ploetz's claim that social development depended upon racial health; he also rejected Ploetz's notion of a *Vitalrasse* as the product of "unbounded subjective valuations," labeling the newly founded journal of racial hygiene (the *Archiv für Rassen- und Gesellschaftsbiologie*) "an arsenal of boundless hypotheses" containing "not a single fact relevant to sociology." Weber maintained that sociology must consider social phenomena sui generis, not as passive reflections of deeply rooted instincts or biological drives.[36]

Weber's position on this matter ultimately came to dominate, despite occasional efforts in subsequent years to found a *Bio-* or *Anthroposozi-ologie*. In Alfred Vierkandt's comprehensive *Handwörterbuch der Soziologie* (1931), Friedrich Hertz rejected Gumplowicz's conception of racial hatred as the driving force of history; Vierkandt himself had explicitly excluded discussion of "Rassenanatomie, -biologie und -hygiene" from scientific sociology as early as 1909.[37] Sociology found little sympathy among Nazi circles in the early 1930s: Its association with socialism, its commonly stated purpose of finding meaning outside human biological process, all worked to make "the science of society" an unlikely candidate for Nazi support.[38]

More lasting bonds were established between racial hygiene and anthropology, especially in Germany, and especially after the rediscovery of Mendelian genetics in 1900 appeared to provide a theoretical foundation for explaining human cultural traits in biological terms.[39] German anthropologists were receptive to the idea of eugenics: *Rassenhygiene* would unite theory and practice; *Rassenkunde* (racial science) would unite the natural and spiritual sciences (*Natur- und Geisteswissenschaften*).[40] Anthropologists were among the founders of the German Society for Racial Hygiene (Richard Thurnwald, for example), and it was an anthropologist, Eugen Fischer, who directed Germany's foremost eugenical institute from 1927 to 1942: the Kaiser Wilhelm Institut für Anthropologie, menschliche Erblehre und Eugenik.[41]

Links between anthropology and eugenics strengthened during the Nazi period. On 23–25 March 1938, at the annual meeting of the Deutsche Gesellschaft für Rassenforschung—DGRf (Germany's leading anthropological body, organized in 1925 as the Deutsche Gesellschaft für Physische Anthropologie), Walter Gross, head of the Rassenpolitisches Amt, proposed a merger of the DGRf and the Gesellschaft für Rassenhygiene, announcing that the chairmen of the two bodies had both been named advisors in the Rassenpolitisches Amt.[42] The merger never took place (the war directed energies elsewhere); nevertheless, by the beginning of the Second World War research efforts in the two communities— anthropological and eugenical—were very close. Anthropology was supposed to provide the theory for which racial hygiene was the practice. Anthropologists and eugenicists therefore collaborated in the administration of the Nuremberg Laws,[43] the sterilization of the *Rheinlandbastarde*, and the elaboration of criteria for sterilization. Eugenicists and anthropologists generally agreed that biology underlies human diversity, that there are superior and inferior kinds of humans, and that it was the duty of the state to encourage the reproduction of the fit and the elimination (e.g., by sterilization) of the unfit.[44]

In America, the relation of anthropology to eugenics was somewhat more complex. American anthropologists were in fact divided over the relevance of eugenics to their field—more so, perhaps, than in Germany.[45] Here it is important to distinguish cultural and physical anthropological traditions (or Boasian versus anti-Boasian traditions). Within the field of physical anthropology, eugenics remained a regular field of interest well into the 1930s.[46] The prefatory remarks of Aleš Hrdlička in the first (1918) volume of the *American Journal of Physical Anthropology* (*AJPA*) cited the relevance of physical anthropology for the "regulation of immigration, eugenic progress, and all other endeavors tending to knowing, safeguarding, and advancing the physical status of man in this country."[47] Defined by Hrdlička as "the study of racial anatomy, physiology, and pathology," physical anthropology was to include research into the health effects of miscegenation: Hrdlička asserted that "the grave problem of mixture of white and negro" was "largely controllable by law and general enlightenment" and that such mixtures "if found detrimental could be reduced to a minimum." Physical anthropologists were concerned about the effects of the war, syphilis, and alcoholism on "racial health"; the *AJPA* reported on the efforts of American and British eugenics societies to address the general question of "race suicide." In 1918, Hrdlička predicted that the new science of eugenics would "essentially become applied anthropology."[48]

American physical anthropologists' fascination with eugenics continued through the 1920s and 1930s. In 1944, when Charles Davenport died, the *American Journal of Physical Anthropology* celebrated the former head of the Eugenics Record Office as "a born leader, a promoter, a director, an organizer; a zoologist, biologist, geneticist, eugenicist and anthropologist."[49] The case of anthropology is complicated, however, by the fact that a strong antieugenicist alternative existed from the last decade of the nineteenth century. Indeed, by the 1920s, a sizable body of American anthropologists (especially cultural anthropologists) were following Franz Boas in distinguishing race, language, and culture as independent variables (a person of any race could speak any language or develop any culture, and so forth). In his 1928 *Anthropology and Modern Society*, Boas rejected the assumption central to mainline eugenics that cultural traits (such as alcoholism or criminality) are heritable; he also doubted whether eugenicists had correctly diagnosed the "degeneration" from which society was said to be suffering: "No amount of eugenic selection will overcome those social conditions that have raised a poverty and disease-stricken proletariat—which will be reborn from even the best stock, so long as the social conditions persist that remorselessly push human beings into helpless and hopeless misery."[50] As a social democrat and outsider to the Anglo-Saxon mainstream celebrated by eugenicists (he had left Germany in the 1880s concerned that, as a Jew, he would never be able to land an academic position in his native land),[51] it is not surprising that Boas found little of value in the eugenics either of Madison Grant ("Nordic nonsense") or of Charles Davenport, a man for whom equality was a "biological absurdity" and traits such as "nomadism," "shiftlessness," and "thalassophilia" (love of the sea) were inherited through the genes.

In the 1930s, Boas and his students helped organize opposition to Nazi racism. Here again, Boas won support more from cultural than from physical anthropologists. On 29 December 1938, at the annual meeting of the American Anthropological Association, Boas managed to have a motion passed denouncing Nazi racism; the statement asserted that "the terms Aryan and Semitic have no racial significance whatsoever" and that "anthropology provides no scientific basis for discrimination against any people on the ground of racial inferiority." By contrast, a similar proposal introduced before the American Association of Physical Anthropologists (by Ashley Montagu in 1939) failed to win support and was never adopted.[52]

Among sociologists, support for eugenics encountered strong opposition early in the century. Unlike anthropology, sociology was not a "four-field science" (physical, cultural, archaeological, and linguistic) and racial or anatomical questions never carried the weight they did in anthropology (apart from a few early treatises such as George Fitzhugh's proslavery *Sociology for the South* [published in 1854]). It is true that, early in the twentieth century, eugenicists in both England and the United States tried to take over sociology (as in Germany): Francis Galton founded the London Sociological Society in 1904, hoping that the society would take up the cause of eugenics. Eugenics was the leading topic of discussion in each of the three volumes of the society's *Sociological Papers* (1905–1907). With the establishment of independent eugenics institutions, however, sociologists began to divorce themselves from the movement. Charles H. Cooley, the "Darwin of sociology" according to Charles Ellwood, signaled the changing climate of mainstream sociological opinion as early as 1897, when he criticized Galton's eugenics for ignoring the fact that genius could never flower without a favorable environment.[53] In 1906, the American Sociological Society debated the relevance of eugenics for sociology; with Lester Frank Ward playing the role of Weber, eugenics suffered a fate similar to that of Ploetz's racial hygiene in German sociology.[54] Ward, the first president of the new society, attacked eugenics as "oligocentric," concentrating as it did upon "an almost infinitesimal fraction of the human race" while ignoring the rest.[55] Ward later warned against the "feverish haste to improve the world" on the part of those who, assuming a wisdom superior to that of nature, seek to breed an "artificial race of hydrocephalous pygmies."[56]

It is true that, in subsequent years, the *American Journal of Sociology* did occasionally publish eugenics proposals;[57] and in 1910 the journal gave a favorable review to Charles Davenport's *Eugenics—The Science of Human Improvement by Better Breeding*.[58] But the journal's cumulative index for the period 1895 to 1945 includes only seven articles on this topic, and several of these are reprints of lectures from England. Frank H. Hankins, professor of sociology at Smith College, considered himself a staunch eugenicist, but even he rejected (in 1928) the "pseudo-scientific bunk" of the Nordic doctrine, irritating the *Eugenical News* by suggesting that "well-endowed Italians, Hebrews, Turks, Chinese, and Negroes" were better materials out of which to forge a nation than "average or below average Nordics."[59]

Given the different reactions of anthropologists and sociologists to racial theory, it is interesting to note the different fates of these two fields in Germany and the United States. American and German anthropology grew apart in the 1920s and 1930s, as the Boasian concept of culture (relativist, environmentalist) came to dominate American research, while an increasingly hereditarian approach came to the fore in Germany. In 1911, Boas's was the voice of the future when he declared that modern anthropologists assumed a "unity of the mind of man" and "the similarity of mental functions in all races."[60] In 1914, Fritz Lenz presaged the German future when he declared that the study of mental differences was the very core of anthropology, a science he defined as the study of "genetic differences in humans," both mental and physical.[61]

Sociology presents quite a different story. Whereas anthropology flourished under the Nazis (in a purely quantitative sense—numbers of faculty, papers published, etc.), sociology, partly because of its association with socialism, collapsed. Anthropologists in Germany generally embraced the Nazi movement (eight out of ten *Ordinariate* joined the Nazi party);[62] the Deutsche Gesellschaft für Soziologie, by contrast, was disbanded. Anthropology by the 1930s had shown its usefulness to Germany's radical right; sociology had not.

Whatever the proclivities of particular disciplines may have been, it was ultimately the triumph of the National Socialist government in 1933 that turned the tide—in opposite directions—for eugenics in Germany and the United States. The Nazi government adopted the racial hygiene program as its own, highlighting those elements consistent with National Socialist ideologies of Nordic supremacy and the imperative to destroy "lives not worth living." Many American eugenicists were at first excited by Nazi eugenics achievements, but eventually they, too, proclaimed their allegiance to the values of the society within which they lived. As we shall see, the outbreak of war in 1939 put American eugenicists in a difficult position, a position from which they were able to extract themselves only by rejecting a substantial portion of their intellectual ancestry.

German-American Relations in the 1930s

I noted earlier that historians do not entirely agree on the role of science in bringing about the collapse of eugenics or the extent of American support for Nazi racial policies. Haller, for example, has emphasized the fact that in the course of the 1930s, geneticists began to realize that eugenicists had underestimated the complexity of hereditary mechanisms and the role of environmental factors in shaping human physical and cultural traits. Haller admits that the specter of Hitler's Germany helped to discredit the eugenics movement, but his emphasis is on an earlier shift. Haller suggests that eugenics after 1930 was of a different character from that from 1905 to 1930: This latter period was characterized "not by legislation, or even propaganda, but by continued and careful research into the heredity of man."[63] American eugenicists (in his view) rejected Nazi eugenics from the outset.

In fact, while it is true that some American eugenicists changed their views as Haller describes, it is also true that many supported Nazi racial hygiene until the onset of hostilities in the Second World War. The *Eugenical News*, for example, praised the Nazis' 1933 sterilization law (allowing the forcible sterilization of persons suffering from feeblemindedness, schizophrenia, manic depressive insanity, epilepsy, Huntington's disease, genetic blindness, deafness, or alcoholism) as "clean-cut, direct, and 'model'. . . . From a legal point of view nothing more could be desired."[64] Paul Popenoe echoed this sentiment in 1934, characterizing the law as "better than the sterilization laws of most American states"; the Hitler regime was taking strong steps to apply "biological principles" to human society.[65] In 1937 Frederick Osborn, secretary of the American Eugenics Society, described the German program as "excellent . . . the most important social experiment . . . ever tried"; the same year, the American Eugenics Society voted to endorse the Nazi sterilization program at a conference on "Eugenics in Relation to Nursing."[66]

Surprisingly, a number of American social science journals also joined in supporting the Nazi law. In 1936, in a review of "Legal and Medical Aspects of Eugenic Sterilization in Germany" for the *American Sociological Review*, Marie E. Kopp wrote that the Nazi law was being administered "in entire fairness" and that "discrimination of class, race, creed, political, or religious belief" did not enter into the matter. Kopp hailed the law as a "great step ahead," a "constructive public health measure," a "method of preventive medicine," and a "contribution to social welfare." Kopp ended her review by citing the now notorious words of Supreme Court Justice Oliver Wendell Holmes, handing down his decision in the case of *Buck v. Bell*, that "three generations of imbeciles are enough"![67]

There were, of course, important differences in the two movements—German and American—especially after the Nazi *Machtergreifung* (seizure of power). Government and foundation support for eugen-

ics grew in Germany after 1933; support for eugenics in America declined. Most (approximately two-thirds) of those sterilized under the
Nazi law were not institutionalized; American sterilization laws were
generally applied only to people incarcerated in prisons or homes for
the mentally ill. In Germany, sterilization was national policy; in the
United States, laws varied from state to state. The Nazi law was far
more aggressive; indeed more were sterilized in the second year of its
operation (73,174 in 1935) than in all of the United States from 1907
(when the first law was enacted in Indiana) through the end of the
Second World War.[68]

German and American eugenicists were united, however, even in
the 1930s on a broad range of themes: in their fears of "race suicide"
and of "racial poisons" (especially alcohol, tobacco, narcotics, and syphilis),[69] in their belief that it was to genetics that we must look for the
causes of crime, mental illness, and social deviance. German and American eugenicists were united in assuming that (1) a broad class of defectives (the criminal, mentally ill, morally dissolute, etc.) is threatening
the race through excessive breeding; (2) these defectives are genetic
defectives, that is, the defects from which they suffer are largely inherited; (3) sterilization can eliminate genetic defectives in a relatively short
period of time; and (4) sterilization should be used to eliminate inferiors
because, as Laughlin once wrote, the human germ plasm belongs to
society and not solely "to the individual who carries it."[70]

German and American eugenicists were also generally united on the
question of the dangers posed by racial miscegenation to the health of
the race. In the 1930s and 1940s, a number of leading geneticists believed
that intermarriage between widely separated races was inadvisable for
biological reasons.[71] The 1935 Nuremberg Law banning sexual relations
between Jews and Germans (the so-called Blood Protection Law) received a measure of support from the German scientific community;
even after the war, in his commentary on the UNESCO statement on
race, anthropologist Hans Weinert wondered whether any of the men
who signed the statement "would be prepared to marry his daughter
to an Australian aboriginal."[72]

Here again, Nazi physicians were able to point to many American
states where laws banning racial intermarriage were even more strict
than in Germany. A 1929 California law banned marriage between
whites and "Negroes, Mongolians, Mulattoes, or members of the Malay
race." A 1926 Indiana law declared null and void marriages between
white persons and "persons having one-eighth or more of negro
blood."[73] By 1940, thirty American states had passed legislation barring
racial miscegenation in one form or another; most of these laws were

not repealed until after World War II. (California's law, for example, was declared unconstitutional by the California Supreme Court in 1948.)

Nazi journals cited these laws as evidence that Germany was not alone in pursuing policies of racial segregation.[74] American eugenicists returned the favor, praising Nazi laws that excluded Jews from civil service. In 1934, the *Eugenical News* reported under the headline "Jewish Physicians in Berlin" that "the excitement caused by the German racial legislation and the adoption of measures directed against Jewish physicians in Germany was, after all, rather ungrounded if we realize that the large German cities were literally swamped by those physicians and that, in spite of careful attempts to limit the Jewish contingent, their numbers actually were but slightly reduced."[75]

I do not mean to imply that all American eugenicists supported views such as this; indeed, there is clear evidence that, in the course of the 1930s, many eugenicists became dissatisfied with the racist elements of the "mainline" movement. In America, the racist rhetoric of Madison Grant, Harry Laughlin, and Charles Davenport is eventually replaced by the more cautious work of Frederick Osborn, Raymond Pearl, and what Daniel Kevles has called "reform eugenics."

Even in Germany, at least until 1933, the Nordic supremacist version of racial hygiene was only one of several strands of eugenics competing for scholarly attention. Until the rise of the Nazis, the German eugenics movement was more nationalist or meritocratic than it was anti-Semitic. Anti-Semitism played only a minor role in the early movement (the father of German racial hygiene, Alfred Ploetz, considered Jews to be part of the superior "Nordic race"). The focus instead was on the dangers of birth control, medical care for the weak, and the disproportionate breeding of the genetically infirm assumed to exist in all races. By the late 1920s, however, this had changed, and the right-wing faction of racial hygiene had merged with National Socialism.[76]

Under the Nazis, racial hygiene came to play a central role in the ideology of the repressive state. In 1930 Fritz Lenz, Germany's foremost human geneticist, praised Hitler as "the first politician of truly great import who has taken racial hygiene as a serious element of state policy"; Hitler himself would later call his revolution "the final step in the overcoming of historicism and the recognition of purely biological values." But if Hitler's revolution gave a luster to eugenics that it never had before, it also tarnished it in a way that would ultimately bring the entire movement into disrepute throughout the world.

The End of Eugenics?

The eugenics movement did not arise unopposed. Opposition came from social scientists, fearing the reduction of their work to biology; from Catholics, fearful of violating the sanctity of life; from socialists and communists, fearful of a new and brutal weapon to combat the "proletarization" of European or American society; from liberals, fearful of state power encroaching into the private lives of individual citizens; from feminists, fearing yet another effort to reduce women to reproductive beings; and from natural scientists, increasingly concerned that many of the assumptions upon which the movement was based were flawed. Just as support for eugenics transcended many traditional political boundaries, so did antieugenics sentiments.

In both Europe and the United States, the most sustained resistance to the eugenics movement came from Catholics. The Vatican's 1930 Encyclical on Marriage (*Casti Connubii*) condemned sterilization as a mutilating, mortal sin against nature (U.S. and European laws were clearly the target); one year before, the National Council of Catholic Women denounced American eugenics legislation as a violation of individual rights.[77] In subsequent years American Catholics stepped up their criticism of eugenics, focusing primarily but not exclusively on the sterilization laws. The editors of the Catholic *Linacre Quarterly* in 1935 denounced sterilization as "un-American and immoral";[78] other physicians warned that "killing the unfortunates will be the next step."[79]

Criticism also came from outside Catholic circles. Clarence Darrow warned in 1926 that those practicing the "cult of eugenics" were allowing big business to create "a race in its own image"; Bertrand Russell warned that the day might come when "rebels of all kinds will be sterilized."[80] In 1927, Harvard University declined a gift of $60,000 from the legacy of Philadelphia surgeon J. Ewing Mears to found a professorship in eugenics, "notably that branch relating to the treatment of the defective and criminal classes by surgical procedures."[81]

Though geneticists were among the most consistent supporters of eugenics, here too there were criticisms, especially in the 1930s, as evidence of genetic or developmental complexity began to mount. In 1932, Lionel Penrose showed that "Mongoloid idiocy" had nothing to do with the "Asiatic race."[82] The 1930s also saw growing evidence for both the idea that single traits may be coded for by more than one gene (polygenism), and that single genes may shape more than one trait (pleiotropy). William E. Castle criticized Davenport's warnings against the biological effects of miscegenation; psychiatrist Smith Ely Jelliffe chided

Davenport for having lumped all types of mental disability into the ambiguous rubric of "insanity."[83]

Interestingly, biologists were sometimes able to attack what they did not like about eugenics by linking the field with softer or more speculative sciences. Raymond Pearl, professor of biometry at Johns Hopkins, wrote in a 1927 issue of *American Mercury* that eugenics had become "a mingled mess of ill-grounded and uncritical sociology, economics, anthropology, and politics, full of emotional appeals to class and race prejudices, solemnly put forth as science, and unfortunately accepted as such by the general public."[84] Editors of the *Eugenics Review*, attempting to distance themselves from racialist thought at the end of the 1930s, ridiculed the naive belief in selection on the basis of superior or inferior characteristics as "sociological bed-time thinking."[85] Complaints such as these persisted alongside the more common criticism, namely, that social scientists had generally failed to appreciate the role of genetics in determining behavior. In 1950 Frank H. Hankins, a member of the board of directors of the American Eugenics Society since the 1930s, lamented the fact that in sociological circles it had become "almost a dogma" that "all races of men . . . are substantially uniform in genetic quality."[86]

Ultimately it was the European war and the American quest to define the place of "eugenics in a democracy" that put a damper on the eugenics movement. In 1939 the Carnegie Institution's Eugenics Record Office was renamed the Genetic Record Office; a year later the office closed down for good. Also in 1939, the American Eugenics Society took over publication of *Eugenical News* from the Galton Society and the Eugenics Research Association; control of the journal shifted from Davenport, Laughlin, and Steggerda, to Frederick Osborn and his colleagues in the reform movement. The journal dropped its subtitle ("Current Record of Human Genetics and Race Hygiene") and began to publish, for the first time, strong criticisms of German racial hygiene. An editorial in the March 1939 issue sought to articulate a distinctively "American Concept of Eugenics" that would harmonize with democratic ideals: The editorial announced that while differences in genetic factors had once been attributed to occupational, regional, or racial groups, there was in fact "hardly any scientific evidence on innate differences between large groups."[87] The journal asserted that "no class, no caste, and no profession can be trusted with dictatorial control of the destiny of their fellow men" and that failure to recognize this fact had led to "a forty-years wandering of eugenics in the wilderness."[88] Alva Myrdal helped launch the revised journal with an essay on "The Swedish Approach to Population Policies," presenting an overview of what population policy in a democratic, rather than a fascist or communist, society should look like.[89]

Eugenicists during the war years continued these efforts to distinguish between "good" eugenics and "bad." Myron Kantorovitz defended Alfred Grotjahn's socialist eugenics against the Nordic supremacist "race-hygiene" that had come to dominate German thinking.[90] Donald L. Custis denounced the antidemocratic government of Germany, warning that "in a country in which 'political' prisoners are given the inhuman treatment afforded in concentration camps, what guarantee has one that 'eugenic' measures will not be used in a similar fashion?" The author of this prize-winning essay, a Catholic premed student at Wabash College in Crawfordsville, Indiana, stressed the need to expand eugenical teaching and research, but only if it could be freed from "the ugly bugaboo of public prejudice."[91] Frederick Osborn's 1940 *Preface to Eugenics* similarly sought to distance the American movement from antidemocratic tendencies abroad. *Time* magazine devoted a full page to his views on "Eugenics for Democracy"; shortly thereafter he was named brigadier general in charge of the Morale Division of the U.S. Army.[92]

After the war, the movement suffered further setbacks. Revelations at the Nuremberg trials gave eugenics a bad name, and though some still tried to separate "genuine eugenics" from the atrocities (those responsible for planning and carrying out the German sterilization program were never tried for war crimes), many also tried to tar them with the same brush.[93] Within the eugenics community, efforts were made to harmonize eugenics rhetoric with postwar sensitivities. Genetics textbooks began to include discussions of the abuse of their science: L. C. Dunn and T. Dobzhansky's 1946 *Heredity, Race and Society*, for example, declared that "most of the ardent eugenists have also been adherents of the Nordic myth, of white superiority, and political conservatives." The *Eugenical News* strongly criticized the work,[94] but eugenicists themselves were also busy repudiating prewar traditions. Frederick Osborn's 1951 *Preface to Eugenics* reasserted his opposition to belief in "the inherent or necessary superiority of one race over another, or of one economic class over another";[95] the fourth (1952) edition of Laurence Snyder's *Principles of Heredity* noted that eugenicists had begun to dissociate themselves from the "unscientific social-class bias" of Galton's England and the "racial prejudice" of early American eugenics.

Concerns for genetic health continued, of course, but now under different names and often in different forms. H. J. Muller introduced terms such as *genetic load* and the *cost of selection* in order to distance himself from tainted eugenics rhetoric.[96] The British *Annals of Eugenics* was rechristened the *Annals of Human Genetics* in 1954; in 1969, the *Eugenics Quarterly* became the *Journal of Social Biology*. Eugenics had a bad name. The objects of eugenic fears also changed. Concerns for the "health of the race" shifted to concerns to ameliorate runaway population growth through "population control," especially in the impoverished countries of the Third World.[97] Fears of racial miscegenation or the dysgenic effects of alcohol or syphilis were replaced by fears of new and alarming forms of environmental hazards. On 30 September 1945, less than two months after Hiroshima, G. I. Burch of the Population Reference Bureau asserted that eugenics would become necessary if atomic warfare, with its mutagenic radiation, were not controlled.[98]

Concern about the effects of radiation on human genetic health becomes in fact one of the more persistent and fundable themes of postwar eugenics. A number of geneticists were employed by government agencies to explore the biological consequences of radiation-induced mutagenesis (James Neel by the U.S. Atomic Bomb Casualty Commission; Otmar von Verschuer by German government officials); military officials in both countries were eager to find out how exposures at the workplace or the bomb site might produce birth defects, cancer, or other biological problems.[99] (Anyone puzzled by the present-day Department of Energy's interest in the Human Genome Project should recall that the Atomic Energy Commission was one of the chief supporters of postwar population genetics.) Social scientists recognized the new face of eugenics: The 1968 article on "Eugenics" for the authoritative *Encyclopedia of the Social Sciences* identified nuclear radiation as one of the central concerns of a legitimate eugenics.[100]

By the 1960s, however, it was rare for social scientists explicitly to advocate eugenics, either in Germany or the United States. Antimiscegenation and sterilization laws had succumbed to the civil rights movement and movements to ensure prisoners' and patients' rights; the hereditarian impulse of the eugenics movement was dealt a strong blow by the UNESCO statements of 1950 and 1952, bringing the entire conception of biological race into disrepute. In 1954, in the landmark case of *Brown v. The Board of Education*, the U.S. Supreme Court was able to cite social scientific works (Gunnar Myrdal's *American Dilemma*, for example) in support of the thesis that racial inequality was due to social, not biological, causes. Ashley Montagu gained a broader audience for his thesis that race was "man's most dangerous myth,"[101] and the Boasian, culturalist approach to anthropology gained a clear upper hand in American universities.

Yet the egalitarian rhetoric of the UNESCO statement on race painted a picture of scientific consensus that was never as solid as the social scientific press made it appear. In the late 1960s, one begins to see a hereditarian backlash against the supposed "environmentalist bias" of much social theory. At issue was not the right of governments to plan the human genetic future (this had been largely discredited) but rather whether there was not in fact some heritable component of human racial or sexual inequality. "Pop ethologists" argued that human sexual and aggressive behavior is rooted in the biology of our primate ancestors; Konrad Lorenz suggested that war, student revolt, and other forms of political behavior are evolutionarily anchored.[102] Arthur Jensen's 1969 article "How Much can We Boost IQ and Scholastic Achievement?" tried to prove that the failure of American blacks to score well on IQ tests could be traced to certain genetic infirmities in the Negro race;[103] E. O. Wilson, author of the influential book *Sociobiology*, suggested that however hard they tried, women were unlikely to ever equal men in the spheres of politics, business, or science.[104] Hereditarian assumptions extended to other spheres as well, as efforts were launched to prove (once again) that alcoholism, crime, manic depression, and a host of other talents or disabilities are genetically based.[105] In 1979, *Science* magazine reported research claiming that "most terrorists probably suffer from faulty vestibular functions in the middle ear";[106] four years later the same magazine published headlines suggesting that "Math Genius May Have Hormonal Basis," and that this might explain why boys do better in math than girls.[107]

Biologists and social theorists from a variety of traditions have criticized these works.[108] Against those who have argued that rape, homosexuality, crime, or even the dislike of spinach are the natural outcome of adaptive evolutionary strategies,[109] critics have argued that simpler and more plausible explanations can be found in the constructs of cultural traditions. Against those who argue that there is homosexuality among worms or rape among mallards,[110] critics have argued that one must resist the temptation to project human qualities into the nonhuman world. Objections have also been voiced against claims by sociobiologists that this particular field of study will revolutionize the social sciences, subsuming sociology, anthropology, and even ethics as "the last branches of biology waiting to be included in the Modern Synthesis."[111]

In short, the hereditarian impulse that guided eugenics research of the 1920s and 1930s is by no means dead. Even in postwar Germany, where eugenics institutions were more forcibly dismantled in the wake of Allied occupation, sporadic calls for eugenical sterilization or even the "renordification" of Europe resumed (especially in the western sectors) soon after the end of the war, albeit in muted tones. Anthropologist Hans Nachtsheim argued for voluntary eugenic sterilization in 1952; Otmar von Verschuer published a book on eugenics in 1966, defending modest and voluntary steps to slow the "degeneration of the race."[112]

More extreme groups have also learned that the prestige of science can help lend respectability to political demands. The Deutsche Gesellschaft für biologische Anthropologie (German Society for Biological Anthropology), a right-wing organization based in Hamburg, has published since 1972 a journal which puts forward an explicitly Nordic supremacist version of eugenics, warning that the Nordic peoples of Europe are threatened by decline—from within, through the increase of alien racial stocks (especially the Turks), and from without, especially from Soviet communism. The journal publishes research purportedly showing that half of all criminals suffer from some inherited genetic defect; "born criminals" in this view are marked with certain "morphological peculiarities," including a thin beard, thick body hair, asymmetric head shape, and irregularities in brain EEG. The journal asserts that there are not only "born criminals" but also "born thieves," "born rapists," and so forth.[113]

The journal combines its "research reports" with regular demands for a halt to Turkish immigration and the return of *Gastarbeiter* (foreign workers) to their countries of origin. The editors call for a "new eugenics" incorporating genetic and marital counseling, getting tough with crime, and promotion of Nordic births and institutions.[114] *Neue Anthropologie* repeats many of the slogans of racial hygiene of the 1920s and 1930s, including the notion that racial struggle is the key to history and that Nordic man instinctively senses "the alien nature of Marxian thought."[115] The journal's editorial board reads like a *Who's Who?* of world scientific racism, including (as of 1982) Donald Swan, head of the International Federation of Eugenics Organizations; Rolf Kosiek, an ex-Nazi and leading member of the neo-Nazi Nationaldemokratische Partei Deutschlands (NPD); H. G. Amsel, a writer for *Mensch und Mass*, a small anti-Semitic Ludendorff society concerned with exposing the "world Jewish conspiracy"; John R. Baker, author of the most ambitious defense of Gobineau's racial theory of history in postwar England;[116] Alan de Benoist, editor of the French journal *Nouvelle Ecole*; and a number of other figures active on the far right of European politics. Earlier advisors included Karl Thums, a former professor of racial science under the Nazis; Karl Kötschau, Germany's premier "organic

Eugenics Congress Announcement

Number 1. History and Purpose of the Congress.

EUGENICS

EUGENICS IS THE SELF DIRECTION OF HUMAN EVOLUTION.

LIKE A TREE EUGENICS DRAWS ITS MATERIALS FROM MANY SOURCES AND ORGANIZES THEM INTO AN HARMONIOUS ENTITY.

Third International Eugenics Congress

New York City, August 21-23, 1932.

Tree from Third International Congress of Eugenics, New York City, 1932
Source: Reprinted from *Medizin historisches Journal* (1980) 15:337. Note that sociology is not included.

physician" during the Nazi regime; Edith Rüdin, daughter of psychiatrist Ernst Rüdin; and Arthur Jensen, professor of educational psychology at Berkeley and author of the notorious 1969 article on the genetic origins of white intellectual superiority. (I asked the journal's editor about Jensen and he assured me that the Berkeley psychologist had been one of their closest American supporters since the beginning of the journal in 1972. Rieger showed me that Jensen was no casual contributor: In four of the first five volumes of the journal Jensen had either published an article or allowed himself to be interviewed.)[117]

The editor of *Neue Anthropologie*, Hamburg lawyer Jürgen Rieger, has himself been active in far-right politics since the 1960s. In 1969 he was a leader in the Bund Heimattreue Jugend (League of Youth True to Homeland), an organization modeled on the Hitler Youth. In 1971, four days before local elections in Schleswig-Holstein, Rieger helped fake a kidnapping of a neo-Nazi professor (Bertholt Rubin) in order to blame it on the left. Two years later, the young Hamburg lawyer was expelled from the Hamburg Senate for right-wing extremist activities, and in 1974 he was arrested for assault with a deadly weapon during a political demonstration. In the same year, he helped to organize Aktion W, a rightist organization with the slogan "Brandt an die Wand!" (Brandt should be shot!). Rieger has spoken at numerous rallies of the far right; in September 1977 he was scheduled to deliver an address with Professor Christian Frey, head of the NPD, on the topic "Ewig Büssen für Hitler?" (Eternal Penitence for Hitler?). The demonstration, scheduled to be held in Munich, was barred by government officials on grounds of national security.[118]

Neue Anthropologie represents one extreme of the German neoeugenics movement; most German anthropologists no doubt consider the group something of an embarrassment, though a number of prestigious human geneticists have written for the journal (Heinrich Schade, for example, former SS officer and director since 1966 of the Institute for Anthropology and Human Genetics in Düsseldorf).[119] Even if the organization is extreme in its particulars, however, it is by no means unique in its more general insistence upon biological determinism—the view that politics must be, in the words of *Neue Anthropologie* co-editor Detlef Promp, "The Continuation of Biology with Other Means."[120]

Biological determinism is only one of the legacies of the eugenics movement; the prospects for human gene therapy, genetic screening, and family planning based on prenatal genetic diagnosis have become another.[121] This latter promises to become a major research frontier in the 1990s, especially with the rapid growth of techniques for identifying genetic illnesses. In 1983 the gene for Huntington's disease was found to reside on chromosome number 4; the gene for cystic fibrosis was traced to chromosome number 7 in 1985. Searches are under way for genes for manic depression and schizophrenia, and plans have been announced to map all 100,000 genes in the human genome—a three billion-dollar effort that is likely to generate entirely new kinds of ethical and political questions.

It might be tempting to see a danger only in the determinism but not in the therapy, especially as most of the new biotechnologies are likely to be offered as voluntary services rather than as state-mandated programs. And surely it is unlikely that modern genetic technologies will ever produce the kinds of horrors that discredited the eugenics movements of the 1930s and 1940s. But as progress in biotechnology brings intervention in the human genetic constitution out of the realm of science fiction, questions of potential abuse and responsibility will become ever more pressing. India has banned amniocentesis for the purposes of identifying sex, but how effective can such a ban ever be? Northern Ireland has started genetic fingerprinting for suspected terrorists, but what guarantees are there that such systems will not be abused? Will employers or insurers be able to deny jobs or insurance to persons found to be suffering from "genetic lesions"? Who owns the human genome?[122] Genetic health is likely to remain a goal toward which humans will strive, but what constitutes health and how or at what costs genetic diseases should be treated are likely to remain in dispute. Whether the experience of the past will be heeded remains an open question, as is the question of what role governments and the public will play in requiring, allowing, or barring these capabilities as they are introduced.

Notes

Epigraphs: Francis Galton, "Hereditary Talent and Character," *Macmillan's Magazine* 12, no. 68 (1865): 165–66; and Franz Boas, *Anthropology and Modern Life* (New York: W. W. Norton, 1928), p. 119.

1. See, for example, Renate Bridenthal, Atina Grossmann, and Marion Kaplan, eds., *When Biology Became Destiny: Women in Weimar and Nazi Germany* (New York: Monthly Review Press, 1984); also Linda Gordon, *Woman's Body, Woman's Right* (New York: Grossman, 1976), esp. pp. 116–35.

2. See, for example, William Brennan's *The Abortion Holocaust: Today's Final Solution* (St. Louis: Landmark, 1983). For the antipsychiatry movement, see Peter Breggin's "The Psychiatric Holocaust," *Penthouse* (January 1979): 81–84, 216; also his "Psychosurgery for Political Purposes," *Duquesne Law Review* 13 (1975): 841–62.

3. Ernst Klee, *"Euthanasie" im NS-Staat, die "Vernichtung lebensunwerten Lebens"* (Frankfurt: S. Fischer Verlag, 1983); Götz Aly et al., *Aussonderung und Tod:*

Die Klinische Hinrichtung der Unbrauchbaren (Berlin: Rotbuch Verlag, 1985).

4. See, for example, Benno Müller-Hill's *Murderous Science: Elimination by Scientific Selection of Jews, Gypsies, and Others. Germany 1933–1945* (New York: Oxford University Press, 1988).

5. There is a large and growing literature on the German eugenics movement. Apart from works already mentioned, this includes Gerhard Baader and Ulrich Schultz, eds., *Medizin und Nationalsozialismus* (West Berlin: Verlagsgesellschaft Gesundheit, 1980); Gisela Bock, *Zwangessterilisation im Nationalsozialismus* (Opladen: Westdeutscher Verlag, 1986); Heidrun Kaupen-Haas, ed., *Der Griff nach der Bevölkerung* (Nördlingen: Delphi Politik, 1986); Georg Lilienthal, "Rassenhygiene im Dritten Reich," *Medizinhistorisches Journal* 14 (1979): 114–37; Hans-Walter Schmuhl, *Rassenhygiene, Nationalsozialismus, Euthanasie* (Göttingen: Vandenhoeck & Ruprecht, 1987); Achim Thom and Horst Spar, eds., *Medizin im Faschismus* (East Berlin: VEB Kongress- und Werbedruck Oberlungwitz, 1983); Paul Weindling, *Health, Race and German Politics between National Unification and Nazism 1870–1945* (Cambridge, England: Cambridge University Press, 1989); and Peter Weingart, Jürgen Kroll, and Kurt Bayertz, *Rasse, Blut und Gene, Geschichte der Eugenik und Rassenhygiene in Deutschland* (Frankfurt: Suhrkamp, 1988).

6. Michael H. Kater, "The Burden of the Past: Problems of a Modern Historiography of Physicians and Medicine in Nazi Germany," *German Studies Review* 10 (1987): 31–56.

7. Eight volumes of the *Beiträge zur Nationalsozialistischen Gesundheits- und Sozialpolitik* have appeared as of 1990; Götz Aly's *Aussonderung und Tod* was vol. 1 of this series.

8. A. H. Sturtevant, *A History of Genetics* (New York: Harper and Row, 1965), pp. 126–32.

9. Benno Müller-Hill, "Genetics after Auschwitz," *Holocaust and Genocide Studies* 2 (1987): 3–20.

10. Christian Pross, unpublished paper delivered to the conference "Medicine without Compassion" in Cologne, 28–30 September 1988.

11. Alexander Mitscherlich and Fred Mielke, *Doctors of Infamy* (New York: Henry Schuman, 1949), p. xx.

12. Mark H. Haller, *Eugenics: Hereditarian Attitudes in American Thought* (New Brunswick, N.J.: Rutgers University Press, 1963); Kenneth M. Ludmerer, *Genetics and American Society* (Baltimore: Johns Hopkins University Press, 1972); Donald K. Pickens, *Eugenics and the Progressives* (Nashville: Vanderbilt University Press, 1968); Daniel J. Kevles, *In the Name of Eugenics: Genetics and the Uses of Human Heredity* (Berkeley: University of California Press, 1985). See also Lyndsay Farrall, "The History of Eugenics: A Bibliographical Review," *Annals of Science* 36 (1979): 111–23; and especially the "Essay on Sources" at the end of Kevles, *In the Name of Eugenics*. Stephen Trombley's *The Right to Reproduce: A History of Coercive Sterilization* (London: Weidenfeld and Nicolson, 1988) is not widely known (the publisher, threatened by libel suits, refused to distribute it), but presents the most comprehensive history of forcible sterilization in the Anglo-American world to date.

13. Loren R. Graham, "Science and Values: The Eugenics Movement in Germany

and Russia in the 1920s," *American Historical Review* 82 (1977): 1133–64; Diane Paul, "Eugenics and the Left," *Journal of the History of Ideas* 45 (1984): 567–90.

14. Garland Allen, "The Eugenics Record Office at Cold Spring Harbor, 1910–1940," *Osiris* 2 (1986): 225–64; Allan Chase, *The Legacy of Malthus* (New York: Knopf, 1977); Barry Mehler, "A History of the American Eugenics Society, 1921–1940," Ph.D. diss., University of Illinois, 1988.

15. The term *eugenics* is first found in Francis Galton's *Inquiries into Human Faculty* (London: Macmillan and Co., 1883), p. 44. Galton had earlier proposed the terms *viriculture* and *stirpiculture*. See his "Hereditary Improvement," *Fraser's Magazine* (January 1873): 119.

16. *Archiv für Rassen- und Gesellschaftsbiologie* 1 (1904): i–iv. The German term *Rassenhygiene* has been variously translated as *eugenics, race hygiene,* or *racial hygiene.* For the latter term, see T. B. Rice, *Racial hygiene: A Practical Discussion of Eugenics and Race Culture* (New York: Macmillan and Co., 1929). *Racial hygiene* was also the translation preferred in the U.S. Office of Strategic Services secret reports on Nazi medical work. I shall be using the terms *eugenics* and *racial hygiene* as roughly synonymous, though a number of theorists in the Nazi movement did try to drive a wedge between home-grown racial hygiene and the more internationalist eugenics. In the most pronounced example of this tendency, Nazi physician Martin Stämmler characterized eugenics as "the racial hygiene of the bastard nations"; pure eugenics was pursued only by those who believed in "the equal worth of the races." Racial hygienists, in his view, recognized by contrast the supremacy of the Nordic race. Stämmler claimed that Jews, Catholics, and Social Democrats were the ones promoting the nonracist eugenics. See his *Rassenpflege im völkischen Staat* (Munich: J. F. Lehmann, 1933), p. 44.

17. In 1926 Alfred Grotjahn defended eugenics as "applicable to each group of individuals connected with each other by procreation, without any dependence on race in the anthropological sense of the word." See Felix Tietze, "Eugenic Measures in the Third Reich," *Eugenics Review* 31 (1939): 105.

18. For the American case, see Rabbi Max Reichler's *Jewish Eugenics* (New York: Bloch, 1916). In 1918, the *American Journal of Physical Anthropology* reported on an article by Maurice Fischberg (first published in the *American Hebrew*) entitled "Eugenic Factors in Jewish Life" asserting among other things that "the Jews are physically puny—a large proportion are feeble, undersized; their muscular system is of deficient development with narrow, flat chests, and of inferior capacity. They make the appearance of a weakly people, often actually decrepit" (*American Journal of Physical Anthropology* 1 [1918]: 106–7). Fischberg suggested that both the talents and the infirmities of Jews were to be explained by the impact of their habits upon their breeding, as in their "giving preference in marriage to the scholar" but also in their "dysgenic" custom of distributing relief to the poor.

19. American historians have tended to contrast laissez-faire Social Darwinism with state planning-oriented eugenics. In Germany, however, laissez-faire was never an important part of Social Darwinian ideology, and the transition to eugenics was probably for this reason somewhat smoother.

20. Left- and right-wing Social Darwinists emphasized different aspects of Darwin's theory. Conservatives tended to emphasize natural selection and the struggle for existence (*Selektionslehre*); progressives tended to stress the continuity of man and ape (*Abstammungslehre*). It was ultimately the conservative emphasis that triumphed in German racial hygiene of the 1920s and 1930s.

21. "Was lernen wir aus den Prinzipien der Descendenztheorie in Beziehung auf die innerpolitische Entwickelung und Gesetzgebung der Staaten?" See Sheila Weiss, *Race Hygiene and National Efficiency* (Berkeley: University of California Press, 1987), for a discussion of the Krupp Prize Contest.

22. Membership in the Deutsche Gesellschaft für Rassenhygiene grew from 350 in 1914 to 1,300 in 1930. Membership continued to grow after the rise of the Nazis: By 1940, the Viennese branch of the society alone (founded by Otto Reche) had more than one thousand members. See the *Archiv für Rassen- und Gesellschaftsbiologie* 33 (1939–40): 375.

23. Cited in Kevles, *In the Name of Eugenics*, p. 47.

24. *Eugenical News* was superceded by the *Eugenics Quarterly* (1954–1968).

25. Kevles, *In the Name of Eugenics*; Garland E. Allen, "The Misuse of Biological Hierarchies: The American Eugenics Movement, 1900–1940," *History and Philosophy of the Life Sciences* 5 (1983): 105–28.

26. Cited in Kevles, *In the Name of Eugenics*, p. 58.

27. Caleb Saleeby first distinguished positive and negative eugenics in the *Sociological Review* 2 (1909): 228.

28. B. G. Jefferis and J. L. Nichols, *Searchlights on Health, the Science of Eugenics* (1919; Naperville, Ill.: J. L. Nichols and Company, 1921), pp. 101–5 and 456–57. Jefferis and Nichols's book sold more than one million copies in its first two years of publication.

29. Roswell Johnson, "Eugenics and So-Called Eugenics," *American Journal of Sociology* 20 (1914–15): 98.

30. Allen, "Misuse of Biological Hierarchies," p. 116.

31. Albion Small, "A Decade of Sociology," *American Journal of Sociology* 11 (1905): 2.

32. Leading works in the German organic sociology movement include Albert Schäffle, *Bau und Leben des socialen Körpers*, 4 vols. (Tübingen: H. Laupp, 1875–78); Paul von Lilienfeld, *Zur Vertheidigung der organischen Methode in der Soziologie* (Berlin: G. Reimer, 1898), also his *Gedanken über die Socialwissenschaft der Zukunft*, 5 vols. (Mitau: E. Behre, 1873–81).

33. Ferdinand Tönnies, "Eugenik," *Schmollers Jahrbuch* 29 (1905): 273–90. See also his contribution to the debate on "Studies in National Eugenics," in *Sociological Papers*, vol. 2 (London: 1906), pp. 40–42.

34. *Verhandlungen des ersten Deutschen Soziologentages* (Tübingen: J. C. B. Mohr, 1911, rep. 1977). Wilhelm Schallmayer also hoped that sociologists would take up the banner of racial hygiene: He wrote his *Vererbung und Auslese* not just for physicians but for "sociologists, educators, and criminologists" (3rd ed. [Jena: Gustav Fischer, 1918], pp. ix–x).

35. Weber's contribution to the first (1910) meeting of the Deutsche Gesellschaft für Soziologie, containing his critique of Ploetz's racial hygiene, has been republished in translation in *Social Research* 38 (1971): 30–41. See also Moritz

Manasse, "Max Weber on Race," *Social Research* 14 (1947): 191–221.

36. *Verhandlungen des zweiten Deutschen Soziologentages* (Tübingen: J. C. B. Mohr, 1913), p. 74.

37. Alfred Vierkandt, "Die Soziologie als empirisch betriebene Einzelwissenschaft," *Monatsschrift für Soziologie* 1 (1909): 92; Friedrich Hertz, "Rasse," in Alfred Vierkandt, *Handwörterbuch der Soziologie* (Stuttgart: F. Enke, 1931), pp. 458–66.

38. The Gesellschaft für Soziologie was disbanded in 1934 and by 1938 some two-thirds of German teachers of sociology had been dismissed. See M. Rainer Lepsius, ed., *Soziologie in Deutschland und Oesterreich 1918–1945*, published as Sonderheft 23 (1981) of the *Kölner Zeitschrift für Soziologie und Sozialpsychologie*, p. 17.

39. See my "From *Anthropologie* to *Rassenkunde*: Concepts of Race in German Physical Anthropology," in *Bones, Bodies, Behavior: Essays on Biological Anthropology*, ed. George Stocking (Madison: University of Wisconsin Press, 1988).

40. Walter Scheidt, *Allgemeine Rassenkunde als Einführung in das Studium der Menschenrassen* (Munich: J. F. Lehmann, 1925), pp. 512–13.

41. Fischer began his career studying anatomy at the University of Jena; his doctoral thesis described the female genitalia of orangutans ("Beiträge zur Anatomie der weiblichen Urogenitalorgane des Orang-Utan" [Jena: 1898]). In 1908 he traveled to the town of Rehoboth in German Southwest Africa, where he studied the mixed-race offspring of native Hottentots and German settlers. His resultant *Rehobother Bastards* (Jena: Gustav Fischer, 1913) was for many years regarded in Germany as the founding treatise on human genetics. Fischer founded a branch of the Society for Racial Hygiene in 1910 at Freiburg, and in 1928 he was named president of the International Congress of Genetics.

42. *Zeitschrift für Rassenkunde* 10 (1939): 301.

43. The Nuremberg Laws, passed in the fall of 1935, ruled that (1) genetically diseased could not marry genetically healthy; (2) Jews could not marry or have sexual intercourse with "Aryans"; and (3) only men and women of "German blood" could be full German citizens. Concerning the Blood Protection Law of 15 September 1935 (banning sex or marriage between Jews and non-Jews), Felix Tietze wrote in 1939 that "every German author on eugenics considers this a eugenic law." See his "Eugenic Measures in the Third Reich," *Eugenics Review* 31 (1939): 106.

44. Interestingly, the distinction between cultural and physical anthropology so important in the United States was not so pronounced in Germany—at least in regard to the question of attitudes toward eugenics. It is true that there were both medically and nonmedically trained anthropologists in Germany, and it is also true that there was a strong ethnological research tradition in that country, following in the footsteps of Adolf Bastian. I have argued elsewhere, however, that there was no substantial difference between German cultural and physical anthropologists in their views of eugenics. The common ground on which cultural and physical anthropologists met in the 1930s was *Rassenkunde*, the racial science that purported to derive cultural traits from physical form and (more importantly) genetic character. See my "From *Anthropologie* to *Rassenkunde*," pp. 140–56.

45. The index of the *American Anthropologist* for the years 1888 to 1928 shows only one entry on eugenics, a brief essay by Anita McGee on human *stirpiculture*—Galton's original term for eugenics ("An Experiment in Human Stirpiculture," *American Anthropologist* 4 [1891]: 319-25). In 1915, Charles Davenport complained that "15 years after the proper way of looking at heredity and 'species' or 'races' has been made clear, there are not half a dozen anthropologists who make use of the new point of view" (that is, eugenics). See Davenport to Aleš Hrdlička, 5 May 1915, cited in Ludmerer, *Genetics*, p. 100.

46. George Stocking has shown that physical anthropologists tended to ignore the Boasian critique until well into the 1930s. See his *Race, Culture and Evolution: Essays in the History of Anthropology* (New York: Free Press, 1968), pp. 161-94, 273-307.

47. *American Journal of Physical Anthropology* 1 (1918): 2.

48. Aleš Hrdlička, "Physical Anthropology: Its Scope and Aims," *American Journal of Physical Anthropology* 1 (1918): 4-21.

49. "Charles Benedict Davenport (1866-1944)," *American Journal of Physical Anthropology* n.s. 2 (1944): 170.

50. Franz Boas, *Anthropology and Modern Life*, p. 115.

51. Stocking, *Race, Culture and Evolution*, p. 139.

52. Elazar Barkan, "Mobilizing Scientists against Nazi Racism," in Stocking, ed., *Bones, Bodies, Behavior*, pp. 201-2. See also the *New York Times* 6 January 1935 and 21 March 1937; also Franz Boas, "Aryan and Non-Aryan," printed as a pamphlet (New York: 1934).

53. Charles H. Cooley, "Genius, Fame, and the Comparison of Races," *Annals of the American Academy of Political and Social Science* 9 (1897): 317-58.

54. Lester Ward, "Social Darwinism," *American Journal of Sociology* 12 (1907): 710.

55. Cited in Richard Hofstadter, *Social Darwinism in American Thought* (Boston: Beacon Press, 1955), p. 82. Much of Ward's *Applied Sociology* (Boston: Ginn and Co., 1906) constituted an attack on the hereditarian conceptions of Galton and eugenicists more generally. Ward's views on race were complex, however. He believed that racial conflict was inevitable, constituting "the most vital of all social phenomena." In 1909 he claimed that the "struggle of races" was to sociology what the "struggle for existence" was to biology. See his "The Status of Sociology," *Monatsschrift für Soziologie* 1 (1909): 36-37.

56. Lester Frank Ward, "Eugenics, Euthenics, Eudemics," *American Journal of Sociology* 18 (1912-13): 746.

57. See, for example, Robert Rentoul, "Proposed Sterilization of Certain Mental Degenerates," *American Journal of Sociology* 12 (1907): 319-27. See also Raymond Pearl, "Some Biological Considerations About War," *American Journal of Sociology*, 46 (1941): 487-503; also Conrad and Irene B. Taeuber, "German Fertility Trends," *American Journal of Sociology* 45 (1940): 150-67.

58. Carol Aronovici's review suggested that Mendelian genetics had opened up the prospect of reducing undesirable characters not by "reckless and cruel elimination" but by "a process of scientific mating which each individual can apply for himself with the least amount of social control." She speculated that Mendelism might well "solve for us the race problem." See the *American Journal of Sociology* 16 (1910-11): 121-23. Not long thereafter Charles Ellwood sug-

gested that eugenics was of relevance to sociology because it called attention to the influence of heredity in human social life, an influence often overlooked by social thinkers. Ellwood also warned, however, that it would be dangerous to exaggerate the role of heredity. See his "The Eugenics Movement from the Standpoint of Sociology," in Morton A. Aldrich et al., *Eugenics: Twelve University Lectures* (New York: Dodd, Mead and Co., 1914), pp. 214–16.

59. See the review of Hankins's *The Racial Basis of Civilization* in the *Eugenics Review* 14 (1929): 51. Hankins proposed a science of "social biology" that would draw from Galton, Ammon, and Lapouge and utilize twin studies, genealogies, and family histories to describe "the association of some physical trait (race, sex, age, intelligence) with socially significant phenomena." See his "Research in Social Biology," *Sociology and Social Research* 17 (1932–33): 514–18.

60. Franz Boas, *The Mind of Primitive Man* (New York: Macmillan and Co., 1911), p. 155.

61. Fritz Lenz, "Die sogenannte Vererbung erworbener Eigenschaften," *Medizinische Klinik* 5 (1914): 202.

62. See my "From *Anthropologie* to *Rassenkunde*," pp. 158–61.

63. Haller, *Eugenics*, p. 7.

64. *Eugenical News* 18 (1933): 89–95. The "Law for the Prevention of Genetically Diseased Offspring" of 14 July 1933 had been drafted in the summer of 1932 in the final months of the Weimar regime; Nazi authorities simply added a clause allowing sterilization without the permission of the patient. German racial hygienists had long called for sterilization: Emil Kraepelin had proposed the sterilization of the unfit in 1883; Alexander Tille in his 1894 *Biologie eines Aristokraten* had advocated the sterilization of the unemployed poor to quiet political unrest. American sterilization laws provided the most important model for German efforts in this area, however. By the late 1920s, U.S. sterilization laws had allowed forcible sterilization of fifteen thousand individuals, mostly inmates of prisons or homes for the mentally ill. German racial hygienists in the Weimar period expressed their envy of American achievements, warning that unless the Germans made progress in this field the Americans would become world racial leaders.

65. Paul Popenoe, "The German Sterilization Law," *Journal of Heredity* 25 (1934): 257–60.

66. Mehler, "History of the American Eugenics Society," p. 241; see also Allen, "Eugenics Record Office," pp. 252–54.

67. Marie E. Kopp, "Legal and Medical Aspects of Eugenic Sterilization in Germany," *American Sociological Review* 1 (1936): 761–70.

68. Bock, *Zwangssterilisation*, pp. 232–33.

69. The expression "race suicide" was first used by Edward A. Ross in his annual address before the American Academy of Political and Social Science in Philadelphia on 12 April 1901. The expression was picked up by the press and popular political figures, including Theodore Roosevelt. Caleb Saleeby used the expression "racial poisons" in his *Parenthood and Race Culture: An Outline of Eugenics* (New York: Moffat, Yard and Co., 1909). See also my *Racial Hygiene*, pp. 237–41.

70. Cited in Mehler, "History of the American Eugenics Society," p. 245.

71. See William B. Provine, "Geneticists and the Biology of Race Crossing," *Science* 182 (1973): 790–96. For an example of the argument against miscegenation, see Charles Davenport, "Race Mixture and Physical Disharmonies," *Science* 71 (1930): 603–6.

72. UNESCO, *The Race Concept, Results of an Inquiry* (Paris: UNESCO, 1952), p. 63.

73. Ashley Montagu, *Man's Most Dangerous Myth: The Fallacy of Race* (1942; New York: Harper, 1952), pp. 304–5. Virginia's "Pure-Race Law" allowed anyone with one-sixteenth Indian ancestry to pass as white but required that anyone with even a trace of Negro blood be considered Negro, "though he be white as snow." See Joseph C. Carroll, "The Race Problem," *Sociology and Social Research* 11 (1927): 267.

74. See, for example, *Neues Volk* 1 March 1936, p. 9. Nazi racial theorists on more than one occasion claimed that Nazi policies toward the Jews were relatively "liberal" compared with how blacks were treated in the United States. Evidence for this was usually taken from the fact that in many American states being one-thirty-second black meant one was legally black, whereas if a person were one-eighth Jewish in Germany (and for many purposes one-quarter Jewish), then he or she was legally Aryan.

75. "Jewish Physicians in Berlin," *Eugenical News* 19 (1934): 126. On 10 May 1934, Alfred Ploetz wrote to the *Eugenical News* protesting that the journal had incorrectly stated that sixty thousand Jews had been "expelled" from Germany. Ploetz claimed that the overwhelming majority of these were not forced to emigrate ("nobody chased them away"); he also claimed that Jews had left Germany because they feared, "unjustly, a pogrom," and that reports of horrors ("with the exception of a few minor cruelties") had been invented in order to embarrass the new government. See the *Eugenical News* 19 (1934): 129.

76. See my *Racial Hygiene*, pp. 20–30.

77. *New York Times* 4 October 1929.

78. *Linacre Quarterly* 3 (June 1935): 48. See also Alexander Fraser, "The Answer of Biology to Proposed Measures of Eugenics," *Linacre Quarterly* 1 (December 1933): 5–8.

79. See Francis J. Dore, "Medicine and Morals," *Linacre Quarterly* 1 (December 1935): 10; also James T. Neary, "Euthanasia," *Lincaré Quarterly* 2 (April 1938): 38–42.

80. Kevles, *In the Name of Eugenics*, p. 120.

81. "Harvard University," *Eugenical News* 12 (1927): 85.

82. Kevles, *In the Name of Eugenics*, pp. 160–63. Davenport had earlier tried to identify feeblemindedness with typically Negro features, just as Dr. J. L. H. Down had identified "Mongolism" with the "Asiatic race."

83. Kevles, *In the Name of Eugenics*, p. 49.

84. Cited in Kevles, *In the Name of Eugenics*, p. 122.

85. Clairette P. Armstrong, review of *American Eugenics Today* (1939) in the *Eugenics Review* 24 (1939): 20.

86. Frank Hankins, "Our Load of Defective Genes," *Eugenical News* 35 (1950): 45.

87. Frederick Osborn, "The American Concept of Eugenics," *Eugenical News* 24 (1939): 2.
88. *Eugenical News* 24 (1939): 19.
89. Alva Myrdal, "The Swedish Approach to Population Policies," *Eugenical News* 24 (1939): 3–8.
90. Myron Kantorovitz, "Alfred Grotjahn as a Eugenist," *Eugenical News* 25 (1940): 15–19.
91. Donald L. Custis, "An Undergraduate Views Eugenics," *Eugenical News* 24 (1939): 58–62. Custis's essay was first-prize winner in the contest sponsored by Mrs. Alfreda M. Gregor.
92. "Eugenics for Democracy," *Time*, 9 September 1940.
93. On 9 December 1948, the General Assembly of the United Nations moved to outlaw genocide, including acts committed with intent to destroy—in whole or in part—a national, ethnic, racial, or religious group by killing, sterilization, relocation, isolation of parents from children, or other means. The *Eugenical News* reported on the convention at length but without comment.
94. *Eugenical News* 31 (1946): 52.
95. Frederick Osborn, preface to *Eugenics* (1951), reviewed by Gardner Murphy in *Eugenical News* 37 (1952): 35.
96. See Diane B. Paul, "'Our Load of Mutations' Revisited," *Journal of the History of Biology* 20 (1987): 321–35.
97. See Bonnie Mass, *Population Target, the Political Economy of Population Control in Latin America* (Toronto: Latin American Working Group, 1976).
98. *New York Times*, 30 September 1945.
99. See Mary S. Lindee, "Mutation, Radiation, and Species Survival: The Genetic Studies of the Atomic Bomb Casualty Commission in Hiroshima and Nagasaki," Ph.D. diss., Cornell University, 1990.
100. Gordon Allen, "Eugenics," *International Encyclopedia of the Social Sciences* (New York: Macmillan and Co., 1968), pp. 193–95. Allen expressed concerns that the mutations induced from the atomic bursts over Hiroshima and Nagasaki were likely to exact a toll "in death and suffering spread over many generations." Interestingly, Allen's 1968 article is no less enthusiastic about the prospects for eugenics than the 1931 article by H. S. Jennings in the first edition of the *Encyclopedia*. Allen denounced the contamination of the early movement by class and race prejudice; he nonetheless claimed that the movement had gained respectability since mid-century "by repudiating its early errors and by assimilating scientific advances" (p. 194).
101. Montagu, *Man's Most Dangerous Myth*.
102. See, for example, Robert Ardrey, *The Territorial Imperative: A Personal Inquiry into the Animal Origins of Property and Nations* (New York: Atheneum, 1966); Desmond Morris, *The Naked Ape: A Zoologist's Study of the Human Animal* (New York: McGraw-Hill, 1967); Konrad Lorenz, *On Aggression* (New York: Harcourt, Brace and World, 1966).
103. Arthur Jensen, "How Much Can We Boost IQ and Scholastic Achievement?" *Harvard Educational Review* 38 (1969): 1–123. Not long after publication, Jensen's entire 123-page article was read into the *Congressional Record* at the request of a southern congressman. Daniel P. Moynihan briefed the Nixon

cabinet on the article, advising that it be taken seriously. See Garland Allen's "History of Eugenics," in *Biology as Destiny: Scientific Fact or Social Bias?*, ed. Science for the People Sociobiology Study Group (Cambridge, Mass.: Science for the People, 1984), p. 18. For criticisms of the Jensen thesis, see the essays collected in N. J. Block and Gerald Dworkin, eds., *The IQ Controversy* (New York: Pantheon, 1976).

In 1980, East German scientists Volkmar Weiss and Hans-Georg Mehlhorn published an article in the *Biologisches Zentralblatt* arguing that the heritability of intelligence is about 80 percent and that "general intelligence" represents the expression of a single gene. The authors argue that there is an autosomal-recessive allele which must be homozygous before one's IQ can exceed 130, given "an abstract, average environment." See Volkmar Weiss and Hans-Georg Mehlhorn, "Der Hauptgenlocus der Allgemeinen Intelligenz: Diskrete und ganzzahlige Unterschiede in der zentralen Informationsverarbeitungsgeschwindigkeit," *Biologisches Zentralblatt* 99 (1980): 297–310.

104. E. O. Wilson, "Human Decency Is Animal," *New York Times Magazine*, 12 October 1975, p. 50.

105. On alcohol, see Sandra Blakeslee, "Scientists Find Key Biological Causes of Alcoholism," *New York Times*, 14 August 1984. On crime, see Richard J. Herrnstein and James Q. Wilson, *Crime and Human Nature* (New York: Simon and Schuster, 1985). On manic depression, see Harold Schmeck, "Defective Gene Tied to Form of Manic-Depressive Illness," *New York Times*, 26 February 1987.

106. Constance Holden, "Study of Terrorism Emerging as an International Endeavor," *Science* 203 (1979): 33–35.

107. Gina Kolata, "Math Genius May Have Hormonal Basis," *Science* 222 (1983): 1312.

108. On the IQ controversy, see the articles by Lewontin and David Layzer in Block and Dworkin, *IQ Controversy*; on sociobiology, see Marshall Sahlins, *The Use and Abuse of Biology: An Anthropological Critique of Sociobiology* (Ann Arbor: University of Michigan Press, 1976); on the existence of a "math gene," see J. Beckwith and M. Woodruff's letter in *Science* 223 (1984): 1247–48. For a more general analysis of biological determinism, see Richard Lewontin, Stephen Rose, and Leon Kamin, *Not in Our Genes* (New York: Pantheon, 1983).

109. For the argument that homosexuality and many other sexual practices have a genetic base, see James D. Weinreich, "Human Sociobiology: Pair Bonding and Resource Predictability (Effects of Social Class and Race)," *Behavioral Ecology and Sociobiology* 2 (1977): 91–118. On rape, see William M. Shields and Lea M. Shields, "Forcible Rape: An Evolutionary Perspective," *Ethology and Sociobiology* 4 (1983): 115–36.

110. See, for example, L. G. Abele and S. Gilchrist, "Homosexual Rape and Sexual Selection in Acanthocephalan Worms," *Science* 197 (1977): 81–83; also D. P. Barash, "Sociobiology of Rape in Mallards," *Science* 197 (1977): 788–89.

111. Edward O. Wilson made this claim in his *Sociobiology: The New Synthesis* (Cambridge, Mass.: Harvard University Press, 1975), p. 4. See also his "Biology and the Social Sciences," *Daedalus* 106 (1977): 127–40. For a critical view, see Richard Lewontin, "Sociobiology: Another Biological Determinism," *International Journal of Health Sciences* 10 (1980): 347–63.

112. Hans Nachtsheim, *Für und wider die Sterilisierung aus eugenischer Indikation* (Stuttgart: G. Thieme, 1952); Otmar von Verschuer, *Eugenik. Kommende Generationen in der Sicht der Genetik* (Witten: Luther-Verlag, 1966); see also Verschuer's article on "Eugenik" for the *Handwörterbuch der Sozialwissenschaften* (Stuttgart: Gustav Fischer, 1961), 3:356–57.

113. *Neue Anthropologie* 2 (1974): 114; also 3 (1975): 49.

114. See Rexilius Günter, "Die 'Neue Anthropologie'—das theoretische Organ der Rechtstradikalen in der Bundesrepublik," *Psychologie und Gesellschaftskritik* 13/14 (March 1980): 104–43.

115. *Neue Anthropologie* 2 (1974): 8 ff.

116. John Randal Baker, *Race* (New York: Oxford University Press, 1980).

117. Jensen has been important for other right-wing extremist groups. In 1973 the journal *Spearhead*, official organ of the British National Front, reflected upon the fact that "the most important factor in the buildup of self-confidence among 'racists' and the collapse of morale among multi-racialists was the publication in 1969 by Professor Arthur Jensen in the *Harvard Educational Review*." See *Spearhead* 63 (1973): 5.

118. See Michael Billig, *Psychology, Racism and Fascism* (Birmingham, England: A.F.R. Publications, 1979), pp. 20–21. In 1981 Rieger defended the former Warsaw police chief, Arpad Wigand, against charges of having shot Jews trying to enter the Warsaw ghetto in 1941–42. Before a Hamburg court, Rieger argued that Wigand's orders to shoot hundreds of Jews was a legitimate police operation initiated as a result of a quarantine imposed upon the camp during a typhus epidemic. See "SS and Polizeiführer von Warschau verurteilt," *Frankfurter Allgemeine Zeitung*, 8 December 1981.

119. Heinrich Schade, "Geburtenschwund in Deutschland: verschleiernde Argumente und Tatsachen," *Neue Anthropologie* 4 (1976).

120. This is the title of *Neue Anthropologie* co-editor Detlef Promp's article "Politik: Die Fortsetzung der Biologie mit anderen Mitteln," *Neue Anthropologie* 10 (1982): 1–7. Promp is playing on Clausewitz's maxim that war represents "a continuation of politics by other means."

121. See Kevles, *In the Name of Eugenics*, pp. 251–68.

122. See John Walsh, "Who Owns the Human Genome?" *Science* 237 (1987): 358–59; also George J. Annas, "Who's Afraid of the Human Genome?" *Hastings Center Report* (July–August 1989): 19–21.

▪ 10 THE "AMERICAN CREED" FROM A SWEDISH PERSPECTIVE

The Wartime Context of Gunnar Myrdal's *An American Dilemma*

WALTER A. JACKSON

Gunnar Myrdal's *An American Dilemma*, published in 1944, dominated discussions of race relations in American social science to the middle of the 1960s.[1] This extraordinary fourteen hundred–page work by a young Swedish economist played a key role in establishing a liberal orthodoxy on the race question that included advocacy of desegregation, equality of opportunity in the marketplace, social engineering to aid the black poor, and the assimilation of blacks into white American culture. As a foreign observer, Myrdal placed the race issue in a global perspective and linked it to the United States' prestige abroad. In contrast to most New Dealers, whose approach to the race question centered on economic programs, Myrdal saw it as fundamentally a moral issue. *An American Dilemma* was notable for its tone of moral immediatism and its insistence that racial prejudice posed an acute psychological problem for white Americans.

Myrdal's central argument was that white Americans experienced a profound psychological conflict between their belief in the "American creed" of democracy, individual rights, and equal opportunity and their prejudices against blacks. The race issue thus posed a "moral dilemma" for Americans, a major test of American democracy. Myrdal's arguments, though persuasive to many American intellectuals for twenty years, underwent serious challenge in the 1960s as empirical studies raised questions about the proposition that most white Americans felt a serious moral dilemma about their racial attitudes and behavior.[2]

This study examines Myrdal's formulation of the moral dilemma thesis in the context of World War II as he moved back and forth between the United States and Sweden from the spring of 1940 to the fall of 1942. In contrast to those historians who argue that Myrdal merely summarized or codified an existing liberal consensus among American social scientists,[3] I argue that Myrdal brought a new perspective to bear on American race relations, a perspective grounded in his work as a social engineer in Sweden in the 1930s and sharpened by his encounter with the Nazi challenge during World War II. In a previous article and in a forthcoming book I have analyzed the political and institutional context of the Myrdal study: the Carnegie Corporation's decision to import a foreign observer to study the so-called Negro problem, Myrdal's recruitment of a staff of scholars of both races representing all the important viewpoints in American social science, and his creation of a persuasive liberal interpretation of race relations just as civil rights was emerging as a major national issue.[4]

Gunnar Myrdal was born in rural Dalarna Province in Sweden in 1898. For three hundred years his ancestors had been farmers in a small valley surrounded by mountains in this poor, Appalachia-like region that was rather isolated from the rest of Sweden. Dalarna had never known feudalism, and the social structure of Myrdal's home village was basically egalitarian, with most families farming small plots of land. To the rest of Sweden, Dalarlians were known for their religious piety, work ethic, rich folklore, and democratic political culture.

Gunnar's father left farming to become a building contractor and moved the family to Stockholm, where he made money building houses and speculating in real estate. As a gymnasium and university student in Stockholm, Gunnar Myrdal came to scorn the religious piety of Dalarna, but he always retained a strong moralistic streak in his temperament that was transmuted into an ethic of public service. For a time, Myrdal turned his back on the democratic values of his rural heritage and embraced the more conservative views of his teachers and fellow students at Stockholm University. The young Myrdal was deeply influenced by the philosophy of the Enlightenment—not the democratic strain of French revolutionary thought, but rather the philosophes' idea of a public-spirited elite that used scientific and technological knowledge to plan for human development in a more rational and prosperous direction. As a university student in the era of World War I, Myrdal was troubled by the advent of universal suffrage and horrified by the Bolshevik revolution in Russia. In response to these developments, he advocated a "party of the intelligent," an intellectual aristocracy that would manipulate the masses and govern in the public interest.[5] Myrdal would soon abandon these extreme antidemocratic sentiments, but he would retain a certain elitism even after becoming a Social Democrat, believing that experts had a key role to play in shaping public policy. The growth of Nazism in the 1930s would lead him to a strong concern with educating the public to its democratic responsibilities so that the people could make informed moral choices.

One of the most important political and intellectual influences on Gunnar Myrdal was his wife, Alva Reimer Myrdal, a bright young woman from a Social Democratic family whom he married in 1924. Alva had to struggle hard for an education because there was no gymnasium for girls in her hometown; after working as a secretary, she persuaded her father to organize a special gymnasium course for young women in her community. She graduated from the University of Stockholm with a degree in Scandinavian literature, but her interests quickly turned to psychology, education, and family policy. Over the years Alva Myrdal exerted a great influence on her husband, pushing him politically in the direction of greater concern for equality and also encouraging his interest in interdisciplinary, applied social science research.[6]

During the 1920s Gunnar Myrdal established a reputation as a brilliant young economist in the neoclassical tradition, but he was not politically active. A turning point in his life came in 1929, when both Myrdals were awarded Rockefeller Foundation fellowships to study in the United States for a year. Gunnar Myrdal completed his book *The Political Element in the Development of Economic Theory,* in which he identified hidden biases and assumptions in classical and neoclassical economic writings.[7] His conversations with Wesley Mitchell, John R. Commons, and other American institutionalists exposed Gunnar Myrdal to new ideas that would eventually lead him to turn away from traditional economics toward institutional economics and interdisciplinary research on social problems. The experience of observing the stock market crash and the helplessness of the U.S. government in the face of the oncoming Depression shocked the Myrdals and made them determined to become politically involved when they returned home to Sweden. Both Myrdals were appalled by the poverty and suffering that they saw in the midst of such an affluent society, and they were troubled by the cynicism that they encountered among American intellectuals, who seemed content to debunk the conventional wisdom and reluctant to involve themselves in working for political change. Gunnar Myrdal in particular was pessimistic about America's chances of effecting thoroughgoing reform.[8]

While America seemed unable to cope with its economic crisis, Sweden proved to be a more fertile soil for the Myrdals' new commitment to political change. On returning home in 1931 Gunnar and Alva

Myrdal plunged into Social Democratic politics. As a member of the Stockholm School of Economics, Gunnar Myrdal advised the Social Democratic government on how to combat the Depression. In 1934 Gunnar and Alva Myrdal wrote *Kris i befolkningsfrågan* (Crisis in the Population Question), an influential book on population policy that had a significant impact on the development of the Swedish welfare state.[9] Many people in Sweden in this period worried about the declining birth rate and feared that Swedes were "dying out." The Myrdals took this traditionally conservative issue and used it to argue for government subsidies for poor families, better public housing, and birth control, so that those families that wanted to have more children could afford to have them. A strong feminist, Alva Myrdal drew up plans for collective houses, apartment buildings in which families enjoyed collective cooking and daycare arrangements designed to free women from housework, and several of these "Myrdal houses" were built in Stockholm. The Myrdals also advocated eugenic policies that would have mandated sterilization for "persons incapable of making a rational decision" about reproduction, but they emphatically rejected eugenics based on race, religion, or class differences. *Kris i befolkningsfrågan* became a bestseller, and the Myrdals' futuristic, rationalistic vision of social engineering ignited debates across the country about population policy and social welfare reforms. Jokes about fertility abounded, and the Swedish language gained a new verb for having sexual intercourse: to myrdal.[10]

By the age of thirty–seven, Gunnar Myrdal held the chair of economics at Stockholm University, was a member of the upper house of the Swedish Parliament, and served as a director of the Bank of Sweden. He declared himself an advocate of "prophylactic reform," a term that referred not only to his advocacy of birth control but more generally to a strategy of arguing to conservatives and centrists that they should take preventive measures to keep social problems from getting worse. As a member of Parliament, Myrdal served on several royal commissions and parliamentary committees and was accustomed to negotiating with top business, labor, and farm leaders in an effort to reach a consensus on carrying out these prophylactic reforms. He also had an extraordinary range of experience with policy-oriented research on unemployment, housing, migration, population, agriculture—all of which would come to be useful in his study of black Americans. For a Dalecarlian boy born in humble circumstances, it was a meteoric rise to prominence—and Gunnar Myrdal developed a rather extraordinary ego to match his rise to fame.

When Frederick Keppel of the Carnegie Corporation wrote Myrdal in 1937 to invite him, as an "objective" outsider, to head a study of the American "Negro problem," Myrdal at first declined this bizarre offer. But he was tired of all the committee work and frustrating compromises of parliamentary politics and he did not foresee any exciting new breakthroughs in social legislation at home, as Sweden was entering a "reform pause" and building up its military defense. The idea of heading a large, interdisciplinary research project appealed to him. To be sure, the United States lagged way behind Sweden in the development of a social welfare state, but the social sciences in America were first-rate, and it would be an intellectual challenge to tackle a major social issue about which he knew nothing. Myrdal wrote his friends Dorothy and W. I. Thomas,

> This was, after all, perhaps the last possibility to get free before we are old and absolutely stationary. Why not the Negro as well as anything else? . . . Carnegie is . . . prepared to pay me on a rather high scale. We are going with the children and a Swedish nurse—just like Abraham and Sarah from the Holy Land. I shall work on the Negro—I will do nothing else: I shall think and dream of the Negro 24 hours a day, for I will really do a good job (not like the Migration [study], which I always defrauded for other things).[11]

The Myrdals arrived in New York in the fall of 1938, expecting to spend two academic years in America while Gunnar Myrdal conducted his study of race relations. Alva Myrdal did not take part in the Carnegie Negro Study. She wrote a book on population policy, studied psychology at Columbia University, and lectured around the country on Scandinavian politics and society. Both of the Myrdals were in demand as speakers, since they had been architects of the Swedish welfare state much admired by American liberals. American audiences greeted them as oracles who had been "over into the future" and helped to make it work.[12]

Gunnar Myrdal plunged into the task of researching American race relations, quickly winning the confidence of Frederick Keppel and expanding his study into a large, cooperative research project with American collaborators writing specialized reports on various aspects of Afro-American life. Drawing on his experiences with royal commissions and parliamentary committees, he shrewdly brought on board social scientists and reformers representing several different points of view. The Swedish visitor was also determined to see much of the country himself, and he traveled throughout the South and visited most of the large cities in the North and West with significant black populations. Myrdal relished his interviews with sheriffs, sharecroppers, prisoners on chain gangs, communists, and Ku Klux Klansmen. His standard line was,

"I'm from Sweden and we don't have any black people there. What can you tell me about the race problem?"[13]

The threatening political situation in Europe was never far from Gunnar Myrdal's thoughts as he traveled through the small towns of the South and the ghettos of the North from the autumn of 1938 to the late summer of 1939. When he had left Sweden, he had believed that Germany lacked the resources to win a war and that Hitler would not dare to start one.[14] Still, he and Alva worried about what might happen to Sweden, and both of them felt anxious about being away from their country during a period of potential danger. When Germany invaded Poland in September 1939, Myrdal wrote to Prime Minister Per Albin Hansson offering to return home if he were needed for government service, but the prime minister did not order him home.[15] By the spring of 1940, Gunnar Myrdal was in despair about the fate of Europe. He wrote a Swedish friend that everything he had spent his life working for seemed to be collapsing and "the whole ideological basis for all of our . . . ideals seems to be breaking down."[16] Although he felt "overwhelmed by misery" because of the European war, Myrdal concentrated on his study of the American race question and kept up a punishing schedule of travel and interviewing. In a letter to his mentor, Swedish economist Gustav Cassel, he explained the broader significance of his study of American race relations:

> In my investigation I have the world's problem in miniature: the whole aggression-complex and the circle of prejudices, violence, and poverty. At the same time, the race problem is even greater than the war. That stands out clearly. For the first time I can grasp the full reality of the whole colonial problem.[17]

The news that Gunnar and Alva Myrdal had long dreaded came on 9 April 1940: German armies had invaded Denmark and Norway. The Myrdals thought that Hitler would attack Sweden next, and they began making plans to return home. Both Alva and Gunnar Myrdal wished to resume an active role in public life in Sweden during the national crisis. The decision to go home entailed considerable risk for both the Myrdals: They had a record for antifascist activities, and they realized that they might be interned in a concentration camp or killed if the German army invaded Sweden. Gunnar Myrdal took the precaution of issuing instructions to his close friend, economist Arthur R. Burns, on how to settle his financial affairs in the event of his death. Traveling to Sweden in the midst of the war was not easy, but after two weeks of frantic negotiating with Swedish, Finnish, British, and American diplomats, the Myrdal family secured passage aboard the *Matilda Thorden*, a Finnish freighter bound for Petsamo, Finland. Once aboard, they discovered that the ship was carrying a load of dynamite and that they would pass near German mine fields off the coast of Norway.[18]

The Myrdals reached Stockholm safely, but they found that there was not much they could do except wait to see what happened. "We had traveled home to a war," Gunnar and Alva Myrdal wrote, "but the war did not come. . . . We had traveled home expecting duties, but no duties sought us."[19] Sweden's strategic position in the spring and early summer of 1940 was extremely precarious. There was a possibility that the war in Norway would spill over onto Swedish territory as well as the danger that Hitler would simply decide to occupy Sweden to ensure total German domination of Scandinavia. In all probability, a German invasion would have overwhelmed Swedish defenses in a matter of days.

Neutrality had been the cornerstone of Swedish foreign policy since the Napoleonic era, and the country had avoided involvement in war for over a hundred years. But after the fall of France in June 1940, Germany established military hegemony over most of Europe, leaving Sweden surrounded by German armies. In this situation, the Swedish government pursued a policy of military mobilization and diplomatic accommodation designed to convince Hitler that an invasion of Sweden would not be worth the cost.[20]

The question of how far to go in making concessions to German demands was an issue that bedeviled Sweden's neutrality policy from 1940 to 1943. The Swedish government departed from a strict neutrality policy in 1940 in three important ways: It allowed a limited number of German troops to travel to and from Norway on Swedish trains; Sweden continued to trade with Germany and exported iron ore and ball bearings; and the government censored newspapers and periodicals that were sharply critical of Germany.[21] It was the Swedish government's policy of limiting freedom of the press that shocked and troubled Gunnar and Alva Myrdal. Swedish officials publicly and privately called on the newspapers to exercise restraint in their discussions of Germany. In September 1940, the Swedish government confiscated issues of a major metropolitan newspaper in Göteborg which had been sharply critical of the Nazi regime, and the government also seized issues of several radical anti-Nazi publications.[22]

Within the Swedish press, a considerable diversity of opinion existed in the summer and fall of 1940. Some newspapers argued that Sweden should accept the reality of German hegemony in Europe and accommodate the country's diplomacy and trade to the New Order. This accommodationist line sometimes included a critique of parliamentary democracy and demands for strengthening the power of the Swedish state.

Other newspapers took an isolationist view that the Swedish government should take whatever practical steps were necessary to keep the country from being invaded and the press and public should avoid debate on foreign policy so as to give the government the broadest possible latitude. Another camp openly sympathized with Britain and held that the Nazi dictatorship would eventually collapse. These advocates of resistance called for a policy of strict neutrality, an active discussion of foreign policy, and a grounding of Swedish policies in ethical principles.[23]

Life in wartime Sweden was frustrating for Gunnar Myrdal. There were severe limits to what he or anyone else could do in the face of German military might. He had interrupted a major research project in the United States to return home when his country was in danger, but this quixotic gesture had not resulted in an offer of a cabinet post or any other high government position. He had given up his seat in Parliament and he had been out of the country for a year and a half— a long time in the tightly knit world of Swedish politics. Myrdal's introduction to political life had been in the 1930s, an era of ambitious long-range planning and bold reform, and he felt out of place in a wartime situation that required crisis planning and reaction to events. His blunt and outspoken style was equally ill-suited to the coalition politics of the war years in which caution and restraint were the virtues of the hour.[24] Shortly after his return to Stockholm, the newspaper *Dagens Nyheter* ran an editorial cartoon that portrayed the leaders of the coalition government in a comic posture aboard a bicycle built for fifteen. Gunnar Myrdal was depicted in a bib and baby clothes riding in a baby-seat at the tail end of the tandem bike.[25]

Facing a strong possibility of failure both in his study of American race relations and in his political career at home, Myrdal identified with Abraham Lincoln, "a man who still at 45 years of age could say of himself that he had failed in everything." "What would Lincoln's destiny have been if he had been born a Swede?" he wondered. After describing all the obstacles that Sweden's "more rigid," bureaucratized society would have placed in Lincoln's path, Myrdal still hoped that Swedes would be willing to listen to a man who, like Lincoln, possessed only "a burning sense of justice, a strong intellect, and a clever tongue."[26]

It was in this context that Gunnar Myrdal entered the debate about Swedish accommodation of Nazi Germany and began trying to make sense of his notes and impressions of American culture and the American race question. Students at Stockholm University jammed into a lecture hall to hear this dynamic professor, dressed in Brooks Brothers suits and elegant ties, deliver his lectures on the American "Negro problem."

Meanwhile, Myrdal gave speeches and wrote articles criticizing the Swedish government's restrictions on freedom of the press and warned of a breakdown of the Swedish legal system, which had protected the freedom of the individual. "We must not let the legal system glide like a glacier," he wrote, "accommodating itself to the pressures of wind and weather." Instead, he urged Swedish intellectuals to write about the fundamental principles of democracy and civil rights so that the Swedish people would know what the nation stood for.[27] Alva Myrdal joined with her husband in criticizing Swedish accommodation of Nazi Germany and worked actively to stimulate an intellectual and ideological resistance to Nazism. She organized forums sponsored by women's groups on topics such as the "war for democracy," the situation in occupied Norway, and help for refugees who had fled to Sweden from Nazi-occupied countries.[28]

As they attempted to respond to the altered world of Swedish politics, Gunnar and Alva Myrdal reflected on their experiences in America and found that their admiration for the United States had increased substantially. During their first visit to the United States in 1929–30, they had felt a strong affection for the American people but had been sharply critical of the vast inequalities in American society and the lack of economic and social planning by the government. When they had returned in 1938, they were perceived by many American intellectuals as experts who had helped to create the Swedish welfare state, visitors from a more advanced society who could help Americans chart a more socially responsible future. Resuming life in wartime Sweden had been a shock. They had encountered not only a grave military emergency but also a society ridden with fear and pessimism, in which civil liberties were curtailed and many influential voices called for a policy of accommodation to Nazi Germany.

In response to this situation, the Myrdals decided to write a book about the United States for a Swedish audience, analyzing American society and government with comparisons to Sweden. They wrote *Kontakt med Amerika* (Contact with America) in the fall of 1940, and the book was published early in 1941. *Kontakt* was a resistance book designed to convince Swedish readers that the triumph of Hitler's vaunted New Order of Europe was not inevitable. The United States, which had not then entered the war, was portrayed as a source of hope for occupied Europe. Addressing a broad audience of Swedish readers, the Myrdals argued that a common belief in democracy and individual freedom united the people of Sweden and the United States.

The central theme of *Kontakt* was the importance of strengthening Sweden's ideological "preparedness." The Myrdals argued that Swedes were not as conscious of their liberties and rights as Americans were. Although they considered Sweden to be one of the most democratic societies in the world, they believed that their fellow countrymen needed to be more vigilant about the erosion of their liberties, particularly in the area of government censorship of the press. As they looked back on their time in America, they were struck by the widespread knowledge among the American people of a U.S. citizen's rights under the Constitution. The Myrdals claimed that an ordinary American could explain his belief in the American creed of democracy, equality of opportunity, and individual freedom, and they argued that this American creed was what held such a vast, heterogeneous nation together.[29] But they questioned whether most Swedes had a belief system strong enough to resist pressures to refrain from criticizing Nazi Germany. The authors sought to make the Swedish people more conscious of their democratic traditions as a counterforce to defeatism and acquiescence in the inevitability of a Nazi-dominated Europe.

The Myrdals praised the American penchant for self-criticism and willingness to publicize America's ills to the world. Referring to Gunnar Myrdal's commission to study the "Negro problem," they inquired whether anyone could imagine "that the German Reich should have called in a foreign researcher to make an unbiased report on the country's most serious race problem—the Jewish question."[30] Gunnar Myrdal then developed what would become the central argument of *An American Dilemma*: "The Negro problem, just like all other difficult social problems, is . . . a problem in the Americans' own heart. One can also say that it represents a conflict between a national ideology—which is described above—and dissimilar local ideologies which diverge from it." Gunnar Myrdal argued that this conflict between the American creed and racial prejudice existed even within the mind of the most racist and reactionary southerner. He reported on a psychological experiment he had tried in conversations with Ku Klux Klansmen, in which he had suggested that they could achieve their ends more effectively by using "modern scientific techniques of physical violence and psychological influence, as demonstrated by Nazism." Myrdal found in every case that these men replied that such methods were unconstitutional and contrary to the American creed.[31]

These experiences led the Myrdals to conclude that "moral ideas really represent social forces [in America], though unfortunately not the only ones and not always the strongest." They criticized the tendency of American social scientists to underestimate the social importance of moral ideals and noted the paradox of this intellectual skepticism about ideals in the midst of a strongly moralistic culture. As foreign observers, the Myrdals believed that they could see clearly that the "moral pulse beats more strongly in the American civilization" than in most European cultures. The American creed, they argued, was growing stronger: "The Supreme Court judges according to it. . . . Churches preach it. Schools teach it. A great part of the whole adult education activities are 'Americanization education.' "[32]

The Myrdals arrived at this exaggerated notion of the American creed's importance partly by listening to American intellectuals in the late 1930s. In response to the Great Depression, many writers had journeyed to the heartland of the United States in an effort to discover "authentic" American voices of protest, in contrast to foreign "isms."[33] During the period of the Popular Front (1935 to 1939), intellectuals on the left had sought to anchor contemporary radicalism in the nation's democratic traditions, and Communist party spokesmen had embraced the slogan, "Communism is twentieth-century Americanism."[34] As Nazism, fascism, and Stalinism grew more powerful in Europe, American liberals also sought to strengthen the "American democratic faith," to develop an American democratic ideology tough enough to stand up to totalitarianism. After the outbreak of World War II in Europe in September 1939, both interventionists and isolationists had framed their arguments in terms of preserving America's democratic values.[35]

The American creed thus meant different things to different intellectuals. To the Myrdals, it meant, above all, civil rights, civil liberties, a free press, and democratic decision making. As Social Democrats, they deemphasized the strain of American thinking that invoked the Founding Fathers to sanction the freedom of business enterprise and the idea of limited government. According to the Myrdals, the American creed, deeply rooted in American culture, was also being strengthened by political and economic forces. A major theme of *Kontakt* was the idea that Franklin Roosevelt had wrought a "social revolution" in the United States. Under Roosevelt's leadership, the Myrdals averred, Americans had reinterpreted their ideals, gradually replacing an earlier economic individualism with a greater sense of social responsibility and commitment to economic planning. The authors asserted that the American people were ready for a continuation of reform. Of particular significance was the fact that "Roosevelt and the New Deal, for the first time in American history, have taught the poor to start asking why they should be poor in this rich land, to demand their rights and to depend upon political means to win them." The Myrdals predicted a steady advance for labor in the wake of the Wagner Act and a party realignment, with the Democrats becoming "a left party in the European sense." They confessed that when they had visited the United States ten years earlier, they had found American politics so corrupted and American reformers so ineffective that they had thought the only hope lay in a new socialist labor party. But FDR, who had become an American "folk hero," had brought about change in a manner that grew out of American traditions and was not associated with European "isms." He was making the Democratic party a "national reform-minded peoples' party" like the Swedish Social Democrats. Roosevelt had also appealed to intellectuals—a group that had been alienated from politics during the 1920s—and had welcomed into the Democratic party a "radical intellectual left wing which is becoming the driving force ideologically."[36]

Yet this advance toward a sense of social responsibility in America had not come at the expense of individual freedom, the Myrdals insisted. They contended that American culture did not attempt "to chisel away human diversity with convention's power. On the contrary, the individual is nowhere as uninhibited and free from convention's pressure as in this land." When the Myrdals contrasted this idealistic interpretation of American politics and culture with the situation in Sweden in 1940, they came up with some harsh criticisms of their own country. Swedes, they argued, were not as passionately committed to free speech as were Americans. The Swedish government thought that it had to suppress dissenting views on the neutrality question, whereas in America, free discussion had produced a stable foreign policy consensus, as evidenced by the basic accord between Roosevelt and Willkie in the 1940 election.[37]

Focussing on the issue of freedom of speech in neutral Sweden, the Myrdals asserted that Swedish intellectuals faced a moral dilemma in deciding how far to go in expressing their opinions while their country was threatened from without. They acknowledged that this dilemma was an acute psychological burden for the Swedish journalists who had to express themselves in print day after day. But they suggested that too many Swedish intellectuals were abandoning the proper role of intellectuals as vigorous critics of government and society and instead embracing a "weak opportunism." "What will happen to the nation's strength of resistance," they asked, "if the intellectual middle classes, who occupy all the key positions and are the nation's voice, give up?" "Our country may need martyrs instead," they warned. "In our defense it is perhaps not just soldiers who must be prepared to die. All must be prepared to lose at least income and position, influence and security, yes—even freedom."[38]

In conclusion, the Myrdals urged their countrymen to devise a Swedish equivalent of the American creed and make the principles of democracy, justice, and freedom "holy national symbols for the people." If the country were invaded, this national creed would serve as the ideological basis for a resistance movement. To those among their compatriots who counseled accommodation to Nazi Germany, the Myrdals replied that Swedes should begin planning for a postwar world based on international cooperation, peace, and social justice. They admitted that "all this sounds terribly utopian in Sweden today. But we shall remember that these things are discussed as serious political problems . . . in America. Utopias are alive there."[39]

After completing the manuscript for this book with its extraordinarily favorable interpretation of American culture, its optimism about the power of the American creed, and its erroneous reading of the New Deal as a nascent social democratic movement, Gunnar Myrdal made plans to return to the United States to resume work on his study of race relations. In January 1941 his transit visa across Germany was canceled by the German government. Myrdal went to the German Embassy in Stockholm to complain and was told by a diplomat, Dr. Werner Dankwort, that the German legation had a complete dossier on both of the Myrdals, knew of their hostility to the Nazi philosophy, and would therefore "do everything possible" to prevent him from going to the United States "to encourage the Americans in their attitude of hostility" to Germany. When Dankwort learned that the Myrdals had just finished a book about America, he asked to see the manuscript and suggested that the matter of the transit visa might be reopened if he could see the manuscript before publication. Gunnar Myrdal exploded into rage at this attempt at censorship and blackmail, told Dankwort that Swedish economists such as his mentor, Gustav Cassel, had come to Germany's aid after the First World War when Germany was "despised by all the other nations of the world," and assured the Nazi official that he and other Swedes would again come to the aid of the German people after the Nazi regime was defeated in the current war. Myrdal then stormed out of the German Embassy, obtained a transit visa across the Soviet Union, and returned to the United States via the trans-Siberian railroad and a flight from Japan to San Francisco, where he landed on 6 March 1941.[40]

Shortly after his return to New York, Myrdal made a speech designed to rebut assertions in the American press that Sweden's neutrality policy was really pro-German and to quash rumors of the growth of an indigenous Swedish Nazi movement like that of Quisling in Norway. Although he had been critical of some of the government's policies at home, he loyally portrayed Swedish policy in a favorable light before an American audience. Myrdal reassured Americans that Sweden was still a bastion of democracy and declared, "The rumors spread in this country that the Nazi ideology is making inroads in Sweden are false."

Swallowing his outrage over the government's censorship policies, he declared that "nobody who follows the Swedish press will deny that public discussion is free and unhampered." And he betrayed a certain defensiveness in insisting that "the American public must realize that we are doing our full part in defending democracy by defending ourselves."[41]

After delivering this speech, Myrdal made a trip to the South to have a final look at Jim Crow, checked into the Robert E. Lee Hotel in Jackson, Mississippi, and read through twenty thousand pages of reports prepared by his American collaborators on nearly every aspect of Afro-American life. He then went into seclusion, first at Dartmouth, then at Princeton, to write his study of American race relations with the assistance of Richard Sterner and Arnold Rose. Myrdal had been through a difficult period, juggling roles as a scholar and publicist and delicately balancing his anti-Nazi principles and his sense of loyalty to his endangered country. Myrdal acknowledged that he felt both a sense of awesome responsibility and a twinge of guilt that he should be writing a book at a cloistered American college campus while so many of his friends in Europe were either in Nazi prisons or had been killed in the war. But he threw himself into the task, convinced that America's resolution of its "race problem" was vital to the future peace of the world. Myrdal considered *An American Dilemma* his "war work," and it was, like *Kontakt*, an attempt to overcome the sense of impotence and irrelevance that he felt as a Swedish intellectual by making a vigorous commitment to the strengthening of ideological defenses against Nazism.[42] As the Allies pushed the war in Europe toward a successful conclusion, Myrdal wrote articles entitled "The Negro and America's Uneasy Conscience" and (in Swedish) "Neutrality and Our Conscience."[43] Both Swedes and Americans, he believed, faced a moral dilemma, a choice between following their conscience and ideals or giving in to an expedient but horrifically destructive alternative.

Ironically, while Gunnar Myrdal was working fifteen hours a day on his critique of racism, he was under surveillance by the Federal Bureau of Investigation as a suspected Nazi sympathizer. On 12 June 1941, an informant in New York had told the FBI that a Swede named "Myrdal Gunnar" was going around making pro-Nazi statements while investigating the condition of black Americans. It took the bureau some months to track down this "Karl Gunnar Myrdal, with aliases Gunnar Myrdal, Myrdal Gunnar." Agents in Boston, New York, and Newark checked up on this mysterious Swede, interviewing officials at Dartmouth and the Carnegie Corporation, as well as neighbors and the postmaster in Princeton. The FBI discovered that he spoke in a "heavy

German accent" and that the Myrdals "entertained Negroes often in their apartment," but they found no conclusive evidence of "un-American activities."[44]

When he finished *An American Dilemma* in the summer of 1942, Gunnar Myrdal confided to Charles Dollard of the Carnegie Corporation that he would not have been able to write the book if he had not returned to Sweden when he felt the call of duty in May 1940. "I should not have been able to come back to the study," he wrote, "if I had not left my children there as hostages. And if I did not return now after the work is finished to swim or sink with my own culture, I could not . . . stand for the book. The book could not have been written by a refugee."[45] Only by participating in the struggle to preserve democracy in his own country, Myrdal believed, could he preserve his status as a foreign observer of American culture, a posture that gave him critical distance and enabled him to make a more plausible case that he spoke for people throughout the world who expected the United States to live up to its democratic principles on the race question.

Returning to Stockholm in September 1942, Gunnar and Alva Myrdal plunged into a variety of political and intellectual activities. Drawing on some of John Dewey's ideas, Alva sought to reform Sweden's educational system to make it less authoritarian and more democratic, while Gunnar, reelected to the upper house of the Swedish Parliament, focused his attention on planning Sweden's postwar economy and contributed ideas to discussions about the political and economic reconstruction of Europe after the war. The Myrdals had aided refugees from Germany and Nazi-occupied countries since the mid-1930s, and in 1942 they joined a Social Democratic discussion group in Stockholm consisting of members from fourteen countries, including Willy Brandt, Bruno Kreisky, and other refugees. Dubbed Die Kleine Internationale, the group discussed plans for a democratic socialist Europe free of national rivalries, debated strategies for ridding Germany of Nazi influence, and urged the Allies not to impose vindictive peace terms on the Axis countries.[46]

Gunnar Myrdal's efforts to defeat Nazi Germany were not limited to the ideological sphere; his ties to Social Democratic German refugees led to contacts with the anti-Nazi underground inside the Third Reich. Before American entry into the war, Myrdal had met in the United States with Adam von Trott zu Solz, a German diplomat who was an influential member of the resistance movement that sought to overthrow Hitler. In the spring of 1944, Trott traveled to Stockholm in an effort to contact American, British, and Soviet diplomats to win their cooperation in Operation Valkyrie, the conspiracy of German military and political leaders to assassinate Hitler and stage a coup d'etat in Berlin. On 23 June 1944, Gunnar Myrdal held a secret meeting in his office in which Trott spoke with Myrdal's friend John Scott, an American correspondent for *Time* magazine. Using Scott as an intermediary, Trott unsuccessfully pleaded with American diplomats to modify the United States' demand for unconditional surrender in the event that the plot against Hitler succeeded. This meeting was one of the last contacts between a top figure in the German resistance and American diplomats before 20 July, when Col. Claus Count von Stauffenberg exploded a bomb in Hitler's headquarters in East Prussia, narrowly missing the führer and igniting an abortive plot to seize control of the government in Berlin. Adam von Trott zu Solz was executed by the Nazis for his part in the conspiracy.[47]

Gunnar Myrdal served as Sweden's minister of commerce from 1945 to 1947 and played a leading role in the reconstruction of war-torn Europe as director of the United Nations Economic Commission for Europe from 1947 to 1957. He seldom spoke about his ties to the anti-Nazi resistance, in part because his actions had overstepped the bounds of propriety for an elected official of a neutral state. Gunnar Myrdal would be remembered instead for his "war work" on *An American Dilemma*, which helped to steer postwar research on American ethnic relations toward a greater concern with psychological issues, especially the study of prejudice, and afforded greater legitimacy to policy-oriented research on race relations. Myrdal's definition of the American "Negro problem" as a "white man's problem" put the focus of attention on white racial prejudice and discrimination but had the unintended effect of directing attention away from further studies of Afro-American culture, social structure, and community life.[48]

Though Myrdal's concept of the American creed would seem nebulous or vapid to a later generation of critics on the left, the creed appeared to many American intellectuals of the 1940s and 1950s to be a very real and palpable social fact that distinguished the United States from other mass societies in which the public had been swayed by totalitarian propaganda. In an era when Afro-Americans were beginning to mobilize their political and economic power, the rhetorical appeal to the conscience of white Americans was an added point of leverage in the struggle against Jim Crow. Myrdal undoubtedly exaggerated the importance of the American creed both in everyday life and in politics, but he did persuade a significant number of American intellectuals that American democracy was gravely weakened by racial discrimination and that the nation needed urgently to take action on civil rights. His wartime perception of the weakness of Swedish democracy and his tortured conscience on the issue of Swedish neutrality policy helped to shape this influential formulation of America's moral dilemma.

Notes

1. Gunnar Myrdal, with the assistance of Richard Sterner and Arnold Rose, *An American Dilemma: The Negro Problem and Modern Democracy* (New York: Harper and Brothers, 1944).
2. Some of these objections to the "moral dilemma" thesis were raised in reviews of Myrdal's book in 1944. See David W. Southern, *Gunnar Myrdal and Black-White Relations: The Use and Abuse of "An American Dilemma,"* 1944–1969 (Baton Rouge: Louisiana State University Press, 1987), pp. 81, 88. Myrdal also made a structural argument that the American creed was embedded in American institutions through the Constitution. He predicted that an increasingly militant black protest on several fronts would disrupt business as usual and cause the United States international embarrassment, thus forcing the federal government to protect the civil rights of Afro-Americans.
3. Harvard Sitkoff, *A New Deal for Blacks: The Emergence of Civil Rights as a National Issue: The Depression Decade* (New York: Oxford University Press, 1978), p. 202; George Fredrickson, *The Black Image in the White Mind: The Debate on Afro-American Character and Destiny, 1817–1914* (New York: Harper and Row, 1971), p. 330; August Meier and Elliott Rudwick, *Black History and the Historical Profession, 1915–1980* (Urbana: University of Illinois Press, 1986), p. 122.
4. Walter A. Jackson, "The Making of a Social Science Classic: Gunnar Myrdal's *An American Dilemma*," *Perspectives in American History* n.s. 2 (1985); Jackson, *Gunnar Myrdal and America's Conscience: Social Engineering and Racial Liberalism, 1938–1987* (Chapel Hill: University of North Carolina Press, 1990).
5. Gunnar Myrdal, "Massan och Intelligensen" (1918), Gunnar Myrdal Papers, Arbetarrörelsens Arkiv, Stockholm (hereafter abbreviated as GMP).
6. Sissela Bok, *Alva: Ett Kvinnoliv* (Stockholm: Bonniers, 1987); Lars Lindskog, *Alva Myrdal* (Stockholm: Sveriges Radios Förlag, 1981).
7. G. Myrdal, *The Political Element in the Development of Economic Theory* (Cambridge, Mass.: Harvard University Press, 1961), originally published in Swedish as *Vetenskap och politik i nationalekonomien* (Stockholm: Kooperative förbundets bokförlag, 1930).
8. G. M. to Gustav Cassel, 29 October 1929 and 18 January 1930, Cassel MSS, Royal Library, Stockholm.
9. Alva Myrdal and Gunnar Myrdal, *Kris i befolkningsfrågan* (Stockholm: Bonniers, 1934).
10. Allan Carlson, "The Roles of Alva and Gunnar Myrdal in the Development of a Social Democratic Response to Europe's 'Population Crisis,' 1929–1938," Ph.D. diss., Ohio University, 1978, pp. 265–71.
11. G. M. to Dorothy S. Thomas, 1 March 1938, GMP.
12. Marquis Childs, "How Fares Democracy?," *St. Louis Post-Dispatch*, 25 June 1939; Ralph McGill, "One Word More," *Atlanta Constitution*, n.d. enclosure, Howard Odum to Frederick Keppel, 27 May 1939, "Negro Study General Correspondence," Carnegie Corporation Archives (CCA), New York; Alva Myrdal,

"Education for Democracy in Sweden," in *Education for Democracy: The Proceedings of the Congress on Education for Democracy, Teachers College, Columbia University, August 15-17, 1939* (New York: Teachers College, 1939), pp. 169–80.

13. Arthur Raper, interview with author, 13 April 1977, Oakton, Virginia.
14. G. M. to Keppel, 22 April 1940, CCA.
15. G. M. to Ernst Wigforss, 2 September 1939, GMP.
16. G. M. to Fredrik Ström, 2 April 1940, GMP.
17. G. M. to Cassel, 5 March 1940, Cassel MSS.
18. G. M. to Arthur R. Burns, 8 May 1940, GMP; G. M. to Frederick Osborn, 6 May 1940, GMP.
19. Alva Myrdal and Gunnar Myrdal, *Kontakt med Amerika* (Stockholm: Bonniers, 1941), p. 27.
20. Wilhelm M. Carlgren, *Swedish Foreign Policy during the Second World War* (New York: St. Martin's Press, 1977), pp. 54–68.
21. Ibid., pp. 68–72, 83.
22. Ibid., pp. 61, 82–86; Louise Drangel, *Den kämpande demokratin: en studie in antinazistisk opinionsrörelse, 1935-45* (Stockholm: Liber Förlag, 1976).
23. Thorsten Nybom, *Motstånd—anpassning—uppslutning: linjer i svensk debatt om utrikespolitik och internationell politik, 1940-1943* (Stockholm: Liber Förlag, 1978), pp. 129–84.
24. G. M. to Richard Sterner, 25 June 1940; G. M. to Samuel Stouffer et al, 26 August 1940, GMP.
25. *Dagens Nyheter*, 23 June 1940.
26. Quoted in Sissela Bok, *Alva, Ett kvinnoliv* (Stockholm: Bonniers, 1987), p. 135.
27. G. M. to Åke Hassler, 25 September 1940, GMP.
28. Lindskog, *Alva Myrdal*, p. 60.
29. Myrdal and Myrdal, *Kontakt med Amerika*, pp. 32–33.
30. Ibid., p. 52.
31. Ibid., pp. 52–53. Myrdal got a similar result when he tried this "experiment" on Mississippi senator Theodore Bilbo. See "Dr. Gunnar Myrdal's Interview with Senator Theodore G. Bilbo, April 8, 1940," Ralph Bunche MSS., Box 85, University of California, Los Angeles.
32. Myrdal and Myrdal, *Kontakt med Amerika*, pp. 54–56.
33. See William Stott, *Documentary Expression and Thirties America* (Chicago: University of Chicago Press, 1973), pp. 171–89.
34. Richard Pells, *Radical Visions and American Dreams* (New York: Harper and Row, 1973), pp. 292–99.
35. In *An American Dilemma*, p. 1182 ff., Myrdal cited Ernest Bates, *American Faith: Its Religious, Political, and Economic Foundations* (New York: Norton, 1940). See also Lewis Mumford, *Faith for Living* (1940); Charles C. Alexander, *Nationalism in American Thought, 1930-1945* (Chicago: Rand McNally, 1969), pp. 164–89; and Edward Purcell, *The Crisis of Democratic Theory: Scientific Naturalism and the Problem of Value* (Lexington: University Press of Kentucky, 1973).
36. Myrdal, *An American Dilemma*, pp. 243–46.
37. Ibid., p. 283.
38. Ibid., p. 312.

39. Ibid., pp. 370–72.
40. F. A. Sterling to Secretary of State Cordell Hull, 29 January 1941, document no. 032/1463, National Archives, Washington, D.C.; Egon Glesinger, "Gunnar Myrdal," unpublished MS., GMP.
41. *New York Times*, 26 March 1941.
42. G. M. to Sven Tunberg, 13 August 1941, GMP; G. M., Interview with author, Stockholm, 19 August 1980.
43. Myrdal, "The Negro and America's Uneasy Conscience," *Free World*, 5 November 1943, pp. 412–22; Myrdal, "Neutralitet och vårt samvete," *Tiden* 37 (1945): 257–70.
44. Federal Bureau of Investigation, File no. 100-2893, "Gunnar Myrdal or Myrdal Gunnar," 19 September 1941; File no. 100-4910, "Gunnar Myrdal," 14 October 1941; File no. 100-15527, "Karl Gunnar Myrdal, with alias Gunnar Myrdal," 7 July 1942; File no. 100-16381, "Gunnar Myrdal, Alva Myrdal," 31 October 1942, FBI Headquarters, Washington, D.C.
45. G. M. to Charles Dollard, 22 July 1942, GMP.
46. Klaus Misgeld, *Die "internationale Gruppe demokratischer Sozialisten" in Stockholm 1942-1945* (Uppsala: Almqvist and Wiksell, 1976); Willy Brandt, *Links und frei: Mein Weg 1930-1950* (Hamburg: Hoffmann and Campe, 1982), pp. 327–46; Bruno Kreisky, *Zwischen den Zeiten: Erinnerungen aus fünf Jahrzehnten* (Berlin: Siedler Verlag, 1986), pp. 365–403.
47. Gunnar Myrdal, calendar, 22, 23 June 1944, GMP; Herschel Johnson to the Secretary of State, 26 June 1944, *Foreign Relations* 1944, vol. 1, pp. 523–25; G. Myrdal to Allen Dulles, 8 August 1947, GMP; Peter Hoffmann, *Widerstand, Staatsstreich, Attentat: Der Kampf der Opposition gegen Hitler* (Munich: R. Piper, 1969), p. 286; Ingeborg Fleischauer, *Die Chance der Sonderfriedens: Deutsch-sowjetische Geheimspräche 1941-1945* (Berlin: Siedler Verlag, 1986), pp. 237–39; Hendrik Lindgren, "Adam von Trott's Reisen nach Schweden, 1941–44," *Vierteljahrshefte für Zeitgeschichte* 18 (1970): 274–91; Henry O. Malone, "Adam von Trott zu Solz," Ph.D. diss., University of Texas, 1980; Christopher Sykes, *Tormented Loyalty: The Story of a German Aristocrat Who Defied Hitler* (New York: Harper and Row, 1969), pp. 425–28; R. Taylor Cole, *The Recollections of R. Taylor Cole: Educator, Emissary, Development Planner* (Durham, N.C.: Duke University Press, 1983), pp. 80–84; Cole, Interview with author; Brandt, *Links und frei*, pp. 364–73.
48. See Jackson, *Gunnar Myrdal and America's Conscience*, chaps. 6 and 7.

▪ 11 THE POLITICS OF ETHNICITY IN SOCIAL SCIENCE

RUBÉN MARTINEZ

During the recent social upheaval and change of the civil rights movement the metatheoretical foundations of the social sciences were once again brought into question by scholars representing different orientations, models, and paradigms.[1] The rise of the New Left, the widespread influence of Thomas Kuhn's treatise *The Structure of Scientific Revolutions*, increased participation by ethnic minorities and women in social scientific activity, and a general loss of public confidence, among other factors, produced yet another "crisis in the social sciences," one that was widely and intensely felt by the members of the social scientific community.[2]

Strong critiques of the philosophical foundations and conclusions of the social sciences generated spirited debates and innovative approaches to the study of individuals, groups, and societies. The autonomy of scientific knowledge and the "sanctity" of the scientific method were repeatedly called into question and, in some cases, plausible alternatives were presented.[3] In this context of questioning, creativity, and debate, many minority scholars sought to come to grips with methodological, epistemological, and ontological issues while at the same time attempting to survive in academic and research contexts that in the main were completely new and generally resistant to most of them.[4] Yet, only by remaining within the ranks of the social scientific community could their views and research results stand any realistic chance of gaining legitimacy as social scientific knowledge. Entry into and retention within the scientific community posed distinct problems for minorities that made and continue to make it difficult for them to influence the production of social scientific knowledge.

It is at both of these levels of social science, its metatheoretical foundations and participation within the social scientific community, that we find critical junctures in the relationship between the social sciences and minority scholars. The purpose of this paper is to examine these two junctures and their implications for understanding the politics of ethnicity in social science, a topic that has received little attention even among philosophers and sociologists of scientific knowledge.[5]

In terms of structure, I first present a discussion of the relationship between science and ideology. This is followed by a discussion of the responses of minority scholars to the general views about minorities found in social scientific literature. Next is a discussion of the problems minorities face in maintaining membership in the social scientific community. I end with a discussion of the notion of objectivity and ethnocentric research interpretations and conclusions.

Science and Ideology

Science is generally influenced by the dynamics of the broader social context in which it is located. Not only are its philosophical foundations more or less specific to time and place, but so are the practices and technologies that generate scientific knowledge and establish it as such. The autonomy of science from extrascientific processes is relative to time and place, and scientific disciplines differ in the degree and nature of their autonomy.[6] They also are likely to differ in their specific relationships with minorities.

The theoretical construct that links social scientific activity and knowledge with broader social practices and beliefs is ideology. Althusser defines ideology as "the imaginary relationship of individuals to their real conditions of existence."[7] In other words, ideologies allude to reality but do not correspond to it. Ideology comprehends the conditions of human existence, but not any "system of real relations." That is, ideological views present our conditions of existence in distorted forms. The distortion is not necessarily intended and probably is due to objective factors rather than to conscious attempts to deceive.

The boundary between scientific knowledge and ideology is implied in the definition of the latter concept as imaginary (i.e., not corresponding to reality). The boundary is purely ideal, however, and its actuality remains problematic for social scientists. Scientific knowledge is generally seen as accurately explaining a delimited domain of reality. At the same time, however, scientific knowledge is ever approaching correspondence to reality. It is more or less accurate at any point in time.

Another important aspect of ideology is its material existence. "An ideology always exists in an apparatus, and its practice, or practices."[8]

Ideology is not merely a set of ideas, it also has an existence in the behaviors of human beings located in specific social and institutional contexts. From this view, the practices of individuals are seen as integral components of the material rituals that characterize social institutions. The practices of concrete subjects are both constitutive of and constituted by ideology. As humans we are ideological creatures; our practices tend to correspond with our understanding of social reality, even though our understanding probably only roughly corresponds to its actual nature.

Social scientific activity in our day is primarily connected to institutions of higher learning, particularly those emphasizing research. Government research units, private foundations, "think tanks," and research units of private industry also are sites linked to the production of social scientific knowledge. Generally, we can say that the more connections a particular social scientific endeavor has to these sites, the more likely it is to contribute to the determination of the boundary(ies) and content of social scientific knowledge.

Social scientists are sustained in their research activities through both private and public funding.[9] Their research and theoretical conclusions are made public through a variety of mechanisms. The primary mechanisms include the monographs and textbooks published by a multiplicity of university presses and companies that emphasize scientific work, the annual conferences held by professional societies, and the journals they publish. These media bring together a multiplicity of scientists and bond them together as a community wherein they experience a sense of belonging to a school of thought, a discipline, or a science, and where they have their work subjected to scrutiny in accordance with the standards and canons of the "scientific community."

The boundaries of scientific communities are fixed yet shifting, crystallized yet amorphous. They are historical boundaries that are connected to the phenomena they circumscribe and to the broader environment in which they exist. It is possible to speak of both a scientific community and scientific communities.[10] In either case, it is important to keep in mind that concrete subjects make decisions in everyday life as they engage in scientific activity. At this level, they pursue hunches and interests, engage in various power plays, and construct scientific knowledge.[11] These activities occur in specific contexts, most of which are characterized by some degree of bureaucracy and professionalism.[12] At the organizational level of science are included the processes of recruiting and training new scientists, hierarchical levels of authority and reward structures, and "systems" of evaluation of scientific results.

Minority participation in scientific communities is especially important because their future depends, among other things, on their ability to develop and put to use accurate knowledge about the natural and social contexts in which they exist. In general, minorities are not in a position to either generate substantial knowledge about the world or effectively put it to use. Explanations for the lack of racial and ethnic minority influence on social scientific knowledge tend to be missing from social science. Such explanations would be part of the explanation of the more general relationship between minorities and the social scientific community. The relationship between minorities and social science has to do with the philosophy of science guiding and influencing the work of social scientists, the paradigms that compete for prominence, the values, norms, ethics, and practices of the social scientific community, the specific ideologies that scientists bring to the workplace of science, and those that already characterize it.

Minority Groups and Social Scientific Knowledge

Racial and ethnic minorities in this country have had little influence on the production of social scientific knowledge about themselves or society in general.[13] To be sure, social scientists such as W.E.B. Du Bois, Charles Johnson, E. Franklin Frazier, Oliver C. Cox, Ernesto Galarza, George I. Sanchez, Julian Samora, and others conducted notable research and produced important scholarship on minority groups, American institutions, and societal processes. Yet, their work neither significantly influenced the basic foundations of social scientific activity nor guided such activity, until recently, in directions that influenced its results (e.g., scientific knowledge). To some extent this is due to the fact that many minority scholars accepted, extended, and reinforced "the fundamental conceptual models and the methodological leads initiated and developed by white scholars."[14] At the same time, however, a few were able to provide crucial correctives to those views, especially as they related to minorities.

Nevertheless, it was not until the 1960s and thereafter that a "critical mass" of minority scholars came into existence in this country and began to develop a body of scholarship containing the promise of contributing to and significantly influencing social scientific perspectives and conclusions.[15] During this period some minority social scientists turned to and extended the critical leads provided by their predecessors. Among those early scholars were W.E.B. Du Bois, George I. Sanchez, and E. Franklin Frazier.

As early as 1908, W.E.B. Du Bois, who was the only black faculty member at a white institution of higher learning just before the turn

of the century, implied that American social science was producing biased knowledge about blacks:

> The data upon which the mass of men, and even intelligent men, are basing
> their conclusions today, the basis which they are putting back of their
> treatment of the Negro, is a most ludicrous and harmful conglomeration
> of myth, falsehood, and desire. It would certainly be a most commendable
> thing if [the American Sociological Society] and other learned societies
> would put themselves on record as favoring a most thorough and unbiased
> scientific study of the race problem in America.[16]

Some years later, during the 1930s, Sanchez questioned the uncritical
application of standardized mental tests to study the abilities of students,
especially bilingual schoolchildren. He took issue with the work of
T. R. Garth, who studied Spanish-speaking students from different communities in three southwestern states and concluded that the median
IQ of these children was seventy-eight. Sanchez posed the following
question: "Who would champion the thesis that half or more of the
Spanish-speaking, or any other such, group is dull, borderline, and
feeble-minded when it is generally accepted that only 7 percent of 'normal' groups may be so classified?"[17]

In 1947, one year before he was elected president of the American
Sociological Society, Frazier, in reviewing sociological theories of race
relations, argued that the theories of the founding fathers of American
sociology were based on racial assumptions. He stated:

> Sociological theories relating to the concrete problems of race relations in
> the United States were implicit in the sociological analysis of the Negro
> problem as a social problem. The analysis of the Negro problem was based
> upon several fairly clear assumptions: that the Negro is an inferior race
> because of either biological or social heredity or both; that the Negro be-
> cause of his physical character cannot be assimilated; and that physical
> amalgamation is bad and undesirable.[18]

Despite the warnings and calls for caution by Du Bois, Sanchez, Frazier,
and other minority scholars, dominant group social scientists continued
to produce negative depictions of and conclusions about minorities. Following the relative demise of biological determinist theories to explain
the "inferiority" of some racial groups, American social scientists began
to look at culture as the primary determinant of their low status and
achievement in society.[19]

The image of minorities that emerged from cultural perspectives
emphasized the negative dimensions of their group existence, and the
new generation of minority scholars of the 1960s and 1970s could not

fail to notice this salient feature of race relations literature. Minority scholars, in responding to this literature, questioned both the conclusions and the methods used to produce social scientific knowledge about minority groups. Although virtually all aspects of minority existence were depicted in negative terms, it is enough to look at the family to gain a sense of how minority scholars perceived such conclusions. Mirande, for example, in reviewing the literature on the Chicano family, stated:

> An examination of social scientific literature on the Mexican-American family reveals a consistently pathological and pejorative view. These negative depictions have resulted from the tendency of social scientists to see the Mexican-American family as a radical departure or deviation from the dominant, egalitarian, Anglo-American Family; Mexican and Mexican-American families appear rigid and authoritarian by comparison.[20]

A similar point was made by Staples in reviewing studies focusing on the black family:

> Until recently almost all studies of Black family life have concentrated on the lower-income stratum of the group, while ignoring middle-class families or even "stable" poor Black families. Moreover, the deviation of Black families from [white] middle-class norms has led to the definition of them as "pathological." Such labels ignore the possibility that while a group's family forms may not fit into the normative model, it may have its own functional organization to meet the needs of the group.[21]

Although comparisons of minority families to middle-stratum white families are not in themselves invidious, what makes them so is that they tend to be based on implicit assumptions that there exists a hierarchy of cultures and that the family form of middle-strata white families is somehow superior to all others. Moreover, such comparisons often fail to take into account the broader social-historical and structural forces which have shaped the forms and experiences of minority families.[22]

Minority scholars included in their critiques of dominant group research on minorities alternative perspectives for studying these groups. Jackson, in discussing the approach of black studies, stated that black studies "assumes that black people can be studied on their own terms—that their behavior can be evaluated with respect to the standards and requirements prevalent within the black community, whether or not they are the same as in the white community.[23] Similarly, Thompson argued that blacks can be studied both on their own terms and within the dynamics of the broader society.[24] He proposed that blacks be studied at four levels: (1) the influence of their presence on the overall nature of American society, (2) the direct and indirect influences of white domination on their experiences, (3) their responses to their oppressed status in society, and (4) their contributions to their own survival and progress and to the larger society.

These perspectives not only treat minorities as participants in the historical process but seek to reconstruct their histories and to analyze their experiences as they have been shaped by broader social forces. Given the views and images of minorities produced by dominant group social science, it was not long before the new generation of minority scholars began to question its basic foundations and functions.

In 1969, Gerald McWorter, in a review of race relations literature, echoed the words of Frazier twenty-five years earlier by arguing that race relations studies have mainly "served a white ideology, while black ideologies have lacked the support of a systematic analysis."[25] Dennis Forsythe and others took this view another step and called for a black sociology, arguing that its task was to "stress the uniqueness of the Black experience and to see that knowledge collected on Blacks is used for change rather than for control."[26] Similarly, Alfredo Mirande rejected American sociology and called for a Chicano sociology. According to him, "the ethos of scientism works to perpetuate the subordination of Chicanos and other socially disadvantaged groups through its undue emphasis on objectivity, value neutrality, and universalism."[27] Many minority social scientists became convinced that their respective disciplines and social science in general were producing knowledge that distorted the actual nature of minority existence. They began to study relationships between minorities and the dominant group using different assumptions, concepts, and questions.[28]

Minorities in the Community of Social Science

Minority participation in the social scientific community has been both limited and marginal.[29] Relatively few minorities have earned the necessary credentials to gain entry to this community, and most have been on its margins rather than within its mainstream. The first minority group to enter in substantial numbers white colleges and universities as faculty was the blacks. Prior to 1900, only three blacks held teaching positions in predominantly white colleges.[30] With the expansion of black colleges during the first half of this century came increased numbers of black college graduates. Between 1926 and 1936, more blacks graduated from college than in the one hundred years prior to 1926.[31] By 1936, approximately 153 blacks had received doctorate degrees, compared to the very few who had obtained them prior to 1900.[32] In the forties black faculty in black colleges numbered over two hundred, and as their numbers increased so did their power and control over those colleges. In a relatively short period of time black faculty and administrators were able to assume control of black colleges (within the parameters of dominant group control, of course). As fewer whites continued to teach in black colleges, black faculty increased in numbers and became more and more concentrated at those institutions. In the midforties a mere seventy-eight blacks were teaching at white colleges, with only twenty-nine on continuing assignments.[33] Their numbers were slightly increased, however, through the efforts of the American Friends Service Committee, the Rosenwald Fund, and the General Education Board. By establishing visiting professorships, supplementing the salaries of black faculty, and calling upon the presidents of white colleges to extend democratic practices into the ranks of faculty, these organizations were instrumental in getting some white colleges to hire black faculty. Still, the prevalent view in society at that time was that when talking about black faculty, it was understood that they taught at black colleges.[34]

Hunter and Abraham, in discussing the career of Oliver C. Cox, make the important observation that although Cox had obtained graduate degrees in economics and sociology from a leading university, "he was unable to secure a position in any of the larger white institutions, with their greater resources, and instead—as was customary for even the brightest young black scholars well into the 1950s—was forced to seek employment in a black college, where the teaching load was heavy, the salary low, and there were few graduate students or resources for carrying out research."[35] Unlike blacks, however, other minorities have not had "their own institutions of higher learning" and, until recently, were virtually denied meaningful participation in the social science community.[36]

Like all other social scientists, once out of graduate school minorities are faced with the challenge of surviving and achieving in their respective fields. Unlike natural scientists, social scientists are concentrated in universities and institutes affiliated with universities. Because tenure-track positions at universities lead not only to job security and seniority but also prestige, young minority scholars are likely to seek such positions. Other (usually weaker) options include postdoctoral fellowships, temporary teaching positions, and working as research associates on research projects.

Data on the number of minority faculty in this country are seriously flawed and provide only rough approximations rather than accurate estimates.[37] Cole and Cole, in studying social stratification in science, had only this to say about blacks in science: "We may feel sure of only one point in addressing this question [on discrimination]: There are almost no detailed, reliable data on the position of blacks in American science."[38] Nevertheless, existing data do provide an opportunity for us to glean a view of the existing numbers of minority faculty in American institutions of higher learning.

In 1971, Ruiz reported that Spanish-surnamed individuals residing in the United States constituted .54 percent of the membership in the American Psychiatric Association.[39] In the American Psychological Association (APA) they comprised .88 percent of the membership, and in the American Board of Professional Psychology they constituted .18 percent. Ruiz further estimated that members of this group comprised .84 percent of the membership of the American Sociological Association (ASA) and 2.21 percent of the full-time faculty in graduate sociology departments. Figures from the 1970 census indicate that Spanish-surnamed persons comprised approximately 5 percent of the general population.

Estimates provided by Russo and others in 1981 showed few changes in the composition of the membership of the American Psychological Association.[40] Estimates of the 1978–79 membership indicated that minorities constituted 3.1 percent of the APA. Blacks (1.2 percent) comprised the largest group, followed by Asians (1.0 percent), Hispanics (0.7 percent), and Native Americans (0.2 percent). Their data included foreign-born members. Their analysis of data from the 1980–81 survey of graduate departments of psychology concluded that minorities comprise almost 5 percent of the graduate faculty. They further concluded that minorities are more likely than their white counterparts "to be represented among jointly appointed and part-time faculty than they are among full-time faculty."[41] With regard to tenure, minorities (and women) are much more concentrated in the lower, untenured ranks than are white males. For example, in doctoral departments, 50.2 percent of minority faculty (in this case, including women) are tenured, compared with 80.2 percent of white male faculty. Overall, Russo found that ethnic minorities comprise 3.1 percent of the tenured faculty members in doctoral departments of psychology.

In the discipline of sociology in 1981, minorities comprised 8 percent of the faculty in academic departments.[42] In contrast, ethnic and racial minorities comprised 20.4 percent of the general population in this country in 1980.[43] Of these academic faculty, approximately two-thirds of them were employed at universities and nearly one-third were at four-year colleges (the pattern differs among the different groups). In general, there is a tendency for the relative frequency of minorities to decrease as institutions become more prestigious and research oriented.

If we assume the most prestigious research universities are more likely than their lower-ranked counterparts to influence the boundaries and content of sociological (and social scientific) knowledge and minorities are not likely to be found at those institutions, then we also can assume that minorities will not significantly influence the production of social scientific knowledge. If we ask ourselves which minority social scientists are most likely to arrive and remain at a prestigious research university, we are forced to see that it is those who produce "significant amounts" of social scientific knowledge in accordance with the standards and views approved by the faculty at those research universities. To a great extent, we can see the faculty at such institutions as elites who not only control academic departments, professional societies, journals, and large-scale research projects but also exercise considerable influence in the determination of what constitutes achievement in the production of social scientific knowledge and who is to receive tenure at their institutions.

A similar dynamic characterizes the relationship between minority and dominant group faculty members across the different levels of colleges and universities. In the main, minority faculty have to compete in academia in accordance with the standards set by the dominant group. And, since prestige and promotion are linked to the "quality of scholarship" produced by the individual scientist, it is not likely that minorities will be substantially rewarded for theoretical and research conclusions that depart substantially from the views of science held by dominant group faculty members.[44] In general, there is a tendency for dominant group faculty to view minority scholarship as being of low quality, especially that which focuses on race and ethnic relations.[45] There also is the tendency for journal editors to be quite selective according to particular theoretical and/or methodological schools in publishing articles. As a result, minorities, in seeking to publish articles addressing their questions, had to found their own professional journals, such as *Black Sociologist, Black Scholar, Review of Black Political Economy, Aztlan, Hispanic Journal of Behavioral Science,* and so on.

Because the view that minority scholarship is of inferior quality prevails in the social scientific community these journals are probably seen in this light. At some universities, for example, when faculty are evaluated their publications are categorized according to a scheme that ranks journals in terms of quality, each category is assigned a numeric value, and finally a total score is generated that is linked directly to rewards. In such a scheme, minority journals are assigned low numeric values, so that faculty publishing in them are not likely to be substantially rewarded for their scholarship. The numeric value assigned to a journal becomes a proxy for critical examination of the specific article in question, and under the guise of objectivity based on the reputational prestige of the journal in question, minorities are confined to the margins of the social scientific community. Somewhere in this process of trivializing social scientific knowledge produced from a minority perspective, the tension between the types of questions asked by minority and dominant group scholars results in the imposition of the latter's views regarding the quality of the former's scholarship. And, in the absence of standard criteria for judging the contribution of a specific scientific article to the progress of a discipline, this outcome is not surprising, especially given the nature of the relationship between the groups.

The retention of minority faculty at universities is related to the different factors that influence perception of the quality of their scholarship as well as to other factors that affect tenure decisions. Such factors include not only the personality traits and general attitude of the person in question and how they are perceived by other faculty, but also the relative absence of mentors and the degree and nature of institutional support and opportunity for development.[46]

The actual experiences of minority faculty in the workplace of academe tend to revolve around affirmative action roles and activities.[47] With regard to Chicanos, for example, Arce argues that their roles as academics involves limited participation in mainstream decision-making sectors while serving as buffers in protecting institutional interests vis-à-vis minority issues. Arce characterizes this situation as one of "academic colonialism." At the same time, minority faculty seem to be overloaded by minority-related institutional demands, service on committees, counseling of students, and so on. The composite picture that emerges from the studies conducted on minority faculty at white colleges and universities is one of relative isolation at both individual and organization levels.[48]

Undoubtedly, there are several factors that influence decisions relating to tenure of minority faculty, not the least of which is the tendency for them to leave an institution prior to a tenure decision being rendered. What is important to keep in mind is the race/ethnic factor and the relationship between retention and the production of social scientific knowledge. Where and when racial factors contribute to, if not determine, low tenure rates among minority faculty, they also indirectly influence the context of social scientific knowledge, for if minorities are not at the worksite of science their questions are not likely to be addressed. Recently, Richard Verdugo and James Blackwell argued that the main reason minority scholarship has not influenced sociological knowledge is that "their representation in the discipline has been and continues to be small."[49] Certainly, there seems to be some merit to their point.

Professional societies are another important arena in which participation by minorities is virtually necessary if their work is to have an impact on the development of social scientific knowledge. Professional societies do much more than provide formal recognition to individuals for their work. They also provide access to important decision-making networks connected to research funds, publishing opportunities, editorships, and reputational prestige. Little is known, however, about the role of minority social scientists within scientific societies in general. The work of James Blackwell offers an important contribution to this area. In 1974, he published the results of his study on black sociologists in the American Sociological Association (formerly the American Sociological Society). He argued that blacks

> have always been in a minority situation within the larger society and in the ASA. The experiences parallel. This situation may be characterized by categorical treatment or structural discrimination in general, denial of access to the major values of the association (controlled participation), social isolation, slights, self-consciousness among black members, role ambiguities, and uncertainties among many members, black and white, concerning the appropriateness of their responses to each other.[50]

He further concluded that the internal and external relations among the membership of this society were characterized by a pattern of dominance-subordination.

To the credit of the American Sociological Association, in 1934 it established the policy that it would not hold its annual meetings in any locale which discriminated against any of its members. This policy was established after Charles Johnson was ordered by hotel management to use the rear elevator when entering a hotel in Atlantic City. And, in 1948, the ASA elected E. Franklin Frazier as its president, marking the first time a racial minority member became the head of a national scientific society.

Still, participation by minorities in the ASA over the years has been minor and marginal. It was not until the 1960s that some change came about as the result of the activities and determination of the members of the Caucus of Black Sociologists, founded in 1968. Through the caucus black sociologists were effective not only in getting the ASA membership to pass resolutions that the organization would make efforts to include blacks in all its activities but in obtaining greater representation on ASA committees and establishing the Du Bois-Johnson-Frazier Award, the Minority Fellowship Program, and the Committee on the Status of Racial and Ethnic Minorities.

In 1981, the ASA council directed the executive office to compile a report on the role of minorities and women in association activities. Since then reports have been submitted in the years 1982, 1985, and 1988. The reports indicate that small but steady gains have been made in the process of including minorities within the organization's decision-making structure. Still, Bettina Huber, in the third report, expressed concern about the slow progress and the possibility of reversals in recent gains.[51] Until the recent election of William Julius Wilson as the eighty-first president of the ASA there had not been a minority group member to serve as an elected officer of the organization since 1982.

Objectivity and Ethnocentrism

Perhaps the most debated concept in the social sciences is that of objectivity. The focus in the early stage of the current crisis tended to center on it and whether or not extrascientific values have a legitimate role in scientific activities and results.[52] The positivist and neopositivist views of objectivity hold that such values do not have a legitimate place in social science (and science in general) and must be eliminated from it, or at least an attempt should be made by all scientists to eliminate them from the domain of scientific activity. The intrusion of extrascientific values in social sciences is seen as resulting in biased knowledge. Adoption of a scientific attitude, use of the scientific method, and mutual criticism are seen as necessary and sufficient in the long run for the production of objective scientific knowledge.[53]

Opponents of these views argue that the intrusion of extrascientific values into the domain of science is inevitable.[54] While some see this as preventing the production of objective scientific knowledge, others argue that extrascientific values are actually necessary for its production. Although proponents of these two positions differ in their conclusions about the production of social scientific knowledge, both agree that extrascientific values enter at several critical points throughout the process.[55] Myrdal, for example, argued that "biases in research are much deeper seated than in the formulation of avowedly practical conclusions. They are not valuations *attached* to research but rather they *permeate* research. They are the unfortunate results of concealed valuations that insinuate themselves in research in all stages, from its planning to its final presentation."[56] Valuations enter scientific activity the moment the individual scientist decides to engage in research and continue to do so until the results are published. Recently, Norbert Elias has argued that

> scientific investigations are very far from "value-free," but the type of valuations prevalent in the works of natural sciences is not determined by extra-scientific factors. This distinguishes the natural sciences from the social sciences at the present stage. In the latter, the influence of valuations entering scientific work from outside, from positions taken up within the conflicts of society at large, that is, the influence of heteronomous valuations, is very great.[57]

If we accept the second of these two positions, that values enter social scientific investigations but that we still can obtain objective knowledge about social reality, then a different understanding of the concept of objectivity may be necessary because the positivist view holds that extrascientific values bias the results of scientific investigations.[58] In its weaker formulation the positivist view prescribes that we *attempt* to maintain a "detached" or a "dispassionate attitude" toward our object of study (or the subject of inquiry).[59] When we accept that extrascientific values enter social scientific activity, the questions that logically arise are, whose values do we assume as we go about our business as scientists? Whose values are to guide the selection of the problem, how is it framed and understood, and which are affirmed in the study itself? Several scholars have addressed these questions. Karl Marx suggested we assume and affirm the values of the working class; Howard Becker suggests we assume the view of the underdogs in society, and some minority and women scholars suggest "insiderism" (i.e., "one must be Caesar to know Caesar").

Marx's solution to this problem directs us intentionally to assume and affirm the values of that group (class) whose structural location in society affords the greatest cognitive opportunity for comprehending social reality.[60] The value for Marx was always humanity; the group with the greatest cognitive potential is the one whose vested *vital* interests are in changing society. According to this view, social scientists should "adopt the perspective of the [universal] proletariat, and hence represent the interests of this particular class by applying its system of valuations in the course of research, and affirm it in the body of research results."[61]

Karl Mannheim, one of the founders of the sociology of knowledge, also pointed out that the process of knowing is bound up with the social position of the individual:

> People . . . act with and against one another in diversely organized groups, and while doing so they think with and against one another. These persons, bound together into groups, strive in accordance with the character and position of the groups to which they belong to change the surrounding world of nature and society or attempt to maintain it in a given condition. It is the direction of this will to change or to maintain; of this collective activity, which produces the guiding thread for the emergence of their problems, their concepts, and their forms of thought.[62]

Mannheim has asked us to consider the influence of social structure and social conflict on the definition of social problems, concepts, and entire modes of thought. When we do, we realize that the very questions posed by social scientists are influenced by extrascientific interests and values. C. Wright Mills, in his examination of the perspectives found in the literature of social pathology, pointed out that "if the members of an academic profession are recruited from similar social contexts and if their backgrounds and careers are relatively similar, there is a tendency for them to be uniformly set for some common perspective."[63]

This feature of social scientific knowledge is our focus here. The sociology of knowledge claims that knowledge is partial and limited rather than universal and, within its framework, it is important to take seriously the statement by minority scholars that American social science has claimed to produce objective knowledge about minorities while producing particularized knowledge about them. In particular, we should consider the product of social scientific activity conducted from the "detached attitude." How does this attitude impact the results of social scientific activity? The argument made here is that it becomes a norm within the scientific community, and individual social scientists conduct their research without seriously questioning whether or not their values or those of their specific groups enter scientific activity. Alvin Gouldner expressed a similar view: "I fear there are many sociologists today who, in conceiving social science to be value-free, mean widely different things, that many hold these beliefs dogmatically without having examined seriously the grounds upon which they are credible, and that some affirm a value-free sociology ritualistically without having any clear idea of what it might mean."[64] There is a tendency, it seems, to let the scientific method purge research investigations of extrascientific bias. Consequently, many social scientists remain unaware of the values affirmed in their research and theories. Yet, few sociologists of knowledge or historians of knowledge would seriously deny the influence of social interests and their attendant values on knowledge formation.

More recently, Troy Duster has pointed out the importance of this relationship in the context of race relations, which are marked by institutionalized social, political, and economic inequalities.[65] He implicitly questions the utility of assuming that a "detached attitude" and a set of technical procedures will necessarily produce unbiased (objective) knowledge and concludes that social scientific questions are framed in the context of "the particular circumstances of a group of people with a particular experience in history."[66] As an example, he discusses the work by Adorno and associates, *The Authoritarian Personality*, and how it addresses questions asked by those persons who escaped the Third Reich. He speculates as to the questions that might have been raised by black ex-slaves had they had access to "the nerve of an academic power center." Had they had such access, we would expect to know much more than we do about the psychology of racial domination. The discipline might have addressed the question, "What are the pathogenic elements of a personality structure that is able to rationalize and sustain a system of such total human degradation [as slavery]?"[67] But the discipline has not seriously addressed this question, and it has not done so primarily because the structural location and cultural outlook of those persons in "control" of the discipline do not lend themselves to generating the question or the motivation to marshal resources to address it. But psychology is not alone. What, for instance, has been geography's contribution to the use of physical space in situations of racial domination?

The feminist critique of science has arrived at a similar view of scientific activity and its results. Sue Rosser, for example, states that "from a feminist perspective, we would insist that women be central to the questions and theories of science and that women be studied for their own sake, not as compared to men; only then does one develop accurate understanding that permits valid comparisons. With a focus on women, entirely different questions might be asked."[68] Clearly, there are whole sets of questions that can be generated from the perspectives of American minorities (such as blacks, Chicanos, Native Americans, Asians, and women) that have not been seriously addressed by the social sciences.

In a context of racial domination, study of the oppressed group by the dominant group has tended to produce knowledge that affirms the world view of the latter group. In other words, it has tended to produce social scientific knowledge that is more or less ethnocentric. This does not mean that members of the dominant group cannot produce accurate knowledge about minority groups; rather, it questions the utility of assuming a detached attitude (at least in the unreflexive and taken-for-granted manner that it commonly assumes) toward the group being studied.

Ultimately, scientific knowledge is objective if it corresponds accurately to reality, but because in science we can never prove any theoretical statement as true (although we may amass considerable empirical evidence to support it), we have to rely on a series of empirical confirmations of our theoretical propositions in order for us to develop a sense that they are indeed "true."

Although theories and research results are critically examined by members of the scientific community, the corrective influence of this activity has been small because members of the dominant group have been and are in control of the production of social scientific knowledge. As such, common assumptions about the nature of society are likely to produce a general affinity in the interpretation of research results. The history of the study of race relations in this country, for example, is marked by disagreement among members of differently situated groups. More specifically, minority and dominant group scholars tend to disagree about the latter's conclusions about the former group.[69] Many minority scholars argue that dominant group scholars have tended to produce pejorative views of minorities in general. Indeed, minority scholars have spent a great amount of effort responding to major social scientific conclusions about their respective groups.[70]

At the same time, however, little research has been conducted on the dominant group and the scientific mechanisms that maintain its dominance. Similarly, John Butler argues that "scholars have not spent enough time doing studies on actual processes of discrimination."[71] The relative absence of such studies is related to the types of questions addressed by dominant group scholars and the general control that they exert over the social sciences.

Their assumptions about society lead to questions that provide limited knowledge about minority groups and race relations in general. For example, a common assumption made is that this is an open society characterized by equality of opportunity for all members to develop their talents and become successful participants.[72] The implication is that if certain groups do not "make it," then there must be something "wrong" with them. The assumption that this is an open society is, of course, vitiated by the very existence of a minority group and is not one that is likely to be made by scholars who are members of such a group. Because of their life experiences and their group life, minorities are more inclined to assume that significant barriers to success (i.e., the good life) exist in society. These assumptions are likely to generate different sorts of questions and thereby place different emphases on certain aspects of reality, emphases that reveal and mask aspects of reality that relate to the vested interests of the respective groups. In a context of racial domination, the "detached attitude" is likely to result in a body of knowledge about minorities that is imbued by ethnocentrism (if not outright racism, as was evident in the last century). Whether or not the views of social science by dominant and minority group scholars are incommensurable in the Kuhnian sense is not entirely clear. We can expect, however, that the issues raised by minority scholars will be included in the general solution that takes us beyond the contemporary crisis.

Summary

The recent civil rights movement greatly influenced the entire society, including academic and scientific communities. Increased educational opportunities led directly to increased numbers of minority college graduates at all levels. At the same time that the first major wave of minorities was entering scientific communities, science, especially social science, experienced an intense crisis that shook its metatheoretical foundations. Minority scientists both contributed to and were greatly influenced by this crisis. Minorities attempted to understand epistemological, ontological, and methodological issues and to survive in academic and research contexts that generally resisted their entry. Additionally, the crisis made salient the relationship between science and ideology.

The view of this relationship presented in this paper is that over time human beings have increased their understanding of social and natural reality. In doing so they have not approached reality without beliefs and without knowledge; rather, they have approached it from commonsensical knowledge imbedded within ideological perspectives (i.e., imaginary views of their conditions of existence). As such, scientific knowledge emerges out of ideology and seeks correspondence with the dynamics of reality. To believe, however, that science has achieved autonomy from ideology through some kind of mental detachment and a set of technical procedures is to oversimplify the relationship between scientific knowledge and ideology. The boundary between social scientific knowledge and ideology is always problematic. It is especially problematic in the context of institutionalized domination, where some groups are systematically denied access to full participation in society.

In such a context, differentially situated and culturally different groups develop particular views of reality. Moreover, differential group access to production sites of social scientific knowledge leads to particularized social scientific knowledge of the social world. The questions typically addressed by dominant group scholars are likely to be different from those that minorities would address. This problem is accentuated by the low numbers and participation levels of minorities in social science and the treatment they receive in the different arenas of social scientific activity.

The relatively few minority social scientists who have achieved job security at research universities and other scientific knowledge production sites tend either to have adopted (through socialization or as a survival strategy) the views and methods of science presented by dominant group scholars or addressed their questions from their own view of science. Those who have sought to produce social scientific knowledge from a minority perspective have faced considerable resistance from their colleagues, who often are less inclined to reflect upon and be critical of the autonomous view of science in general and their own values in particular. The result is a tendency to view minority scholarship that is explicitly value-guided as "ideological" and thus inferior. Such a view, along with its attendant practices and the small number of minority scholars, ensures that minority scholarship has little influence on social scientific knowledge.

Still, the social sciences remain in a crisis, and the issues raised by minority social scientists, along with those raised by other scholars, remain to be addressed. As the number of minority scholars increases, the issues will probably become more salient. And, as the social scientific community comes to grips with its treatment of minority scholars, it may open its doors to them with congeniality rather than with arrogance and contempt. Should this happen, there emerges the promise of the revitalization of social science through the views and enrichment activities of minorities and the openness of social scientists in general to different views of social science and alternative practices in the workplace. Moreover, minorities may come to know more about themselves and their natural and social contexts. Through their examinations and critiques of dominant group social scientific conclusions about minorities, this group of scholars has moved slowly in the direction of an alternative philosophy of science, and one day they may develop a coherent one. In one sense, only through the development of a coherent philosophy of science, one that overcomes the problems of neopositivism, will the promise of the crisis and the incorporation of minority scientists be realized.

Notes

Revised version of a paper presented at "The Estate of Social Knowledge, a Symposium on the History and Historiography of the Social Sciences," Department of History, Johns Hopkins University, May 1988. I want to thank David K. van Keuren,

George W. Stocking, Jr., Ronald Walters, and an anonymous reviewer for their critical comments on earlier drafts of this paper.

1. It was during this period that the sociology of science gained recognition as a specialty within the discipline of sociology and the debate on sociology of knowledge was reopened. For a good discussion on these topics, see Joseph Ben-David, "Sociology of Scientific Knowledge," in *The State of Sociology*, ed. James F. Short, Jr. (Beverly Hills: Sage Publications, 1981), pp. 40–59.

2. When the debate on the sociology of knowledge was taking place in France and Germany in the thirties and forties, American sociologist Robert S. Lynd viewed social science in crisis and argued that "social science is neither as 'neutral' nor as 'pure' as it pretends to be." See Robert S. Lynd, *Knowledge for What?* (New York: Grove Press, 1964 [1939]), p. 182.

3. See Richard J. Bernstein, *Beyond Objectivism and Relativism* (Philadelphia: University of Pennsylvania Press, 1983); Harold I. Brown, *Perception, Theory and Commitment* (Chicago: University of Chicago Press, 1977); S. N. Eisenstadt and M. Cureleau, *The Form of Sociology—Paradigms and Crises* (New York: John Wiley, 1976); Piotr Sztompka, *Sociological Dilemmas* (New York: Academic Press, 1979); Dell Hymes, ed., *Reinventing Anthropology* (New York: Pantheon Books, 1972); George E. Marcus and Michael M. J. Fisher, *Anthropology as Cultural Critique* (Chicago: University of Chicago Press, 1986).

4. In the early seventies Robert Blauner wrote that dominant group faculty members were hesitant and fearful of having minority faculty in their midst. See Robert Blauner, *Racial Oppression in America* (New York: Harper and Row, 1972).

5. Among the studies that have focused on the relationship between minorities and social scientific knowledge and activities are those by Jonathan R. Cole and Stephen Cole, *Social Stratification in Science* (Chicago: University of Chicago Press, 1973), and Jonathan R. Cole, *Fair Science, Women in the Scientific Community* (New York: Free Press, 1979).

6. Walter Hirsch, "The Autonomy of Science," in *Comparative Studies in Science and Society*, ed. Sal P. Restivo and Christopher K. Vanderpool (Columbus, Ohio: Charles E. Merrill, 1974), pp. 144–57.

7. Louis Althusser, "Ideology and Ideological State Apparatuses (Notes towards an Investigation)," in *Lenin and Philosophy and Other Essays* (New York: Monthly Review Press, 1972), p. 162. Although Althusser stresses the methodological differences between science and nonscience and views science as autonomous, it is not necessary to accept this part of his work when using his definition of ideology. For critical discussions of his view of science, see Nicholas Abercrombie, *Class, Structure and Knowledge* (New York: New York University Press, 1980), and Stanley Aronowitz, *Science as Power* (Minneapolis: University of Minnesota Press, 1988).

8. Althusser, "Ideology and Ideological State Apparatuses," p. 166.

9. For an important discussion of the relationship between the focus of research and the source of its funding, see Robert S. Broadhead and Ray C. Rist, "Gatekeepers and the Social Control of Social Research," *Social Problems* 23, no. 3 (1976): 325–35.

10. For a critique of the concept "scientific community," see Struan Jacobs, "Scien-

tific Community: Formulation and Critique of a Sociological Motif," *British Journal of Sociology* 38, no. 2 (1987): 266–76.

11. Karin D. Knorr, "Tinkering toward Success: Prelude to a Theory of Scientific Practice," *Theory and Society* 8, no. 3 (1979): 347–76.

12. John J. Beer and W. Daniel Lewis, "Aspects of the Professionalization of Science," in *Comparative Studies in Science and Society*, pp. 197–216.

13. The minority groups referred to in this paper are blacks, Chicanos, native Americans, Asians, and other indigenous "Third World" groups in this country. Each of these groups has its own historical relationship with the dominant group, some being "colonized" and others "middlemen" minorities. The specific relationship between each group and dominant group institutions differs from that of others. Because Jewish Americans have a significantly different relationship with institutions of higher learning from that of the aforementioned groups, they are not included in this analysis. This does not deny the fact that Jewish Americans have been the victims of discrimination, but in general they have had greater access to such institutions and the scientific community. Additionally, there is little evidence that Jewish American scholars have developed a distinctive minority perspective of social reality.

14. James A. Tillman and Mary Norman Tillman, "Black Intellectuals, White Liberals and Race Relations: An Analytic Overview," *Phylon* 33, no. 1 (1972): 54–66. For a related but less extensive discussion, see Irene I. Blea, *Toward a Chicano Social Science* (New York: Praeger, 1988), p. 9.

15. Increases in the number of minorities receiving their doctorates were greatest from 1966 to 1973. Since then the numbers have decreased somewhat, and the general view is that the overall size of this population is relatively stable, with very small increases taking place. See Nancy Felipe Russo, Esteban L. Olmedo, Joy Stapp, and Robert Fulcher, "Women and Minorities in Psychology," *American Psychologist* 36, no. 11 (1981): 1315–63, and E. C. Ladd, Jr., and S. M. Lipset, "Professors' Religious and Ethnic Backgrounds," *Chronicle of Higher Education*, 22 September 1975, p. 2.

16. W. E. B. Du Bois, "Race Friction between Black and White," *American Journal of Sociology* 13 (1908): 836.

17. George I. Sanchez, "Bilingualism and Mental Measures: A Word of Caution," in *Introduction to Chicano Studies*, ed. Livie Isauro Duran and H. Russell Bernard, 2d ed. (New York: Macmillan Publishing, 1982 [1934]), pp. 400–405.

18. E. Franklin Frazier, "Sociological Theory and Race Relations," in *Intergroup Relations*, ed. Pierre van den Berghe (New York: Basic Books, 1972), p. 23.

19. For an excellent examination of the various perspectives on race relations, see Jonathan H. Turner and Royce Singleton, Jr., "A Theory of Ethnic Oppression: Toward a Reintegration of Cultural and Structural Concepts in Ethnic Relations Theory," *Social Forces* 56, no. 4 (1978): 1001–18.

20. Alfredo Mirande, "The Chicano Family: A Reanalysis of Conflicting Views," *Journal of Marriage and the Family* 39 (1977): 748.

21. Robert Staples, *Introduction to Black Sociology* (San Francisco: McGraw-Hill, 1976), pp. 113–14.

22. For some of the works seen by minority scholars as exemplary in terms of bias

and distortion, see Daniel Moynihan, *The Negro Family: The Case for National Action* (Washington, D.C.: Department of Labor, U.S. Government Printing Office, 1965); Arthur R. Jensen, "How Much Can We Boost I.Q. and Scholastic Achievement?," *Harvard Educational Review* 39, no. 1 (1969): 1–123; R. J. Herrnstein, *I.Q. in the Meritocracy* (Boston: Atlantic–Little, Brown, 1973); Celia S. Keller, *Mexican American Youth: Forgotten Youth at the Crossroads* (New York: Random House, 1966); William Madsen, *The Mexican-Americans of South Texas* (New York: Holt, Rinehart and Winston, 1964).

23. Maurice Jackson, "Toward a Sociology of Black Studies," *Journal of Black Studies* 1, no. 1 (1970): 137.

24. Daniel C. Thompson, *Sociology of the Black Experience* (Westport, Conn.: Greenwood, 1974).

25. Gerald McWorter, "The Ideology of Black Social Science," *Black Scholar* 1, no. 2 (1969): 28–29.

26. Dennis Forsythe, "Radical Sociology and Blacks," in *The Death of White Sociology*, ed. Joyce A. Ladner (New York: Vintage, 1973), p. 233.

27. Alfredo Mirande, "Chicano Sociology: A New Paradigm for Social Science," *Pacific Sociological Review* 21, no. 3 (1978): 307.

28. As Octavio Romano-V so aptly put it, "This situation is unique in the annals of American social science. It is unique because a population heretofore studied is now studying the studiers." "Social Science, Objectivity, and the Chicanos," in *Voices, Readings from El Grito*, ed. Octavio I. Romano-V (Berkeley, Calif.: Quinto Sol, 1973), p. 38.

29. See Carlos H. Arce, "Chicanos in Higher Education," *Integrated Education* 14, no. 3 (1976): 14–18; Adalberto Aguirre, Jr., "An Interpretative Analysis of Chicano Faculty in Academe," *Social Science Journal* 24, no. 1 (1987): 71–81; and Evelyn Hu-DeHart, "Women, Minorities and Academic Freedom," in *Regulating the Intellectuals*, ed. Craig Kaplan and Ellen Schrencker (New York: Praeger, 1983), pp. 141–59.

30. James Allen Moss, "Negro Teachers in Predominantly White Colleges," *Journal of Negro Education* 27 (1958): 451–62. According to Moss, the three were Du Bois, Charles Reason (1830s), and R. T. Greener (1870s).

31. Charles Johnson, *The Negro Graduate* (Chapel Hill: University of North Carolina Press, 1938).

32. Moss, "Negro Teachers in Predominantly White Colleges," p. 453.

33. Ibid., p. 457.

34. Fred Wale, "Chosen for Ability," *Atlantic Monthly* (July, 1947): 82.

35. Herbert M. Hunter and Sameer Y. Abraham, Introduction to *Race, Class, and the World System: The Sociology of Oliver C. Cox*, ed. Herbert M. Hunter and Sameer Y. Abraham (New York: Monthly Review Press, 1987), p. xxi.

36. The number of minorities enrolled in institutions of higher learning has been declining over the past decade. It is doubtful that their numbers in graduate school are going to increase over the next few years. Consequently, we can expect the number of minority social scientists to remain small. Cole and Cole, in *Social Stratification in Science*, p. 154, point out that blacks face a set of social and psychological barriers prior to entrance into the scientific community. This point

can be generalized to the other groups. For a discussion of problems surrounding the training of minorities, see Paul R. Williams, "Some Issues in the Training and Professional Development of Minorities in Sociology," *Black Sociologist* 8, nos. 1–4 (1978): 109–13.

37. Robert J. Menges and William H. Exum, "Barriers to the Progress of Women and Minority Faculty," *Journal of Higher Education* 54, no. 2 (1983): 123–44.
38. Cole and Cole, *Social Stratification in Science*, p. 152.
39. Rene Ruiz, "Relative Frequency of Americans with Spanish Surnames in Associations of Psychology, Psychiatry, and Sociology," *American Psychologist* 26 (1971): 1022–24.
40. Russo et al., "Women and Minorities in Psychology."
41. Ibid., p. 1320.
42. American Sociological Association, *Minority Sociologists and Their Status in Academia* (Washington, D.C.: American Sociological Association, 1985).
43. Bureau of the Census, *1980 General Population Characteristics: U.S. Summary* (Washington, D.C.: U.S. Government Printing Office, 1983).
44. For a discussion of social science organizational dynamics, see Stephen Fuchs, "The Social Organization of Scientific Knowledge," *Sociological Theory* 4, no. 2 (1986): 126–42, and Stephen Fuchs and Jonathan H. Turner, "What Makes a Science 'Mature'?: Organizational Control in Scientific Production," *Sociological Theory* 4, no. 2 (1986): 143–50.
45. See Maria de la Luz Reyes and John J. Halcon, "Racism in Academia: The Old Wolf Revisited," *Harvard Educational Review* 58, no. 3 (1988): 299–314.
46. For a critique of mentoring, see Roger L. Collins, "Colonialism on Campus: A Critique of Mentoring to Achieve Equity in Higher Education," *Journal of Educational Equity and Leadership* 3, no. 4 (1983): 277–87. Other important works on minority participation in academia include Jeffrey M. Jacques, "The Split Labor Market and Ethnic Antagonism: A Case Study in Higher Education," *Sociology of Education* 53 (October 1980): 225–36; Carl Jorgensen, Albert W. Black, Jr., and Gordon Morgan, "Crisis in Academia: The Plight of Third World Scholars," *Black Sociologist* 6, no. 4 (1977): 225–36; W. M. Phillips, Jr., and Rhoda L. Blumberg, "Tokenism and Organizational Change," *Integrated Education* 20, nos. 1–2 (1983): 34–39.
47. Hu-DeHart, "Women, Minorities and Academic Freedom"; Carlos H. Arce, "Chicano Participation in Academe: A Case of Academic Colonialism," *Grito del Sol* 3 (1978): 75–104.
48. Arce, "Chicano Participation in Academe;" Aguirre, "An Interpretative Analysis of Chicano Faculty in Academe"; Phillips and Blumberg, "Tokenism and Organizational Change." In contrast, the following authors argue that black faculty are as satisfied with workplace considerations as are white faculty: Charles J. Elmore and Robert T. Blackburn, "Black and White Faculty in White Research Universities," *Journal of Higher Education* 54, no. 1 (1983): 1–15.
49. Richard R. Verdugo and James E. Blackwell, "The Presentation of Minorities in Sociology," *Footnotes* 16, no. 1 (1988): 4.
50. James E. Blackwell, "Role Behavior in a Corporate Structure: Black Sociologists in the ASA," in *Black Sociologists*, ed. James E. Blackwell and Morris Janowitz (Chicago: University of Chicago Press, 1974), p. 341.

51. Bettina J. Huber, "The Status of Minorities and Women within ASA," *Footnotes* 16, no. 6 (1988): 4, 8.
52. See C. W. Mills, *The Sociological Imagination* (London: Oxford University Press, 1959); Gunnar Myrdal, *An American Dilemma: the Negro Social Structure*, 2 (New York: McGraw-Hill, 1964 [1944]); R. Bierstedt, *The Social Order* (New York: McGraw-Hill, 1957); R. K. Merton, *The Sociology of Science* (Chicago: University of Chicago Press, 1973).
53. Bernard Cohen, *Developing Sociological Knowledge* (Englewood Cliffs, N.J.: Prentice-Hall, 1980); E. Nagel, *The Structure of Science* (New York: Harcourt Brace Jovanovich, 1961): R. Dahrendorf, *Essays in the Theory of Society* (Stanford: Stanford University Press, 1968).
54. Mills, *The Sociological Imagination*; Myrdal, *An American Dilemma*; A. Gouldner, *The Coming Crisis of Western Sociology* (London: Heinemann, 1971).
55. Actual involvement by social scientists in specific events on behalf of the government or other social entities or groups remains to be studied. The internment of Japanese Americans during World War II, for example, involved anthropologists. See Orin Starn, "Engineering Internment: Anthropologists and the War Relocation Authority," *American Ethnologist* 13 (1986): 700–20.
56. Myrdal, *An American Dilemma*, p. 1043.
57. Norbert Elias, *Involvement and Detachment* (New York: Basil Blackwell, 1987), p. 34.
58. Sztompka, *Sociological Dilemmas*.
59. Cohen, *Developing Sociological Knowledge*.
60. Sztompka, *Sociological Dilemmas*, p. 237.
61. Ibid., pp. 229–40.
62. Karl Mannheim, *Ideology and Utopia* (London: Routledge and Kegan Paul, 1959), p. 6.
63. C. Wright Mills, "The Professional Ideology of Social Pathologists," *American Journal of Sociology* 49 (1942): 165–80.
64. Alvin W. Gouldner, "Anti-Minotaur: The Myth of a Value-Free Sociology," *Social Problems* 9 (1962): 199–213.
65. Troy Duster, "Purpose and Bias," *Society* 24, no. 2 (1987): 8–12.
66. Ibid., p. 12.
67. Troy Duster, "A Social Frame for Biological Knowledge," in *Cultural Perspectives on Biological Knowledge*, ed. Troy Duster and Karen Garrett (Norwood, N.J.: Ablex, 1984), p. 7.
68. Sue V. Rosser, *Teaching Science and Health from a Feminist Perspective* (New York: Pergamon, 1986), p. 24.
69. Ruben Martinez, "Internal Colonialism: A Reconceptualization of Race Relations in the United States," *Humboldt Journal of Social Relations* 10, no. 1 (1982–83): 163–76.
70. See, for example, the works of Alfredo Mirande, Robert Staples, Raymond Padilla, Octavio Romano, Edgar Epps, Raymond Rocco, Rodolfo Acuña, Daniel Thompson, Joyce Ladner, etc.
71. John Sibley Butler, "Social Research and Scholarly Interpretation," *Society* 24, no. 2 (1987): 13–18. The emphasis here is on the actual processes of discrim-

ination, especially its different historical forms. It is not my intention to minimize the good studies that have been conducted on discrimination.

72. This assumption is vitiated by the very existence of racism, sexism, and other forms of oppression, yet it is implicit in the works of many scholars, especially those adopting assimilation theories and functional perspectives.

■ Contributors

JEFF E. BIDDLE is associate professor in the Department of Economics at Michigan State University. His research interests include the history of American institutional economics and the labor supply decision. His work on these topics has appeared in *History of Political Economy, Review of Political Economy,* and the *Journal of Labor Economics.*

JOANNE BROWN is assistant professor in the Department of History at the Johns Hopkins University. Her research interests include history of the professions, language theory, and historiography. She has published articles on the cultural impact of the atomic bomb and on professional language. Her forthcoming book, "The Semantics of Profession," will be published by Princeton University Press.

JAMES FARR is associate professor of political science at the University of Minnesota. He is co-editor of *Political Innovation and Conceptual Change* (Cambridge University Press, 1989) and of *After Marx* (Cambridge University Press, 1984), and is the author of a number of essays in the history and philosophy of political science.

JOHN (SHANKLIN) GILKESON, JR., is a fellow at the Charles Warren Center for Studies in American History at Harvard University. He is author of *Middle Class Providence, 1820–1940* (Princeton University Press, 1986) and is currently at work on a study of the impact of the social sciences, and anthropology in particular, on academic and popular thought in America from 1920 to 1960.

GAIL A. HORNSTEIN is associate professor of psychology and chair of the Women's Studies Program at Mount Holyoke College. She has published on a variety of topics in the history of social psychology and contributed the chapter on the history of quantitative methods to *The Rise of Experimentation in American Psychology* (Yale University Press, 1988). She is currently at work on a historical study of the development of psychotherapeutic approaches to the treatment of psychosis, with a special focus on the contributions of Frieda Fromm-Reichmann.

WALTER A. JACKSON is assistant professor in the History Department at North Carolina State University, Raleigh. His research interests are in American intellectual history. He is the author of *Gunnar Myrdal and America's Conscience: Social Engineering and Racial Liberalism, 1938–1987* (University of North Carolina Press, 1990) and is currently working on a study of American intellectuals and the civil rights movement.

ANDREW KIRBY is currently professor of geography and regional development at the University of Arizona. His main research interests lie in social theory, urbanization, and the evolution of the modern state. He has written a number of books, including *The Politics of Location* and *Education, Health and Housing,* and co-edited a number of volumes, including *Resources and Planning, The Human Geography of Contemporary Britain,* and *Public Service Provision and Urban Development.* His most recent publications include *Nothing to Fear,* an edited collection which deals with the nature of risk, and *The Pentagon and the Cities,* to be published by Sage in 1991.

RUBÉN MARTINEZ is assistant professor in the Sociology Department at the University of Colorado at Colorado Springs. His research interests are in the philosophy of science, race relations, and the education of minorities. His recent publications include articles on self-esteem among high school students, Chicano faculty in higher education, and minority high school dropouts.

JILL G. MORAWSKI is associate professor of psychology at Wesleyan University. She is editor of the *Rise of Experimentation in American Psychology* (Yale University Press, 1988) and author of numerous articles on the history of nineteenth- and twentieth-century American psychology.

ROBERT N. PROCTOR is associate professor of history at Pennsylvania State University. He is author of *Racial Hygiene: Medicine under the Nazis* (Harvard University Press, 1988) and the forthcoming "Value Free Science? The Origins of an Ideal." He has written a number of essays on the history of the social sciences, the philosophy of ecology, and the political philosophy of science.

MARGARET SCHABAS is assistant professor in the Department of History at the University of Wisconsin–Madison. Her research interests are in the history of economics and the philosophy of science. She is the author of *A World Ruled by Number: William Stanley Jevons and the Rise of Mathematical Economics* (Princeton University Press, 1990). She serves on the editorial boards of *History of Political Economy* and *The Journal of Labor Economics.*

DAVID K. VAN KEUREN is historian with the Naval Research Laboratory in Washington, D.C. His research interests are in the history of nineteenth- and twentieth-century social science, particularly anthropology, and twentieth-century American science. He is the author of several articles on the history of British anthropology and is currently editing a collected study on "Science and the Federal Patron: Post–World War II Government Support of American Science."

■ Index

Abortion, 176
Abraham, Sameer, 235
Acland, Henry W., 56
Adams, Grace, 109, 116–17, 124
Adams, Jane, xviii
Adams, John, 5
Adolescence, 163
Adorno, Theodor W., 243; *The Authoritarian Personality*, 243
Advertising, 147
Alcoholism, 207
Allen, Garland, 177
Althusser, Louis, 37, 229, 247
Aly, Götz, 176
American Anthropological Association, 184
American Association of Physical Anthropologists, 185
American Board of Professional Psychology, 236
American Constitution, 3, 5, 7, 9–14, 43
American creed, 209, 218–21, 224
American Economic Association, 79–80
American Eugenics Society, 187
American exceptionalism, 27, 29, 41
American Friends Service Committee, 235
American Historical Association, 167
American Journal of Sociology, 185
American Political Science Review, 23
American pragmatism, xxi
American Psychological Association, 116, 127
American Revolution, 3, 5, 7

American Sociological Association, 236–40; role of minorities and women in, 236, 240
American Sociological Review, 23
American Sociological Society, 181, 185, 239
Annales school, xix, 34–36
Anthropological diploma program, 56–57
Anthropological Institute of Great Britain and Ireland, 48, 50–53, 59
Anthropological synthesis, 48, 51
Anthropology, evolutionary, 49, 155; fieldwork, 155; mental, 58; methodology, 157; physical, 52, 55, 59, 183–84; social, 47, 58
Antifederalists, 6–7, 11
Antihistoricism, xx
Antiquarianism, 48, 51
Antiquity of man, 53
Anti-Semitism, 179, 189
Arce, Carlos, 238
Archaeology, 51, 55–56; prehistoric, 52
Areal differentiation, 32
Army testing program, 143
Arnold, Matthew, 153
Aronovici, Carol, 203
Articles of Confederation, 7
Ash, Mitchell, xiii–xiv
Association of American Geographers, 29
Atomic Energy Commission, 193
Atomic warfare, 193
Autonomy of science, 229
Ayers, Leonard P., 140, 145
Aztlan, 237

Babbage, Charles, 69
Bagehot, Walter, 69
Baker, John R., 195
Balfour, A. J., 80
Balfour, Henry, 53
Barnes, Harry E., 159
Bastian, Adolf, 202
Becker, Howard, 241
Beecher, Catherine, xviii
Beeton, Henry, 79
Behavorial genetics, 175
Behavorial sciences, 26, 32
Behaviorism, 24, 32, 114
Benedict, Ruth, 158, 165–69
Bentham, Jeremy, 11, 75
Berger, Peter, 27
Bernard, Jessie, 160
Bias, 137, 240
Binet, Alfred, 146; Scale of Intelligence, 142
Biological determinism, 175–76, 188
Biology, developmental, 48, 50
Biotechnology, 198
Black Scholar, 237
Black Sociologist, 237
Black Sociologists, Caucus of, 239
Black sociology, 234
Blackmar, Frank W., 22
Blauner, Robert, 247
Blurred genres, 23, 39
Boas, Franz, xxiii, 154–57, 167, 175, 183–84, 203; school of, xii
Bodin, Jean, 6
Boole, George, 73
Boring, E. G., 113
Bowley, Arthur, 74
Bowman, Isaiah, 41
Boyer, Paul S., 149
Brabrook, E. B., 52
Brandt, Willie, 223
Braudel, Fernand, 34–35, 38
British Association for the Advancement of Science, 69, 71, 79; section H, 50–53
British Economic Association, 68, 79
British National Front, 208
Bronze Age, of Greece, 53
Brown v. The Board of Education, 193
Bureaucracy, 230
Burgess, John W., 1–2, 12–14, 42
Burns, Arthur R., 324

Burt, Cyril, 144
Busk, George, 48
Butler, John, 244
Butterfield, Herbert, 98–99

Cairnes, John Elliott, 77, 80
Calhoun, John C., 9
Callahan, Raymond, 149
Calvin, Jean, 6
Cannan, Edwin, 70
Capitalism, 34–35
Carlyle, Thomas, 70
Carnegie Corporation, 210, 212–13, 222–23
Carnegie Foundation, 145
Cartography, 28, 33
Cassedy, James H., 149
Cassel, Gustav, 214, 221
Catholic Church: Encyclical on Marriage, 190; National Council of Catholic Women, 190
Cattell, James McKeen, 107, 145
Center for Advanced Study in the Behavioral Sciences, xv, xix, 39
Chase, Allan, 177
Chase, Stuart, 165–68
Chicano sociology, 234
Child hygiene, 141
Childers, H.C.E., 80
Chipman, Nathaniel, 7
Citizen education, 3, 5, 10, 12
Civil rights movement, 245
Civil War, 2–3, 8, 10, 12–13, 42
Claggett, Marshall, Critical Problems, xii
Clark University, 29
Coats, A. W., 80–81, 85, 89, 101
Cole, Jonathan, 235, 249
Cole, Stephen, 235, 249
Collective action, 34, 90–93, 95; Adam Smith and, 94–98
Collective bargaining, xxii
Colleges: black faculty and administrators of, 235, 238; dominant group faculty in, 237; minority faculty of, 235–36, participation in decision making, 238; promotion within, 237; tenure in, 235, 237
Columbia University, 8, 10, 12, 26, 136
Committee on the Status of Racial and Ethnic Minorities, 240
Common sense, 106, 108, 122–26, 245

Commons, J. R., xii, 211; assessment of Adam Smith by, 94–98; business cycle theory of, 89–90; epistemological beliefs of, 87–88; *Institutional Economics*, 86–90, 94; on relationship between historiography and general methodology, 93–94, 101; theory of the active mind, 87
Communalism, 28, 39
Communism, 219
Comparative anatomy, 48, 51, 55, 59
Comparative historical method, 49–51, 57
Comparative history, 38
Comparative method, 155
Comparative philology, 48
Comparative religion, 46,51, 56–57
Comte, Auguste, xii, 52; sociology of, 52
Consensus, 135, 146
Continental Congress, 28
Cooke, Morris Llewellyn, 145
Cooley, Charles H., 185
Cordorcet, Marquis de, xi
Corruption, 134
Courtney, Leonard, 80
Cox, Oliver C., 231
Cravens, Hamilton, xii–xiv
Cubberley, Ellwood P., 142
Cultural change, 49, 164
Cultural criticism, 161, 163, 165
Cultural development, 155
Cultural lag, 160, 165
Cultural perspectives, 232
Culture, xxiii, 46, 48–49, 52, 54, 56, 59, 153, 158–68, 184, 186, 220, 223, 232; American, 153, 162–67; centers of, 159; complex, 47; concept of, xxiii, 186; context of, 138; hierarchy of, 233; material, 49, 51, 53, 58; science of, 58
Culture-area concept, 159
Cunningham, William, 67
Curti, Merle, xii
Curtis, Hinsley, xiii
Custis, Donald L., 192

Dankwort, Werner, 221
Darrow, Charles, 190
Darwin, Charles, 25, 50, 179; *The Origin of Species*, 50, 155; theory of, 48
Darwinism, 53, 58, 182
Davenport, Charles, 185, 189, 191, 203
de Mably, Abbé, 6

De Morgan, Augustus, 73
Deconstructionism, xvi–xvii
Demand *vs.* supply, 74
Democratic Party, 219–20
Democratic revival, 167
Department of Energy, 193
Dependency theories, xvii
Deutsche Gesellschaft für biologische Anthropologie, 195
Deutsche Gesellschaft für Physische Anthropologie, 183
Deutsche Gesellschaft für Rassenforschung, 179
Deutsche Gesellschaft für Rassenhygiene, 179
Deutsche Gesellschaft für Soziologie, 181, 182, 186, 201–2
Dewey, John, xviii, xix, 146–47, 167–69, 223
Disciplines, xiv, xvi–xxi, 1–3, 12, 14–15, 23–26, 29, 31–33, 38, 40–41, 43–44, 106, 127; boundaries between, 230; turf battles, 24, 29, 31
Discrimination, 244
"Dismal science," 70
Dobu, 166
Dobzhansky, T., 192
Dollard, Charles, 223
Du Bois, W.E.B., 231
Du Bois-Johnson-Frazier Award, 240
Duhem-Quine problem, 72
Dunn, L. C., 192
Dunning, William, 2

Economic Circle, 79
Economics, institutional, 211
Edgeworth, Francis Ysidro, 67, 74–75, 78–80
Edwardian era, 58
Elias, Norbert, 241
Ellwood, Charles, 185, 203–4
Ely, Richard T., 86
Encyclopedia of the Social Sciences, 160, 193
Engineering, 134
Engineers, xxii
Enlightenment, 49, 210; French, xi; Scottish, 5
Environment, 28, 38
Epistemology, xv, 26, 31, 72, 87

Estates General, xi
Ethnocentrism, xxiv, 243
Ethnography, 37, 48–49, 51–52
Ethnological Society of London, 48
Ethnology, 48, 51–52, 55; collections of, 155; taxonomy of, 48
Euclid, 72
Eugenical News, 187
Eugenics Record Office, 180, 191
Eugenics Review, 180, 191
Eugenics, xxiii–xxiv, 180, 200; American, 175–208; German, 181–89; German American relations in, 186–89; history of, 175–78, 186–87; negative, 180; opposition to, 190; positive, 180; *vs.* racial hygene, 200
Eupsychia, 117
Evolution, xx, 48–51, 53–55, 58, 154
Experimental science, 118–20
Experimental Station for the Study of Evolution, 180

Family: black, 233; chicano, 233
Farnell, Lewis, 56
Federal Bureau of Investigation, 222
Federalists, 6–7, 11
Feminism, 37, 179, 212; critique of science by, 243
Fermi, Enrico, 109
Fieldwork, 29–30, 40, 43
Fischberg, Maurice, 200
Fischer, Eugene, 183, 202
Fisher, Irving, 70
Flower, William Henry, 51
Ford, Henry, 120
Forsythe, Dennis, 234
Forum, 140
Foucault, Michel, 23, 26, 36–37, 148
Fowler, Robert Booth, 149
Foxwell, Herbert S., 67–68, 74, 79–80
Franklin, Christine Ladd, 112
Franks, Augustus W., 48
Frazer, James George, 57–59; *The Golden Bough*, 57
Frazier, E. Franklin, 231–32, 239
Freud, Sigmund, 25, 109, 115, 120
Frontier, 42, thesis of, 139
Furner, Mary, xii

Galarza, Ernesto, 231
Galton, Francis, xviii, 48–51, 135, 175, 179, 181, 185, 192–204
Gardiner, Stanley, 56
Garth, T. R., 232
Geertz, Clifford, 23–24
Geison, Gerald, 149
Gender, 164
Gene therapy, 197
General Education Board, 235
Genetic health, 198; constitution, xxiii
Genetics, 177–78, 182, 190–92
Genocide, 177, 206
Geographical Institute, 29
Geography, 24–36, 243; cultural, 23; departments of, 23; exceptionalist stance, 25, 29, 31, 33; geographical imagination, 38–39; marginality of, 23, 33; relations of, with sociology, 24; unity myth, 29–31; as Ur-discipline, xxiii, 24
George, Henry, 78, 85
Germany, 214–18, 221, 223
Giddens, Anthony, 36
Giffen, Robert, 70
Gleason, Philip, 167
Glick, Thomas, 32–32
Goff, John W., 146
Goldenweiser, Alexander, 158, 162
Goodnow, Frank J., 13
Gortjahn, Alfred, 192
Goschen, Viscount, 68, 79–80
Gouldner, Alvin, 242
Gove, Mary, 125
Graham, Loren, 177
Grant, Madison, 157, 184, 189
Great American Desert, 22, 38
Great Depression, 121, 125, 219
Great Exhibition of 1851, 69
Green Moral Philosophy Prize, 45
Gross, Walter, 183
Gulick, Luther Halsey, 140
Gypsy, 176

Haddon, Alfred C., 53; Torres Straits expedition of, 53
Hall, G. Stanley, 106–7, 118
Haller, Karl Ludwig von, 9
Haller, Mark, 177, 186
Hamilton, Alexander, 6, 9
Hankins, Frank H., 185, 191, 204

Hansson, Per Albin, 214
Harvard University, 41, 142, 190
Haskell, Thomas, xii
Hayes, E. C., 23, 29
Hermeneutics, 5, 8–9, 12
Hershel, John, 69
Herskovits, Melville, J., 157, 160
Hewins, William, 77
Higgs, Henry, 79–80
Higham, John, 159
Hilts, Victor, xiv
Hispanic Journal of Behavioral Science, 237
Historical method, 26
Historical presentism, 87–99
Historical sensibility, 84–85
Historicism, xii, 5, 42
Historiography, xiii, xv, xvii, xix–xx, 4
History: of civilization, 47; disciplinary,
   xv, xviii, xxiii; economic, xxii; institu-
   tional, xxi, xxiii; intellectual, xiii–xiv,
   xx, 26; of science, xii–xiii
Hitler, Adolph, 187, 189, 197, 214–15, 217,
   223–24
Hobbes, Thomas, 6, 9
Hobhouse, L. T., 46, 52, 57, 59
Hoffman, Frank S., 15
Hofstadter, Richard, xii
Hollinger, David, xix
Holmes, Oliver Wendell, 187
Holocaust, 177
Hooker, Joseph, 48
Hoover, President Herbert, 159
Hrdlička, Aleš, 183–84
Huber, Bettina, 240
Hughes, H. Stuart, xii
Human engineering, 139
Human Genome Project, 193, 198
Humboldt, Alexander von, 8–9
Hume, David, 4, 7, 9–10
Hunter, Herbert, 235
Huntington's disease, 197
Hutchins, Robert M., 159
Hutchinson, Terence, 71
Hutter, Edward, 125
Huxley, Thomas Henry, 50–51; *Zoological
   Evidences as to Man's Place in Nature*,
   50
Hygiene, in schools, 140

Ideology, 27–28, 229–30, 234, 245–46;
   black, 234; white, 234
Indian Mutiny of 1857, 34
Indian, American, 163
Ingram, John Kells, 77
Institute for Anthropology and Human
   Genetics, 197
Institutions, xv, xix, 26
Instrumental presentism, xxi, 88, 98, 102
Intelligence: homogeneous grouping, 143;
   tests, 142, 147
Interdisciplinary tension, xviii
IQ, 175, 194, 207, 232; controversy over,
   207

Jackson, Maurice, 233
Jacobs, Struan, 247
James, William, 118
Jameson, Fredric, 37
Jastrow, Joseph, 107, 122
Jefferson, Thomas, 9
Jenks, Albert E., 158
Jennings, H. S., 206
Jensen, Arthur, 194, 197, 208
Jevons, William Stanley, xxi, 67, 71–78,
   80–81
Jewish people, 176, 179, 189, 205, eugen-
   ics, 200
Johns Hopkins University, 41
Johnson, Charles, 231, 239
Jones, Richard, 70

Kaiser Wilhelm Institut für Anthropolo-
   gie, menschliche Erblehre und Eugenik,
   183
Kant, Immanuel, 25, 29, 40
Kantorovitz, Myron, 192
Kazin, Alfred, 166
Kent, James, 9
Keppel, Frederick, 212–13
Kern, Stephen, 36
Kevles, Daniel, xiv, 152, 177–89
Keynes, John Neville, 79
Klee, Ernst, 176
Klineberg, Otto, 157
Kloppenberg, James, 84
Kopp, Marie E., 187
Kraepelin, Emil, 204
Kreisky, Bruno, 223
Kroeber, Arthur L., 158, 160

Krupp Prize Essay, 179
Kuhn, Thomas, 25, 32, 228; *The Structure of Scientific Revolutions,* 228
Kuklick, Henrika, xiii
Kwakiutl, 154, 166

Labor, 35; theory of value in, 88, 98
LaFollette, Robert, 86
Laissez-faire, 77, 200
Language, xiv, xvi-xx, xxii, 4, 13, 28, 32-33, 37, 147, 184; professional, 135
Lasswell, Harold, 2
Laughlin, Harry, 188-89, 191
Law for the Prevention of Genetically Diseased Offspring, 204
Law, 3-4, 7, 10-13
Leary, David, xiii
Lecky, W., 46
Lenz, Fritz, 186, 189
Leslie, T. E. Cliffe, 77
Lewis, Sinclair, 161-65
Liberalism, 2, 6, 11, 14, 179, 209, 213
Lieber, Francis, 3, 8-12, 14
Limerick, Patricia N., 39
Lincoln, Abraham, 216
Linear model of explanation, 34
Lippmann, Walter, 142
Localism, 28-29
Locke, John, 2
London School of Economics, 68
London Sociological Association, 181
London Sociological Society, 185
London Statistical Society, 79
Lorenz, Konrad, 194
Lowie, Robert H., 158, 162, 168
Lubbock, John, 48, 51, 53; circle of, 48, 50-51, 53, 58; *Prehistoric Times,* 50
Luckmann, Thomas, 27
Ludmerer, Kenneth, xiv, 177
Lynd, Robert S., and Helen Merrell, 153, 164-65, 167-69

Machiavelli, Niccoló, 6
Madison, James, 6, 9
Maine, Henry Sumner, 51
Malthus, Thomas Robert, 67, 69-70, 89
Manifest Destiny, 27
Mannheim, Karl, 241-42
Marett, Ronald R., 46, 53-54, 56, 58-59
Marshall, Alfred, 67-68, 72-75, 77-81

Martin White Chair of Sociology, 46
Marx, Karl, 1, 8, 25, 78-79, 88, 241
Marxism, 179, 241
Mason, Otis T., 155
Mathematics, xxi, 32; symbolism of, 147
Maxwell, James Clerk, 71
McDougall, W., 122
McLennan, John, 51
McWorter, Gerald, 234
Mead, George Herbert, xviii; *Mind, Self, and Society,* xix
Mead, Margaret, 154, 157-58, 163-65, 168
Medical inspection, 138; of schools, 143
Medicine, 134
Mehler, Barry, 177
Mehlhorn, Hans-George, 207
Mencken, H. L., 123-24, 165
Mendelism, 203
Mental age, 144, 151
Mental testing, xxii, 134, 232
Merton, Thomas, 26
Metaphor, xxii, 137, 146-48
Methodology, xi, xiii-xiv, xxi, xxiii, 5, 12-13, 23-24, 28, 34, 59, 72-73, 115
Mill, John Stuart, 67, 70-72, 75-77, 80
Mills, C. Wright, 242
Minorities, xxiv; negative depictions of, 232; in social scientific community, 228, 230, 238; quality of scholarship from, 237-38; scholars from, 231
Mirande, Alfredo, 233
Miscegenation, American laws barring, 182, 188-89
Mitchell, Weir, 111
Mitchell, Wesley, 211
Modernism, 37
Modernization theory, xvii
Monogenist *vs.* polygenist, 50
Montagu, Ashley, 193
Montesquieu, Baron de, 7, 9
Moral sciences, xi, xvii, 8, 68, 70
Morgan, Mary S., 81
Morley, John, 80
Mower, O. H., 114
Moynihan, Daniel P., 206
Muller, H. J., 192
Munsterberg, Hugo, 107
Museums, 47, 53
Myers, John Linton, 57

Myrdal, Alva Reimer, 191, 211–12, 214–15, 217, 219, 223
Myrdal, Gunnar, xxiv, 193, 209–10, 212–13, 217, 221–23, 240
Myres, John L., 58–59

Nachtsheim, Hans, 195
National Research Council, 157
Nationaldemokratische Partei Deutschlands, 195, 197
Nation, 145
Natural History Museum, 51
Natural history of mankind, xx, 47, 52, 58
Natural inheritance, xxiii
Nazis, 176–77, 186, 205, 210–11, 215–19, 221–24
Neel, James, 193
Negro, 205, 213, 216, 281, 221, 224
Neue Anthropologie, 195, 197
Neurath, Otto, 182
New Deal, 2, 209, 219–20
"New geography," 32
New Republic, 142
New School for Social Research, 162
New York City, 143
Newton, Isaac, 5, 68–69
Newtonianism, 69–70
Nicholson, Joseph Shield, 70
Niebuhr, Barthold, 8
Nixon, Richard, 206
Nordic supremacy, 185–86, 189, 192, 200
Northwestern University, 26
Nuremberg: Laws, 183, 188, 202; trials, 177, 192

Ogburn, William Fielding, 160–65
Osborn, Frederick, 187, 189, 191–92
Owens College, 71

Palgrave, Henry, 79
Parsons, Talcott, 149
Pearl, Raymond, 189, 191
Pearson, Karl, xviii, 135
Pedagogy, 140
Peirce, Charles, xix, 84, 100
Penrose, Lionel, 190
Philogy, 51
Physicians, xxii
Physiography, 25, 30, 40
Pickens, Donald, 177

Pitt-Rivers Museum, 53
Pitt-Rivers, Autustus, 47, 51
Plato, 9
Pleistocene, 50
Ploetz, Alfred, 179, 182, 185, 189, 201, 205
Political Economy Club, 69, 79
Political parties, 3, 11
Political science, 1–15, 28
Politics, 134
Popular culture, xx, xxiii
Popular Front, 219
Popular science, 108, 158
Popularization, xxiii, 108–9, 116, 125, 126
Population policy, 212–13
Porter, Ted, xiv
Positivism, xiii, 240–41
Postmodernism, 37
Pragmatism, 84, 87
Pred, Allan, 43
Prehistory, 49–51
President's Research Committee on Social Trends, 159
Profession, xii, xv, 4, 134
Professional associations, 137, 239
Professional culture, xx
Professionalization, xiv, xxi–xxiii, 58, 68
Progressive era, xxii
Progressivism, 12, 84, 127, 134, 144
Pross, Christian, 177
Psychoanalysis, xxii, 109–15; co-optation of, 114
Psychological testing, 135
Psychology, experimental, 110, 115, 117, 124; laboratory practice, 107; popular, 107–9, 120, 126–27
Public opinion, 1, 3–4, 11
Pufendorf, Samuel, 9

Quantification, 32, 73, 138, 147; methods of, 134; revolution, 32
Queen Victoria, 27
Quetelet, Adolphe, 70

Race, 51, 156–57, 183–84, 192–93, 195, 209, 212, 222, 224; relations, xxiv, 209–10; suicide, 204
Racial domination, 243
Racial formalism, 156
Racial hygiene, 176, 179–80, 182, 185–86, 189, 191, 195, 200–201

Racial inferiority, 156
Racial poisons, 188
Racial segregation, 189
Ramsay, David, 6
Ramstad, Yngve, 88
Rassenkunde, 183, 202
Rassenpolitisches Amt, 183
Read, Charles H., 53
Reche, Otto, 201
Redfield, Robert, 165
Republicanism, 3, 6, 8–12, 15
Research, interdisciplinary, 211; policy, 224
Review of Black Political Economy, 237
Revolution, marginal, xxi, 67
Rhetorical style, xxii
Ricardo, David, 67, 69, 71, 77, 81, 89
Rice, Joseph Mayer, 140
Richards, Robert, xiii
Richards, William, xiii
Ridgeway, William, 53
Rieger, Jurgen, 197, 208
Roback, A. A., 108–16
Rockefeller Foundation, 211
Rodgers, Daniel, 13
Rolleston, George, 48
Romano-V, Octavio, 249
Roosevelt, Franklin Delano, 219–20
Roosevelt, Theodore, 139
Roscoe, Henry Enfield, 71
Rose, Arnold, 221
Rosenberg, Charles, xiii
Rosenwald Fund, 235
Ross, Dorothy, xii, 42
Ross, Edward A., 204
Rosser, Sue, 243
Rourke, Constance, 166–67, 169
Royal Geographical Society, 27
Rudin, Ernst, 197
Ruiz, Rene, 236
Russell, Bertrand, 190
Russo, Nancy F., 236

Sachs, Hanns, 113
Saint-Simon, C. H., xii
Saleeby, Caleb, 180, 201
Samora, Julian, 231
Sanchez, George I., 231—32
Sanger, Margaret, xviii
Sapir, Edward, 157–58, 162–63

Savage peoples, 47, 50, 54, 58
Savigny, Friedrich Karl von, 8
Scarcity value, 92
Schade, Heinrich, 197
Schallmayer, Wilheim, 201
Schapire-Neurath, Anna, 182
Schleiermacher, Friedrich, E. D., 8–9
School surveys, 138, 140–41, 143
Schumpeter, Joseph, 70
Scientific management, 145
Scientific method, xi, 4–5, 9, 12, 119, 135–36, 228, 240, 242
Scientific objectivity, xxii–xxiii
Scientific popularization, xxii
Scientism, 12, 234
Scott, John, 224
Self-improvement literature, 108
Senior, Nassau, 69, 77
Shaw, George Bernard, 78–79, 81
Sidgwick, Henry, 67, 80
Sitwell, Osbert, 27
Skinner, Quentin, 33
Small, Albion, 28, 181
Smith, Adam, 69–70, 75–77, 94–98;
    Theory of Moral Sentiments, 96–97;
    Wealth of Nations, 96–97
Snyder, Laurence, 192
Social anthropology, 47, 58
Social construction of reality, 26–27
Social darwinism, 79, 179, 200
Social Democrats, 211, 212, 219–20
Social engineering, 161, 164, 168, 210, 212
Socialism, 41, 179, 182
Social Science Quarterly, 23
Social Science Research Council, 25, 159
Social science: crisis in, 228, 246; interpretive, xi–xii
Social scientific knowledge, 237, 242;
    boundary of, 237; minority influence on, 231; production of, 230, 237–39, 246
Society of 1789, xi
Sociobiology, 175
Sociological Society, 45–46, 232
Sociology, 24–25, 34, 58; Durkheimian, 59; historical, 23; of knowledge, xv, 241–42; value-free, 242
Sokal, Michael, xiii
South Carolina College, 10
Sovereignty, 3–4, 7, 10–13
Space, 28, 32–33, 35–36, 39, 42

Specialization, xviii
Spencer, Herbert, 49, 51
Spock, Benjamin, 124
Spottiswoode, William, 48
SS (*Schutzstaffel*), 176, 197
Staatswissenschaft, 2–3
Stammler, Martin, 200
Stanford University, 142
Stanford-Binet Test, 144
Staples, Robert, 233
Starr, Paul, 149
State, xx, 1–15, 28, 36, 42
Statistics, 4, 9, 12, 142
Stauffenberg, Claus Count von, 224
Sterilization, 183, 192, 195; laws, 188,
    193, 204
Sterner, Richard, 221
Stigler, George, 69
Stirpiculture, 203
Stockholm School of Economics, 212
Stocking, George, xiii, 99, 203
Stoddart, David, 25, 43
Story, Joseph, 9, 11
Structuralism, 37
Structuration, 35, 37
Structure and agency, 35
Sturtevant, A. H., 177
Susman, Warren, 154
Sweden, 210–18, 221, 223

Taylor, Frederick, 145
Terman Group Test, 143
Terman, Lewis, 119, 141
Thomas, Dorothy, 213
Thomas, W. I., 160
Thomas, W. J., 213
Thompson, Daniel C., 233
Thorndike, Edward L., 136, 138, 145–46
Thurnwald, Richard, 183
Tille, Alexander, 204
Tilly, Charles, 37
Titchener, E. B., 106, 117, 120–23
Tocqueville, Alexis de, 1, 8
Tonnies, Ferdinand, 181
Torres Straits, 53
Toynbee, Arnold, 77
Trant, Luther, 110
Trott zu Solz, Adam von, 223
Truth: as social consensus, 100; in the
    social sciences, 100–101

Turner, Frederick Jackson, 22, 29, 38, 139
Tyack, David, 151
Tyler, Edward Burnett, 46–48, 51–53,
    55–56, 58; *Anthropology*, 47; *Researches
    into the Early History of Mankind*, 47

U.S. Atomic Bomb Casualty Commission,
    193
U.S. Immigration Commission, 157
UNESCO, 193; statement on race, 188,
    194
University Museum, 47
University of Cambridge, 27; Trinity
    College, 57
University of Chicago, 24, 26, 41
University of Liverpool, 57
University of London, 46; Department of
    Sociology, 59
University of Oxford, xx, 46; Committee
    for Anthropology, 45; Congregation,
    56; Convocation, 55; Finals School in
    Natural Science, 55; Greats School, 45,
    56; Hebdomadal Council, 55; *Literae
    Humaniores*, 45, 55; "non-placet soci-
    ety," 55
Utilitarianism, 75–76
Utility theory of value, 75

Veblen, Thorstein, 84, 161
Verschuer, Otmar von, 193, 195, 208
Vierkandt, Alfred, 182
Vietnam War, 30
Virginia, "Pure-Race Law," 205

Wallace, Alfred Russel, 48, 50
Walras, Léon, 70
Ward, Lester Frank, 185, 203
Ware, Caroline, 167, 169
Warsaw ghetto, 208
Waterstone, Penny, 43
Watson, John B., 107, 114, 118–20, 122
Webb, Sidney, 79
Webb, Walter Prescott, 23
Weber, Max, 182
Weinert, Hans, 188
Weiss, Volkmar, 207
Welfare state, 213, 217
Whewell, William, 9, 69
Whittlesey, Derwent, 41
Wicksteed, Philip H., 67, 74–75

Wiebe, Robert, 139, 149; *The Wisconsin Idea*, 139
Wiese, Leopold von, 182
Willey, Malcolm, 160
Willoughby, W. W., 2, 12–13
Wilson, E. O., 194; *Sociobiology*, 194
Wilson, William Julius, 240
Wilson, Woodrow, 12
Wissler, Clark, 158–59, 164, 166
Women social scientists, 125
Woodworth, Robert, 112
Woolsey, Theodore Dwight, 2, 12–13

Working rules, 91–92, 96
World systems analysis, xvii
World War I, 30, 135, 143, 210, 221
World War II, 219

Yale University, 2
Yerkes, Robert, 107, 151
Young, Ella Flagg, xviii
Young, Robert, xii

Zuni, 166

The Estate of Social Knowledge

Designed by Ann Walston

Composed by Blue Heron
in Plantin with Franklin Gothic display

Printed by The Maple Press Company
on 55-lb. MV Antique Cream
and bound in Holliston Aqualite